MW00996004

The G.K. Chesterton Collection

Volume 2

Tremendous Trifles
Orthodoxy
What's Wrong with the World

By G.K. Chesterton

Henderson Publishing

All rights reserved. No part of this book may be reproduced, stored in a retrieval system, or transmitted, in any form or by any means, electronic, mechanical, photocopying, recording, or otherwise, without the prior permission of Henderson Publishing.

Copyright ©2024 by Henderson Publishing.
Published July 2024.
Version: 1.0.
ISBN: 978-1-964170-81-7.

If you have a question or have found an error concerning this manuscript, please email: contact@hendersonpublishing.com

Book cover designed by Christian Caudill.
Book designed by Jeremy Hausotter.
This book is typeset in IM FELL English.
The Fell Types are digitally reproduced by Igino Marini. www.iginomarini.com

Henderson Publishing | San Antonio, Texas

Table of Contents

Orthodoxy

What's Wrong with the World

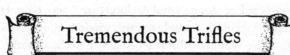

Tremendous Trifles

Preface

hese fleeting sketches are all republished by kind permission of the Editor of the DAILY NEWS, in which paper they appeared. They amount to no more than a sort of sporadic diary—a diary recording one day in twenty which happened to stick in the fancy—the only kind of diary the author has ever been able to keep. Even that diary he could only keep by keeping it in public, for bread and cheese. But trivial as are the topics they are not utterly without a connecting thread of motive. As the reader's eye strays, with hearty relief, from these pages, it probably alights on something, a bed-post or a lamp-post, a window blind or a wall. It is a thousand to one that the reader is looking at something that he has never seen: that is, never realised. He could not write an essay on such a post or wall: he does not know what the post or wall mean. He could not even write the synopsis of an essay; as "The Bed-Post; Its Significance—Security Essential to Idea of Sleep—Night Felt as Infinite—Need of Monumental Architecture," and so on. He could not sketch in outline his theoretic attitude towards window-blinds, even in the form of a summary. "The Window-Blind—Its Analogy to the Curtain and Veil—Is Modesty Natural?—Worship of and Avoidance of the Sun, etc., etc." None of us think enough of these things on which the eye rests. But don't let us let the eye rest. Why should the eye be so lazy? Let us exercise the eye until it learns to see startling facts that run across the landscape as plain as a painted fence. Let us be ocular athletes. Let us learn to write essays on a stray cat or a coloured cloud. I have attempted some such thing in what follows; but anyone else may do it better, if anyone else will only try.

Chapter 1
Tremendous Trifles

nce upon a time there were two little boys who lived chiefly in the front garden, because their villa was a model one. The front garden was about the same size as the dinner table; it consisted of four strips of gravel, a square of turf with some mysterious pieces of cork standing up in the middle and one flower bed with a row of red daisies. One morning while they were at play in these romantic grounds, a passing individual, probably the milkman, leaned over the railing and engaged them in philosophical conversation. The boys, whom we will call Paul and Peter, were at least sharply interested in his remarks. For the milkman (who was, I need say, a fairy) did his duty in that state of life by offering them in the regulation manner anything that they chose to ask for. And Paul closed with the offer with a business-like abruptness, explaining that he had long wished to be a giant that he might stride across continents and oceans and visit Niagara or the Himalayas in an afternoon dinner stroll. The milkman producing a wand from his breast pocket, waved it in a hurried and perfunctory manner; and in an instant the model villa with its front garden was like a tiny doll's house at Paul's colossal feet. He went striding away with his head above the clouds to visit Niagara and the Himalayas. But when he came to the Himalayas, he found they were quite small and silly-looking, like the little cork rockery in the garden; and when he found Niagara it was no bigger than the tap turned on in the bathroom. He wandered round the world for several minutes trying to find something really large and finding everything small, till in sheer boredom he lay down on four or five prairies and fell asleep. Unfortunately his head was just outside the hut of an intellectual backwoodsman who came out of it at that moment with an axe in one hand and a book of Neo-Catholic Philosophy in the other. The man looked at the book and then at the giant, and then at the book again. And in the book it said, "It can be maintained that the evil of pride consists in being out of proportion to the universe." So the backwoodsman put down his book, took his axe and, working eight hours a day for about a week, cut the giant's head off; and there was an end of him.

Such is the severe yet salutary history of Paul. But Peter, oddly enough, made exactly the opposite request; he said he had long wished to be a pigmy about half an inch high; and of course he immediately became one. When the transformation was over he found himself in the midst of an immense plain, covered with a tall green jungle and above which, at intervals, rose strange trees each with a head like the sun in symbolic pictures, with gigantic rays of silver and a huge heart of gold. Toward the middle of this prairie stood up a mountain of such romantic and impossible shape, yet of such stony height and dominance, that it looked like some incident of the end of the world. And far away on the faint horizon he could see the line of another forest, taller and yet more mystical, of a terrible crimson colour, like a forest on fire for ever. He set out on his adventures across that coloured plain; and he has not come to the end of it yet.

Such is the story of Peter and Paul, which contains all the highest qualities of a modern fairy tale, including that of being wholly unfit for children; and indeed the motive with which I have introduced it is not childish, but rather full of subtlety and reaction. It is in fact the almost desperate motive of excusing or palliating the pages that follow. Peter and Paul are the two primary influences upon European literature to-day; and I may be permitted to put my own preference in its most favourable shape, even if I can only do it by what little girls call telling a story.

I need scarcely say that I am the pigmy. The only excuse for the scraps that follow is that they show what can be achieved with a commonplace existence and the sacred spectacles of exaggeration. The other great literary theory, that which is roughly represented in England by Mr. Rudyard Kipling, is that we moderns are to regain the primal zest by sprawling all over the world growing used to travel and geographical variety, being at home everywhere, that is being at home nowhere. Let it be granted that a man in a frock coat is a heartrending sight; and the two alternative methods still remain. Mr. Kipling's school advises us to go to Central Africa in order to find a man without a frock coat. The school to which I belong suggests that we should stare steadily at the man until we see the man inside the frock coat. If we stare at him long enough he may even be moved to take off his coat to us; and that is a far greater compliment than his taking off his hat. In other words, we may, by fixing our attention almost fiercely on the facts actually before us, force them to turn into adventures; force them to give up their meaning and fulfil their mysterious purpose. The purpose of the Kipling literature is to show how many extraordinary things a man may see if he is active and strides from continent to continent like the giant in my tale. But the object of my school is to show how many extraordinary things even a lazy and ordinary man may see if he can spur himself to the single activity of seeing. For this purpose I have taken the laziest person of my acquaintance, that is myself; and made an idle diary of such odd things as I have fallen over by accident, in walking in a very limited area at a very indolent pace. If anyone says that these are very small affairs talked about in very big language, I can only gracefully compliment him upon seeing the joke. If anyone says that I am making mountains out of molehills, I confess with pride that it is so. I can imagine no more successful and productive form of manufacture than that of making mountains out of molehills. But I would add this not unimportant fact, that molehills are mountains; one has only to become a pigmy like Peter to discover that.

I have my doubts about all this real value in mountaineering, in getting to the top of everything and overlooking everything. Satan was the most celebrated of Alpine guides, when he took Jesus to the top of an exceeding high mountain and showed him all the kingdoms of the earth. But the joy of Satan in standing on a peak is not a joy in largeness, but a joy in beholding smallness, in the fact that all men look like insects at his feet. It is from the valley that things look large; it is from the level that things look high; I am a child of the level and have no need of that celebrated Alpine guide. I will lift up my eyes to the hills, from whence cometh my help; but I will not lift up my carcass to the hills, unless it is absolutely necessary. Everything is in an attitude of mind; and at this moment I am in a comfortable attitude. I will sit still and let the marvels and the adventures settle on me like flies. There are plenty of them, I assure you. The world will never starve for want of wonders; but only for want of wonder.

Chapter 2
A Piece of Chalk

remember one splendid morning, all blue and silver, in the summer holidays when I reluctantly tore myself away from the task of doing nothing in particular, and put on a hat of some sort and picked up a walking-stick, and put six very bright-coloured chalks in my pocket. I then went into the kitchen (which, along with the rest of the house, belonged to a very square and sensible old woman in a Sussex village), and asked the owner and occupant of the kitchen if she had any brown paper. She had a great deal; in fact, she had too much; and she mistook the purpose and the rationale of the existence of brown paper. She seemed to have an idea that if a person wanted brown paper he must be wanting to tie up parcels; which was the last thing I wanted to do; indeed, it is a thing which I have found to be beyond my mental capacity. Hence she dwelt very much on the varying qualities of toughness and endurance in the material. I explained to her that I only wanted to draw pictures on it, and that I did not want them to endure in the least; and that from my point of view, therefore, it was a question, not of tough consistency, but of responsive surface, a thing comparatively irrelevant in a parcel. When she understood that I wanted to draw she offered to overwhelm me with note-paper, apparently supposing that I did my notes and correspondence on old brown paper wrappers from motives of economy.

I then tried to explain the rather delicate logical shade, that I not only liked brown paper, but liked the quality of brownness in paper, just as I liked the quality of brownness in October woods, or in beer, or in the peat-streams of the North. Brown paper represents the primal twilight of the first toil of creation, and with a bright-coloured chalk or two you can pick out points of fire in it, sparks of gold, and blood-red, and sea-green, like the first fierce stars that sprang out of divine darkness. All this I said (in an off-hand way) to the old woman; and I put the brown paper in my pocket along with the chalks, and possibly other things. I suppose every one must have reflected how primeval and how poetical are the things that one carries in one's pocket; the pocket-knife, for instance, the type of all human tools, the infant of the sword. Once I planned to write a book of poems entirely about the things in my pockets. But I found it would be too long; and the age of the great epics is past.

With my stick and my knife, my chalks and my brown paper, I went out on to the great downs. I crawled across those colossal contours that express the best quality of England, because they are at the same time soft and strong. The smoothness of them has the same meaning as the smoothness of great cart-horses, or the smoothness of the beech-tree; it declares in the teeth of our timid and cruel theories that the mighty are merciful. As my eye swept the landscape, the landscape was as kindly as any of its cottages, but for power it was like an earthquake. The villages in the immense valley were safe, one could see, for centuries; yet the lifting of the whole land was like the lifting of one enormous wave to wash them all away.

I crossed one swell of living turf after another, looking for a place to sit down and draw. Do not, for heaven's sake, imagine I was going to sketch from Nature. I was going to draw devils and seraphim, and blind old gods that men worshipped before the dawn of right, and saints in robes of angry crimson, and seas of strange green, and all the sacred or monstrous symbols that look so well in bright colours on brown paper. They are much better worth drawing than Nature; also they are much easier to draw. When a cow came slouching by in the field next to me, a mere artist might have drawn it; but I always get wrong in the hind legs of quadrupeds. So I drew the soul of the cow; which I saw there plainly walking before me in the sunlight; and the soul was all purple and silver, and had seven horns and the mystery that belongs to all the beasts. But though I could not with a crayon get the best out of the landscape, it does not follow that the landscape was not getting the best out of me. And this, I think, is the mistake that people make about the old poets who lived before Wordsworth, and were supposed not to care very much about Nature because they did not describe it much.

They preferred writing about great men to writing about great hills; but they sat on the great hills to write it. They gave out much less about Nature, but they drank in, perhaps, much more. They painted the white robes of their holy virgins with the blinding snow, at which they had stared all day. They blazoned the shields of their paladins with the purple and gold of many heraldic sunsets. The greenness of a thousand green leaves clustered into the live green figure of Robin Hood. The blueness of a score of forgotten skies became the blue robes of the Virgin. The inspiration went in like sunbeams and came out like Apollo.

But as I sat scrawling these silly figures on the brown paper, it began to dawn on me, to my great disgust, that I had left one chalk, and that a most exquisite and essential chalk, behind. I searched all my pockets, but I could not find any white chalk. Now, those who are acquainted with all the philosophy (nay, religion) which is typified in the art of drawing on brown paper, know that white is positive and essential. I cannot avoid remarking here upon a moral significance. One of the wise and awful truths which this brown-paper art reveals, is this, that white is a colour. It is not a mere absence of colour; it is a shining and affirmative thing, as fierce as red, as definite as black. When, so to speak, your pencil grows red-hot, it draws roses; when it grows white-hot, it draws stars. And one of the two or three defiant verities of the best religious morality, of real Christianity, for example, is exactly this same thing; the chief assertion of religious morality is that white is a colour. Virtue is not the absence of vices or the avoidance of moral dangers; virtue is a vivid and separate thing, like pain or a particular smell. Mercy does not mean not being cruel or sparing people revenge or punishment; it means a plain and positive thing like the sun, which one has either seen or not seen.

Chastity does not mean abstention from sexual wrong; it means something flaming, like Joan of Arc. In a word, God paints in many colours; but He never paints so gorgeously, I had almost said so gaudily, as when He paints in white. In a sense our age has realised this fact, and expressed it in our sullen costume. For if it were really true that white was a blank and colourless thing, negative and non-committal, then white would be used instead of black and grey for the funeral dress of this pessimistic period. We should see city gentlemen in frock coats of spotless silver linen, with top hats as white as wonderful arum lilies. Which is not the case.

Meanwhile, I could not find my chalk.

I sat on the hill in a sort of despair. There was no town nearer than Chichester at which it was even remotely probable that there would be such a thing as an artist's colourman. And yet, without white, my absurd little pictures would be as pointless as the world would be if there were no good people in it. I stared stupidly round, racking my brain for expedients. Then I suddenly stood up and roared with laughter, again and again, so that the cows stared at me and called a committee. Imagine a man in the Sahara regretting that he had no sand for his hour-glass. Imagine a gentleman in mid-ocean wishing that he had brought some salt water with him for his chemical experiments. I was sitting on an immense warehouse of white chalk. The landscape was made entirely out of white chalk. White chalk was piled more miles until it met the sky. I stooped and broke a piece off the rock I sat on; it did not mark so well as the shop chalks do; but it gave the effect. And I stood there in a trance of pleasure, realising that this Southern England is not only a grand peninsula, and a tradition and a civilisation; it is something even more admirable. It is a piece of chalk.

Chapter 3
The Secret of a Train

ll this talk of a railway mystery has sent my mind back to a loose memory. I will not merely say that this story is true: because, as you will soon see, it is all truth and no story. It has no explanation and no conclusion; it is, like most of the other things we encounter in life, a fragment of something else which would be intensely exciting if it were not too large to be seen. For the perplexity of life arises from there being too many interesting things in it for us to be interested properly in any of them; what we call its triviality is really the tag-ends of numberless tales; ordinary and unmeaning existence is like ten thousand thrilling detective stories mixed up with a spoon. My experience was a fragment of this nature, and it is, at any rate, not fictitious. Not only am I not making up the incidents (what there were of them), but I am not making up the atmosphere of the landscape, which were the whole horror of the thing. I remember them vividly, and they were as I shall now describe.

About noon of an ashen autumn day some years ago I was standing outside the station at Oxford intending to take the train to London. And for some reason, out of idleness or the emptiness of my mind or the emptiness of the pale grey sky, or the cold, a kind of caprice fell upon me that I would not go by that train at all, but would step out on the road and walk at least some part of the way to London. I do not know if other people are made like me in this matter; but to me it is always dreary weather, what may be called useless weather, that slings into life a sense of action and romance. On bright blue days I do not want anything to happen; the world is complete and beautiful, a thing for contemplation. I no more ask for adventures under that turquoise dome than I ask for adventures in church. But when the background of man's life is a grey background, then, in the name of man's sacred supremacy, I desire to paint on it in fire and gore. When the heavens fail man refuses to fail; when the sky seems to have written on it, in letters of lead and pale silver, the decree that nothing shall happen, then the immortal soul, the prince of the creatures, rises up and decrees that something shall happen, if it be only the slaughter of a policeman. But this is a digressive way of stating what I have said already—that the bleak sky awoke in me a hunger for some change of plans, that the monotonous weather seemed to render unbearable the use of the monotonous train, and that I set out into the country lanes, out of the town of Oxford. It was, perhaps, at that moment that a strange curse came upon me out of the city and the sky, whereby it was decreed that years afterwards I should, in an article in the DAILY NEWS, talk about Sir George Trevelyan in connection with Oxford, when I knew perfectly well that he went to Cambridge.

As I crossed the country everything was ghostly and colourless. The fields that should have been green were as grey as the skies; the tree-tops that should have been green were as grey as the clouds and as cloudy. And when I had walked for some hours the evening was closing in. A sickly sunset clung weakly to the horizon, as if pale with reluctance to leave the world in the dark. And as it faded more and more the skies seemed to come closer and to threaten. The clouds which had been merely sullen became swollen; and then they loosened and let down the dark curtains of the rain. The rain was blinding and seemed to beat like blows from an enemy at close quarters; the skies seemed bending over and bawling in my ears. I walked on many more miles before I met a man, and in that distance my mind had been made up; and when I met him I asked him if anywhere in the neighbourhood I could pick up the train for Paddington. He directed me to a small silent station (I cannot even remember the name of it) which stood well away from the road and looked as lonely as a hut on the Andes. I do not think I have ever seen such a type of time and sadness and scepticism and everything devilish as that station was: it looked as if it had always been raining there ever since the creation of the world. The water streamed from the soaking wood of it as if it were not water at all, but some loathsome liquid corruption of the wood itself; as if the solid station were eternally falling to pieces and pouring away in filth. It took me nearly ten minutes to find a man in the station. When I did he was a dull one, and when I asked him if there was a train to Paddington his answer was sleepy and vague. As far as I understood him, he said there would be a train in half an hour. I sat down and lit a cigar and waited, watching the last tail of the tattered sunset and listening to the everlasting rain. It may have been in half an hour or less, but a train came rather slowly into the station. It was an unnaturally dark train; I could not see a light anywhere in the long black body of it; and I could not see any guard running beside it. I was reduced to walking up to the engine and calling out to the stoker to ask if the train was going to London. "Well—yes, sir," he said, with an unaccountable kind of reluctance. "It is going to London; but—— " It was just starting, and I jumped into the first carriage; it was pitch dark. I sat there smoking and wondering, as we steamed through the continually darkening landscape, lined with desolate poplars, until we slowed down and stopped, irrationally, in the middle of a field. I heard a heavy noise as of some one clambering off the train, and a dark, ragged head suddenly put itself into my window. "Excuse me, sir," said the stoker, "but I think, perhaps—well, perhaps you ought to know—there's a dead man in this train."

Had I been a true artist, a person of exquisite susceptibilities and nothing else, I should have been bound, no doubt, to be finally overwhelmed with this sensational touch, and to have insisted on getting out and walking. As it was, I regret to say, I expressed myself politely, but firmly, to the effect that I didn't care particularly if the train took me to Paddington. But when the train had started with its unknown burden I did do one thing, and do it quite instinctively, without stopping to think, or to think more than a flash. I threw away my cigar. Something that is as old as man and has to do with all mourning and ceremonial told me to do it. There was something unnecessarily horrible, it seemed to me, in the idea of there being only two men in that train, and one of them dead and the other smoking a cigar. And as the red and gold of the butt end of it faded like a funeral torch trampled out at some symbolic moment of a procession, I realised how immortal ritual is. I realised (what is the origin and essence of all ritual) that in the presence of those sacred riddles about which we can say nothing it is more decent merely to do something. And I realised that ritual will always mean throwing away something; DESTROYING our corn or wine upon the altar of our gods.

When the train panted at last into Paddington Station I sprang out of it with a suddenly released curiosity. There was a barrier and officials guarding the rear part of the train; no one was allowed to press towards it. They were guarding and hiding something; perhaps death in some too shocking form, perhaps something like the Merstham matter, so mixed up with human mystery and wickedness that the land has to give it a sort of sanctity; perhaps something worse than either. I went out gladly enough into the streets and saw the lamps shining on the laughing faces. Nor have I ever known from that day to this into what strange story I wandered or what frightful thing was my companion in the dark.

Chapter 4
The Perfect Game

e have all met the man who says that some odd things have happened to him, but that he does not really believe that they were supernatural. My own position is the opposite of this. I believe in the supernatural as a matter of intellect and reason, not as a matter of personal experience. I do not see ghosts; I only see their inherent probability. But it is entirely a matter of the mere intelligence, not even of the motions; my nerves and body are altogether of this earth, very earthy. But upon people of this temperament one weird incident will often leave a peculiar impression. And the weirdest circumstance that ever occurred to me occurred a little while ago. It consisted in nothing less than my playing a game, and playing it quite well for some seventeen consecutive minutes. The ghost of my grandfather would have astonished me less.

On one of these blue and burning afternoons I found myself, to my inexpressible astonishment, playing a game called croquet. I had imagined that it belonged to the epoch of Leach and Anthony Trollope, and I had neglected to provide myself with those very long and luxuriant side whiskers which are really essential to such a scene. I played it with a man whom we will call Parkinson, and with whom I had a semi-philosophical argument which lasted through the entire contest. It is deeply implanted in my mind that I had the best of the argument; but it is certain and beyond dispute that I had the worst of the game.

"Oh, Parkinson, Parkinson!" I cried, patting him affectionately on the head with a mallet, "how far you really are from the pure love of the sport—you who can play. It is only we who play badly who love the Game itself. You love glory; you love applause; you love the earthquake voice of victory; you do not love croquet. You do not love croquet until you love being beaten at croquet. It is we the bunglers who adore the occupation in the abstract. It is we to whom it is art for art's sake. If we may see the face of Croquet herself (if I may so express myself) we are content to see her face turned upon us in anger. Our play is called amateurish; and we wear proudly the name of amateur, for amateurs is but the French for Lovers. We accept all adventures from our Lady, the most disastrous or the most dreary. We wait outside her iron gates (I allude to the hoops), vainly essaying to enter. Our devoted balls, impetuous and full of chivalry, will not be confined within the pedantic boundaries of the mere croquet ground. Our balls seek honour in the ends of the earth; they turn up in the flower-beds and the conservatory; they are to be found in the front garden and the next street. No, Parkinson! The good painter has skill. It is the bad painter who loves his art. The good musician loves being a musician, the bad musician loves music. With such a pure and hopeless passion do I worship croquet. I love the game itself. I love the parallelogram of grass marked out with chalk or tape, as if its limits were the frontiers of my sacred Fatherland, the four seas of Britain. I love the mere swing of the mallets, and the click of the balls is music. The four colours are to me sacramental and symbolic, like the red of martyrdom, or the white of Easter Day. You lose all this, my poor Parkinson. You have to solace yourself for the absence of this vision by the paltry consolation of being able to go through hoops and to hit the stick."

And I waved my mallet in the air with a graceful gaiety.

"Don't be too sorry for me," said Parkinson, with his simple sarcasm. "I shall get over it in time. But it seems to me that the more a man likes a game the better he would want to play it. Granted that the pleasure in the thing itself comes first, does not the pleasure of success come naturally and inevitably afterwards? Or, take your own simile of the Knight and his Lady-love. I admit the gentleman does first and foremost want to be in the lady's presence. But I never yet heard of a gentleman who wanted to look an utter ass when he was there."

"Perhaps not; though he generally looks it," I replied. "But the truth is that there is a fallacy in the simile, although it was my own. The happiness at which the lover is aiming is an infinite happiness, which can be extended without limit. The more he is loved, normally speaking, the jollier he will be. It is definitely true that the stronger the love of both lovers, the stronger will be the happiness. But it is not true that the stronger the play of both croquet players the stronger will be the game. It is logically possible—(follow me closely here, Parkinson!)—it is logically possible, to play croquet too well to enjoy it at all. If you could put this blue ball through that distant hoop as easily as you could pick it up with your hand, then you would not put it through that hoop any more than you pick it up with your hand; it would not be worth doing. If you could play unerringly you would not play at all. The moment the game is perfect the game disappears."

"I do not think, however," said Parkinson, "that you are in any immediate danger of effecting that sort of destruction. I do not think your croquet will vanish through its own faultless excellence. You are safe for the present."

I again caressed him with the mallet, knocked a ball about, wired myself, and resumed the thread of my discourse.

The long, warm evening had been gradually closing in, and by this time it was almost twilight. By the time I had delivered four more fundamental principles, and my companion had gone through five more hoops, the dusk was verging upon dark.

"We shall have to give this up," said Parkinson, as he missed a ball almost for the first time, "I can't see a thing."

"Nor can I," I answered, "and it is a comfort to reflect that I could not hit anything if I saw it."

With that I struck a ball smartly, and sent it away into the darkness towards where the shadowy figure of Parkinson moved in the hot haze. Parkinson immediately uttered a loud and dramatic cry. The situation, indeed, called for it. I had hit the right ball.

Stunned with astonishment, I crossed the gloomy ground, and hit my ball again. It went through a hoop. I could not see the hoop; but it was the right hoop. I shuddered from head to foot.

Words were wholly inadequate, so I slouched heavily after that impossible ball. Again I hit it away into the night, in what I supposed was the vague direction of the quite invisible stick. And in the dead silence I heard the stick rattle as the ball struck it heavily.

I threw down my mallet. "I can't stand this," I said. "My ball has gone right three times. These things are not of this world."

"Pick your mallet up," said Parkinson, "have another go."

"I tell you I daren't. If I made another hoop like that I should see all the devils dancing there on the blessed grass."

"Why devils?" asked Parkinson; "they may be only fairies making fun of you. They are sending you the 'Perfect Game,' which is no game."

I looked about me. The garden was full of a burning darkness, in which the faint glimmers had the look of fire. I stepped across the grass as if it burnt me, picked up the mallet, and hit the ball somewhere—somewhere where another ball might be. I heard the dull click of the balls touching, and ran into the house like one pursued.

Chapter 5
The Extraordinary Cabman

rom time to time I have introduced into this newspaper column the narration of incidents that have really occurred. I do not mean to insinuate that in this respect it stands alone among newspaper columns. I mean only that I have found that my meaning was better expressed by some practical parable out of daily life than by any other method; therefore I propose to narrate the incident of the extraordinary cabman, which occurred to me only three days ago, and which, slight as it apparently is, aroused in me a moment of genuine emotion bordering upon despair.

On the day that I met the strange cabman I had been lunching in a little restaurant in Soho in company with three or four of my best friends. My best friends are all either bottomless sceptics or quite uncontrollable believers, so our discussion at luncheon turned upon the most ultimate and terrible ideas. And the whole argument worked out ultimately to this: that the question is whether a man can be certain of anything at all. I think he can be certain, for if (as I said to my friend, furiously brandishing an empty bottle) it is impossible intellectually to entertain certainty, what is this certainty which it is impossible to entertain? If I have never experienced such a thing as certainty I cannot even say that a thing is not certain. Similarly, if I have never experienced such a thing as green I cannot even say that my nose is not green. It may be as green as possible for all I know, if I have really no experience of greenness. So we shouted at each other and shook the room; because metaphysics is the only thoroughly emotional thing. And the difference between us was very deep, because it was a difference as to the object of the whole thing called broad-mindedness or the opening of the intellect. For my friend said that he opened his intellect as the sun opens the fans of a palm tree, opening for opening's sake, opening infinitely for ever. But I said that I opened my intellect as I opened my mouth, in order to shut it again on something solid. I was doing it at the moment. And as I truly pointed out, it would look uncommonly silly if I went on opening my mouth infinitely, for ever and ever.

Now when this argument was over, or at least when it was cut short (for it will never be over), I went away with one of my companions, who in the confusion and comparative insanity of a General Election had somehow become a member of Parliament, and I drove with him in a cab from the corner of Leicester-square to the members' entrance of the House of Commons, where the police received me with a quite unusual tolerance. Whether they thought that he was my keeper or that I was his keeper is a discussion between us which still continues.

It is necessary in this narrative to preserve the utmost exactitude of detail. After leaving my friend at the House I took the cab on a few hundred yards to an office in Victoria-street which I had to visit. I then got out and offered him more than his fare. He looked at it, but not with the surly doubt and general disposition to try it on which is not unknown among normal cabmen. But this was no normal, perhaps, no human, cabman. He looked at it with a dull and infantile astonishment, clearly quite genuine. "Do you know, sir," he said, "you've only given me 1s.8d?" I remarked, with some surprise, that I did know it. "Now you know, sir," said he in a kindly, appealing, reasonable way, "you know that ain't the fare from Euston." "Euston," I repeated vaguely, for the phrase at that moment sounded to me like China or Arabia. "What on earth has Euston got to do with it?" "You hailed me just outside Euston Station," began the man with astonishing precision, "and then you said—— " "What in the name of Tartarus are you talking about?" I said with Christian forbearance; "I took you at the south-west corner of Leicester-square." "Leicester-square," he exclaimed, loosening a kind of cataract of scorn, "why we ain't been near Leicester-square to-day. You hailed me outside Euston Station, and you said—— " "Are you mad, or am I?" I asked with scientific calm.

I looked at the man. No ordinary dishonest cabman would think of creating so solid and colossal and creative a lie. And this man was not a dishonest cabman. If ever a human face was heavy and simple and humble, and with great big blue eyes protruding like a frog's, if ever (in short) a human face was all that a human face should be, it was the face of that resentful and respectful cabman. I looked up and down the street; an unusually dark twilight seemed to be coming on. And for one second the old nightmare of the sceptic put its finger on my nerve. What was certainty? Was anybody certain of anything? Heavens! to think of the dull rut of the sceptics who go on asking whether we possess a future life. The exciting question for real scepticism is whether we possess a past life. What is a minute ago, rationalistically considered, except a tradition and a picture? The darkness grew deeper from the road. The cabman calmly gave me the most elaborate details of the gesture, the words, the complex but consistent course of action which I had adopted since that remarkable occasion when I had hailed him outside Euston Station. How did I know (my sceptical friends would say) that I had not hailed him outside Euston. I was firm about my assertion; he was quite equally firm about his. He was obviously quite as honest a man as I, and a member of a much more respectable profession. In that moment the universe and the stars swung just a hair's breadth from their balance, and the foundations of the earth were moved. But for the same reason that I believe in Democracy, for the same reason that I believe in free will, for the same reason that I believe in fixed character of virtue, the reason that could only be expressed by saying that I do not choose to be a lunatic, I continued to believe that this honest cabman was wrong, and I repeated to him that I had really taken him at the corner of Leicester-square. He began with the same evident and ponderous sincerity, "You hailed me outside Euston Station, and you said—— "

And at this moment there came over his features a kind of frightful transfiguration of living astonishment, as if he had been lit up like a lamp from the inside. "Why, I beg your pardon, sir," he said. "I beg your pardon. I beg your pardon. You took me from Leicester-square. I remember now. I beg your pardon." And with that this astonishing man let out his whip with a sharp crack at his horse and went trundling away. The whole of which interview, before the banner of St. George I swear, is strictly true.

I looked at the strange cabman as he lessened in the distance and the mists. I do not know whether I was right in fancying that although his face had seemed so honest there was something unearthly and demoniac about him when seen from behind. Perhaps he had been sent to tempt me from my adherence to those sanities and certainties which I had defended earlier in the day. In any case it gave me pleasure to remember that my sense of reality, though it had rocked for an instant, had remained erect.

Chapter 6
An Accident

ome time ago I wrote in these columns an article called "The Extraordinary Cabman." I am now in a position to contribute my experience of a still more extraordinary cab. The extraordinary thing about the cab was that it did not like me; it threw me out violently in the middle of the Strand. If my friends who read the DAILY NEWS are as romantic (and as rich) as I take them to be, I presume that this experience is not uncommon. I suppose that they are all being thrown out of cabs, all over London. Still, as there are some people, virginal and remote from the world, who have not yet had this luxurious experience, I will give a short account of the psychology of myself when my hansom cab ran into the side of a motor omnibus, and I hope hurt it.

I do not need to dwell on the essential romance of the hansom cab—that one really noble modern thing which our age, when it is judged, will gravely put beside the Parthenon. It is really modern in that it is both secret and swift. My particular hansom cab was modern in these two respects; it was also very modern in the fact that it came to grief. But it is also English; it is not to be found abroad; it belongs to a beautiful, romantic country where nearly everybody is pretending to be richer than they are, and acting as if they were. It is comfortable, and yet it is reckless; and that combination is the very soul of England. But although I had always realised all these good qualities in a hansom cab, I had not experienced all the possibilities, or, as the moderns put it, all the aspects of that vehicle. My enunciation of the merits of a hansom cab had been always made when it was the right way up. Let me, therefore, explain how I felt when I fell out of a hansom cab for the first and, I am happy to believe, the last time. Polycrates threw one ring into the sea to propitiate the Fates. I have thrown one hansom cab into the sea (if you will excuse a rather violent metaphor) and the Fates are, I am quite sure, propitiated. Though I am told they do not like to be told so.

I was driving yesterday afternoon in a hansom cab down one of the sloping streets into the Strand, reading one of my own admirable articles with continual pleasure, and still more continual surprise, when the horse fell forward, scrambled a moment on the scraping stones, staggered to his feet again, and went forward. The horses in my cabs often do this, and I have learnt to enjoy my own articles at any angle of the vehicle. So I did not see anything at all odd about the way the horse went on again. But I saw it suddenly in the faces of all the people on the pavement. They were all turned towards me, and they were all struck with fear suddenly, as with a white flame out of the sky. And one man half ran out into the road with a movement of the elbow as if warding off a blow, and tried to stop the horse. Then I knew that the reins were lost, and the next moment the horse was like a living thunder-bolt. I try to describe things exactly as they seemed to me; many details I may have missed or mis-stated; many details may have, so to speak, gone mad in the race down the road. I remember that I once called one of my experiences narrated in this paper "A Fragment of Fact." This is, at any rate, a fragment of fact. No fact could possibly be more fragmentary than the sort of fact that I expected to be at the bottom of that street.

I believe in preaching to the converted; for I have generally found that the converted do not understand their own religion. Thus I have always urged in this paper that democracy has a deeper meaning than democrats understand; that is, that common and popular things, proverbs, and ordinary sayings always have something in them unrealised by most who repeat them. Here is one. We have all heard about the man who is in momentary danger, and who sees the whole of his life pass before him in a moment. In the cold, literal, and common sense of words, this is obviously a thundering lie. Nobody can pretend that in an accident or a mortal crisis he elaborately remembered all the tickets he had ever taken to Wimbledon, or all the times that he had ever passed the brown bread and butter.

But in those few moments, while my cab was tearing towards the traffic of the Strand, I discovered that there is a truth behind this phrase, as there is behind all popular phrases. I did really have, in that short and shrieking period, a rapid succession of a number of fundamental points of view. I had, so to speak, about five religions in almost as many seconds. My first religion was pure Paganism, which among sincere men is more shortly described as extreme fear. Then there succeeded a state of mind which is quite real, but for which no proper name has ever been found. The ancients called it Stoicism, and I think it must be what some German lunatics mean (if they mean anything) when they talk about Pessimism. It was an empty and open acceptance of the thing that happens—as if one had got beyond the value of it. And then, curiously enough, came a very strong contrary feeling—that things mattered very much indeed, and yet that they were something more than tragic. It was a feeling, not that life was unimportant, but that life was much too important ever to be anything but life. I hope that this was Christianity. At any rate, it occurred at the moment when we went crash into the omnibus.

It seemed to me that the hansom cab simply turned over on top of me, like an enormous hood or hat. I then found myself crawling out from underneath it in attitudes so undignified that they must have added enormously to that great cause to which the Anti-Puritan League and I have recently dedicated ourselves. I mean the cause of the pleasures of the people. As to my demeanour when I emerged, I have two confessions to make, and they are both made merely in the interests of mental science. The first is that whereas I had been in a quite pious frame of mind the moment before the collision, when I got to my feet and found I had got off with a cut or two I began (like St. Peter) to curse and to swear. A man offered me a newspaper or something that I had dropped. I can distinctly remember consigning the paper to a state of irremediable spiritual ruin. I am very sorry for this now, and I apologise both to the man and to the paper. I have not the least idea what was the meaning of this unnatural anger; I mention it as a psychological confession. It was immediately followed by extreme hilarity, and I made so many silly jokes to the policeman that he disgraced himself by continual laughter before all the little boys in the street, who had hitherto taken him seriously.

There is one other odd thing about the matter which I also mention as a curiosity of the human brain or deficiency of brain. At intervals of about every three minutes I kept on reminding the policeman that I had not paid the cabman, and that I hoped he would not lose his money. He said it would be all right, and the man would appear. But it was not until about half an hour afterwards that it suddenly struck me with a shock intolerable that the man might conceivably have lost more than half a crown; that he had been in danger as well as I. I had instinctively regarded the cabman as something uplifted above accidents, a god. I immediately made inquiries, and I am happy to say that they seemed to have been unnecessary.

But henceforward I shall always understand with a darker and more delicate charity those who take tythe of mint, and anise, and cumin, and neglect the weightier matters of the law; I shall remember how I was once really tortured with owing half a crown to a man who might have been dead. Some admirable men in white coats at the Charing Cross Hospital tied up my small injury, and I went out again into the Strand. I felt upon me even a kind of unnatural youth; I hungered for something untried. So to open a new chapter in my life I got into a hansom cab.

Chapter 7
The Advantages of Having One Leg

 friend of mine who was visiting a poor woman in bereavement and casting about for some phrase of consolation that should not be either insolent or weak, said at last, "I think one can live through these great sorrows and even be the better. What wears one is the little worries." "That's quite right, mum," answered the old woman with emphasis, "and I ought to know, seeing I've had ten of 'em." It is, perhaps, in this sense that it is most true that little worries are most wearing. In its vaguer significance the phrase, though it contains a truth, contains also some possibilities of self-deception and error. People who have both small troubles and big ones have the right to say that they find the small ones the most bitter; and it is undoubtedly true that the back which is bowed under loads incredible can feel a faint addition to those loads; a giant holding up the earth and all its animal creation might still find the grasshopper a burden. But I am afraid that the maxim that the smallest worries are the worst is sometimes used or abused by people, because they have nothing but the very smallest worries. The lady may excuse herself for reviling the crumpled rose leaf by reflecting with what extraordinary dignity she would wear the crown of thorns—if she had to. The gentleman may permit himself to curse the dinner and tell himself that he would behave much better if it were a mere matter of starvation. We need not deny that the grasshopper on man's shoulder is a burden; but we need not pay much respect to the gentleman who is always calling out that he would rather have an elephant when he knows there are no elephants in the country. We may concede that a straw may break the camel's back, but we like to know that it really is the last straw and not the first.

I grant that those who have serious wrongs have a real right to grumble, so long as they grumble about something else. It is a singular fact that if they are sane they almost always do grumble about something else. To talk quite reasonably about your own quite real wrongs is the quickest way to go off your head. But people with great troubles talk about little ones, and the man who complains of the crumpled rose leaf very often has his flesh full of the thorns. But if a man has commonly a very clear and happy daily life then I think we are justified in asking that he shall not make mountains out of molehills. I do not deny that molehills can sometimes be important. Small annoyances have this evil about them, that they can be more abrupt because they are more invisible; they cast no shadow before, they have no atmosphere. No one ever had a mystical premonition that he was going to tumble over a hassock. William III. died by falling over a molehill; I do not suppose that with all his varied abilities he could have managed to fall over a mountain. But when all this is allowed for, I repeat that we may ask a happy man (not William III.) to put up with pure inconveniences, and even make them part of his happiness. Of positive pain or positive poverty I do not here speak. I speak of those innumerable accidental limitations that are always falling across our path—bad weather, confinement to this or that house or room, failure of appointments or arrangements, waiting at railway stations, missing posts, finding unpunctuality when we want punctuality, or, what is worse, finding punctuality when we don't. It is of the poetic pleasures to be drawn from all these that I sing—I sing with confidence because I have recently been experimenting in the poetic pleasures which arise from having to sit in one chair with a sprained foot, with the only alternative course of standing on one leg like a stork—a stork is a poetic simile; therefore I eagerly adopted it.

To appreciate anything we must always isolate it, even if the thing itself symbolise something other than isolation. If we wish to see what a house is it must be a house in some uninhabited landscape. If we wish to depict what a man really is we must depict a man alone in a desert or on a dark sea sand. So long as he is a single figure he means all that humanity means; so long as he is solitary he means human society; so long as he is solitary he means sociability and comradeship. Add another figure and the picture is less human—not more so. One is company, two is none. If you wish to symbolise human building draw one dark tower on the horizon; if you wish to symbolise light let there be no star in the sky. Indeed, all through that strangely lit season which we call our day there is but one star in the sky—a large, fierce star which we call the sun. One sun is splendid; six suns would be only vulgar. One Tower Of Giotto is sublime; a row of Towers of Giotto would be only like a row of white posts. The poetry of art is in beholding the single tower; the poetry of nature in seeing the single tree; the poetry of love in following the single woman; the poetry of religion in worshipping the single star. And so, in the same pensive lucidity, I find the poetry of all human anatomy in standing on a single leg. To express complete and perfect leggishness the leg must stand in sublime isolation, like the tower in the wilderness. As Ibsen so finely says, the strongest leg is that which stands most alone.

This lonely leg on which I rest has all the simplicity of some Doric column. The students of architecture tell us that the only legitimate use of a column is to support weight. This column of mine fulfils its legitimate function. It supports weight. Being of an animal and organic consistency, it may even improve by the process, and during these few days that I am thus unequally balanced, the helplessness or dislocation of the one leg may find compensation in the astonishing strength and classic beauty of the other leg. Mrs. Mountstuart Jenkinson in Mr. George Meredith's novel might pass by at any moment, and seeing me in the stork-like attitude would exclaim, with equal admiration and a more literal exactitude, "He has a leg." Notice how this famous literary phrase supports my contention touching this isolation of any admirable thing. Mrs. Mountstuart Jenkinson, wishing to make a clear and perfect picture of human grace, said that

Sir Willoughby Patterne had a leg. She delicately glossed over and concealed the clumsy and offensive fact that he had really two legs. Two legs were superfluous and irrelevant, a reflection, and a confusion. Two legs would have confused Mrs. Mountstuart Jenkinson like two Monuments in London. That having had one good leg he should have another—this would be to use vain repetitions as the Gentiles do. She would have been as much bewildered by him as if he had been a centipede.

All pessimism has a secret optimism for its object. All surrender of life, all denial of pleasure, all darkness, all austerity, all desolation has for its real aim this separation of something so that it may be poignantly and perfectly enjoyed. I feel grateful for the slight sprain which has introduced this mysterious and fascinating division between one of my feet and the other. The way to love anything is to realise that it might be lost. In one of my feet I can feel how strong and splendid a foot is; in the other I can realise how very much otherwise it might have been. The moral of the thing is wholly exhilarating. This world and all our powers in it are far more awful and beautiful than even we know until some accident reminds us. If you wish to perceive that limitless felicity, limit yourself if only for a moment. If you wish to realise how fearfully and wonderfully God's image is made, stand on one leg. If you want to realise the splendid vision of all visible things—wink the other eye.

Chapter 8
The End of the World

or some time I had been wandering in quiet streets in the curious town of Besançon, which stands like a sort of peninsula in a horseshoe of river. You may learn from the guide books that it was the birthplace of Victor Hugo, and that it is a military station with many forts, near the French frontier. But you will not learn from guide books that the very tiles on the roofs seem to be of some quainter and more delicate colour than the tiles of all the other towns of the world; that the tiles look like the little clouds of some strange sunset, or like the lustrous scales of some strange fish. They will not tell you that in this town the eye cannot rest on anything without finding it in some way attractive and even elvish, a carved face at a street corner, a gleam of green fields through a stunted arch, or some unexpected colour for the enamel of a spire or dome.

Evening was coming on and in the light of it all these colours so simple and yet so subtle seemed more and more to fit together and make a fairy tale. I sat down for a little outside a café with a row of little toy trees in front of it, and presently the driver of a fly (as we should call it) came to the same place. He was one of those very large and dark Frenchmen, a type not common but yet typical of France; the Rabelaisian Frenchman, huge, swarthy, purple-faced, a walking wine-barrel; he was a sort of Southern Falstaff, if one can imagine Falstaff anything but English. And, indeed, there was a vital difference, typical of two nations. For while Falstaff would have been shaking with hilarity like a huge jelly, full of the broad farce of the London streets, this Frenchman was rather solemn and dignified than otherwise— as if pleasure were a kind of pagan religion. After some talk which was full of the admirable civility and equality of French civilisation, he suggested without either eagerness or embarrassment that he should take me in his fly for an hour's ride in the hills beyond the town. And though it was growing late I consented; for there was one long white road under an archway and round a hill that dragged me like a long white cord. We drove through the strong, squat gateway that was made by Romans, and I remember the coincidence like a sort of omen that as we passed out of the city I heard simultaneously the three sounds which are the trinity of France. They make what some poet calls "a tangled trinity," and I am not going to disentangle it. Whatever those three things mean, how or why they co-exist; whether they can be reconciled or perhaps are reconciled already; the three sounds I heard then by an accident all at once make up the French mystery. For the brass band in the Casino gardens behind me was playing with a sort of passionate levity some ramping tune from a Parisian comic opera, and while this was going on I heard also the bugles on the hills above, that told of terrible loyalties and men always arming in the gate of France; and I heard also, fainter than these sounds and through them all, the Angelus.

After this coincidence of symbols I had a curious sense of having left France behind me, or, perhaps, even the civilised world. And, indeed, there was something in the landscape wild enough to encourage such a fancy. I have seen perhaps higher mountains, but I have never seen higher rocks; I have never seen height so near, so abrupt and sensational, splinters of rock that stood up like the spires of churches, cliffs that fell sudden and straight as Satan fell from heaven. There was also a quality in the ride which was not only astonishing, but rather bewildering; a quality which many must have noticed if they have driven or ridden rapidly up mountain roads. I mean a sense of gigantic gyration, as of the whole earth turning about one's head. It is quite inadequate to say that the hills rose and fell like enormous waves. Rather the hills seemed to turn about me like the enormous sails of a windmill, a vast wheel of monstrous archangelic wings. As we drove on and up into the gathering purple of the sunset this dizziness increased, confounding things above with things below. Wide walls of wooded rock stood out above my head like a roof. I stared at them until I fancied that I was staring down at a wooded plain. Below me steeps of green swept down to the river. I stared at them until I fancied that they swept up to the sky. The purple darkened, night drew nearer; it seemed only to cut clearer the chasms and draw higher the spires of that nightmare landscape. Above me in the twilight was the huge black hulk of the driver, and his broad, blank back was as mysterious as the back of Death in Watts' picture. I felt that I was growing too fantastic, and I sought to speak of ordinary things. I called out to the driver in French, "Where are you taking me?" and it is a literal and solemn fact that he answered me in the same language without turning around, "To the end of the world."

I did not answer. I let him drag the vehicle up dark, steep ways, until I saw lights under a low roof of little trees and two children, one oddly beautiful, playing at ball. Then we found ourselves filling up the strict main street of a tiny hamlet, and across the wall of its inn was written in large letters, LE BOUT DU MONDE—the end of the world.

The driver and I sat down outside that inn without a word, as if all ceremonies were natural and understood in that ultimate place. I ordered bread for both of us, and red wine, that was good but had no name. On the other side of the road was a little plain church with a cross on top of it and a cock on top of the cross. This seemed to me a very good end of the world; if the story of the world ended here it ended well. Then I wondered whether I myself should really be content to end here, where most certainly there were the best things of Christendom—a church and children's games and decent soil and a tavern for men to talk with men. But as I thought a singular doubt and desire grew slowly in me, and at last I started up.

"Are you not satisfied?" asked my companion. "No," I said, "I am not satisfied even at the end of the world."

Then, after a silence, I said, "Because you see there are two ends of the world. And this is the wrong end of the world; at least the wrong one for me. This is the French end of the world. I want the other end of the world. Drive me to the other end of the world."

"The other end of the world?" he asked. "Where is that?"

"It is in Walham Green," I whispered hoarsely. "You see it on the London omnibuses. 'World's End and Walham Green.' Oh, I know how good this is; I love your vineyards and your free peasantry, but I want the English end of the world. I love you like a brother, but I want an English cabman, who will be funny and ask me what his fare 'is.' Your bugles stir my blood, but I want to see a London policeman. Take, oh, take me to see a London policeman."

He stood quite dark and still against the end of the sunset, and I could not tell whether he understood or not. I got back into his carriage.

"You will understand," I said, "if ever you are an exile even for pleasure. The child to his mother, the man to his country, as a countryman of yours once said. But since, perhaps, it is rather too long a drive to the English end of the world, we may as well drive back to Besançon."

Only as the stars came out among those immortal hills I wept for Walham Green.

Chapter 9
In the Place de La Bastille

On the first of May I was sitting outside a café in the Place de la Bastille in Paris staring at the exultant column, crowned with a capering figure, which stands in the place where the people destroyed a prison and ended an age. The thing is a curious example of how symbolic is the great part of human history. As a matter of mere material fact, the Bastille when it was taken was not a horrible prison; it was hardly a prison at all. But it was a symbol, and the people always go by a sure instinct for symbols; for the Chinaman, for instance, at the last General Election, or for President Kruger's hat in the election before; their poetic sense is perfect. The Chinaman with his pigtail is not an idle flippancy. He does typify with a compact precision exactly the thing the people resent in African policy, the alien and grotesque nature of the power of wealth, the fact that money has no roots, that it is not a natural and familiar power, but a sort of airy and evil magic calling monsters from the ends of the earth. The people hate the mine owner who can bring a Chinaman flying across the sea, exactly as the people hated the wizard who could fetch a flying dragon through the air. It was the same with Mr. Kruger's hat. His hat (that admirable hat) was not merely a joke. It did symbolise, and symbolise extremely well, the exact thing which our people at that moment regarded with impatience and venom; the old-fashioned, dingy, Republican simplicity, the unbeautiful dignity of the bourgeois, and the heavier truisms of political morality. No; the people are sometimes wrong on the practical side of politics; they are never wrong on the artistic side.

So it was, certainly, with the Bastille. The destruction of the Bastille was not a reform; it was something more important than a reform. It was an iconoclasm; it was the breaking of a stone image. The people saw the building like a giant looking at them with a score of eyes, and they struck at it as at a carved fact. For of all the shapes in which that immense illusion called materialism can terrify the soul, perhaps the most oppressive are big buildings. Man feels like a fly, an accident, in the thing he has himself made. It requires a violent effort of the spirit to remember that man made this confounding thing and man could unmake it. Therefore the mere act of the ragged people in the street taking and destroying a huge public building has a spiritual, a ritual meaning far beyond its immediate political results. It is a religious service. If, for instance, the Socialists were numerous or courageous enough to capture and smash up the Bank of England, you might argue for ever about the inutility of the act, and how it really did not touch the root of the economic problem in the correct manner. But mankind would never forget it. It would change the world.

Architecture is a very good test of the true strength of a society, for the most valuable things in a human state are the irrevocable things—marriage, for instance. And architecture approaches nearer than any other art to being irrevocable, because it is so difficult to get rid of. You can turn a picture with its face to the wall; it would be a nuisance to turn that Roman cathedral with its face to the wall. You can tear a poem to pieces; it is only in moments of very sincere emotion that you tear a town-hall to pieces. A building is akin to dogma; it is insolent, like a dogma. Whether or no it is permanent, it claims permanence like a dogma. People ask why we have no typical architecture of the modern world, like impressionism in painting. Surely it is obviously because we have not enough dogmas; we cannot bear to see anything in the sky that is solid and enduring, anything in the sky that does not change like the clouds of the sky. But along with this decision which is involved in creating a building, there goes a quite similar decision in the more delightful task of smashing one. The two of necessity go together. In few places have so many fine public buildings been set up as here in Paris, and in few places have so many been destroyed. When people have finally got into the horrible habit of preserving buildings, they have got out of the habit of building them. And in London one mingles, as it were, one's tears because so few are pulled down.

As I sat staring at the column of the Bastille, inscribed to Liberty and Glory, there came out of one corner of the square (which, like so many such squares, was at once crowded and quiet) a sudden and silent line of horsemen. Their dress was of a dull blue, plain and prosaic enough, but the sun set on fire the brass and steel of their helmets; and their helmets were carved like the helmets of the Romans. I had seen them by twos and threes often enough before. I had seen plenty of them in pictures toiling through the snows of Friedland or roaring round the squares at Waterloo. But now they came file after file, like an invasion, and something in their numbers, or in the evening light that lit up their faces and their crests, or something in the reverie into which they broke, made me inclined to spring to my feet and cry out, "The French soldiers!" There were the little men with the brown faces that had so often ridden through the capitals of Europe as coolly as they now rode through their own. And when I looked across the square I saw that the two other corners were choked with blue and red; held by little groups of infantry. The city was garrisoned as against a revolution.

Of course, I had heard all about the strike, chiefly from a baker. He said he was not going to "Chomer." I said, "Qu'est-ce que c'est que le chome?" He said, "Ils ne veulent pas travailler." I said, "Ni moi non plus," and he thought I was a class-conscious collectivist proletarian. The whole thing was curious, and the true moral of it one not easy for us, as a nation, to grasp, because our own faults are so deeply and dangerously in the other direction. To me, as an Englishman (personally steeped in the English optimism and the English dislike of severity), the whole thing seemed a fuss about nothing. It looked like turning out one of the best armies in Europe against ordinary people walking about the street. The cavalry charged us once or twice, more or less harmlessly. But, of course, it is hard to say how far in such criticisms one is assuming the French populace to be (what it is not) as docile as the English. But the deeper truth of the matter tingled, so to speak, through the whole noisy night. This people has a natural faculty for feeling itself on the eve of something—of the Bartholomew or the Revolution or the Commune or the Day of Judgment. It is this sense of crisis that makes France eternally young. It is perpetually pulling down and building up, as it pulled down the prison and put up the column in the Place de La Bastille. France has always been at the point of dissolution. She has found the only method of immortality. She dies daily.

Chapter 10
On Lying in Bed

ying in bed would be an altogether perfect and supreme experience if only one had a coloured pencil long enough to draw on the ceiling. This, however, is not generally a part of the domestic apparatus on the premises. I think myself that the thing might be managed with several pails of Aspinall and a broom. Only if one worked in a really sweeping and masterly way, and laid on the colour in great washes, it might drip down again on one's face in floods of rich and mingled colour like some strange fairy rain; and that would have its disadvantages. I am afraid it would be necessary to stick to black and white in this form of artistic composition. To that purpose, indeed, the white ceiling would be of the greatest possible use; in fact, it is the only use I think of a white ceiling being put to.

But for the beautiful experiment of lying in bed I might never have discovered it. For years I have been looking for some blank spaces in a modern house to draw on. Paper is much too small for any really allegorical design; as Cyrano de Bergerac says, "Il me faut des géants." But when I tried to find these fine clear spaces in the modern rooms such as we all live in I was continually disappointed. I found an endless pattern and complication of small objects hung like a curtain of fine links between me and my desire. I examined the walls; I found them to my surprise to be already covered with wallpaper, and I found the wallpaper to be already covered with uninteresting images, all bearing a ridiculous resemblance to each other. I could not understand why one arbitrary symbol (a symbol apparently entirely devoid of any religious or philosophical significance) should thus be sprinkled all over my nice walls like a sort of small-pox. The Bible must be referring to wallpapers, I think, when it says, "Use not vain repetitions, as the Gentiles do." I found the Turkey carpet a mass of unmeaning colours, rather like the Turkish Empire, or like the sweetmeat called Turkish Delight. I do not exactly know what Turkish Delight really is; but I suppose it is Macedonian Massacres. Everywhere that I went forlornly, with my pencil or my paint brush, I found that others had unaccountably been before me, spoiling the walls, the curtains, and the furniture with their childish and barbaric designs.

Nowhere did I find a really clear space for sketching until this occasion when I prolonged beyond the proper limit the process of lying on my back in bed. Then the light of that white heaven broke upon my vision, that breadth of mere white which is indeed almost the definition of Paradise, since it means purity and also means freedom. But alas! like all heavens, now that it is seen it is found to be unattainable; it looks more austere and more distant than the blue sky outside the window. For my proposal to paint on it with the bristly end of a broom has been discouraged—never mind by whom; by a person debarred from all political rights—and even my minor proposal to put the other end of the broom into the kitchen fire and turn it to charcoal has not been conceded. Yet I am certain that it was from persons in my position that all the original inspiration came for covering the ceilings of palaces and cathedrals with a riot of fallen angels or victorious gods. I am sure that it was only because Michael Angelo was engaged in the ancient and honourable occupation of lying in bed that he ever realized how the roof of the Sistine Chapel might be made into an awful imitation of a divine drama that could only be acted in the heavens.

The tone now commonly taken toward the practice of lying in bed is hypocritical and unhealthy. Of all the marks of modernity that seem to mean a kind of decadence, there is none more menacing and dangerous than the exultation of very small and secondary matters of conduct at the expense of very great and primary ones, at the expense of eternal ties and tragic human morality. If there is one thing worse than the modern weakening of major morals, it is the modern strengthening of minor morals. Thus it is considered more withering to accuse a man of bad taste than of bad ethics. Cleanliness is not next to godliness nowadays, for cleanliness is made essential and godliness is regarded as an offence. A playwright can attack the institution of marriage so long as he does not misrepresent the manners of society, and I have met Ibsenite pessimists who thought it wrong to take beer but right to take prussic acid. Especially this is so in matters of hygiene; notably such matters as lying in bed. Instead of being regarded, as it ought to be, as a matter of personal convenience and adjustment, it has come to be regarded by many as if it were a part of essential morals to get up early in the morning. It is upon the whole part of practical wisdom; but there is nothing good about it or bad about its opposite.

Misers get up early in the morning; and burglars, I am informed, get up the night before. It is the great peril of our society that all its mechanisms may grow more fixed while its spirit grows more fickle. A man's minor actions and arrangements ought to be free, flexible, creative; the things that should be unchangeable are his principles, his ideals. But with us the reverse is true; our views change constantly; but our lunch does not change. Now, I should like men to have strong and rooted conceptions, but as for their lunch, let them have it sometimes in the garden, sometimes in bed, sometimes on the roof, sometimes in the top of a tree. Let them argue from the same first principles, but let them do it in a bed, or a boat, or a balloon. This alarming growth of good habits really means a too great emphasis on those virtues which mere custom can ensure, it means too little emphasis on those virtues which custom can never quite ensure, sudden and splendid virtues of inspired pity or of inspired candour. If ever that abrupt appeal is made to us we may fail. A man can get use to getting up at five o'clock in the morning. A man cannot very well get used to being burnt for his opinions; the first experiment is commonly fatal. Let us pay a little more attention to these possibilities of the heroic and unexpected. I dare say that when I get out of this bed I shall do some deed of an almost terrible virtue.

For those who study the great art of lying in bed there is one emphatic caution to be added. Even for those who can do their work in bed (like journalists), still more for those whose work cannot be done in bed (as, for example, the professional harpooners of whales), it is obvious that the indulgence must be very occasional. But that is not the caution I mean. The caution is this: if you do lie in bed, be sure you do it without any reason or justification at all. I do not speak, of course, of the seriously sick. But if a healthy man lies in bed, let him do it without a rag of excuse; then he will get up a healthy man. If he does it for some secondary hygienic reason, if he has some scientific explanation, he may get up a hypochondriac.

Chapter 11
The Twelve Men

he other day, while I was meditating on morality and Mr. H. Pitt, I was, so to speak, snatched up and put into a jury box to try people. The snatching took some weeks, but to me it seemed something sudden and arbitrary. I was put into this box because I lived in Battersea, and my name began with a C. Looking round me, I saw that there were also summoned and in attendance in the court whole crowds and processions of men, all of whom lived in Battersea, and all of whose names began with a C.

It seems that they always summon jurymen in this sweeping alphabetical way. At one official blow, so to speak, Battersea is denuded of all its C's, and left to get on as best it can with the rest of the alphabet. A Cumberpatch is missing from one street—a Chizzolpop from another—three Chucksterfields from Chucksterfield House; the children are crying out for an absent Cadgerboy; the woman at the street corner is weeping for her Coffintop, and will not be comforted. We settle down with a rollicking ease into our seats (for we are a bold, devil-may-care race, the C's of Battersea), and an oath is administered to us in a totally inaudible manner by an individual resembling an Army surgeon in his second childhood. We understand, however, that we are to well and truly try the case between our sovereign lord the King and the prisoner at the bar, neither of whom has put in an appearance as yet.

Just when I was wondering whether the King and the prisoner were, per-haps, coming to an amicable understanding in some adjoining public house, the prisoner's head appears above the barrier of the dock; he is accused of stealing bicycles, and he is the living image of a great friend of mine. We go into the matter of the stealing of the bicycles. We do well and truly try the case between the King and the prisoner in the affair of the bicycles. And we come to the conclusion, after a brief but reasonable discussion, that the King is not in any way implicated. Then we pass on to a woman who neglected her children, and who looks as if somebody or something had neglected her. And I am one of those who fancy that something had.

All the time that the eye took in these light appearances and the brain passed these light criticisms, there was in the heart a barbaric pity and fear which men have never been able to utter from the beginning, but which is the power behind half the poems of the world. The mood cannot even adequately be suggested, except faintly by this statement that tragedy is the highest expression of the infinite value of human life. Never had I stood so close to pain; and never so far away from pessimism. Ordinarily, I should not have spoken of these dark emotions at all, for speech about them is too difficult; but I mention them now for a specific and particular reason to the statement of which I will proceed at once. I speak these feelings because out of the furnace of them there came a curious realisation of a political or social truth. I saw with a queer and indescribable kind of clearness what a jury really is, and why we must never let it go.

The trend of our epoch up to this time has been consistently towards specialism and professionalism. We tend to have trained soldiers because they fight better, trained singers because they sing better, trained dancers because they dance better, specially instructed laughers because they laugh better, and so on and so on. The principle has been applied to law and politics by innumerable modern writers. Many Fabians have insisted that a greater part of our political work should be performed by experts. Many legalists have declared that the untrained jury should be altogether supplanted by the trained Judge.

Now, if this world of ours were really what is called reasonable, I do not know that there would be any fault to find with this. But the true result of all experience and the true foundation of all religion is this. That the four or five things that it is most practically essential that a man should know, are all of them what people call paradoxes. That is to say, that though we all find them in life to be mere plain truths, yet we cannot easily state them in words without being guilty of seeming verbal contradictions. One of them, for instance, is the unimpeachable platitude that the man who finds most pleasure for himself is often the man who least hunts for it. Another is the paradox of courage; the fact that the way to avoid death is not to have too much aversion to it. Whoever is careless enough of his bones to climb some hopeful cliff above the tide may save his bones by that carelessness. Whoever will lose his life, the same shall save it; an entirely practical and prosaic statement.

Now, one of these four or five paradoxes which should be taught to every infant prattling at his mother's knee is the following: That the more a man looks at a thing, the less he can see it, and the more a man learns a thing the less he knows it. The Fabian argument of the expert, that the man who is trained should be the man who is trusted would be absolutely unanswerable if it were really true that a man who studied a thing and practiced it every day went on seeing more and more of its significance. But he does not. He goes on seeing less and less of its significance. In the same way, alas! we all go on every day, unless we are continually goading ourselves into gratitude and humility, seeing less and less of the significance of the sky or the stones.

Now it is a terrible business to mark a man out for the vengeance of men. But it is a thing to which a man can grow accustomed, as he can to other terrible things; he can even grow accustomed to the sun. And the horrible thing about all legal officials, even the best, about all judges, magistrates, barristers, detectives, and policemen, is not that they are wicked (some of them are good), not that they are stupid (several of them are quite intelligent), it is simply that they have got used to it.

Strictly they do not see the prisoner in the dock; all they see is the usual man in the usual place. They do not see the awful court of judgment; they only see their own workshop. Therefore, the instinct of Christian civilisation has most wisely declared that into their judgments there shall upon every occasion be infused fresh blood and fresh thoughts from the streets. Men shall come in who can see the court and the crowd, and coarse faces of the policeman and the professional criminals, the wasted faces of the wastrels, the unreal faces of the gesticulating counsel, and see it all as one sees a new picture or a play hitherto unvisited.

Our civilisation has decided, and very justly decided, that determining the guilt or innocence of men is a thing too important to be trusted to trained men. It wishes for light upon that awful matter, it asks men who know no more law than I know, but who can feel the things that I felt in the jury box. When it wants a library catalogued, or the solar system discovered, or any trifle of that kind, it uses up specialists. But when it wishes anything done which is really serious, it collects twelve of the ordinary men standing round. The same thing was done, if I remember right, by the Founder of Christianity.

Chapter 12
The Wind and the Trees

 am sitting under tall trees, with a great wind boiling like surf about the tops of them, so that their living load of leaves rocks and roars in something that is at once exultation and agony. I feel, in fact, as if I were actually sitting at the bottom of the sea among mere anchors and ropes, while over my head and over the green twilight of water sounded the everlasting rush of waves and the toil and crash and shipwreck of tremendous ships. The wind tugs at the trees as if it might pluck them root and all out of the earth like tufts of grass. Or, to try yet another desperate figure of speech for this unspeakable energy, the trees are straining and tearing and lashing as if they were a tribe of dragons each tied by the tail.

As I look at these top-heavy giants tortured by an invisible and violent witchcraft, a phrase comes back into my mind. I remember a little boy of my acquaintance who was once walking in Battersea Park under just such torn skies and tossing trees. He did not like the wind at all; it blew in his face too much; it made him shut his eyes; and it blew off his hat, of which he was very proud. He was, as far as I remember, about four. After complaining repeatedly of the atmospheric unrest, he said at last to his mother, "Well, why don't you take away the trees, and then it wouldn't wind."

Nothing could be more intelligent or natural than this mistake. Any one looking for the first time at the trees might fancy that they were indeed vast and titanic fans, which by their mere waving agitated the air around them for miles. Nothing, I say, could be more human and excusable than the belief that it is the trees which make the wind. Indeed, the belief is so human and excusable that it is, as a matter of fact, the belief of about ninety-nine out of a hundred of the philosophers, reformers, sociologists, and politicians of the great age in which we live. My small friend was, in fact, very like the principal modern thinkers; only much nicer.

In the little apologue or parable which he has thus the honour of inventing, the trees stand for all visible things and the wind for the invisible. The wind is the spirit which bloweth where it listeth; the trees are the material things of the world which are blown where the spirit lists. The wind is philosophy, religion, revolution; the trees are cities and civilisations. We only know that there is a wind because the trees on some distant hill suddenly go mad. We only know that there is a real revolution because all the chimney-pots go mad on the whole skyline of the city.

Just as the ragged outline of a tree grows suddenly more ragged and rises into fantastic crests or tattered tails, so the human city rises under the wind of the spirit into toppling temples or sudden spires. No man has ever seen a revolution. Mobs pouring through the palaces, blood pouring down the gutters, the guillotine lifted higher than the throne, a prison in ruins, a people in arms—these things are not revolution, but the results of revolution.

You cannot see a wind; you can only see that there is a wind. So, also, you cannot see a revolution; you can only see that there is a revolution. And there never has been in the history of the world a real revolution, brutally active and decisive, which was not preceded by unrest and new dogma in the reign of invisible things. All revolutions began by being abstract. Most revolutions began by being quite pedantically abstract.

The wind is up above the world before a twig on the tree has moved. So there must always be a battle in the sky before there is a battle on the earth. Since it is lawful to pray for the coming of the kingdom, it is lawful also to pray for the coming of the revolution that shall restore the kingdom. It is lawful to hope to hear the wind of Heaven in the trees. It is lawful to pray "Thine anger come on earth as it is in Heaven."

The great human dogma, then, is that the wind moves the trees. The great human heresy is that the trees move the wind. When people begin to say that the material circumstances have alone created the moral circumstances, then they have prevented all possibility of serious change. For if my circumstances have made me wholly stupid, how can I be certain even that I am right in altering those circumstances?

The man who represents all thought as an accident of environment is simply smashing and discrediting all his own thoughts—including that one. To treat the human mind as having an ultimate authority is necessary to any kind of thinking, even free thinking. And nothing will ever be reformed in this age or country unless we realise that the moral fact comes first.

For example, most of us, I suppose, have seen in print and heard in debating clubs an endless discussion that goes on between Socialists and total abstainers. The latter say that drink leads to poverty; the former say that poverty leads to drink. I can only wonder at their either of them being content with such simple physical explanations. Surely it is obvious that the thing which among the English proletariat leads to poverty is the same as the thing which leads to drink; the absence of strong civic dignity, the absence of an instinct that resists degradation.

When you have discovered why enormous English estates were not long ago cut up into small holdings like the land of France, you will have discovered why the Englishman is more drunken than the Frenchman. The Englishman, among his million delightful virtues, really has this quality, which may strictly be called "hand to mouth," because under its influence a man's hand automatically seeks his own mouth, instead of seeking (as it sometimes should do) his oppressor's nose. And a man who says that the English inequality in land is due only to economic causes, or that the drunkenness of England is due only to economic causes, is saying something so absurd that he cannot really have thought what he was saying.

Yet things quite as preposterous as this are said and written under the influence of that great spectacle of babyish helplessness, the economic theory of history. We have people who represent that all great historic motives were economic, and then have to howl at the top of their voices in order to induce the modern democracy to act on economic motives. The extreme Marxian politicians in England exhibit themselves as a small, heroic minority, trying vainly to induce the world to do what, according to their theory, the world always does. The truth is, of course, that there will be a social revolution the moment the thing has ceased to be purely economic. You can never have a revolution in order to establish a democracy. You must have a democracy in order to have a revolution.

I get up from under the trees, for the wind and the slight rain have ceased. The trees stand up like golden pillars in a clear sunlight. The tossing of the trees and the blowing of the wind have ceased simultaneously. So I suppose there are still modern philosophers who will maintain that the trees make the wind.

Chapter 13
The Dickensian

e was a quiet man, dressed in dark clothes, with a large limp straw hat; with something almost military in his moustache and whiskers, but with a quite unmilitary stoop and very dreamy eyes. He was gazing with a rather gloomy interest at the cluster, one might almost say the tangle, of small shipping which grew thicker as our little pleasure boat crawled up into Yarmouth Harbour. A boat entering this harbour, as every one knows, does not enter in front of the town like a foreigner, but creeps round at the back like a traitor taking the town in the rear. The passage of the river seems almost too narrow for traffic, and in consequence the bigger ships look colossal. As we passed under a timber ship from Norway, which seemed to block up the heavens like a cathedral, the man in a straw hat pointed to an odd wooden figurehead carved like a woman, and said, like one continuing a conversation, "Now, why have they left off having them. They didn't do any one any harm?"

I replied with some flippancy about the captain's wife being jealous; but I knew in my heart that the man had struck a deep note. There has been something in our most recent civilisation which is mysteriously hostile to such healthy and humane symbols.

"They hate anything like that, which is human and pretty," he continued, exactly echoing my thoughts. "I believe they broke up all the jolly old figureheads with hatchets and enjoyed doing it."

"Like Mr. Quilp," I answered, "when he battered the wooden Admiral with the poker."

His whole face suddenly became alive, and for the first time he stood erect and stared at me.

"Do you come to Yarmouth for that?" he asked.

"For what?"

"For Dickens," he answered, and drummed with his foot on the deck.

"No," I answered; "I come for fun, though that is much the same thing."

"I always come," he answered quietly, "to find Peggotty's boat. It isn't here."

And when he said that I understood him perfectly.

There are two Yarmouths; I daresay there are two hundred to the people who live there. I myself have never come to the end of the list of Batterseas. But there are two to the stranger and tourist; the poor part, which is dignified, and the prosperous part, which is savagely vulgar. My new friend haunted the first of these like a ghost; to the latter he would only distantly allude.

"The place is very much spoilt now . . . trippers, you know," he would say, not at all scornfully, but simply sadly. That was the nearest he would go to an admission of the monstrous watering place that lay along the front, outblazing the sun, and more deafening than the sea. But behind—out of earshot of this uproar—there are lanes so narrow that they seem like secret entrances to some hidden place of repose. There are squares so brimful of silence that to plunge into one of them is like plunging into a pool. In these places the man and I paced up and down talking about Dickens, or, rather, doing what all true Dickensians do, telling each other verbatim long passages which both of us knew quite well already. We were really in the atmosphere of the older England. Fishermen passed us who might well have been characters like Peggotty; we went into a musty curiosity shop and bought pipe-stoppers carved into figures from Pickwick. The evening was settling down between all the buildings with that slow gold that seems to soak everything when we went into the church.

In the growing darkness of the church, my eye caught the coloured windows which on that clear golden evening were flaming with all the passionate heraldry of the most fierce and ecstatic of Christian arts. At length I said to my companion:

"Do you see that angel over there? I think it must be meant for the angel at the sepulchre."

He saw that I was somewhat singularly moved, and he raised his eyebrows.

"I daresay," he said. "What is there odd about that?"

After a pause I said, "Do you remember what the angel at the sepulchre said?"

"Not particularly," he answered; "but where are you off to in such a hurry?"

I walked him rapidly out of the still square, past the fishermen's almshouses, towards the coast, he still inquiring indignantly where I was going.

"I am going," I said, "to put pennies in automatic machines on the beach. I am going to listen to the niggers. I am going to have my photograph taken. I am going to drink ginger-beer out of its original bottle. I will buy some picture postcards. I do want a boat. I am ready to listen to a concertina, and but for the defects of my education should be ready to play it. I am willing to ride on a donkey; that is, if the donkey is willing. I am willing to be a donkey; for all this was commanded me by the angel in the stained-glass window."

"I really think," said the Dickensian, "that I had better put you in charge of your relations."

"Sir," I answered, "there are certain writers to whom humanity owes much, whose talent is yet of so shy or delicate or retrospective a type that we do well to link it with certain quaint places or certain perishing associations. It would not be unnatural to look for the spirit of Horace Walpole at Strawberry Hill, or even for the shade of Thackeray in Old Kensington. But let us have no antiquarianism about Dickens, for Dickens is not an antiquity. Dickens looks not backward, but forward; he might look at our modern mobs with satire, or with fury, but he would love to look at them. He might lash our democracy, but it would be because, like a democrat, he asked much from it. We will not have all his books bound up under the title of 'The Old Curiosity Shop.' Rather we will have them all bound up under the title of 'Great Expectations.' Wherever humanity is he would have us face it and make something of it, swallow it with a holy cannibalism, and assimilate it with the digestion of a giant. We must take these trippers as he would have taken them, and tear out of them their tragedy and their farce. Do you remember now what the angel said at the sepulchre? 'Why seek ye the living among the dead? He is not here; he is risen.'"

With that we came out suddenly on the wide stretch of the sands, which were black with the knobs and masses of our laughing and quite desperate democracy. And the sunset, which was now in its final glory, flung far over all of them a red flush and glitter like the gigantic firelight of Dickens. In that strange evening light every figure looked at once grotesque and attractive, as if he had a story to tell. I heard a little girl (who was being throttled by another little girl) say by way of self-vindication, "My sister-in-law 'as got four rings aside her weddin' ring!"

I stood and listened for more, but my friend went away.

Chapter 14
In Topsy-Turvy Land

ast week, in an idle metaphor, I took the tumbling of trees and the secret energy of the wind as typical of the visible world moving under the violence of the invisible. I took this metaphor merely because I happened to be writing the article in a wood. Nevertheless, now that I return to Fleet Street (which seems to me, I confess, much better and more poetical than all the wild woods in the world), I am strangely haunted by this accidental comparison. The people's figures seem a forest and their soul a wind. All the human personalities which speak or signal to me seem to have this fantastic character of the fringe of the forest against the sky. That man that talks to me, what is he but an articulate tree? That driver of a van who waves his hands wildly at me to tell me to get out of the way, what is he but a bunch of branches stirred and swayed by a spiritual wind, a sylvan object that I can continue to contemplate with calm? That policeman who lifts his hand to warn three omnibuses of the peril that they run in encountering my person, what is he but a shrub shaken for a moment with that blast of human law which is a thing stronger than anarchy? Gradually this impression of the woods wears off. But this black-and-white contrast between the visible and invisible, this deep sense that the one essential belief is belief in the invisible as against the visible, is suddenly and sensationally brought back to my mind. Exactly at the moment when Fleet Street has grown most familiar (that is, most bewildering and bright), my eye catches a poster of vivid violet, on which I see written in large black letters these remarkable words: "Should Shop Assistants Marry?"

When I saw those words everything might just as well have turned upside down. The men in Fleet Street might have been walking about on their hands. The cross of St. Paul's might have been hanging in the air upside down. For I realise that I have really come into a topsy-turvy country; I have come into the country where men do definitely believe that the waving of the trees makes the wind. That is to say, they believe that the material circumstances, however black and twisted, are more important than the spiritual realities, however powerful and pure. "Should Shop Assistants Marry?" I am puzzled to think what some periods and schools of human history would have made of such a question. The ascetics of the East or of some periods of the early Church would have thought that the question meant, "Are not shop assistants too saintly, too much of another world, even to feel the emotions of the sexes?" But I suppose that is not what the purple poster means. In some pagan cities it might have meant, "Shall slaves so vile as shop assistants even be allowed to propagate their abject race?" But I suppose that is not what the purple poster meant. We must face, I fear, the full insanity of what it does mean. It does really mean that a section of the human race is asking whether the primary relations of the two human sexes are particularly good for modern shops. The human race is asking whether Adam and Eve are entirely suitable for Marshall and Snelgrove. If this is not topsy-turvy I cannot imagine what would be. We ask whether the universal institution will improve our (please God) temporary institution. Yet I have known many such questions. For instance, I have known a man ask seriously, "Does Democracy help the Empire?" Which is like saying, "Is art favourable to frescoes?"

I say that there are many such questions asked. But if the world ever runs short of them, I can suggest a large number of questions of precisely the same kind, based on precisely the same principle.

"Do Feet Improve Boots?"—"Is Bread Better when Eaten?"—"Should Hats have Heads in them?"—"Do People Spoil a Town?"—"Do Walls Ruin Wall-papers?" —"Should Neckties enclose Necks?"—"Do Hands Hurt Walking-sticks?"—"Does Burning Destroy Firewood?"—"Is Cleanliness Good for Soap?"—"Can Cricket Really Improve Cricket-bats?"—"Shall We Take Brides with our Wedding Rings?" and a hundred others.

Not one of these questions differs at all in intellectual purport or in intellectual value from the question which I have quoted from the purple poster, or from any of the typical questions asked by half of the earnest economists of our times. All the questions they ask are of this character; they are all tinged with this same initial absurdity. They do not ask if the means is suited to the end; they all ask (with profound and penetrating scepticism) if the end is suited to the means. They do not ask whether the tail suits the dog. They all ask whether a dog is (by the highest artistic canons) the most ornamental appendage that can be put at the end of a tail. In short, instead of asking whether our modern arrangements, our streets, trades, bargains, laws, and concrete institutions are suited to the primal and permanent idea of a healthy human life, they never admit that healthy human life into the discussion at all, except suddenly and accidentally at odd moments; and then they only ask whether that healthy human life is suited to our streets and trades. Perfection may be attainable or unattainable as an end. It may or may not be possible to talk of imperfection as a means to perfection. But surely it passes toleration to talk of perfection as a means to imperfection. The New Jerusalem may be a reality. It may be a dream. But surely it is too outrageous to say that the New Jerusalem is a reality on the road to Birmingham.

This is the most enormous and at the same time the most secret of the modern tyrannies of materialism. In theory the thing ought to be simple enough. A really human human being would always put the spiritual things first. A walking and speaking statue of God finds himself at one particular moment employed as a shop assistant. He has in himself a power of terrible love, a promise of paternity, a thirst for some loyalty that shall unify life, and in the ordinary course of things he asks himself, "How far do the existing conditions of those assisting in shops fit in with my evident and epic destiny in the matter of love and marriage?" But here, as I have said, comes in the quiet and crushing power of modern materialism. It prevents him rising in rebellion, as he would otherwise do. By perpetually talking about environment and visible things, by perpetually talking about economics and physical necessity, painting and keeping repainted a perpetual picture of iron machinery and merciless engines, of rails of steel, and of towers of stone, modern materialism at last produces this tremendous impression in which the truth is stated upside down. At last the result is achieved. The man does not say as he ought to have said, "Should married men endure being modern shop assistants?" The man says, "Should shop assistants marry?" Triumph has completed the immense illusion of materialism. The slave does not say, "Are these chains worthy of me?" The slave says scientifically and contentedly, "Am I even worthy of these chains?"

Chapter 15
What I Found in My Pocket

nce when I was very young I met one of those men who have made the Empire what it is—a man in an astracan coat, with an astracan moustache—a tight, black, curly moustache. Whether he put on the moustache with the coat or whether his Napoleonic will enabled him not only to grow a moustache in the usual place, but also to grow little moustaches all over his clothes, I do not know. I only remember that he said to me the following words: "A man can't get on nowadays by hanging about with his hands in his pockets." I made reply with the quite obvious flippancy that perhaps a man got on by having his hands in other people's pockets; whereupon he began to argue about Moral Evolution, so I suppose what I said had some truth in it. But the incident now comes back to me, and connects itself with another incident—if you can call it an incident—which happened to me only the other day.

I have only once in my life picked a pocket, and then (perhaps through some absent-mindedness) I picked my own. My act can really with some reason be so described. For in taking things out of my own pocket I had at least one of the more tense and quivering emotions of the thief; I had a complete ignorance and a profound curiosity as to what I should find there. Perhaps it would be the exaggeration of eulogy to call me a tidy person. But I can always pretty satisfactorily account for all my possessions. I can always tell where they are, and what I have done with them, so long as I can keep them out of my pockets. If once anything slips into those unknown abysses, I wave it a sad Virgilian farewell. I suppose that the things that I have dropped into my pockets are still there; the same presumption applies to the things that I have dropped into the sea. But I regard the riches stored in both these bottomless chasms with the same reverent ignorance. They tell us that on the last day the sea will give up its dead; and I suppose that on the same occasion long strings of extraordinary things will come running out of my pockets. But I have quite forgotten what any of them are; and there is really nothing (excepting the money) that I shall be at all surprised at finding among them.

Such at least has hitherto been my state of innocence. I here only wish briefly to recall the special, extraordinary, and hitherto unprecedented circumstances which led me in cold blood, and being of sound mind, to turn out my pockets. I was locked up in a third-class carriage for a rather long journey. The time was towards evening, but it might have been anything, for everything resembling earth or sky or light or shade was painted out as if with a great wet brush by an unshifting sheet of quite colourless rain. I had no books or newspapers. I had not even a pencil and a scrap of paper with which to write a religious epic. There were no advertisements on the walls of the carriage, otherwise I could have plunged into the study, for any collection of printed words is quite enough to suggest infinite complexities of mental ingenuity. When I find myself opposite the words "Sunlight Soap" I can exhaust all the aspects of Sun Worship, Apollo, and Summer poetry before I go on to the less congenial subject of soap. But there was no printed word or picture anywhere; there was nothing but blank wood inside the carriage and blank wet without. Now I deny most energetically that anything is, or can be, uninteresting. So I stared at the joints of the walls and seats, and began thinking hard on the fascinating subject of wood. Just as I had begun to realise why, perhaps, it was that Christ was a carpenter, rather than a bricklayer, or a baker, or anything else, I suddenly started upright, and remembered my pockets. I was carrying about with me an unknown treasury. I had a British Museum and a South Kensington collection of unknown curios hung all over me in different places. I began to take the things out.

The first thing I came upon consisted of piles and heaps of Battersea tram tickets. There were enough to equip a paper chase. They shook down in showers like confetti. Primarily, of course, they touched my patriotic emotions, and brought tears to my eyes; also they provided me with the printed matter I required, for I found on the back of them some short but striking little scientific essays about some kind of pill. Comparatively speaking, in my then destitution, those tickets might be regarded as a small but well-chosen scientific library. Should my railway journey continue (which seemed likely at the time) for a few months longer, I could imagine myself throwing myself into the controversial aspects of the pill, composing replies and rejoinders pro and con upon the data furnished to me. But after all it was the symbolic quality of the tickets that moved me most. For as certainly as the cross of St. George means English patriotism, those scraps of paper meant all that municipal patriotism which is now, perhaps, the greatest hope of England.

The next thing that I took out was a pocket-knife. A pocket-knife, I need hardly say, would require a thick book full of moral meditations all to itself. A knife typifies one of the most primary of those practical origins upon which as upon low, thick pillows all our human civilisation reposes. Metals, the mystery of the thing called iron and of the thing called steel, led me off half-dazed into a kind of dream. I saw into the intrails of dim, damp wood, where the first man among all the common stones found the strange stone. I saw a vague and violent battle, in which stone axes broke and stone knives were splintered against something shining and new in the hand of one desperate man. I heard all the hammers on all the anvils of the earth. I saw all the swords of Feudal and all the weals of Industrial war. For the knife is only a short sword; and the pocket-knife is a secret sword. I opened it and looked at that brilliant and terrible tongue which we call a blade; and I thought that perhaps it was the symbol of the oldest of the needs of man. The next moment I knew that I was wrong; for the thing that came next out of my pocket was a box of matches. Then I saw fire, which is stronger even than steel, the old, fierce female thing, the thing we all love, but dare not touch.

The next thing I found was a piece of chalk; and I saw in it all the art and all the frescoes of the world. The next was a coin of a very modest value; and I saw in it not only the image and superscription of our own Caesar, but all government and order since the world began. But I have not space to say what were the items in the long and splendid procession of poetical symbols that came pouring out. I cannot tell you all the things that were in my pocket. I can tell you one thing, however, that I could not find in my pocket. I allude to my railway ticket.

Chapter 16
The Dragon's Grandmother

 met a man the other day who did not believe in fairy tales. I do not mean that he did not believe in the incidents narrated in them—that he did not believe that a pumpkin could turn into a coach. He did, indeed, entertain this curious disbelief. And, like all the other people I have ever met who entertained it, he was wholly unable to give me an intelligent reason for it. He tried the laws of nature, but he soon dropped that. Then he said that pumpkins were unalterable in ordinary experience, and that we all reckoned on their infinitely protracted pumpkinity. But I pointed out to him that this was not an attitude we adopt specially towards impossible marvels, but simply the attitude we adopt towards all unusual occurrences. If we were certain of miracles we should not count on them. Things that happen very seldom we all leave out of our calculations, whether they are miraculous or not. I do not expect a glass of water to be turned into wine; but neither do I expect a glass of water to be poisoned with prussic acid. I do not in ordinary business relations act on the assumption that the editor is a fairy; but neither do I act on the assumption that he is a Russian spy, or the lost heir of the Holy Roman Empire. What we assume in action is not that the natural order is unalterable, but simply that it is much safer to bet on uncommon incidents than on common ones. This does not touch the credibility of any attested tale about a Russian spy or a pumpkin turned into a coach. If I had seen a pumpkin turned into a Panhard motor-car with my own eyes that would not make me any more inclined to assume that the same thing would happen again. I should not invest largely in pumpkins with an eye to the motor trade. Cinderella got a ball dress from the fairy; but I do not suppose that she looked after her own clothes any the less after it.

But the view that fairy tales cannot really have happened, though crazy, is common. The man I speak of disbelieved in fairy tales in an even more amazing and perverted sense. He actually thought that fairy tales ought not to be told to children. That is (like a belief in slavery or annexation) one of those intellectual errors which lie very near to ordinary mortal sins. There are some refusals which, though they may be done what is called conscientiously, yet carry so much of their whole horror in the very act of them, that a man must in doing them not only harden but slightly corrupt his heart. One of them was the refusal of milk to young mothers when their husbands were in the field against us. Another is the refusal of fairy tales to children.

The man had come to see me in connection with some silly society of which I am an enthusiastic member; he was a fresh-coloured, short-sighted young man, like a stray curate who was too helpless even to find his way to the Church of England. He had a curious green necktie and a very long neck; I am always meeting idealists with very long necks. Perhaps it is that their eternal aspiration slowly lifts their heads nearer and nearer to the stars. Or perhaps it has something to do with the fact that so many of them are vegetarians: perhaps they are slowly evolving the neck of the giraffe so that they can eat all the tops of the trees in Kensington Gardens. These things are in every sense above me. Such, anyhow, was the young man who did not believe in fairy tales; and by a curious coincidence he entered the room when I had just finished looking through a pile of contemporary fiction, and had begun to read "Grimm's Fairy tales" as a natural consequence.

The modern novels stood before me, however, in a stack; and you can imagine their titles for yourself. There was "Suburban Sue: A Tale of Psychology," and also "Psychological Sue: A Tale of Suburbia"; there was "Trixy: A Temperament," and "Man-Hate: A Monochrome," and all those nice things. I read them with real interest, but, curiously enough, I grew tired of them at last, and when I saw "Grimm's Fairy Tales" lying accidentally on the table, I gave a cry of indecent joy. Here at least, here at last, one could find a little common sense. I opened the book, and my eyes fell on these splendid and satisfying words, "The Dragon's Grandmother." That at least was reasonable; that at least was true. "The Dragon's Grandmother!" While I was rolling this first touch of ordinary human reality upon my tongue, I looked up suddenly and saw this monster with a green tie standing in the doorway.

I listened to what he said about the society politely enough, I hope; but when he incidentally mentioned that he did not believe in fairy tales, I broke out beyond control. "Man," I said, "who are you that you should not believe in fairy tales? It is much easier to believe in Blue Beard than to believe in you. A blue beard is a misfortune; but there are green ties which are sins. It is far easier to believe in a million fairy tales than to believe in one man who does not like fairy tales. I would rather kiss Grimm instead of a Bible and swear to all his stories as if they were thirty-nine articles than say seriously and out of my heart that there can be such a man as you; that you are not some temptation of the devil or some delusion from the void. Look at these plain, homely, practical words. 'The Dragon's Grandmother,' that is all right; that is rational almost to the verge of rationalism. If there was a dragon, he had a grandmother. But you—you had no grandmother! If you had known one, she would have taught you to love fairy tales. You had no father, you had no mother; no natural causes can explain you. You cannot be. I believe many things which I have not seen; but of such things as you it may be said, 'Blessed is he that has seen and yet has disbelieved.' "

It seemed to me that he did not follow me with sufficient delicacy, so I moderated my tone. "Can you not see," I said, "that fairy tales in their essence are quite solid and straightforward; but that this everlasting fiction about modern life is in its nature essentially incredible? Folk-lore means that the soul is sane, but that the universe is wild and full of marvels. Realism means that the world is dull and full of routine, but that the soul is sick and screaming. The problem of the fairy tale is—what will a healthy man do with a fantastic world? The problem of the modern novel is—what will a madman do with a dull world? In the fairy tales the cosmos goes mad; but the hero does not go mad. In the modern novels the hero is mad before the book begins, and suffers from the harsh steadiness and cruel sanity of the cosmos. In the excellent tale of 'The Dragon's Grandmother,' in all the other tales of Grimm, it is assumed that the young man setting out on his travels will have all substantial truths in him; that he will be brave, full of faith, reasonable, that he will respect his parents, keep his word, rescue one kind of people, defy another kind, 'parcere subjectis et debellare,' etc. Then, having assumed this centre of sanity, the writer entertains himself by fancying what would happen if the whole world went mad all round it, if the sun turned green and the moon blue, if horses had six legs and giants had two heads. But your modern literature takes insanity as its centre. Therefore, it loses the interest even of insanity. A lunatic is not startling to himself, because he is quite serious; that is what makes him a lunatic. A man who thinks he is a piece of glass is to himself as dull as a piece of glass. A man who thinks he is a chicken is to himself as common as a chicken. It is only sanity that can see even a wild poetry in insanity. Therefore, these wise old tales made the hero ordinary and the tale extraordinary. But you have made the hero extraordinary and the tale ordinary—so ordinary—oh, so very ordinary."

I saw him still gazing at me fixedly. Some nerve snapped in me under the hypnotic stare. I leapt to my feet and cried, "In the name of God and Democracy and the Dragon's grandmother—in the name of all good things—I charge you to avaunt and haunt this house no more." Whether or no it was the result of the exorcism, there is no doubt that he definitely went away.

Chapter 17
The Red Angel

find that there really are human beings who think fairy tales bad for children. I do not speak of the man in the green tie, for him I can never count truly human. But a lady has written me an earnest letter saying that fairy tales ought not to be taught to children even if they are true. She says that it is cruel to tell children fairy tales, because it frightens them. You might just as well say that it is cruel to give girls sentimental novels because it makes them cry. All this kind of talk is based on that complete forgetting of what a child is like which has been the firm foundation of so many educational schemes. If you keep bogies and goblins away from children they would make them up for themselves. One small child in the dark can invent more hells than Swedenborg. One small child can imagine monsters too big and black to get into any picture, and give them names too unearthly and cacophonous to have occurred in the cries of any lunatic. The child, to begin with, commonly likes horrors, and he continues to indulge in them even when he does not like them. There is just as much difficulty in saying exactly where pure pain begins in his case, as there is in ours when we walk of our own free will into the torture-chamber of a great tragedy. The fear does not come from fairy tales; the fear comes from the universe of the soul.

The timidity of the child or the savage is entirely reasonable; they are alarmed at this world, because this world is a very alarming place. They dislike being alone because it is verily and indeed an awful idea to be alone. Barbarians fear the unknown for the same reason that Agnostics worship it—because it is a fact. Fairy tales, then, are not responsible for producing in children fear, or any of the shapes of fear; fairy tales do not give the child the idea of the evil or the ugly; that is in the child already, because it is in the world already. Fairy tales do not give the child his first idea of bogey. What fairy tales give the child is his first clear idea of the possible defeat of bogey. The baby has known the dragon intimately ever since he had an imagination. What the fairy tale provides for him is a St. George to kill the dragon.

Exactly what the fairy tale does is this: it accustoms him for a series of clear pictures to the idea that these limitless terrors had a limit, that these shapeless enemies have enemies in the knights of God, that there is something in the universe more mystical than darkness, and stronger than strong fear. When I was a child I have stared at the darkness until the whole black bulk of it turned into one negro giant taller than heaven. If there was one star in the sky it only made him a Cyclops. But fairy tales restored my mental health, for next day I read an authentic account of how a negro giant with one eye, of quite equal dimensions, had been baffled by a little boy like myself (of similar inexperience and even lower social status) by means of a sword, some bad riddles, and a brave heart. Sometimes the sea at night seemed as dreadful as any dragon. But then I was acquainted with many youngest sons and little sailors to whom a dragon or two was as simple as the sea.

Take the most horrible of Grimm's tales in incident and imagery, the excellent tale of the "Boy who Could not Shudder," and you will see what I mean. There are some living shocks in that tale. I remember specially a man's legs which fell down the chimney by themselves and walked about the room, until they were rejoined by the severed head and body which fell down the chimney after them. That is very good. But the point of the story and the point of the reader's feelings is not that these things are frightening, but the far more striking fact that the hero was not frightened at them. The most fearful of all these fearful wonders was his own absence of fear. He slapped the bogies on the back and asked the devils to drink wine with him; many a time in my youth, when stifled with some modern morbidity, I have prayed for a double portion of his spirit. If you have not read the end of his story, go and read it; it is the wisest thing in the world. The hero was at last taught to shudder by taking a wife, who threw a pail of cold water over him. In that one sentence there is more of the real meaning of marriage than in all the books about sex that cover Europe and America.

At the four corners of a child's bed stand Perseus and Roland, Sigurd and St. George. If you withdraw the guard of heroes you are not making him rational; you are only leaving him to fight the devils alone. For the devils, alas, we have always believed in. The hopeful element in the universe has in modern times continually been denied and reasserted; but the hopeless element has never for a moment been denied. As I told "H. N. B." (whom I pause to wish a Happy Christmas in its most superstitious sense), the one thing modern people really do believe in is damnation. The greatest of purely modern poets summed up the really modern attitude in that fine Agnostic line—

"There may be Heaven; there must be Hell."

The gloomy view of the universe has been a continuous tradition; and the new types of spiritual investigation or conjecture all begin by being gloomy. A little while ago men believed in no spirits. Now they are beginning rather slowly to believe in rather slow spirits.

Some people objected to spiritualism, table rappings, and such things, because they were undignified, because the ghosts cracked jokes or waltzed with dinner-tables. I do not share this objection in the least. I wish the spirits were more farcical than they are. That they should make more jokes and better ones, would be my suggestion. For almost all the spiritualism of our time, in so far as it is new, is solemn and sad. Some Pagan gods were lawless, and some Christian saints were a little too serious; but the spirits of modern spiritualism are both lawless and serious—a disgusting combination. The specially contemporary spirits are not only devils, they are blue devils. This is, first and last, the real value of Christmas; in so far as the mythology remains at all it is a kind of happy mythology. Personally, of course, I believe in Santa Claus; but it is the season of forgiveness, and I will forgive others for not doing so. But if there is anyone who does not comprehend the defect in our world which I am civilising, I should recommend him, for instance, to read a story by Mr. Henry James, called "The Turn of the Screw." It is one of the most powerful things ever written, and it is one of the things about which I doubt most whether it ought ever to have been written at all. It describes two innocent children gradually growing at once omniscient and half-witted under the influence of the foul ghosts of a groom and a governess. As I say, I doubt whether Mr. Henry James ought to have published it (no, it is not indecent, do not buy it; it is a spiritual matter), but I think the question so doubtful that I will give that truly great man a chance. I will approve the thing as well as admire it if he will write another tale just as powerful about two children and Santa Claus. If he will not, or cannot, then the conclusion is clear; we can deal strongly with gloomy mystery, but not with happy mystery; we are not rationalists, but diabolists.

I have thought vaguely of all this staring at a great red fire that stands up in the room like a great red angel. But, perhaps, you have never heard of a red angel. But you have heard of a blue devil. That is exactly what I mean.

Chapter 18
The Tower

 have been standing where everybody has stood, opposite the great Belfry Tower of Bruges, and thinking, as every one has thought (though not, perhaps, said), that it is built in defiance of all decencies of architecture. It is made in deliberate disproportion to achieve the one startling effect of height. It is a church on stilts. But this sort of sublime deformity is characteristic of the whole fancy and energy of these Flemish cities. Flanders has the flattest and most prosaic landscapes, but the most violent and extravagant of buildings. Here Nature is tame; it is civilisation that is untamable. Here the fields are as flat as a paved square; but, on the other hand, the streets and roofs are as uproarious as a forest in a great wind. The waters of wood and meadow slide as smoothly and meekly as if they were in the London water-pipes. But the parish pump is carved with all the creatures out of the wilderness. Part of this is true, of course, of all art. We talk of wild animals, but the wildest animal is man. There are sounds in music that are more ancient and awful than the cry of the strangest beast at night. And so also there are buildings that are shapeless in their strength, seeming to lift themselves slowly like monsters from the primal mire, and there are spires that seem to fly up suddenly like a startled bird.

This savagery even in stone is the expression of the special spirit in humanity. All the beasts of the field are respectable; it is only man who has broken loose. All animals are domestic animals; only man is ever undomestic. All animals are tame animals; it is only we who are wild. And doubtless, also, while this queer energy is common to all human art, it is also generally characteristic of Christian art among the arts of the world. This is what people really mean when they say that Christianity is barbaric, and arose in ignorance. As a matter of historic fact, it didn't; it arose in the most equably civilised period the world has ever seen.

But it is true that there is something in it that breaks the outline of perfect and conventional beauty, something that dots with anger the blind eyes of the Apollo and lashes to a cavalry charge the horses of the Elgin Marbles. Christianity is savage, in the sense that it is primeval; there is in it a touch of the nigger hymn. I remember a debate in which I had praised militant music in ritual, and some one asked me if I could imagine Christ walking down the street before a brass band. I said I could imagine it with the greatest ease; for Christ definitely approved a natural noisiness at a great moment. When the street children shouted too loud, certain priggish disciples did begin to rebuke them in the name of good taste. He said: "If these were silent the very stones would cry out." With these words He called up all the wealth of artistic creation that has been founded on this creed. With those words He founded Gothic architecture. For in a town like this, which seems to have grown Gothic as a wood grows leaves, anywhere and anyhow, any odd brick or moulding may be carved off into a shouting face. The front of vast buildings is thronged with open mouths, angels praising God, or devils defying Him. Rock itself is racked and twisted, until it seems to scream. The miracle is accomplished; the very stones cry out.

But though this furious fancy is certainly a specialty of men among creatures, and of Christian art among arts, it is still most notable in the art of Flanders. All Gothic buildings are full of extravagant things in detail; but this is an extravagant thing in design. All Christian temples worth talking about have gargoyles; but Bruges Belfry is a gargoyle. It is an unnaturally long-necked animal, like a giraffe. The same impression of exaggeration is forced on the mind at every corner of a Flemish town. And if any one asks, "Why did the people of these flat countries instinctively raise these riotous and towering monuments?" the only answer one can give is, "Because they were the people of these flat countries." If any one asks, "Why the men of Bruges sacrificed architecture and everything to the sense of dizzy and divine heights?" we can only answer, "Because Nature gave them no encouragement to do so."

As I stare at the Belfry, I think with a sort of smile of some of my friends in London who are quite sure of how children will turn out if you give them what they call "the right environment." It is a troublesome thing, environment, for it sometimes works positively and sometimes negatively, and more often between the two. A beautiful environment may make a child love beauty; it may make him bored with beauty; most likely the two effects will mix and neutralise each other. Most likely, that is, the environment will make hardly any difference at all. In the scientific style of history (which was recently fashionable, and is still conventional) we always had a list of countries that had owed their characteristics to their physical conditions.

The Spaniards (it was said) are passionate because their country is hot; Scandinavians adventurous because their country is cold; Englishmen naval because they are islanders; Switzers free because they are mountaineers. It is all very nice in its way. Only unfortunately I am quite certain that I could make up quite as long a list exactly contrary in its argument point-blank against the influence of their geographical environment. Thus Spaniards have discovered more continents than Scandinavians because their hot climate discouraged them from exertion. Thus Dutchmen have fought for their freedom quite as bravely as Switzers because the

Dutch have no mountains. Thus Pagan Greece and Rome and many Mediterranean peoples have specially hated the sea because they had the nicest sea to deal with, the easiest sea to manage. I could extend the list for ever. But however long it was, two examples would certainly stand up in it as pre-eminent and unquestionable. The first is that the Swiss, who live under staggering precipices and spires of eternal snow, have produced no art or literature at all, and are by far the most mundane, sensible, and business-like people in Europe. The other is that the people of Belgium, who live in a country like a carpet, have, by an inner energy, desired to exalt their towers till they struck the stars.

As it is therefore quite doubtful whether a person will go specially with his environment or specially against his environment, I cannot comfort myself with the thought that the modern discussions about environment are of much practical value. But I think I will not write any more about these modern theories, but go on looking at the Belfry of Bruges. I would give them the greater attention if I were not pretty well convinced that the theories will have disappeared a long time before the Belfry.

Chapter 19
How I Met the President

everal years ago, when there was a small war going on in South Africa and a great fuss going on in England, when it was by no means so popular and convenient to be a Pro-Boer as it is now, I remember making a bright suggestion to my Pro-Boer friends and allies, which was not, I regret to say, received with the seriousness it deserved. I suggested that a band of devoted and noble youths, including ourselves, should express our sense of the pathos of the President's and the Republic's fate by growing Kruger beards under our chins. I imagined how abruptly this decoration would alter the appearance of Mr. John Morley; how startling it would be as it emerged from under the chin of Mr. Lloyd-George. But the younger men, my own friends, on whom I more particularly urged it, men whose names are in many cases familiar to the readers of this paper—Mr. Masterman's for instance, and Mr. Conrad Noel—they, I felt, being young and beautiful, would do even more justice to the Kruger beard, and when walking down the street with it could not fail to attract attention. The beard would have been a kind of counterblast to the Rhodes hat. An appropriate counterblast; for the Rhodesian power in Africa is only an external thing, placed upon the top like a hat; the Dutch power and tradition is a thing rooted and growing like a beard; we have shaved it, and it is growing again. The Kruger beard would represent time and the natural processes. You cannot grow a beard in a moment of passion.

After making this proposal to my friends I hurriedly left town. I went down to a West Country place where there was shortly afterwards an election, at which I enjoyed myself very much canvassing for the Liberal candidate. The extraordinary thing was that he got in. I sometimes lie awake at night and meditate upon that mystery; but it must not detain us now. The rather singular incident which happened to me then, and which some recent events have recalled to me, happened while the canvassing was still going on. It was a burning blue day, and the warm sunshine, settling everywhere on the high hedges and the low hills, brought out into a kind of heavy bloom that HUMANE quality of the landscape which, as far as I know, only exists in England; that sense as if the bushes and the roads were human, and had kindness like men; as if the tree were a good giant with one wooden leg; as if the very line of palings were a row of good-tempered gnomes. On one side of the white, sprawling road a low hill or down showed but a little higher than the hedge, on the other the land tumbled down into a valley that opened towards the Mendip hills. The road was very erratic, for every true English road exists in order to lead one a dance; and what could be more beautiful and beneficent than a dance? At an abrupt turn of it I came upon a low white building, with dark doors and dark shuttered windows, evidently not inhabited and scarcely in the ordinary sense inhabitable—a thing more like a toolhouse than a house of any other kind. Made idle by the heat, I paused, and, taking a piece of red chalk out of my pocket, began drawing aimlessly on the back door—drawing goblins and Mr. Chamberlain, and finally the ideal Nationalist with the Kruger beard. The materials did not permit of any delicate rendering of his noble and national expansion of countenance (stoical and yet hopeful, full of tears for man, and yet of an element of humour); but the hat was finely handled. Just as I was adding the finishing touches to the Kruger fantasy, I was frozen to the spot with terror. The black door, which I thought no more of than the lid of an empty box, began slowly to open, impelled from within by a human hand. And President Kruger himself came out into the sunlight!

He was a shade milder of eye than he was in his portraits, and he did not wear that ceremonial scarf which was usually, in such pictures, slung across his ponderous form. But there was the hat which filled the Empire with so much alarm; there were the clumsy dark clothes, there was the heavy, powerful face; there, above all, was the Kruger beard which I had sought to evoke (if I may use the verb) from under the features of Mr. Masterman. Whether he had the umbrella or not I was too much emotionally shaken to observe; he had not the stone lions with him, or Mrs. Kruger; and what he was doing in that dark shed I cannot imagine, but I suppose he was oppressing an Outlander.

I was surprised, I must confess, to meet President Kruger in Somersetshire during the war. I had no idea that he was in the neighbourhood. But a yet more arresting surprise awaited me. Mr. Kruger regarded me for some moments with a dubious grey eye, and then addressed me with a strong Somersetshire accent. A curious cold shock went through me to hear that inappropriate voice coming out of that familiar form. It was as if you met a Chinaman, with pigtail and yellow jacket, and he began to talk broad Scotch. But the next moment, of course, I understood the situation. We had much underrated the Boers in supposing that the Boer education was incomplete. In pursuit of his ruthless plot against our island home, the terrible President had learnt not only English, but all the dialects at a moment's notice to win over a Lancashire merchant or seduce a Northumberland Fusilier. No doubt, if I asked him, this stout old gentleman could grind out Sussex, Essex, Norfolk, Suffolk, and so on, like the tunes in a barrel organ. I could not wonder if our plain, true-hearted German millionaires fell before a cunning so penetrated with culture as this.

And now I come to the third and greatest surprise of all that this strange old man gave me. When he asked me, dryly enough, but not without a certain steady civility that belongs to old-fashioned country people, what I wanted and what I was doing, I told him the facts of the case, explaining my political mission and the almost angelic qualities of the Liberal candidate. Whereupon, this old man became suddenly transfigured in the sunlight into a devil of wrath. It was some time before I could understand a word he said, but the one word that kept on recurring was the word "Kruger," and it was invariably accompanied with a volley of violent terms. Was I for old Kruger, was I? Did I come to him and want him to help old Kruger? I ought to be ashamed, I was . . . and here he became once more obscure. The one thing that he made quite clear was that he wouldn't do anything for Kruger.

"But you ARE Kruger," burst from my lips, in a natural explosion of reasonableness. "You ARE Kruger, aren't you?"

After this innocent CRI DE COEUR of mine, I thought at first there would be a fight, and I remembered with regret that the President in early life had had a hobby of killing lions. But really I began to think that I had been mistaken, and that it was not the President after all. There was a confounding sincerity in the anger with which he declared that he was Farmer Bowles, and everybody knowed it. I appeased him eventually and parted from him at the door of his farmhouse, where he left me with a few tags of religion, which again raised my suspicions of his identity. In the coffee-room to which I returned there was an illustrated paper with a picture of President Kruger, and he and Farmer Bowles were as like as two peas. There was a picture also of a group of Outlander leaders, and the faces of them, leering and triumphant, were perhaps unduly darkened by the photograph, but they seemed to me like the faces of a distant and hostile people.

I saw the old man once again on the fierce night of the poll, when he drove down our Liberal lines in a little cart ablaze with the blue Tory ribbons, for he was a man who would carry his colours everywhere. It was evening, and the warm western light was on the grey hair and heavy massive features of that good old man. I knew as one knows a fact of sense that if Spanish and German stockbrokers had flooded his farm or country he would have fought them for ever, not fiercely like an Irishman, but with the ponderous courage and ponderous cunning of the Boer. I knew that without seeing it, as certainly as I knew without seeing it that when he went into the polling room he put his cross against the Conservative name. Then he came out again, having given his vote and looking more like Kruger than ever. And at the same hour on the same night thousands upon thousands of English Krugers gave the same vote. And thus Kruger was pulled down and the dark-faced men in the photograph reigned in his stead.

Chapter 20
The Giant

sometimes fancy that every great city must have been built by night. At least, it is only at night that every part of a great city is great. All architecture is great architecture after sunset; perhaps architecture is really a nocturnal art, like the art of fireworks. At least, I think many people of those nobler trades that work by night (journalists, policemen, burglars, coffee-stall keepers, and such mistaken enthusiasts as refuse to go home till morning) must often have stood admiring some black bulk of building with a crown of battlements or a crest of spires and then burst into tears at daybreak to discover that it was only a haberdasher's shop with huge gold letters across the face of it.

I had a sensation of this sort the other day as I happened to be wandering in the Temple Gardens towards the end of twilight. I sat down on a bench with my back to the river, happening to choose such a place that a huge angle and façade of building jutting out from the Strand sat above me like an incubus. I dare say that if I took the same seat to-morrow by daylight I should find the impression entirely false. In sunlight the thing might seem almost distant; but in that half-darkness it seemed as if the walls were almost falling upon me. Never before have I had so strongly the sense which makes people pessimists in politics, the sense of the hopeless height of the high places of the earth. That pile of wealth and power, whatever was its name, went up above and beyond me like a cliff that no living thing could climb. I had an irrational sense that this thing had to be fought, that I had to fight it; and that I could offer nothing to the occasion but an indolent journalist with a walking-stick.

Almost as I had the thought, two windows were lit in that black, blind face. It was as if two eyes had opened in the huge face of a sleeping giant; the eyes were too close together, and gave it the suggestion of a bestial sneer. And either by accident of this light or of some other, I could now read the big letters which spaced themselves across the front; it was the Babylon Hotel. It was the perfect symbol of everything that I should like to pull down with my hands if I could. Reared by a detected robber, it is framed to be the fashionable and luxurious home of undetected robbers. In the house of man are many mansions; but there is a class of men who feel normal nowhere except in the Babylon Hotel or in Dartmoor Gaol. That big black face, which was staring at me with its flaming eyes too close together, that was indeed the giant of all epic and fairy tales. But, alas!

I was not the giant-killer; the hour had come, but not the man. I sat down on the seat again (I had had one wild impulse to climb up the front of the hotel and fall in at one of the windows), and I tried to think, as all decent people are thinking, what one can really do. And all the time that oppressive wall went up in front of me, and took hold upon the heavens like a house of the gods.

It is remarkable that in so many great wars it has been the defeated who have won. The people who were left worst at the end of the war were generally the people who were left best at the end of the whole business. For instance, the Crusades ended in the defeat of the Christians. But they did not end in the decline of the Christians; they ended in the decline of the Saracens. That huge prophetic wave of Moslem power which had hung in the very heavens above the towns of Christendom, that wave was broken, and never came on again. The Crusaders had saved Paris in the act of losing Jerusalem. The same applies to that epic of Republican war in the eighteenth century to which we Liberals owe our political creed. The French Revolution ended in defeat: the kings came back across a carpet of dead at Waterloo. The Revolution had lost its last battle; but it had gained its first object. It had cut a chasm. The world has never been the same since. No one after that has ever been able to treat the poor merely as a pavement.

These jewels of God, the poor, are still treated as mere stones of the street; but as stones that may sometimes fly. If it please God, you and I may see some of the stones flying again before we see death. But here I only remark the interesting fact that the conquered almost always conquer. Sparta killed Athens with a final blow, and she was born again. Sparta went away victorious, and died slowly of her own wounds. The Boers lost the South African War and gained South Africa.

And this is really all that we can do when we fight something really stronger than ourselves; we can deal it its death-wound one moment; it deals us death in the end. It is something if we can shock and jar the unthinking impetus and enormous innocence of evil; just as a pebble on a railway can stagger the Scotch express. It is enough for the great martyrs and criminals of the French revolution, that they have surprised for all time the secret weakness of the strong. They have awakened and set leaping and quivering in his crypt for ever the coward in the hearts of kings.

When Jack the Giant-Killer really first saw the giant his experience was not such as has been generally supposed. If you care to hear it I will tell you the real story of Jack the Giant-Killer. To begin with, the most awful thing which Jack first felt about the giant was that he was not a giant. He came striding across an interminable wooded plain, and against its remote horizon the giant was quite a small figure, like a figure in a picture—he seemed merely a man walking across the grass. Then Jack was shocked by remembering that the grass which the man was treading down was one of the tallest forests upon that plain. The man came nearer and nearer, growing bigger and bigger, and at the instant when he passed the possible stature of humanity Jack almost screamed. The rest was an intolerable apocalypse.

The giant had the one frightful quality of a miracle; the more he became incredible the more he became solid. The less one could believe in him the more plainly one could see him. It was unbearable that so much of the sky should be occupied by one human face. His eyes, which had stood out like bow windows, became bigger yet, and there was no metaphor that could contain their bigness; yet still they were human eyes. Jack's intellect was utterly gone under that huge hypnotism of the face that filled the sky; his last hope was submerged, his five wits all still with terror.

But there stood up in him still a kind of cold chivalry, a dignity of dead honour that would not forget the small and futile sword in his hand. He rushed at one of the colossal feet of this human tower, and when he came quite close to it the ankle-bone arched over him like a cave. Then he planted the point of his sword against the foot and leant on it with all his weight, till it went up to the hilt and broke the hilt, and then snapped just under it. And it was plain that the giant felt a sort of prick, for he snatched up his great foot into his great hand for an instant; and then, putting it down again, he bent over and stared at the ground until he had seen his enemy.

Then he picked up Jack between a big finger and thumb and threw him away; and as Jack went through the air he felt as if he were flying from system to system through the universe of stars. But, as the giant had thrown him away carelessly, he did not strike a stone, but struck soft mire by the side of a distant river. There he lay insensible for several hours; but when he awoke again his horrible conqueror was still in sight. He was striding away across the void and wooded plain towards where it ended in the sea; and by this time he was only much higher than any of the hills. He grew less and less indeed; but only as a really high mountain grows at last less and less when we leave it in a railway train. Half an hour afterwards he was a bright blue colour, as are the distant hills; but his outline was still human and still gigantic. Then the big blue figure seemed to come to the brink of the big blue sea, and even as it did so it altered its attitude. Jack, stunned and bleeding, lifted himself laboriously upon one elbow to stare. The giant once more caught hold of his ankle, wavered twice as in a wind, and then went over into the great sea which washes the whole world, and which, alone of all things God has made, was big enough to drown him.

Chapter 21
A Great Man

eople accuse journalism of being too personal; but to me it has always seemed far too impersonal. It is charged with tearing away the veils from private life; but it seems to me to be always dropping diaphanous but blinding veils between men and men. The Yellow Press is abused for exposing facts which are private; I wish the Yellow Press did anything so valuable. It is exactly the decisive individual touches that it never gives; and a proof of this is that after one has met a man a million times in the newspapers it is always a complete shock and reversal to meet him in real life. The Yellow Pressman seems to have no power of catching the first fresh fact about a man that dominates all after impressions. For instance, before I met Bernard Shaw I heard that he spoke with a reckless desire for paradox or a sneering hatred of sentiment; but I never knew till he opened his mouth that he spoke with an Irish accent, which is more important than all the other criticisms put together.

Journalism is not personal enough. So far from digging out private personalities, it cannot even report the obvious personalities on the surface. Now there is one vivid and even bodily impression of this kind which we have all felt when we met great poets or politicians, but which never finds its way into the newspapers. I mean the impression that they are much older than we thought they were. We connect great men with their great triumphs, which generally happened some years ago, and many recruits enthusiastic for the thin Napoleon of Marengo must have found themselves in the presence of the fat Napoleon of Leipzic.

I remember reading a newspaper account of how a certain rising politician confronted the House of Lords with the enthusiasm almost of boyhood. It described how his "brave young voice" rang in the rafters. I also remember that I met him some days after, and he was considerably older than my own father. I mention this truth for only one purpose: all this generalisation leads up to only one fact—the fact that I once met a great man who was younger than I expected.

I had come over the wooded wall from the villages about Epsom, and down a stumbling path between trees towards the valley in which Dorking lies. A warm sunlight was working its way through the leafage; a sunlight which though of saintless gold had taken on the quality of evening. It was such sunlight as reminds a man that the sun begins to set an instant after noon. It seemed to lessen as the wood strengthened and the road sank.

I had a sensation peculiar to such entangled descents; I felt that the treetops that closed above me were the fixed and real things, certain as the level of the sea; but that the solid earth was every instant failing under my feet. In a little while that splendid sunlight showed only in splashes, like flaming stars and suns in the dome of green sky. Around me in that emerald twilight were trunks of trees of every plain or twisted type; it was like a chapel supported on columns of every earthly and unearthly style of architecture.

Without intention my mind grew full of fancies on the nature of the forest; on the whole philosophy of mystery and force. For the meaning of woods is the combination of energy with complexity. A forest is not in the least rude or barbarous; it is only dense with delicacy. Unique shapes that an artist would copy or a philosopher watch for years if he found them in an open plain are here mingled and confounded; but it is not a darkness of deformity. It is a darkness of life; a darkness of perfection. And I began to think how much of the highest human obscurity is like this, and how much men have misunderstood it. People will tell you, for instance, that theology became elaborate because it was dead. Believe me, if it had been dead it would never have become elaborate; it is only the live tree that grows too many branches.

These trees thinned and fell away from each other, and I came out into deep grass and a road. I remember being surprised that the evening was so far advanced; I had a fancy that this valley had a sunset all to itself. I went along that road according to directions that had been given me, and passed the gateway in a slight paling beyond which the wood changed only faintly to a garden. It was as if the curious courtesy and fineness of that character I was to meet went out from him upon the valley; for I felt on all these things the finger of that quality which the old English called "faërie"; it is the quality which those can never understand who think of the past as merely brutal; it is an ancient elegance such as there is in trees. I went through the garden and saw an old man sitting by a table, looking smallish in his big chair. He was already an invalid, and his hair and beard were both white; not like snow, for snow is cold and heavy, but like something feathery, or even fierce; rather they were white like the white thistledown. I came up quite close to him; he looked at me as he put out his frail hand, and I saw of a sudden that his eyes were startlingly young. He was the one great man of the old world whom I have met who was not a mere statue over his own grave.

He was deaf and he talked like a torrent. He did not talk about the books he had written; he was far too much alive for that. He talked about the books he had not written. He unrolled a purple bundle of romances which he had never had time to sell. He asked me to write one of the stories for him, as he would have asked the milkman, if he had been talking to the milkman. It was a splendid and frantic story, a sort of astronomical farce. It was all about a man who was rushing up to the Royal Society with the only possible way of avoiding an earth-destroying comet; and it showed how, even on this huge errand, the man was tripped up at every other minute by his own weakness and vanities; how he lost a train by trifling or was put in gaol for brawling. That is only one of them; there were ten or twenty more. Another, I dimly remember, was a version of the fall of Parnell; the idea that a quite honest man might be secret from a pure love of secrecy, of solitary self-control. I went out of that garden with a blurred sensation of the million possibilities of creative literature. The feeling increased as my way fell back into the wood; for a wood is a palace with a million corridors that cross each other everywhere. I really had the feeling that I had seen the creative quality; which is supernatural. I had seen what Virgil calls the Old Man of the Forest: I had seen an elf. The trees thronged behind my path; I have never seen him again; and now I shall not see him, because he died last Tuesday.

Chapter 22
The Orthodox Barber

hose thinkers who cannot believe in any gods often assert that the love of humanity would be in itself sufficient for them; and so, perhaps, it would, if they had it. There is a very real thing which may be called the love of humanity; in our time it exists almost entirely among what are called uneducated people; and it does not exist at all among the people who talk about it.

A positive pleasure in being in the presence of any other human being is chiefly remarkable, for instance, in the masses on Bank Holiday; that is why they are so much nearer Heaven (despite appearances) than any other part of our population.

I remember seeing a crowd of factory girls getting into an empty train at a wayside country station. There were about twenty of them; they all got into one carriage; and they left all the rest of the train entirely empty. That is the real love of humanity. That is the definite pleasure in the immediate proximity of one's own kind. Only this coarse, rank, real love of men seems to be entirely lacking in those who propose the love of humanity as a substitute for all other love; honourable, rationalistic idealists.

I can well remember the explosion of human joy which marked the sudden starting of that train; all the factory girls who could not find seats (and they must have been the majority) relieving their feelings by jumping up and down. Now I have never seen any rationalistic idealists do this. I have never seen twenty modern philosophers crowd into one third-class carriage for the mere pleasure of being together. I have never seen twenty Mr. McCabes all in one carriage and all jumping up and down.

Some people express a fear that vulgar trippers will overrun all beautiful places, such as Hampstead or Burnham Beeches. But their fear is unreasonable; because trippers always prefer to trip together; they pack as close as they can; they have a suffocating passion of philanthropy.

But among the minor and milder aspects of the same principle, I have no hesitation in placing the problem of the colloquial barber. Before any modern man talks with authority about loving men, I insist (I insist with violence) that he shall always be very much pleased when his barber tries to talk to him. His barber is humanity: let him love that. If he is not pleased at this, I will not accept any substitute in the way of interest in the Congo or the future of Japan. If a man cannot love his barber whom he has seen, how shall he love the Japanese whom he has not seen?

It is urged against the barber that he begins by talking about the weather; so do all dukes and diplomatists, only that they talk about it with ostentatious fatigue and indifference, whereas the barber talks about it with an astonishing, nay incredible, freshness of interest. It is objected to him that he tells people that they are going bald. That is to say, his very virtues are cast up against him; he is blamed because, being a specialist, he is a sincere specialist, and because, being a tradesman, he is not entirely a slave. But the only proof of such things is by example; therefore I will prove the excellence of the conversation of barbers by a specific case. Lest any one should accuse me of attempting to prove it by fictitious means, I beg to say quite seriously that though I forget the exact language employed, the following conversation between me and a human (I trust), living barber really took place a few days ago.

I had been invited to some At Home to meet the Colonial Premiers, and lest I should be mistaken for some partly reformed bush-ranger out of the interior of Australia I went into a shop in the Strand to get shaved. While I was undergoing the torture the man said to me:

"There seems to be a lot in the papers about this new shaving, sir. It seems you can shave yourself with anything—with a stick or a stone or a pole or a poker" (here I began for the first time to detect a sarcastic intonation) "or a shovel or a—— "

Here he hesitated for a word, and I, although I knew nothing about the matter, helped him out with suggestions in the same rhetorical vein.

"Or a button-hook," I said, "or a blunderbuss or a battering-ram or a piston-rod—— "

He resumed, refreshed with this assistance, "Or a curtain rod or a candle-stick, or a—— "

"Cow-catcher," I suggested eagerly, and we continued in this ecstatic duet for some time. Then I asked him what it was all about, and he told me. He explained the thing eloquently and at length.

"The funny part of it is," he said, "that the thing isn't new at all. It's been talked about ever since I was a boy, and long before. There is always a notion that the razor might be done without somehow. But none of those schemes ever came to anything; and I don't believe myself that this will."

"Why, as to that," I said, rising slowly from the chair and trying to put on my coat inside out, "I don't know how it may be in the case of you and your new shaving. Shaving, with all respect to you, is a trivial and materialistic thing, and in such things startling inventions are sometimes made. But what you say reminds me in some dark and dreamy fashion of something else. I recall it especially when you tell me, with such evident experience and sincerity, that the new shaving is not really new. My friend, the human race is always trying this dodge of making everything entirely easy; but the difficulty which it shifts off one thing it shifts on to another. If one man has not the toil of preparing a man's chin, I suppose that some other man has the toil of preparing something very curious to put on a man's chin. It would be nice if we could be shaved without troubling anybody. It would be nicer still if we could go unshaved without annoying anybody—

" 'But, O wise friend, chief Barber of the Strand,
Brother, nor you nor I have made the world.'

"Whoever made it, who is wiser, and we hope better than we, made it under strange limitations, and with painful conditions of pleasure.

"In the first and darkest of its books it is fiercely written that a man shall not eat his cake and have it; and though all men talked until the stars were old it would still be true that a man who has lost his razor could not shave with it. But every now and then men jump up with the new something or other and say that everything can be had without sacrifice, that bad is good if you are only enlightened, and that there is no real difference between being shaved and not being shaved. The difference, they say, is only a difference of degree; everything is evolutionary and relative. Shavedness is immanent in man. Every ten-penny nail is a Potential Razor. The superstitious people of the past (they say) believed that a lot of black bristles standing out at right angles to one's face was a positive affair. But the higher criticism teaches us better. Bristles are merely negative. They are a Shadow where Shaving should be.

"Well, it all goes on, and I suppose it all means something. But a baby is the Kingdom of God, and if you try to kiss a baby he will know whether you are shaved or not. Perhaps I am mixing up being shaved and being saved; my democratic sympathies have always led me to drop my 'h's.' In another moment I may suggest that goats represent the lost because goats have long beards. This is growing altogether too allegorical.

"Nevertheless," I added, as I paid the bill, "I have really been profoundly interested in what you told me about the New Shaving. Have you ever heard of a thing called the New theology?"

He smiled and said that he had not.

Chapter 23
The Toy Theatre

here is only one reason why all grown-up people do not play with toys; and it is a fair reason. The reason is that playing with toys takes so very much more time and trouble than anything else. Playing as children mean playing is the most serious thing in the world; and as soon as we have small duties or small sorrows we have to abandon to some extent so enormous and ambitious a plan of life. We have enough strength for politics and commerce and art and philosophy; we have not enough strength for play. This is a truth which every one will recognize who, as a child, has ever played with anything at all; any one who has played with bricks, any one who has played with dolls, any one who has played with tin soldiers. My journalistic work, which earns money, is not pursued with such awful persistency as that work which earned nothing.

Take the case of bricks. If you publish a book to-morrow in twelve volumes (it would be just like you) on "The Theory and Practice of European Architecture," your work may be laborious, but it is fundamentally frivolous. It is not serious as the work of a child piling one brick on the other is serious; for the simple reason that if your book is a bad book no one will ever be able ultimately and entirely to prove to you that it is a bad book. Whereas if his balance of bricks is a bad balance of bricks, it will simply tumble down. And if I know anything of children, he will set to work solemnly and sadly to build it up again. Whereas, if I know anything of authors, nothing would induce you to write your book again, or even to think of it again if you could help it.

Take the case of dolls. It is much easier to care for an educational cause than to care for a doll. It is as easy to write an article on education as to write an article on toffee or tramcars or anything else. But it is almost as difficult to look after a doll as to look after a child. The little girls that I meet in the little streets of Battersea worship their dolls in a way that reminds one not so much of play as idolatry. In some cases the love and care of the artistic symbol has actually become more important than the human reality which it was, I suppose, originally meant to symbolize.

I remember a Battersea little girl who wheeled her large baby sister stuffed into a doll's perambulator. When questioned on this course of conduct, she replied: "I haven't got a dolly, and Baby is pretending to be my dolly." Nature was indeed imitating art. First a doll had been a substitute for a child; afterwards a child was a mere substitute for a doll. But that opens other matters; the point is here that such devotion takes up most of the brain and most of the life; much as if it were really the thing which it is supposed to symbolize. The point is that the man writing on motherhood is merely an educationalist; the child playing with a doll is a mother.

Take the case of soldiers. A man writing an article on military strategy is simply a man writing an article; a horrid sight. But a boy making a campaign with tin soldiers is like a General making a campaign with live soldiers. He must to the limit of his juvenile powers think about the thing; whereas the war correspondent need not think at all. I remember a war correspondent who remarked after the capture of Methuen: "This renewed activity on the part of Delarey is probably due to his being short of stores." The same military critic had mentioned a few paragraphs before that Delarey was being hard pressed by a column which was pursuing him under the command of Methuen. Methuen chased Delarey; and Delarey's activity was due to his being short of stores. Otherwise he would have stood quite still while he was chased. I run after Jones with a hatchet, and if he turns round and tries to get rid of me the only possible explanation is that he has a very small balance at his bankers. I cannot believe that any boy playing at soldiers would be as idiotic as this. But then any one playing at anything has to be serious. Whereas, as I have only too good reason to know, if you are writing an article you can say anything that comes into your head.

Broadly, then, what keeps adults from joining in children's games is, generally speaking, not that they have no pleasure in them; it is simply that they have no leisure for them. It is that they cannot afford the expenditure of toil and time and consideration for so grand and grave a scheme. I have been myself attempting for some time past to complete a play in a small toy theatre, the sort of toy theatre that used to be called Penny Plain and Twopence Coloured; only that I drew and coloured the figures and scenes myself. Hence I was free from the degrading obligation of having to pay either a penny or twopence; I only had to pay a shilling a sheet for good cardboard and a shilling a box for bad water colours. The kind of miniature stage I mean is probably familiar to every one; it is never more than a development of the stage which Skelt made and Stevenson celebrated.

But though I have worked much harder at the toy theatre than I ever worked at any tale or article, I cannot finish it; the work seems too heavy for me. I have to break off and betake myself to lighter employments; such as the biographies of great men. The play of "St. George and the Dragon," over which I have burnt the midnight oil (you must colour the thing by lamplight because that is how it will be seen), still lacks most conspicuously, alas! two wings of the Sultan's Palace, and also some comprehensible and workable way of getting up the curtain.

All this gives me a feeling touching the real meaning of immortality. In this world we cannot have pure pleasure. This is partly because pure pleasure would be dangerous to us and to our neighbours. But it is partly because pure pleasure is a great deal too much trouble. If I am ever in any other and better world, I hope that I shall have enough time to play with nothing but toy theatres; and I hope that I shall have enough divine and superhuman energy to act at least one play in them without a hitch.

Meanwhile the philosophy of toy theatres is worth any one's consideration. All the essential morals which modern men need to learn could be deduced from this toy. Artistically considered, it reminds us of the main principle of art, the principle which is in most danger of being forgotten in our time. I mean the fact that art consists of limitation; the fact that art is limitation. Art does not consist in expanding things. Art consists of cutting things down, as I cut down with a pair of scissors my very ugly figures of St. George and the Dragon. Plato, who liked definite ideas, would like my cardboard dragon; for though the creature has few other artistic merits he is at least dragonish. The modern philosopher, who likes infinity, is quite welcome to a sheet of the plain cardboard. The most artistic thing about the theatrical art is the fact that the spectator looks at the whole thing through a window. This is true even of theatres inferior to my own; even at the Court Theatre or His Majesty's you are looking through a window; an unusually large window. But the advantage of the small theatre exactly is that you are looking through a small window. Has not every one noticed how sweet and startling any landscape looks when seen through an arch? This strong, square shape, this shutting off of everything else is not only an assistance to beauty; it is the essential of beauty. The most beautiful part of every picture is the frame.

This especially is true of the toy theatre; that, by reducing the scale of events it can introduce much larger events. Because it is small it could easily represent the earthquake in Jamaica. Because it is small it could easily represent the Day of Judgment. Exactly in so far as it is limited, so far it could play easily with falling cities or with falling stars. Meanwhile the big theatres are obliged to be economical because they are big. When we have understood this fact we shall have understood something of the reason why the world has always been first inspired by small nationalities. The vast Greek philosophy could fit easier into the small city of Athens than into the immense Empire of Persia. In the narrow streets of Florence Dante felt that there was room for Purgatory and Heaven and Hell. He would have been stifled by the British Empire. Great empires are necessarily prosaic; for it is beyond human power to act a great poem upon so great a scale. You can only represent very big ideas in very small spaces. My toy theatre is as philosophical as the drama of Athens.

Chapter 24
A Tragedy of Twopence

y relations with the readers of this page have been long and pleasant, but—perhaps for that very reason—I feel that the time has come when I ought to confess the one great crime of my life. It happened a long time ago; but it is not uncommon for a belated burst of remorse to reveal such dark episodes long after they have occurred. It has nothing to do with the orgies of the Anti-Puritan League. That body is so offensively respectable that a newspaper, in describing it the other day, referred to my friend Mr. Edgar Jepson as Canon Edgar Jepson; and it is believed that similar titles are intended for all of us. No; it is not by the conduct of Archbishop Crane, of Dean Chesterton, of the Rev. James Douglas, of Monsignor Bland, and even of that fine and virile old ecclesiastic, Cardinal Nesbit, that I wish (or rather, am driven by my conscience) to make this declaration. The crime was committed in solitude and without accomplices. Alone I did it. Let me, with the characteristic thirst of penitents to get the worst of the confession over, state it first of all in its most dreadful and indefensible form. There is at the present moment in a town in Germany (unless he has died of rage on discovering his wrong), a restaurant-keeper to whom I still owe twopence. I last left his open-air restaurant knowing that I owed him twopence. I carried it away under his nose, despite the fact that the nose was a decidedly Jewish one. I have never paid him, and it is highly improbable that I ever shall. How did this villainy come to occur in a life which has been, generally speaking, deficient in the dexterity necessary for fraud? The story is as follows—and it has a moral, though there may not be room for that.

It is a fair general rule for those travelling on the Continent that the easiest way of talking in a foreign language is to talk philosophy. The most difficult kind of talking is to talk about common necessities. The reason is obvious. The names of common necessities vary completely with each nation and are generally somewhat odd and quaint. How, for instance, could a Frenchman suppose that a coalbox would be called a "scuttle"? If he has ever seen the word scuttle it has been in the Jingo Press, where the "policy of scuttle" is used whenever we give up something to a small Power like Liberals, instead of giving up everything to a great Power, like Imperialists. What Englishman in Germany would be poet enough to guess that the Germans call a glove a "hand-shoe." Nations name their necessities by nicknames, so to speak. They call their tubs and stools by quaint, elvish, and almost affectionate names, as if they were their own children! But any one can argue about abstract things in a foreign language who has ever got as far as Exercise IV. in a primer. For as soon as he can put a sentence together at all he finds that the words used in abstract or philosophical discussions are almost the same in all nations. They are the same, for the simple reason that they all come from the things that were the roots of our common civilisation. From Christianity, from the Roman Empire, from the mediaeval Church, or the French Revolution. "Nation," "citizen," "religion," "philosophy," "authority," "the Republic," words like these are nearly the same in all the countries in which we travel. Restrain, therefore, your exuberant admiration for the young man who can argue with six French atheists when he first lands at Dieppe. Even I can do that. But very likely the same young man does not know the French for a shoe-horn. But to this generalisation there are three great exceptions. (1) In the case of countries that are not European at all, and have never had our civic conceptions, or the old Latin scholarship. I do not pretend that the Patagonian phrase for "citizenship" at once leaps to the mind, or that a Dyak's word for "the Republic" has been familiar to me from the nursery. (2) In the case of Germany, where, although the principle does apply to many words such as "nation" and "philosophy," it does not apply so generally, because Germany has had a special and deliberate policy of encouraging the purely German part of its language. (3) In the case where one does not know any of the language at all, as is generally the case with me.

Such at least was my situation on the dark day on which I committed my crime. Two of the exceptional conditions which I have mentioned were combined. I was walking about a German town, and I knew no German. I knew, however, two or three of those great and solemn words which hold our European civilisation together—one of which is "cigar." As it was a hot and dreamy day, I sat down at a table in a sort of beer-garden, and ordered a cigar and a pot of lager. I drank the lager, and paid for it. I smoked the cigar, forgot to pay for it, and walked away, gazing rapturously at the royal outline of the Taunus mountains. After about ten minutes, I suddenly remembered that I had not paid for the cigar. I went back to the place of refreshment, and put down the money. But the proprietor also had forgotten the cigar, and he merely said guttural things in a tone of query, asking me, I suppose, what I wanted. I said "cigar," and he gave me a cigar. I endeavoured while putting down the money to wave away the cigar with gestures of refusal. He thought that my rejection was of the nature of a condemnation of that particular cigar, and brought me another. I whirled my arms like a windmill, seeking to convey by the sweeping universality of my gesture that my rejection was a rejection of cigars in general, not of that particular article. He mistook this for the ordinary impatience of common men, and rushed forward, his hands filled with miscellaneous cigars, pressing them upon me. In desperation I tried other kinds of pantomime, but the more cigars I refused the more and more rare and precious cigars were brought out of the deeps and recesses of the establishment. I tried in vain to think of a way of conveying to him the fact that I had already had the cigar. I imitated the action of a citizen smoking, knocking off and throwing away a cigar. The watchful proprietor only thought I was rehearsing (as in an ecstasy of anticipation) the joys of the cigar he was going to give me. At last I retired baffled: he would not take the money and leave the cigars alone. So that this restaurant-keeper (in whose face a love of money shone like the sun at noonday) flatly and firmly refused to receive the twopence that I certainly owed him; and I took that twopence of his away with me and rioted on it for months. I hope that on the last day the angels will break the truth very gently to that unhappy man.

This is the true and exact account of the Great Cigar Fraud, and the moral of it is this—that civilisation is founded upon abstractions. The idea of debt is one which cannot be conveyed by physical motions at all, because it is an abstract idea. And civilisation obviously would be nothing without debt. So when hard-headed fellows who study scientific sociology (which does not exist) come and tell you that civilisation is material or indifferent to the abstract, just ask yourselves how many of the things that make up our Society, the Law, or the Stocks and Shares, or the National Debt, you would be able to convey with your face and your ten fingers by grinning and gesticulating to a German innkeeper.

Chapter 25
A Cab Ride Across Country

own somewhere far off in the shallow dales of Hertfordshire there lies a village of great beauty, and I doubt not of admirable virtue, but of eccentric and unbalanced literary taste, which asked the present writer to come down to it on Sunday afternoon and give an address.

But the absurdity of the modern English convention is that it does not let a man sit still; it only perpetually trips him up when it has forced him to walk about. Our Sabbatarianism does not forbid us to ask a man in Battersea to come and talk in Hertfordshire; it only prevents his getting there. I can understand that a deity might be worshipped with joys, with flowers, and fireworks in the old European style. I can understand that a deity might be worshipped with sorrows. But I cannot imagine any deity being worshipped with inconveniences. Let the good Moslem go to Mecca, or let him abide in his tent, according to his feelings for religious symbols. But surely Allah cannot see anything particularly dignified in his servant being misled by the time-table, finding that the old Mecca express is not running, missing his connection at Bagdad, or having to wait three hours in a small side station outside Damascus.

So it was with me on this occasion. I found there was no telegraph service at all to this place; I found there was only one weak thread of train-service. Now if this had been the authority of real English religion, I should have submitted to it at once. If I believed that the telegraph clerk could not send the telegram because he was at that moment rigid in an ecstasy of prayer, I should think all telegrams unimportant in comparison. If I could believe that railway porters when relieved from their duties rushed with passion to the nearest place of worship, I should say that all lectures and everything else ought to give way to such a consideration. I should not complain if the national faith forbade me to make any appointments of labour or self-expression on the Sabbath. But, as it is, it only tells me that I may very probably keep the Sabbath by not keeping the appointment.

But I must resume the real details of my tale. I found that there was only one train in the whole of that Sunday by which I could even get within several hours or several miles of the time or place. I therefore went to the telephone, which is one of my favourite toys, and down which I have shouted many valuable, but prematurely arrested, monologues upon art and morals. I remember a mild shock of surprise when I discovered that one could use the telephone on Sunday;

I did not expect it to be cut off, but I expected it to buzz more than on ordinary days, to the advancement of our national religion. Through this instrument, in fewer words than usual, and with a comparative economy of epigram, I ordered a taxi-cab to take me to the railway station. I have not a word to say in general either against telephones or taxi-cabs; they seem to me two of the purest and most poetic of the creations of modern scientific civilisation. Unfortunately, when the taxi-cab started, it did exactly what modern scientific civilisation has done—it broke down. The result of this was that when I arrived at King's Cross my only train was gone; there was a Sabbath calm in the station, a calm in the eyes of the porters, and in my breast, if calm at all, if any calm, a calm despair.

There was not, however, very much calm of any sort in my breast on first making the discovery; and it was turned to blinding horror when I learnt that I could not even send a telegram to the organisers of the meeting. To leave my entertainers in the lurch was sufficiently exasperating; to leave them without any intimation was simply low. I reasoned with the official. I said: "Do you really mean to say that if my brother were dying and my mother in this place, I could not communicate with her?" He was a man of literal and laborious mind; he asked me if my brother was dying. I answered that he was in excellent and even offensive health, but that I was inquiring upon a question of principle. What would happen if England were invaded, or if I alone knew how to turn aside a comet or an earthquake. He waved away these hypotheses in the most irresponsible spirit, but he was quite certain that telegrams could not reach this particular village. Then something exploded in me; that element of the outrageous which is the mother of all adventures sprang up ungovernable, and I decided that I would not be a cad merely because some of my remote ancestors had been Calvinists. I would keep my appointment if I lost all my money and all my wits. I went out into the quiet London street, where my quiet London cab was still waiting for its fare in the cold misty morning. I placed myself comfortably in the London cab and told the London driver to drive me to the other end of Hertfordshire. And he did.

I shall not forget that drive. It was doubtful whether, even in a motor-cab, the thing was possible with any consideration for the driver, not to speak of some slight consideration for the people in the road. I urged the driver to eat and drink something before he started, but he said (with I know not what pride of profession or delicate sense of adventure) that he would rather do it when we arrived—if we ever did. I was by no means so delicate; I bought a varied selection of pork-pies at a little shop that was open (why was that shop open?—it is all a mystery), and ate them as we went along. The beginning was sombre and irritating. I was annoyed, not with people, but with things, like a baby; with the motor for breaking down and with Sunday for being Sunday. And the sight of the northern slums expanded and ennobled, but did not decrease, my gloom: Whitechapel has an Oriental gaudiness in its squalor; Battersea and Camberwell have an indescribable bustle of democracy; but the poor parts of North London ... well, perhaps I saw them wrongly under that ashen morning and on that foolish errand.

It was one of those days which more than once this year broke the retreat of winter; a winter day that began too late to be spring. We were already clear of the obstructing crowds and quickening our pace through a borderland of market gardens and isolated public-houses, when the grey showed golden patches and a good light began to glitter on everything. The cab went quicker and quicker. The open land whirled wider and wider; but I did not lose my sense of being battled with and thwarted that I had felt in the thronged slums. Rather the feeling increased, because of the great difficulty of space and time. The faster went the car, the fiercer and thicker I felt the fight.

The whole landscape seemed charging at me—and just missing me. The tall, shining grass went by like showers of arrows; the very trees seemed like lances hurled at my heart, and shaving it by a hair's breadth. Across some vast, smooth valley I saw a beech-tree by the white road stand up little and defiant. It grew bigger and bigger with blinding rapidity. It charged me like a tilting knight, seemed to hack at my head, and pass by. Sometimes when we went round a curve of road, the effect was yet more awful. It seemed as if some tree or windmill swung round to smite like a boomerang. The sun by this time was a blazing fact; and I saw that all Nature is chivalrous and militant. We do wrong to seek peace in Nature; we should rather seek the nobler sort of war; and see all the trees as green banners.

I gave my address, arriving just when everybody was deciding to leave. When my cab came reeling into the market-place they decided, with evident disappointment, to remain. Over the lecture I draw a veil. When I came back home I was called to the telephone, and a meek voice expressed regret for the failure of the motor-cab, and even said something about any reasonable payment. "Whom can I pay for my own superb experience? What is the usual charge for seeing the clouds shattered by the sun? What is the market price of a tree blue on the sky-line and then blinding white in the sun? Mention your price for that windmill that stood behind the hollyhocks in the garden. Let me pay you for ... " Here it was, I think, that we were cut off.

Chapter 26
The Two Noises

or three days and three nights the sea had charged England as Napoleon charged her at Waterloo. The phrase is instinctive, because away to the last grey line of the sea there was only the look of galloping squadrons, impetuous, but with a common purpose. The sea came on like cavalry, and when it touched the shore it opened the blazing eyes and deafening tongues of the artillery. I saw the worst assault at night on a seaside parade where the sea smote on the doors of England with the hammers of earthquake, and a white smoke went up into the black heavens. There one could thoroughly realise what an awful thing a wave really is. I talk like other people about the rushing swiftness of a wave. But the horrible thing about a wave is its hideous slowness. It lifts its load of water laboriously: in that style at once slow and slippery in which a Titan might lift a load of rock and then let it slip at last to be shattered into shock of dust. In front of me that night the waves were not like water: they were like falling city walls. The breaker rose first as if it did not wish to attack the earth; it wished only to attack the stars. For a time it stood up in the air as naturally as a tower; then it went a little wrong in its outline, like a tower that might some day fall. When it fell it was as if a powder magazine blew up.

I have never seen such a sea. All the time there blew across the land one of those stiff and throttling winds that one can lean up against like a wall. One expected anything to be blown out of shape at any instant; the lamp-post to be snapped like a green stalk, the tree to be whirled away like a straw. I myself should certainly have been blown out of shape if I had possessed any shape to be blown out of; for I walked along the edge of the stone embankment above the black and battering sea and could not rid myself of the idea that it was an invasion of England. But as I walked along this edge I was somewhat surprised to find that as I neared a certain spot another noise mingled with the ceaseless cannonade of the sea.

Somewhere at the back, in some pleasure ground or casino or place of entertainment, an undaunted brass band was playing against the cosmic uproar. I do not know what band it was. Judging from the boisterous British Imperialism of most of the airs it played, I should think it was a German band. But there was no doubt about its energy, and when I came quite close under it it really drowned the storm. It was playing such things as "Tommy Atkins" and "You Can Depend on

Young Australia," and many others of which I do not know the words, but I should think they would be "John, Pat, and Mac, With the Union Jack," or that fine though unwritten poem, "Wait till the Bull Dog gets a bite of you." Now, I for one detest Imperialism, but I have a great deal of sympathy with Jingoism. And there seemed something so touching about this unbroken and innocent bragging under the brutal menace of Nature that it made, if I may so put it, two tunes in my mind. It is so obvious and so jolly to be optimistic about England, especially when you are an optimist—and an Englishman. But through all that glorious brass came the voice of the invasion, the undertone of that awful sea. I did a foolish thing. As I could not express my meaning in an article, I tried to express it in a poem—a bad one. You can call it what you like. It might be called "Doubt," or "Brighton." It might be called "The Patriot," or yet again "The German Band." I would call it "The Two Voices," but that title has been taken for a grossly inferior poem. This is how it began—

> "They say the sun is on your knees
> A lamp to light your lands from harm,
> They say you turn the seven seas
> To little brooks about your farm.
> I hear the sea and the new song
> that calls you empress all day long.
>
> "(O fallen and fouled! O you that lie
> Dying in swamps—you shall not die,
> Your rich have secrets, and stronge lust,
> Your poor are chased about like dust,
> Emptied of anger and surprise—
> And God has gone out of their eyes,
> Your cohorts break—your captains lie,
> I say to you, you shall not die.)"

Then I revived a little, remembering that after all there is an English country that the Imperialists have never found. The British Empire may annex what it likes, it will never annex England. It has not even discovered the island, let alone conquered it. I took up the two tunes again with a greater sympathy for the first—

> "I know the bright baptismal rains,
> I love your tender troubled skies,
> I know your little climbing lanes,
> Are peering into Paradise,
> From open hearth to orchard cool,
> How bountiful and beautiful.
>
> "(O throttled and without a cry,
> O strangled and stabbed, you shall not die,

The frightful word is on your walls,
The east sea to the west sea calls,
The stars are dying in the sky,
You shall not die; you shall not die.)"

Then the two great noises grew deafening together, the noise of the peril of England and the louder noise of the placidity of England. It is their fault if the last verse was written a little rudely and at random—

"I see you how you smile in state
Straight from the Peak to Plymouth Bar,
You need not tell me you are great,
I know how more than great you are.
I know what William Shakespeare was,
I have seen Gainsborough and the grass.

"(O given to believe a lie,
O my mad mother, do do not die,
Whose eyes turn all ways but within,
Whose sin is innocence of sin,
Whose eyes, blinded with beams at noon,
Can see the motes upon the moon,
You shall your lover still pursue.
To what last madhouse shelters you
I will uphold you, even I.
You that are dead. You shall not die.)"

But the sea would not stop for me any more than for Canute; and as for the German band, that would not stop for anybody.

Chapter 27
Some Policemen and a Moral

he other day I was nearly arrested by two excited policemen in a wood in Yorkshire. I was on a holiday, and was engaged in that rich and intricate mass of pleasures, duties, and discoveries which for the keeping off of the profane, we disguise by the exoteric name of Nothing. At the moment in question I was throwing a big Swedish knife at a tree, practising (alas, without success) that useful trick of knife-throwing by which men murder each other in Stevenson's romances.

Suddenly the forest was full of two policemen; there was something about their appearance in and relation to the greenwood that reminded me, I know not how, of some happy Elizabethan comedy. They asked what the knife was, who I was, why I was throwing it, what my address was, trade, religion, opinions on the Japanese war, name of favourite cat, and so on. They also said I was damaging the tree; which was, I am sorry to say, not true, because I could not hit it. The peculiar philosophical importance, however, of the incident was this. After some half-hour's animated conversation, the exhibition of an envelope, an unfinished poem, which was read with great care, and, I trust, with some profit, and one or two other subtle detective strokes, the elder of the two knights became convinced that I really was what I professed to be, that I was a journalist, that I was on the DAILY NEWS (this was the real stroke; they were shaken with a terror common to all tyrants), that I lived in a particular place as stated, and that I was stopping with particular people in Yorkshire, who happened to be wealthy and well-known in the neighbourhood.

In fact the leading constable became so genial and complimentary at last that he ended up by representing himself as a reader of my work. And when that was said, everything was settled. They acquitted me and let me pass.

"But," I said, "what of this mangled tree? It was to the rescue of that Dryad, tethered to the earth, that you rushed like knight-errants. You, the higher human-itarians, are not deceived by the seeming stillness of the green things, a stillness like the stillness of the cataract, a headlong and crashing silence. You know that a tree is but a creature tied to the ground by one leg. You will not let assassins with their Swedish daggers shed the green blood of such a being. But if so, why am I not in custody; where are my gyves? Produce, from some portion of your persons, my mouldy straw and my grated window. The facts of which I have just convinced you, that my name is Chesterton, that I am a journalist, that I am living with the well-known and philanthropic Mr. Blank of Ilkley, cannot have anything to do with the question of whether I have been guilty of cruelty to vegetables. The tree is none the less damaged even though it may reflect with a dark pride that it was wounded by a gentleman connected with the Liberal press. Wounds in the bark do not more rapidly close up because they are inflicted by people who are stopping with Mr. Blank of Ilkley. That tree, the ruin of its former self, the wreck of what was once a giant of the forest, now splintered and laid low by the brute superiority of a Swedish knife, that tragedy, constable, cannot be wiped out even by stopping for several months more with some wealthy person. It is incredible that you have no legal claim to arrest even the most august and fashionable persons on this charge. For if so, why did you interfere with me at all?"

I made the later and larger part of this speech to the silent wood, for the two policemen had vanished almost as quickly as they came. It is very possible, of course, that they were fairies. In that case the somewhat illogical character of their view of crime, law, and personal responsibility would find a bright and elfish explanation; perhaps if I had lingered in the glade till moonrise I might have seen rings of tiny policemen dancing on the sward; or running about with glow-worm belts, arresting grasshoppers for damaging blades of grass. But taking the bolder hypothesis, that they really were policemen, I find myself in a certain difficulty. I was certainly accused of something which was either an offence or was not. I was let off because I proved I was a guest at a big house. The inference seems painfully clear; either it is not a proof of infamy to throw a knife about in a lonely wood, or else it is a proof of innocence to know a rich man. Suppose a very poor person, poorer even than a journalist, a navvy or unskilled labourer, tramping in search of work, often changing his lodgings, often, perhaps, failing in his rent. Suppose he had been intoxicated with the green gaiety of the ancient wood. Suppose he had thrown knives at trees and could give no description of a dwelling-place except that he had been fired out of the last. As I walked home through a cloudy and purple twilight I wondered how he would have got on.

Moral. We English are always boasting that we are very illogical; there is no great harm in that. There is no subtle spiritual evil in the fact that people always brag about their vices; it is when they begin to brag about their virtues that they become insufferable. But there is this to be said, that illogicality in your constitution or your legal methods may become very dangerous if there happens to be some great national vice or national temptation which many take advantage of the chaos. Similarly, a drunkard ought to have strict rules and hours; a temperate man may obey his instincts.

Take some absurd anomaly in the British law—the fact, for instance, that a man ceasing to be an M. P. has to become Steward of the Chiltern Hundreds, an office which I believe was intended originally to keep down some wild robbers near Chiltern, wherever that is. Obviously this kind of illogicality does not matter very much, for the simple reason that there is no great temptation to take advantage of it. Men retiring from Parliament do not have any furious impulse to hunt robbers in the hills. But if there were a real danger that wise, white-haired, venerable politicians taking leave of public life would desire to do this (if, for instance, there were any money in it), then clearly, if we went on saying that the illogicality did not matter, when (as a matter of fact) Sir Michael Hicks-Beach was hanging Chiltern shop-keepers every day and taking their property, we should be very silly. The illogicality would matter, for it would have become an excuse for indulgence. It is only the very good who can live riotous lives.

Now this is exactly what is present in cases of police investigation such as the one narrated above. There enters into such things a great national sin, a far greater sin than drink—the habit of respecting a gentleman. Snobbishness has, like drink, a kind of grand poetry. And snobbishness has this peculiar and devilish quality of evil, that it is rampant among very kindly people, with open hearts and houses. But it is our great English vice; to be watched more fiercely than small-pox. If a man wished to hear the worst and wickedest thing in England summed up in casual English words, he would not find it in any foul oaths or ribald quarrelling. He would find it in the fact that the best kind of working man, when he wishes to praise any one, calls him "a gentleman." It never occurs to him that he might as well call him "a marquis," or "a privy councillor"—that he is simply naming a rank or class, not a phrase for a good man. And this perennial temptation to a shameful admiration, must, and, I think, does, constantly come in and distort and poison our police methods.

In this case we must be logical and exact; for we have to keep watch upon ourselves. The power of wealth, and that power at its vilest, is increasing in the modern world. A very good and just people, without this temptation, might not need, perhaps, to make clear rules and systems to guard themselves against the power of our great financiers. But that is because a very just people would have shot them long ago, from mere native good feeling.

Chapter 28
The Lion

In the town of Belfort I take a chair and I sit down in the street. We talk in a cant phrase of the Man in the Street, but the Frenchman is the man in the street. Things quite central for him are connected with these lamp-posts and pavements; everything from his meals to his martyrdoms. When first an Englishman looks at a French town or village his first feeling is simply that it is uglier than an English town or village; when he looks again he sees that this comparative absence of the picturesque is chiefly expressed in the plain, precipitous frontage of the houses standing up hard and flat out of the street like the cardboard houses in a pantomime—a hard angularity allied perhaps to the harshness of French logic. When he looks a third time he sees quite simply that it is all because the houses have no front gardens. The vague English spirit loves to have the entrance to its house softened by bushes and broken by steps. It likes to have a little anteroom of hedges half in the house and half out of it; a green room in a double sense. The Frenchman desires no such little pathetic ramparts or halting places, for the street itself is a thing natural and familiar to him.

The French have no front gardens; but the street is every man's front garden. There are trees in the street, and sometimes fountains. The street is the Frenchman's tavern, for he drinks in the street. It is his dining-room, for he dines in the street. It is his British Museum, for the statues and monuments in French streets are not, as with us, of the worst, but of the best, art of the country, and they are often actually as historical as the Pyramids. The street again is the Frenchman's Parliament, for France has never taken its Chamber of Deputies so seriously as we take our House of Commons, and the quibbles of mere elected nonentities in an official room seem feeble to a people whose fathers have heard the voice of Desmoulins like a trumpet under open heaven, or Victor Hugo shouting from his carriage amid the wreck of the second Republic. And as the Frenchman drinks in the street and dines in the street so also he fights in the street and dies in the street, so that the street can never be commonplace to him.

Take, for instance, such a simple object as a lamp-post. In London a lamp-post is a comic thing. We think of the intoxicated gentleman embracing it, and recalling ancient friendship. But in Paris a lamp-post is a tragic thing. For we think of tyrants hanged on it, and of an end of the world. There is, or was, a bitter Republican paper in Paris called LA LANTERNE. How funny it would be if there were a Progressive paper in England called THE LAMP POST! We have said, then, that the Frenchman is the man in the street; that he can dine in the street, and die in the street. And if I ever pass through Paris and find him going to bed in the street, I shall say that he is still true to the genius of his civilisation. All that is good and all that is evil in France is alike connected with this open-air element. French democracy and French indecency are alike part of the desire to have everything out of doors. Compared to a café, a public-house is a private house.

There were two reasons why all these fancies should float through the mind in the streets of this especial town of Belfort. First of all, it lies close upon the boundary of France and Germany, and boundaries are the most beautiful things in the world. To love anything is to love its boundaries; thus children will always play on the edge of anything. They build castles on the edge of the sea, and can only be restrained by public proclamation and private violence from walking on the edge of the grass. For when we have come to the end of a thing we have come to the beginning of it.

Hence this town seemed all the more French for being on the very margin of Germany, and although there were many German touches in the place—German names, larger pots of beer, and enormous theatrical barmaids dressed up in outrageous imitation of Alsatian peasants—yet the fixed French colour seemed all the stronger for these specks of something else. All day long and all night long troops of dusty, swarthy, scornful little soldiers went plodding through the streets with an air of stubborn disgust, for German soldiers look as if they despised you, but French soldiers as if they despised you and themselves even more than you. It is a part, I suppose, of the realism of the nation which has made it good at war and science and other things in which what is necessary is combined with what is nasty. And the soldiers and the civilians alike had most of them cropped hair, and that curious kind of head which to an Englishman looks almost brutal, the kind that we call a bullet-head. Indeed, we are speaking very appropriately when we call it a bullet-head, for in intellectual history the heads of Frenchmen have been bullets—yes, and explosive bullets.

But there was a second reason why in this place one should think particularly of the open-air politics and the open-air art of the French. For this town of Belfort is famous for one of the most typical and powerful of the public monuments of France. From the café table at which I sit I can see the hill beyond the town on which hangs the high and flat-faced citadel, pierced with many windows, and warmed in the evening light. On the steep hill below it is a huge stone lion, itself as large as a hill. It is hacked out of the rock with a sort of gigantic impression. No trivial attempt has been made to make it like a common statue; no attempt to carve the mane into curls, or to distinguish the monster minutely from the earth out of which he rises, shaking the world. The face of the lion has something of the bold conventionality of Assyrian art. The mane of the lion is left like a shapeless cloud of tempest, as if it might literally be said of him that God had clothed his neck with thunder. Even at this distance the thing looks vast, and in some sense prehistoric. Yet it was carved only a little while ago. It commemorates the fact that this town was never taken by the Germans through all the terrible year, but only laid down its arms at last at the command of its own Government. But the spirit of it has been in this land from the beginning—the spirit of something defiant and almost defeated.

As I leave this place and take the railway into Germany the news comes thicker and thicker up the streets that Southern France is in a flame, and that there perhaps will be fought out finally the awful modern battle of the rich and poor. And as I pass into quieter places for the last sign of France on the sky-line, I see the Lion of Belfort stand at bay, the last sight of that great people which has never been at peace.

Chapter 29
Humanity: an Interlude

xcept for some fine works of art, which seem to be there by accident, the City of Brussels is like a bad Paris, a Paris with everything noble cut out, and everything nasty left in. No one can understand Paris and its history who does not understand that its fierceness is the balance and justification of its frivolity. It is called a city of pleasure; but it may also very specially be called a city of pain. The crown of roses is also a crown of thorns. Its people are too prone to hurt others, but quite ready also to hurt themselves. They are martyrs for religion, they are martyrs for irreligion; they are even martyrs for immorality. For the indecency of many of their books and papers is not of the sort which charms and seduces, but of the sort that horrifies and hurts; they are torturing themselves. They lash their own patriotism into life with the same whips which most men use to lash foreigners to silence. The enemies of France can never give an account of her infamy or decay which does not seem insipid and even polite compared with the things which the Nationalists of France say about their own nation. They taunt and torment themselves; sometimes they even deliberately oppress themselves. Thus, when the mob of Paris could make a Government to please itself, it made a sort of sublime tyranny to order itself about. The spirit is the same from the Crusades or St. Bartholomew to the apotheosis of Zola. The old religionists tortured men physically for a moral truth. The new realists torture men morally for a physical truth.

Now Brussels is Paris without this constant purification of pain. Its indecencies are not regrettable incidents in an everlasting revolution. It has none of the things which make good Frenchmen love Paris; it has only the things which make unspeakable Englishmen love it. It has the part which is cosmopolitan—and narrow; not the part which is Parisian—and universal. You can find there (as commonly happens in modern centres) the worst things of all nations—the *Daily Mail* from England, the cheap philosophies from Germany, the loose novels of France, and the drinks of America. But there is no English broad fun, no German kindly ceremony, no American exhilaration, and, above all, no French tradition of fighting for an idea. Though all the boulevards look like Parisian boulevards, though all the shops look like Parisian shops, you cannot look at them steadily for two minutes without feeling the full distance between, let us say, King Leopold and fighters like Clemenceau and Deroulède.

For all these reasons, and many more, when I had got into Brussels I began to make all necessary arrangements for getting out of it again; and I had impulsively got into a tram which seemed to be going out of the city. In this tram there were two men talking; one was a little man with a black French beard; the other was a baldish man with bushy whiskers, like the financial foreign count in a three-act farce. And about the time that we reached the suburb of the city, and the traffic grew thinner, and the noises more few, I began to hear what they were saying. Though they spoke French quickly, their words were fairly easy to follow, because they were all long words. Anybody can understand long words because they have in them all the lucidity of Latin.

The man with the black beard said: "It must that we have the Progress."

The man with the whiskers parried this smartly by saying: "It must also that we have the Consolidation International."

This is a sort of discussion which I like myself, so I listened with some care, and I think I picked up the thread of it. One of the Belgians was a Little Belgian, as we speak of a Little Englander. The other was a Belgian Imperialist, for though Belgium is not quite strong enough to be altogether a nation, she is quite strong enough to be an empire. Being a nation means standing up to your equals, whereas being an empire only means kicking your inferiors. The man with whiskers was the Imperialist, and he was saying: "The science, behold there the new guide of humanity."

And the man with the beard answered him: "It does not suffice to have progress in the science; one must have it also in the sentiment of the human justice."

This remark I applauded, as if at a public meeting, but they were much too keen on their argument to hear me. The views I have often heard in England, but never uttered so lucidly, and certainly never so fast. Though Belgian by nation they must both have been essentially French. Whiskers was great on education, which, it seems, is on the march. All the world goes to make itself instructed. It must that the more instructed enlighten the less instructed. Eh, well then, the European must impose upon the savage the science and the light. Also (apparently) he must impose himself on the savage while he is about it. To-day one travelled quickly. The science had changed all. For our fathers, they were religious, and (what was worse) dead. To-day humanity had electricity to the hand; the machines came from triumphing; all the lines and limits of the globe effaced themselves. Soon there would not be but the great Empires and confederations, guided by the science, always the science.

Here Whiskers stopped an instant for breath; and the man with the sentiment for human justice had "la parole" off him in a flash. Without doubt Humanity was on the march, but towards the sentiments, the ideal, the methods moral and pacific. Humanity directed itself towards Humanity. For your wars and empires on behalf of civilisation, what were they in effect? The war, was it not itself an affair of the barbarism? The Empires were they not things savage? The Humanity had passed all that; she was now intellectual. Tolstoy had refined all human souls with the sentiments the most delicate and just. Man was become a spirit; the wings pushed . . .

At this important point of evolution the tram came to a jerky stoppage; and staring around I found, to my stunned consternation, that it was almost dark, that I was far away from Brussels, that I could not dream of getting back to dinner; in short, that through the clinging fascination of this great controversy on Humanity and its recent complete alteration by science or Tolstoy, I had landed myself Heaven knows where. I dropped hastily from the suburban tram and let it go on without me.

I was alone in the flat fields out of sight of the city. On one side of the road was one of those small, thin woods which are common in all countries, but of which, by a coincidence, the mystical painters of Flanders were very fond. The night was closing in with cloudy purple and grey; there was one ribbon of silver, the last rag of the sunset. Through the wood went one little path, and somehow it suggested that it might lead to some sign of life—there was no other sign of life on the horizon. I went along it, and soon sank into a sort of dancing twilight of all those tiny trees. There is something subtle and bewildering about that sort of frail and fantastic wood. A forest of big trees seems like a bodily barrier; but somehow that mist of thin lines seems like a spiritual barrier. It is as if one were caught in a fairy cloud or could not pass a phantom. When I had well lost the last gleam of the high road a curious and definite feeling came upon me. Now I suddenly felt something much more practical and extraordinary—the absence of humanity: inhuman loneliness. Of course, there was nothing really lost in my state; but the mood may hit one anywhere. I wanted men—any men; and I felt our awful alliance over all the globe. And at last, when I had walked for what seemed a long time, I saw a light too near the earth to mean anything except the image of God.

I came out on a clear space and a low, long cottage, the door of which was open, but was blocked by a big grey horse, who seemed to prefer to eat with his head inside the sitting-room. I got past him, and found he was being fed by a young man who was sitting down and drinking beer inside, and who saluted me with heavy rustic courtesy, but in a strange tongue. The room was full of staring faces like owls, and these I traced at length as belonging to about six small children. Their father was still working in the fields, but their mother rose when I entered. She smiled, but she and all the rest spoke some rude language, Flamand, I suppose; so that we had to be kind to each other by signs. She fetched me beer, and pointed out my way with her finger; and I drew a picture to please the children; and as it was a picture of two men hitting each other with swords, it pleased them very much. Then I gave a Belgian penny to each child, for as I said on chance in French, "It must be that we have the economic equality." But they had never heard of economic equality, while all Battersea workmen have heard of economic equality, though it is true that they haven't got it.

I found my way back to the city, and some time afterwards I actually saw in the street my two men talking, no doubt still saying, one that Science had changed all in Humanity, and the other that Humanity was now pushing the wings of the purely intellectual. But for me Humanity was hooked on to an accidental picture. I thought of a low and lonely house in the flats, behind a veil or film of slight trees, a man breaking the ground as men have broken from the first morning, and a huge grey horse champing his food within a foot of a child's head, as in the stable where Christ was born.

Chapter 30
The Little Birds Who Won't Sing

n my last morning on the Flemish coast, when I knew that in a few hours I should be in England, my eye fell upon one of the details of Gothic carving of which Flanders is full. I do not know whether the thing is old, though it was certainly knocked about and indecipherable, but at least it was certainly in the style and tradition of the early Middle Ages. It seemed to represent men bending themselves (not to say twisting themselves) to certain primary employments. Some seemed to be sailors tugging at ropes; others, I think, were reaping; others were energetically pouring something into something else. This is entirely characteristic of the pictures and carvings of the early thirteenth century, perhaps the most purely vigorous time in all history. The great Greeks preferred to carve their gods and heroes doing nothing. Splendid and philosophic as their composure is there is always about it something that marks the master of many slaves. But if there was one thing the early mediaevals liked it was representing people doing something—hunting or hawking, or rowing boats, or treading grapes, or making shoes, or cooking something in a pot. "Quicquid agunt homines, votum, timor, ira voluptas." (I quote from memory.) The Middle Ages is full of that spirit in all its monuments and manuscripts. Chaucer retains it in his jolly insistence on everybody's type of trade and toil. It was the earliest and youngest resurrection of Europe, the time when social order was strengthening, but had not yet become oppressive; the time when religious faiths were strong, but had not yet been exasperated. For this reason the whole effect of Greek and Gothic carving is different. The figures in the Elgin marbles, though often reining their steeds for an instant in the air, seem frozen for ever at that perfect instant. But a mass of mediaeval carving seems actually a sort of bustle or hubbub in stone. Sometimes one cannot help feeling that the groups actually move and mix, and the whole front of a great cathedral has the hum of a huge hive.

But about these particular figures there was a peculiarity of which I could not be sure. Those of them that had any heads had very curious heads, and it seemed to me that they had their mouths open. Whether or no this really meant anything or was an accident of nascent art I do not know; but in the course of wondering I recalled to my mind the fact that singing was connected with many of the tasks there suggested, that there were songs for reapers and songs for sailors hauling ropes. I was still thinking about this small problem when I walked along the pier at Ostend; and I heard some sailors uttering a measured shout as they laboured, and I remembered that sailors still sing in chorus while they work, and even sing different songs according to what part of their work they are doing. And a little while afterwards, when my sea journey was over, the sight of men working in the English fields reminded me again that there are still songs for harvest and for many agricultural routines. And I suddenly wondered why if this were so it should be quite unknown, for any modern trade to have a ritual poetry. How did people come to chant rude poems while pulling certain ropes or gathering certain fruit, and why did nobody do anything of the kind while producing any of the modern things? Why is a modern newspaper never printed by people singing in chorus? Why do shopmen seldom, if ever, sing?

If reapers sing while reaping, why should not auditors sing while auditing and bankers while banking? If there are songs for all the separate things that have to be done in a boat, why are there not songs for all the separate things that have to be done in a bank? As the train from Dover flew through the Kentish gardens, I tried to write a few songs suitable for commercial gentlemen. Thus, the work of bank clerks when casting up columns might begin with a thundering chorus in praise of Simple Addition.

"Up my lads and lift the ledgers, sleep and ease are o'er. Hear the Stars of Morning shouting: 'Two and Two are four.' Though the creeds and realms are reeling, though the sophists roar, Though we weep and pawn our watches, Two and Two are Four."

"There's a run upon the Bank—Stand away! For the Manager's a crank and the Secretary drank, and the

Upper Tooting Bank
Turns to bay!
Stand close: there is a run
On the Bank.
Of our ship, our royal one, let the ringing legend run,
That she fired with every gun
Ere she sank."

And as I came into the cloud of London I met a friend of mine who actually is in a bank, and submitted these suggestions in rhyme to him for use among his colleagues. But he was not very hopeful about the matter. It was not (he assured me) that he underrated the verses, or in any sense lamented their lack of polish.

No; it was rather, he felt, an indefinable something in the very atmosphere of the society in which we live that makes it spiritually difficult to sing in banks. And I think he must be right; though the matter is very mysterious. I may observe here that I think there must be some mistake in the calculations of the Socialists. They put down all our distress, not to a moral tone, but to the chaos of private enterprise. Now, banks are private; but post-offices are Socialistic: therefore I naturally expected that the post-office would fall into the collectivist idea of a chorus. Judge of my surprise when the lady in my local post-office (whom I urged to sing) dismissed the idea with far more coldness than the bank clerk had done. She seemed indeed, to be in a considerably greater state of depression than he. Should any one suppose that this was the effect of the verses themselves, it is only fair to say that the specimen verse of the Post-Office Hymn ran thus:

"O'er London our letters are shaken like snow,
Our wires o'er the world like the thunderbolts go.
The news that may marry a maiden in Sark,
Or kill an old lady in Finsbury Park."
Chorus (with a swing of joy and energy):
"Or kill an old lady in Finsbury Park."

And the more I thought about the matter the more painfully certain it seemed that the most important and typical modern things could not be done with a chorus. One could not, for instance, be a great financier and sing; because the essence of being a great financier is that you keep quiet. You could not even in many modern circles be a public man and sing; because in those circles the essence of being a public man is that you do nearly everything in private. Nobody would imagine a chorus of money-lenders. Every one knows the story of the solicitors' corps of volunteers who, when the Colonel on the battlefield cried "Charge!" all said simultaneously, "Six-and-eightpence." Men can sing while charging in a military, but hardly in a legal sense. And at the end of my reflections I had really got no further than the sub-conscious feeling of my friend the bank-clerk—that there is something spiritually suffocating about our life; not about our laws merely, but about our life. Bank-clerks are without songs, not because they are poor, but because they are sad. Sailors are much poorer. As I passed homewards I passed a little tin building of some religious sort, which was shaken with shouting as a trumpet is torn with its own tongue. THEY were singing anyhow; and I had for an instant a fancy I had often had before: that with us the super-human is the only place where you can find the human. Human nature is hunted and has fled into sanctuary.

Chapter 31
The Riddle of the Ivy

ore than a month ago, when I was leaving London for a holiday, a friend walked into my flat in Battersea and found me surrounded with half-packed luggage.

"You seem to be off on your travels," he said. "Where are you going?"

With a strap between my teeth I replied, "To Battersea."

"The wit of your remark," he said, "wholly escapes me."

"I am going to Battersea," I repeated, "to Battersea viâ Paris, Belfort, Heidelberg, and Frankfort. My remark contained no wit. It contained simply the truth. I am going to wander over the whole world until once more I find Battersea. Somewhere in the seas of sunset or of sunrise, somewhere in the ultimate archipelago of the earth, there is one little island which I wish to find: an island with low green hills and great white cliffs. Travellers tell me that it is called England (Scotch travellers tell me that it is called Britain), and there is a rumour that somewhere in the heart of it there is a beautiful place called Battersea."

"I suppose it is unnecessary to tell you," said my friend, with an air of intellectual comparison, "that this is Battersea?"

"It is quite unnecessary," I said, "and it is spiritually untrue. I cannot see any Battersea here; I cannot see any London or any England. I cannot see that door. I cannot see that chair: because a cloud of sleep and custom has come across my eyes. The only way to get back to them is to go somewhere else; and that is the real object of travel and the real pleasure of holidays. Do you suppose that I go to France in order to see France? Do you suppose that I go to Germany in order to see Germany? I shall enjoy them both; but it is not them that I am seeking. I am seeking Battersea. The whole object of travel is not to set foot on foreign land; it is at last to set foot on one's own country as a foreign land. Now I warn you that this Gladstone bag is compact and heavy, and that if you utter that word 'paradox' I shall hurl it at your head. I did not make the world, and I did not make it paradoxical. It is not my fault, it is the truth, that the only way to go to England is to go away from it."

But when, after only a month's travelling, I did come back to England, I was startled to find that I had told the exact truth. England did break on me at once beautifully new and beautifully old. To land at Dover is the right way to approach England (most things that are hackneyed are right), for then you see first the full, soft gardens of Kent, which are, perhaps, an exaggeration, but still a typical exaggeration, of the rich rusticity of England. As it happened, also, a fellow-traveller with whom I had fallen into conversation felt the same freshness, though for another cause. She was an American lady who had seen Europe, and had never yet seen England, and she expressed her enthusiasm in that simple and splendid way which is natural to Americans, who are the most idealistic people in the whole world. Their only danger is that the idealist can easily become the idolator. And the American has become so idealistic that he even idealises money. But (to quote a very able writer of American short stories) that is another story.

"I have never been in England before," said the American lady, "yet it is so pretty that I feel as if I have been away from it for a long time."

"So you have," I said; "you have been away for three hundred years."

"What a lot of ivy you have," she said. "It covers the churches and it buries the houses. We have ivy; but I have never seen it grow like that."

"I am interested to hear it," I replied, "for I am making a little list of all the things that are really better in England. Even a month on the Continent, combined with intelligence, will teach you that there are many things that are better abroad. All the things that the DAILY MAIL calls English are better abroad. But there are things entirely English and entirely good. Kippers, for instance, and Free Trade, and front gardens, and individual liberty, and the Elizabethan drama, and hansom cabs, and cricket, and Mr. Will Crooks. Above all, there is the happy and holy custom of eating a heavy breakfast. I cannot imagine that Shakespeare began the day with rolls and coffee, like a Frenchman or a German. Surely he began with bacon or bloaters. In fact, a light bursts upon me; for the first time I see the real meaning of Mrs. Gallup and the Great Cipher. It is merely a mistake in the matter of a capital letter. I withdraw my objections; I accept everything; bacon did write Shakespeare."

"I cannot look at anything but the ivy," she said, "it looks so comfortable."

While she looked at the ivy I opened for the first time for many weeks an English newspaper, and I read a speech of Mr. Balfour in which he said that the House of Lords ought to be preserved because it represented something in the nature of permanent public opinion of England, above the ebb and flow of the parties. Now Mr. Balfour is a perfectly sincere patriot, a man who, from his own point of view, thinks long and seriously about the public needs, and he is, moreover, a man of entirely exceptional intellectual power. But alas, in spite of all this, when I had read that speech I thought with a heavy heart that there was one more thing that I had to add to the list of the specially English things, such as kippers and cricket; I had to add the specially English kind of humbug. In France things are attacked and defended for what they are. The Catholic Church is attacked because it is Catholic, and defended because it is Catholic. The Republic is defended because it is Republican, and attacked because it is Republican. But here is the ablest of English politicians consoling everybody by telling them that the House of Lords is not really the House of Lords, but something quite different, that the foolish accidental peers whom he meets every night are in some mysterious way experts upon the psychology of the democracy; that if you want to know what the very poor want you must ask the very rich, and that if you want the truth about Hoxton, you must ask for it at Hatfield. If the Conservative defender of the House of Lords were a logical French politician he would simply be a liar. But being an English politician he is simply a poet. The English love of believing that all is as it should be, the English optimism combined with the strong English imagination, is too much even for the obvious facts. In a cold, scientific sense, of course, Mr. Balfour knows that nearly all the Lords who are not Lords by accident are Lords by bribery. He knows, and (as Mr. Belloc excellently said) everybody in Parliament knows the very names of the peers who have purchased their peerages. But the glamour of comfort, the pleasure of reassuring himself and reassuring others, is too strong for this original knowledge; at last it fades from him, and he sincerely and earnestly calls on Englishmen to join with him in admiring an august and public-spirited Senate, having wholly forgotten that the Senate really consists of idiots whom he has himself despised; and adventurers whom he has himself ennobled.

"Your ivy is so beautifully soft and thick," said the American lady, "it seems to cover almost everything. It must be the most poetical thing in England."

"It is very beautiful," I said, "and, as you say, it is very English. Charles Dickens, who was almost more English than England, wrote one of his rare poems about the beauty of ivy. Yes, by all means let us admire the ivy, so deep, so warm, so full of a genial gloom and a grotesque tenderness. Let us admire the ivy; and let us pray to God in His mercy that it may not kill the tree."

Chapter 32
The Travellers in State

he other day, to my great astonishment, I caught a train; it was a train going into the Eastern Counties, and I only just caught it. And while I was running along the train (amid general admiration) I noticed that there were a quite peculiar and unusual number of carriages marked "Engaged." On five, six, seven, eight, nine carriages was pasted the little notice: at five, six, seven, eight, nine windows were big bland men staring out in the conscious pride of possession. Their bodies seemed more than usually impenetrable, their faces more than usual placid. It could not be the Derby, if only for the minor reasons that it was the opposite direction and the wrong day. It could hardly be the King. It could hardly be the French President. For, though these distinguished persons naturally like to be private for three hours, they are at least public for three minutes. A crowd can gather to see them step into the train; and there was no crowd here, or any police ceremonial.

Who were those awful persons, who occupied more of the train than a brick-layer's beanfeast, and yet were more fastidious and delicate than the King's own suite? Who were these that were larger than a mob, yet more mysterious than a monarch? Was it possible that instead of our Royal House visiting the Tsar, he was really visiting us? Or does the House of Lords have a breakfast? I waited and wondered until the train slowed down at some station in the direction of Cambridge. Then the large, impenetrable men got out, and after them got out the distinguished holders of the engaged seats. They were all dressed decorously in one colour; they had neatly cropped hair; and they were chained together.

I looked across the carriage at its only other occupant, and our eyes met. He was a small, tired-looking man, and, as I afterwards learnt, a native of Cambridge; by the look of him, some working tradesman there, such as a journeyman tailor or a small clock-mender. In order to make conversation I said I wondered where the convicts were going. His mouth twitched with the instinctive irony of our poor, and he said: "I don't s'pose they're goin' on an 'oliday at the seaside with little spades and pails." I was naturally delighted, and, pursuing the same vein of literary invention, I suggested that perhaps dons were taken down to Cambridge chained together like this. And as he lived in Cambridge, and had seen several dons, he was pleased with such a scheme. Then when we had ceased to laugh, we suddenly became quite silent; and the bleak, grey eyes of the little man grew sadder and emptier than an open sea. I knew what he was thinking, because I was thinking the same, because all modern sophists are only sophists, and there is such a thing as mankind. Then at last (and it fell in as exactly as the right last note of a tune one is trying to remember) he said: "Well, I s'pose we 'ave to do it."

And in those three things, his first speech and his silence and his second speech, there were all the three great fundamental facts of the English democracy, its profound sense of humour, its profound sense of pathos, and its profound sense of helplessness.

It cannot be too often repeated that all real democracy is an attempt (like that of a jolly hostess) to bring the shy people out. For every practical purpose of a political state, for every practical purpose of a tea-party, he that abaseth himself must be exalted. At a tea-party it is equally obvious that he that exalteth himself must be abased, if possible without bodily violence. Now people talk of democracy as being coarse and turbulent: it is a self-evident error in mere history. Aristocracy is the thing that is always coarse and turbulent: for it means appealing to the self-confident people. Democracy means appealing to the different people. Democracy means getting those people to vote who would never have the cheek to govern: and (according to Christian ethics) the precise people who ought to govern are the people who have not the cheek to do it. There is a strong example of this truth in my friend in the train. The only two types we hear of in this argument about crime and punishment are two very rare and abnormal types.

We hear of the stark sentimentalist, who talks as if there were no problem at all: as if physical kindness would cure everything: as if one need only pat Nero and stroke Ivan the Terrible. This mere belief in bodily humanitarianism is not sentimental; it is simply snobbish. For if comfort gives men virtue, the comfortable classes ought to be virtuous—which is absurd. Then, again, we do hear of the yet weaker and more watery type of sentimentalists: I mean the sentimentalist who says, with a sort of splutter, "Flog the brutes!" or who tells you with innocent obscenity "what he would do" with a certain man—always supposing the man's hands were tied.

This is the more effeminate type of the two; but both are weak and unbalanced. And it is only these two types, the sentimental humanitarian and the sentimental brutalitarian, whom one hears in the modern babel. Yet you very rarely meet either of them in a train. You never meet anyone else in a controversy. The man you meet in a train is like this man that I met: he is emotionally decent, only he is intellectually doubtful. So far from luxuriating in the loathsome things that could be "done" to criminals, he feels bitterly how much better it would be if nothing need be done. But something must be done. "I s'pose we 'ave to do it." In short, he is simply a sane man, and of a sane man there is only one safe definition. He is a man who can have tragedy in his heart and comedy in his head.

Now the real difficulty of discussing decently this problem of the proper treatment of criminals is that both parties discuss the matter without any direct human feeling. The denouncers of wrong are as cold as the organisers of wrong. Humanitarianism is as hard as inhumanity.

Let me take one practical instance. I think the flogging arranged in our modern prisons is a filthy torture; all its scientific paraphernalia, the photographing, the medical attendance, prove that it goes to the last foul limit of the boot and rack. The cat is simply the rack without any of its intellectual reasons. Holding this view strongly, I open the ordinary humanitarian books or papers and I find a phrase like this, "The lash is a relic of barbarism." So is the plough. So is the fishing net. So is the horn or the staff or the fire lit in winter. What an inexpressibly feeble phrase for anything one wants to attack—a relic of barbarism! It is as if a man walked naked down the street to-morrow, and we said that his clothes were not quite in the latest fashion. There is nothing particularly nasty about being a relic of barbarism. Man is a relic of barbarism. Civilisation is a relic of barbarism.

But torture is not a relic of barbarism at all. In actuality it is simply a relic of sin; but in comparative history it may well be called a relic of civilisation. It has always been most artistic and elaborate when everything else was most artistic and elaborate. Thus it was detailed exquisite in the late Roman Empire, in the complex and gorgeous sixteenth century, in the centralised French monarchy a hundred years before the Revolution, and in the great Chinese civilisation to this day. This is, first and last, the frightful thing we must remember. In so far as we grow instructed and refined we are not (in any sense whatever) naturally moving away from torture. We may be moving towards torture. We must know what we are doing, if we are to avoid the enormous secret cruelty which has crowned every historic civilisation.

The train moves more swiftly through the sunny English fields. They have taken the prisoners away, and I do not know what they have done with them.

Chapter 33
The Prehistoric Railway Station

railway station is an admirable place, although Ruskin did not think so; he did not think so because he himself was even more modern than the railway station. He did not think so because he was himself feverish, irritable, and snorting like an engine. He could not value the ancient silence of the railway station.

"In a railway station," he said, "you are in a hurry, and therefore, miserable"; but you need not be either unless you are as modern as Ruskin. The true philosopher does not think of coming just in time for his train except as a bet or a joke.

The only way of catching a train I have ever discovered is to be late for the one before. Do this, and you will find in a railway station much of the quietude and consolation of a cathedral. It has many of the characteristics of a great ecclesiastical building; it has vast arches, void spaces, coloured lights, and, above all, it has recurrence or ritual. It is dedicated to the celebration of water and fire the two prime elements of all human ceremonial. Lastly, a station resembles the old religions rather than the new religions in this point, that people go there. In connection with this it should also be remembered that all popular places, all sites, actually used by the people, tend to retain the best routine of antiquity very much more than any localities or machines used by any privileged class. Things are not altered so quickly or completely by common people as they are by fashionable people. Ruskin could have found more memories of the Middle Ages in the Underground Railway than in the grand hotels outside the stations. The great palaces of pleasure which the rich build in London all have brazen and vulgar names. Their names are either snobbish, like the Hotel Cecil, or (worse still) cosmopolitan like the Hotel Metropole. But when I go in a third-class carriage from the nearest circle station to Battersea to the nearest circle station to the DAILY NEWS, the names of the stations are one long litany of solemn and saintly memories. Leaving Victoria I come to a park belonging especially to St. James the Apostle; thence I go to Westminster Bridge, whose very name alludes to the awful Abbey; Charing Cross holds up the symbol of Christendom; the next station is called a Temple; and Blackfriars remembers the mediaeval dream of a Brotherhood.

If you wish to find the past preserved, follow the million feet of the crowd. At the worst the uneducated only wear down old things by sheer walking. But the educated kick them down out of sheer culture.

I feel all this profoundly as I wander about the empty railway station, where I have no business of any kind. I have extracted a vast number of chocolates from automatic machines; I have obtained cigarettes, toffee, scent, and other things that I dislike by the same machinery; I have weighed myself, with sublime results; and this sense, not only of the healthiness of popular things, but of their essential antiquity and permanence, is still in possession of my mind. I wander up to the bookstall, and my faith survives even the wild spectacle of modern literature and journalism. Even in the crudest and most clamorous aspects of the newspaper world I still prefer the popular to the proud and fastidious. If I had to choose between taking in the DAILY MAIL and taking in the TIMES (the dilemma reminds one of a nightmare), I should certainly cry out with the whole of my being for the DAILY MAIL. Even mere bigness preached in a frivolous way is not so irritating as mere meanness preached in a big and solemn way. People buy the DAILY MAIL, but they do not believe in it. They do believe in the TIMES, and (apparently) they do not buy it. But the more the output of paper upon the modern world is actually studied, the more it will be found to be in all its essentials ancient and human, like the name of Charing Cross. Linger for two or three hours at a station bookstall (as I am doing), and you will find that it gradually takes on the grandeur and historic allusiveness of the Vatican or Bodleian Library. The novelty is all superficial; the tradition is all interior and profound. The DAILY MAIL has new editions, but never a new idea. Everything in a newspaper that is not the old human love of altar or fatherland is the old human love of gossip. Modern writers have often made game of the old chronicles because they chiefly record accidents and prodigies; a church struck by lightning, or a calf with six legs. They do not seem to realise that this old barbaric history is the same as new democratic journalism. It is not that the savage chronicle has disappeared. It is merely that the savage chronicle now appears every morning.

As I moved thus mildly and vaguely in front of the bookstall, my eye caught a sudden and scarlet title that for the moment staggered me. On the outside of a book I saw written in large letters, "Get On or Get Out." The title of the book recalled to me with a sudden revolt and reaction all that does seem unquestionably new and nasty; it reminded me that there was in the world of to-day that utterly idiotic thing, a worship of success; a thing that only means surpassing anybody in anything; a thing that may mean being the most successful person in running away from a battle; a thing that may mean being the most successfully sleepy of the whole row of sleeping men. When I saw those words the silence and sanctity of the railway station were for the moment shadowed. Here, I thought, there is at any rate something anarchic and violent and vile. This title, at any rate, means the most disgusting individualism of this individualistic world. In the fury of my bitterness and passion I actually bought the book, thereby ensuring that my enemy would get some of my money. I opened it prepared to find some brutality, some blasphemy, which would really be an exception to the general silence and sanctity of the railway station. I was prepared to find something in the book that was as infamous as its title.

I was disappointed. There was nothing at all corresponding to the furious decisiveness of the remarks on the cover. After reading it carefully I could not discover whether I was really to get on or to get out; but I had a vague feeling that I should prefer to get out. A considerable part of the book, particularly towards the end, was concerned with a detailed description of the life of Napoleon Bonaparte. Undoubtedly Napoleon got on. He also got out. But I could not discover in any way how the details of his life given here were supposed to help a person aiming at success. One anecdote described how Napoleon always wiped his pen on his knee-breeches. I suppose the moral is: always wipe your pen on your knee-breeches, and you will win the battle of Wagram. Another story told that he let loose a gazelle among the ladies of his Court. Clearly the brutal practical inference is—loose a gazelle among the ladies of your acquaintance, and you will be Emperor of the French. Get on with a gazelle or get out. The book entirely reconciled me to the soft twilight of the station. Then I suddenly saw that there was a symbolic division which might be paralleled from biology. Brave men are vertebrates; they have their softness on the surface and their toughness in the middle. But these modern cowards are all crustaceans; their hardness is all on the cover and their softness is inside. But the softness is there; everything in this twilight temple is soft.

Chapter 34
The Diabolist

very now and then I have introduced into my essays an element of truth. Things that really happened have been mentioned, such as meeting President Kruger or being thrown out of a cab. What I have now to relate really happened; yet there was no element in it of practical politics or of personal danger. It was simply a quiet conversation which I had with another man. But that quiet conversation was by far the most terrible thing that has ever happened to me in my life. It happened so long ago that I cannot be certain of the exact words of the dialogue, only of its main questions and answers; but there is one sentence in it for which I can answer absolutely and word for word. It was a sentence so awful that I could not forget it if I would. It was the last sentence spoken; and it was not spoken to me.

The thing befell me in the days when I was at an art school. An art school is different from almost all other schools or colleges in this respect: that, being of new and crude creation and of lax discipline, it presents a specially strong contrast between the industrious and the idle. People at an art school either do an atrocious amount of work or do no work at all. I belonged, along with other charming people, to the latter class; and this threw me often into the society of men who were very different from myself, and who were idle for reasons very different from mine. I was idle because I was very much occupied; I was engaged about that time in discovering, to my own extreme and lasting astonishment, that I was not an atheist. But there were others also at loose ends who were engaged in discovering what Carlyle called (I think with needless delicacy) the fact that ginger is hot in the mouth.

I value that time, in short, because it made me acquainted with a good representative number of blackguards. In this connection there are two very curious things which the critic of human life may observe. The first is the fact that there is one real difference between men and women; that women prefer to talk in twos, while men prefer to talk in threes. The second is that when you find (as you often do) three young cads and idiots going about together and getting drunk together every day you generally find that one of the three cads and idiots is (for some extraordinary reason) not a cad and not an idiot. In these small groups devoted to a drivelling dissipation there is almost always one man who seems to have condescended to his company; one man who, while he can talk a foul triviality with his fellows, can also talk politics with a Socialist, or philosophy with a Catholic.

It was just such a man whom I came to know well. It was strange, perhaps, that he liked his dirty, drunken society; it was stranger still, perhaps, that he liked my society. For hours of the day he would talk with me about Milton or Gothic architecture; for hours of the night he would go where I have no wish to follow him, even in speculation. He was a man with a long, ironical face, and close and red hair; he was by class a gentleman, and could walk like one, but preferred, for some reason, to walk like a groom carrying two pails. He looked like a sort of Super-jockey; as if some archangel had gone on the Turf. And I shall never forget the half-hour in which he and I argued about real things for the first and the last time.

Along the front of the big building of which our school was a part ran a huge slope of stone steps, higher, I think, than those that lead up to St. Paul's Cathedral. On a black wintry evening he and I were wandering on these cold heights, which seemed as dreary as a pyramid under the stars. The one thing visible below us in the blackness was a burning and blowing fire; for some gardener (I suppose) was burning something in the grounds, and from time to time the red sparks went whirling past us like a swarm of scarlet insects in the dark. Above us also it was gloom; but if one stared long enough at that upper darkness, one saw vertical stripes of grey in the black and then became conscious of the colossal façade of the Doric building, phantasmal, yet filling the sky, as if Heaven were still filled with the gigantic ghost of Paganism.

The man asked me abruptly why I was becoming orthodox. Until he said it, I really had not known that I was; but the moment he had said it I knew it to be literally true. And the process had been so long and full that I answered him at once out of existing stores of explanation.

"I am becoming orthodox," I said, "because I have come, rightly or wrongly, after stretching my brain till it bursts, to the old belief that heresy is worse even than sin. An error is more menacing than a crime, for an error begets crimes. An Imperialist is worse than a pirate. For an Imperialist keeps a school for pirates; he teaches piracy disinterestedly and without an adequate salary. A Free Lover is worse than a profligate. For a profligate is serious and reckless even in his shortest love; while a Free Lover is cautious and irresponsible even in his longest devotion. I hate modern doubt because it is dangerous."

"You mean dangerous to morality," he said in a voice of wonderful gentleness. "I expect you are right. But why do you care about morality?"

I glanced at his face quickly. He had thrust out his neck as he had a trick of doing; and so brought his face abruptly into the light of the bonfire from below, like a face in the footlights. His long chin and high cheek-bones were lit up infernally from underneath; so that he looked like a fiend staring down into the flaming pit. I had an unmeaning sense of being tempted in a wilderness; and even as I paused a burst of red sparks broke past.

"Aren't those sparks splendid?" I said.

"Yes," he replied.

"That is all that I ask you to admit," said I. "Give me those few red specks and I will deduce Christian morality. Once I thought like you, that one's pleasure in a flying spark was a thing that could come and go with that spark. Once I thought that the delight was as free as the fire. Once I thought that red star we see was alone in space. But now I know that the red star is only on the apex of an invisible pyramid of virtues. That red fire is only the flower on a stalk of living habits, which you cannot see. Only because your mother made you say 'Thank you' for a bun are you now able to thank Nature or chaos for those red stars of an instant or for the white stars of all time. Only because you were humble before fireworks on the fifth of November do you now enjoy any fireworks that you chance to see. You only like them being red because you were told about the blood of the martyrs; you only like them being bright because brightness is a glory. That flame flowered out of virtues, and it will fade with virtues. Seduce a woman, and that spark will be less bright. Shed blood, and that spark will be less red. Be really bad, and they will be to you like the spots on a wall-paper."

He had a horrible fairness of the intellect that made me despair of his soul. A common, harmless atheist would have denied that religion produced humility or humility a simple joy: but he admitted both. He only said, "But shall I not find in evil a life of its own? Granted that for every woman I ruin one of those red sparks will go out: will not the expanding pleasure of ruin . . . "

"Do you see that fire?" I asked. "If we had a real fighting democracy, some one would burn you in it; like the devil-worshipper that you are."

"Perhaps," he said, in his tired, fair way. "Only what you call evil I call good."

He went down the great steps alone, and I felt as if I wanted the steps swept and cleaned. I followed later, and as I went to find my hat in the low, dark passage where it hung, I suddenly heard his voice again, but the words were inaudible. I stopped, startled: then I heard the voice of one of the vilest of his associates saying, "Nobody can possibly know." And then I heard those two or three words which I remember in every syllable and cannot forget. I heard the Diabolist say, "I tell you I have done everything else. If I do that I shan't know the difference between right and wrong." I rushed out without daring to pause; and as I passed the fire I did not know whether it was hell or the furious love of God.

I have since heard that he died: it may be said, I think, that he committed suicide; though he did it with tools of pleasure, not with tools of pain. God help him, I know the road he went; but I have never known, or even dared to think, what was that place at which he stopped and refrained.

Chapter 35
A Glimpse of My Country

hatever is it that we are all looking for? I fancy that it is really quite close. When I was a boy I had a fancy that Heaven or Fairyland or whatever I called it, was immediately behind my own back, and that this was why I could never manage to see it, however often I twisted and turned to take it by surprise. I had a notion of a man perpetually spinning round on one foot like a teetotum in the effort to find that world behind his back which continually fled from him. Perhaps this is why the world goes round. Perhaps the world is always trying to look over its shoulder and catch up the world which always escapes it, yet without which it cannot be itself.

In any case, as I have said, I think that we must always conceive of that which is the goal of all our endeavours as something which is in some strange way near. Science boasts of the distance of its stars; of the terrific remoteness of the things of which it has to speak. But poetry and religion always insist upon the proximity, the almost menacing closeness of the things with which they are concerned. Always the Kingdom of Heaven is "At Hand"; and Looking-glass Land is only through the looking-glass. So I for one should never be astonished if the next twist of a street led me to the heart of that maze in which all the mystics are lost. I should not be at all surprised if I turned one corner in Fleet Street and saw a yet queerer-looking lamp; I should not be surprised if I turned a third corner and found myself in Elfland.

I should not be surprised at this; but I was surprised the other day at something more surprising. I took a turn out of Fleet Street and found myself in England.

The singular shock experienced perhaps requires explanation. In the darkest or the most inadequate moments of England there is one thing that should always be remembered about the very nature of our country. It may be shortly stated by saying that England is not such a fool as it looks. The types of England, the externals of England, always misrepresent the country. England is an oligarchical country, and it prefers that its oligarchy should be inferior to itself.

The speaking in the House of Commons, for instance, is not only worse than the speaking was, it is worse than the speaking is, in all or almost all other places in small debating clubs or casual dinners. Our countrymen probably prefer this solemn futility in the higher places of the national life. It may be a strange sight to see the blind leading the blind; but England provides a stranger. England shows us the blind leading the people who can see. And this again is an under-statement of the case. For the English political aristocrats not only speak worse than many other people; they speak worse than themselves. The ignorance of statesmen is like the ignorance of judges, an artificial and affected thing. If you have the good fortune really to talk with a statesman, you will be constantly startled with his saying quite intelligent things. It makes one nervous at first. And I have never been sufficiently intimate with such a man to ask him why it was a rule of his life in Parliament to appear sillier than he was.

It is the same with the voters. The average man votes below himself; he votes with half a mind or with a hundredth part of one. A man ought to vote with the whole of himself as he worships or gets married. A man ought to vote with his head and heart, his soul and stomach, his eye for faces and his ear for music; also (when sufficiently provoked) with his hands and feet. If he has ever seen a fine sunset, the crimson colour of it should creep into his vote. If he has ever heard splendid songs, they should be in his ears when he makes the mystical cross. But as it is, the difficulty with English democracy at all elections is that it is something less than itself. The question is not so much whether only a minority of the electorate votes. The point is that only a minority of the voter votes.

This is the tragedy of England; you cannot judge it by its foremost men. Its types do not typify. And on the occasion of which I speak I found this to be so especially of that old intelligent middle class which I had imagined had almost vanished from the world. It seemed to me that all the main representatives of the middle class had gone off in one direction or in the other; they had either set out in pursuit of the Smart Set or they had set out in pursuit of the Simple Life. I cannot say which I dislike more myself; the people in question are welcome to have either of them, or, as is more likely, to have both, in hideous alternations of disease and cure. But all the prominent men who plainly represent the middle class have adopted either the single eye-glass of Mr. Chamberlain or the single eye of Mr. Bernard Shaw.

The old class that I mean has no representative. Its food was plentiful; but it had no show. Its food was plain; but it had no fads. It was serious about politics; and when it spoke in public it committed the solecism of trying to speak well. I thought that this old earnest political England had practically disappeared. And as I say, I took one turn out of Fleet Street and I found a room full of it.

At the top of the room was a chair in which Johnson had sat. The club was a club in which Wilkes had spoken, in a time when even the ne'er-do-weel was virile.

But all these things by themselves might be merely archaism. The extraordinary thing was that this hall had all the hubbub, the sincerity, the anger, the oratory of the eighteenth century. The members of this club were of all shades of opinion, yet there was not one speech which gave me that jar of unreality which I often have in listening to the ablest men uttering my own opinion. The Toryism of this club was like the Toryism of Johnson, a Toryism that could use humour and appealed to humanity. The democracy of this club was like the democracy of Wilkes, a democracy that can speak epigrams and fight duels; a democracy that can face things out and endure slander; the democracy of Wilkes, or, rather, the democracy of Fox.

One thing especially filled my soul with the soul of my fathers. Each man speaking, whether he spoke well or ill, spoke as well as he could from sheer fury against the other man. This is the greatest of our modern descents, that nowadays a man does not become more rhetorical as he becomes more sincere. An eighteenth-century speaker, when he got really and honestly furious, looked for big words with which to crush his adversary. The new speaker looks for small words to crush him with. He looks for little facts and little sneers. In a modern speech the rhetoric is put into the merely formal part, the opening to which nobody listens. But when Mr. Chamberlain, or a Moderate, or one of the harder kind of Socialists, becomes really sincere, he becomes Cockney. "The destiny of the Empire," or "The destiny of humanity," do well enough for mere ornamental preliminaries, but when the man becomes angry and honest, then it is a snarl, "Where do we come in?" or "It's your money they want."

The men in this eighteenth-century club were entirely different; they were quite eighteenth century. Each one rose to his feet quivering with passion, and tried to destroy his opponent, not with sniggering, but actually with eloquence. I was arguing with them about Home Rule; at the end I told them why the English aristocracy really disliked an Irish Parliament; because it would be like their club.

I came out again into Fleet Street at night, and by a dim lamp I saw pasted up some tawdry nonsense about Wastrels and how London was rising against something that London had hardly heard of. Then I suddenly saw, as in one obvious picture, that the modern world is an immense and tumultuous ocean, full of monstrous and living things. And I saw that across the top of it is spread a thin, a very thin, sheet of ice, of wicked wealth and of lying journalism.

And as I stood there in the darkness I could almost fancy that I heard it crack.

Chapter 36
A Somewhat Improbable Story

cannot remember whether this tale is true or not. If I read it through very carefully I have a suspicion that I should come to the conclusion that it is not. But, unfortunately, I cannot read it through very carefully, because, you see, it is not written yet. The image and the idea of it clung to me through a great part of my boyhood; I may have dreamt it before I could talk; or told it to myself before I could read; or read it before I could remember. On the whole, however, I am certain that I did not read it, for children have very clear memories about things like that; and of the books which I was really fond I can still remember, not only the shape and bulk and binding, but even the position of the printed words on many of the pages. On the whole, I incline to the opinion that it happened to me before I was born.

At any rate, let us tell the story now with all the advantages of the atmosphere that has clung to it. You may suppose me, for the sake of argument, sitting at lunch in one of those quick-lunch restaurants in the City where men take their food so fast that it has none of the quality of food, and take their half-hour's vacation so fast that it has none of the qualities of leisure; to hurry through one's leisure is the most unbusiness-like of actions. They all wore tall shiny hats as if they could not lose an instant even to hang them on a peg, and they all had one eye a little off, hypnotised by the huge eye of the clock. In short, they were the slaves of the modern bondage, you could hear their fetters clanking. Each was, in fact, bound by a chain; the heaviest chain ever tied to a man—it is called a watch-chain.

Now, among these there entered and sat down opposite to me a man who almost immediately opened an uninterrupted monologue. He was like all the other men in dress, yet he was startlingly opposite to them in all manner. He wore a high shiny hat and a long frock coat, but he wore them as such solemn things were meant to be worn; he wore the silk hat as if it were a mitre, and the frock coat as if it were the ephod of a high priest. He not only hung his hat up on the peg, but he seemed (such was his stateliness) almost to ask permission of the hat for doing so, and to apologise to the peg for making use of it. When he had sat down on a wooden chair with the air of one considering its feelings and given a sort of slight stoop or bow to the wooden table itself, as if it were an altar, I could not help some comment springing to my lips. For the man was a big, sanguine-faced, prosperous-looking man, and yet he treated everything with a care that almost amounted to nervousness.

For the sake of saying something to express my interest I said, "This furniture is fairly solid; but, of course, people do treat it much too carelessly."

As I looked up doubtfully my eye caught his, and was fixed as his was fixed in an apocalyptic stare. I had thought him ordinary as he entered, save for his strange, cautious manner; but if the other people had seen him then they would have screamed and emptied the room. They did not see him, and they went on making a clatter with their forks, and a murmur with their conversation. But the man's face was the face of a maniac.

"Did you mean anything particular by that remark?" he asked at last, and the blood crawled back slowly into his face.

"Nothing whatever," I answered. "One does not mean anything here; it spoils people's digestions."

He limped back and wiped his broad forehead with a big handkerchief; and yet there seemed to be a sort of regret in his relief.

"I thought perhaps," he said in a low voice, "that another of them had gone wrong."

"If you mean another digestion gone wrong," I said, "I never heard of one here that went right. This is the heart of the Empire, and the other organs are in an equally bad way."

"No, I mean another street gone wrong," and he said heavily and quietly, "but as I suppose that doesn't explain much to you, I think I shall have to tell you the story. I do so with all the less responsibility, because I know you won't believe it. For forty years of my life I invariably left my office, which is in Leadenhall Street, at half-past five in the afternoon, taking with me an umbrella in the right hand and a bag in the left hand. For forty years two months and four days I passed out of the side office door, walked down the street on the left-hand side, took the first turning to the left and the third to the right, from where I bought an evening paper, followed the road on the right-hand side round two obtuse angles, and came out just outside a Metropolitan station, where I took a train home. For forty years two months and four days I fulfilled this course by accumulated habit: it was not a long street that I traversed, and it took me about four and a half minutes to do it. After forty years two months and four days, on the fifth day I went out in the same manner, with my umbrella in the right hand and my bag in the left, and I began to notice that walking along the familiar street tired me somewhat more than usual; and when I turned it I was convinced that I had turned down the wrong one. For now the street shot up quite a steep slant, such as one only sees in the hilly parts of London, and in this part there were no hills at all. Yet it was not the wrong street; the name written on it was the same; the shuttered shops were the same; the lamp-posts and the whole look of the perspective was the same; only it was tilted upwards like a lid. Forgetting any trouble about breathlessness or fatigue I ran furiously forward, and reached the second of my accustomed turnings, which ought to bring me almost within sight of the station. And as I turned that corner I nearly fell on the pavement. For now the street went up straight in front of my face like a steep staircase or the side of a pyramid. There was not for miles round that place so much as a slope like that of Ludgate Hill. And this was a slope like that of the Matterhorn. The whole street had lifted itself like a single wave, and yet every speck and detail of it was the same, and I saw in the high distance, as at the top of an Alpine pass, picked out in pink letters the name over my paper shop.

"I ran on and on blindly now, passing all the shops and coming to a part of the road where there was a long grey row of private houses. I had, I know not why, an irrational feeling that I was a long iron bridge in empty space. An impulse seized me, and I pulled up the iron trap of a coal-hole. Looking down through it I saw empty space and the stars.

"When I looked up again a man was standing in his front garden, having apparently come out of his house; he was leaning over the railings and gazing at me. We were all alone on that nightmare road; his face was in shadow; his dress was dark and ordinary; but when I saw him standing so perfectly still I knew somehow that he was not of this world. And the stars behind his head were larger and fiercer than ought to be endured by the eyes of men.

" 'If you are a kind angel,' I said, 'or a wise devil, or have anything in common with mankind, tell me what is this street possessed of devils.'

"After a long silence he said, 'What do you say that it is?'

" 'It is Bumpton Street, of course,' I snapped. 'It goes to Oldgate Station.'

" 'Yes,' he admitted gravely; 'it goes there sometimes. Just now, however, it is going to heaven.'

" 'To heaven?' I said. 'Why?'

" 'It is going to heaven for justice,' he replied. 'You must have treated it badly. Remember always that there is one thing that cannot be endured by anybody or anything. That one unendurable thing is to be overworked and also neglected. For instance, you can overwork women—everybody does. But you can't neglect women—I defy you to. At the same time, you can neglect tramps and gypsies and all the apparent refuse of the State so long as you do not overwork it. But no beast of the field, no horse, no dog can endure long to be asked to do more than his work and yet have less than his honour. It is the same with streets. You have worked this street to death, and yet you have never remembered its existence. If you had a healthy democracy, even of pagans, they would have hung this street with garlands and given it the name of a god. Then it would have gone quietly. But at last the street has grown tired of your tireless insolence; and it is bucking and rearing its head to heaven. Have you never sat on a bucking horse?'

"I looked at the long grey street, and for a moment it seemed to me to be exactly like the long grey neck of a horse flung up to heaven. But in a moment my sanity returned, and I said, 'But this is all nonsense. Streets go to the place they have to go. A street must always go to its end.'

" 'Why do you think so of a street?' he asked, standing very still.

" 'Because I have always seen it do the same thing,' I replied, in reasonable anger. 'Day after day, year after year, it has always gone to Oldgate Station; day after . . . '

"I stopped, for he had flung up his head with the fury of the road in revolt.

" 'And you?' he cried terribly. 'What do you think the road thinks of you? Does the road think you are alive? Are you alive? Day after day, year after year, you have gone to Oldgate Station . . . ' Since then I have respected the things called inanimate."

And bowing slightly to the mustard-pot, the man in the restaurant withdrew.

Chapter 37
The Shop Of Ghosts

early all the best and most precious things in the universe you can get for a halfpenny. I make an exception, of course, of the sun, the moon, the earth, people, stars, thunderstorms, and such trifles. You can get them for nothing. Also I make an exception of another thing, which I am not allowed to mention in this paper, and of which the lowest price is a penny halfpenny. But the general principle will be at once apparent. In the street behind me, for instance, you can now get a ride on an electric tram for a halfpenny. To be on an electric tram is to be on a flying castle in a fairy tale. You can get quite a large number of brightly coloured sweets for a halfpenny. Also you can get the chance of reading this article for a halfpenny; along, of course, with other and irrelevant matter.

But if you want to see what a vast and bewildering array of valuable things you can get at a halfpenny each you should do as I was doing last night. I was gluing my nose against the glass of a very small and dimly lit toy shop in one of the greyest and leanest of the streets of Battersea. But dim as was that square of light, it was filled (as a child once said to me) with all the colours God ever made. Those toys of the poor were like the children who buy them; they were all dirty; but they were all bright. For my part, I think brightness more important than cleanliness; since the first is of the soul, and the second of the body. You must excuse me; I am a democrat; I know I am out of fashion in the modern world.

As I looked at that palace of pigmy wonders, at small green omnibuses, at small blue elephants, at small black dolls, and small red Noah's arks, I must have fallen into some sort of unnatural trance. That lit shop-window became like the brilliantly lit stage when one is watching some highly coloured comedy. I forgot the grey houses and the grimy people behind me as one forgets the dark galleries and the dim crowds at a theatre. It seemed as if the little objects behind the glass were small, not because they were toys, but because they were objects far away. The green omnibus was really a green omnibus, a green Bayswater omnibus, passing across some huge desert on its ordinary way to Bayswater. The blue elephant was no longer blue with paint; he was blue with distance. The black doll was really a negro relieved against passionate tropic foliage in the land where every weed is flaming and only man is black. The red Noah's ark was really the enormous ship of earthly salvation riding on the rain-swollen sea, red in the first morning of hope.

Every one, I suppose, knows such stunning instants of abstraction, such brilliant blanks in the mind. In such moments one can see the face of one's own best friend as an unmeaning pattern of spectacles or moustaches. They are commonly marked by the two signs of the slowness of their growth and the suddenness of their termination. The return to real thinking is often as abrupt as bumping into a man. Very often indeed (in my case) it is bumping into a man. But in any case the awakening is always emphatic and, generally speaking, it is always complete. Now, in this case, I did come back with a shock of sanity to the consciousness that I was, after all, only staring into a dingy little toy-shop; but in some strange way the mental cure did not seem to be final. There was still in my mind an unmanageable something that told me that I had strayed into some odd atmosphere, or that I had already done some odd thing. I felt as if I had worked a miracle or committed a sin. It was as if I had at any rate, stepped across some border in the soul.

To shake off this dangerous and dreamy sense I went into the shop and tried to buy wooden soldiers. The man in the shop was very old and broken, with confused white hair covering his head and half his face, hair so startlingly white that it looked almost artificial. Yet though he was senile and even sick, there was nothing of suffering in his eyes; he looked rather as if he were gradually falling asleep in a not unkindly decay. He gave me the wooden soldiers, but when I put down the money he did not at first seem to see it; then he blinked at it feebly, and then he pushed it feebly away.

"No, no," he said vaguely. "I never have. I never have. We are rather old-fashioned here."

"Not taking money," I replied, "seems to me more like an uncommonly new fashion than an old one."

"I never have," said the old man, blinking and blowing his nose; "I've always given presents. I'm too old to stop."

"Good heavens!" I said. "What can you mean? Why, you might be Father Christmas."

"I am Father Christmas," he said apologetically, and blew his nose again.

The lamps could not have been lighted yet in the street outside. At any rate, I could see nothing against the darkness but the shining shop-window. There were no sounds of steps or voices in the street; I might have strayed into some new and sunless world. But something had cut the chords of common sense, and I could not feel even surprise except sleepily. Something made me say, "You look ill, Father Christmas."

"I am dying," he said.

I did not speak, and it was he who spoke again.

"All the new people have left my shop. I cannot understand it. They seem to object to me on such curious and inconsistent sort of grounds, these scientific men, and these innovators. They say that I give people superstitions and make them too visionary; they say I give people sausages and make them too coarse.

They say my heavenly parts are too heavenly; they say my earthly parts are too earthly; I don't know what they want, I'm sure. How can heavenly things be too heavenly, or earthly things too earthly? How can one be too good, or too jolly? I don't understand. But I understand one thing well enough. These modern people are living and I am dead."

"You may be dead," I replied. "You ought to know. But as for what they are doing, do not call it living."

A silence fell suddenly between us which I somehow expected to be unbroken. But it had not fallen for more than a few seconds when, in the utter stillness, I distinctly heard a very rapid step coming nearer and nearer along the street. The next moment a figure flung itself into the shop and stood framed in the doorway. He wore a large white hat tilted back as if in impatience; he had tight black old-fashioned pantaloons, a gaudy old-fashioned stock and waistcoat, and an old fantastic coat. He had large, wide-open, luminous eyes like those of an arresting actor; he had a pale, nervous face, and a fringe of beard. He took in the shop and the old man in a look that seemed literally a flash and uttered the exclamation of a man utterly staggered.

"Good lord!" he cried out; "it can't be you! It isn't you! I came to ask where your grave was."

"I'm not dead yet, Mr. Dickens," said the old gentleman, with a feeble smile; "but I'm dying," he hastened to add reassuringly.

"But, dash it all, you were dying in my time," said Mr. Charles Dickens with animation; "and you don't look a day older."

"I've felt like this for a long time," said Father Christmas.

Mr. Dickens turned his back and put his head out of the door into the darkness.

"Dick," he roared at the top of his voice; "he's still alive."

Another shadow darkened the doorway, and a much larger and more full-blooded gentleman in an enormous periwig came in, fanning his flushed face with a military hat of the cut of Queen Anne. He carried his head well back like a soldier, and his hot face had even a look of arrogance, which was suddenly contradicted by his eyes, which were literally as humble as a dog's. His sword made a great clatter, as if the shop were too small for it.

"Indeed," said Sir Richard Steele, " 'tis a most prodigious matter, for the man was dying when I wrote about Sir Roger de Coverley and his Christmas Day."

My senses were growing dimmer and the room darker. It seemed to be filled with newcomers.

"It hath ever been understood," said a burly man, who carried his head humorously and obstinately a little on one side—I think he was Ben Jonson—"It hath ever been understood, consule Jacobo, under our King James and her late Majesty, that such good and hearty customs were fallen sick, and like to pass from the world. This grey beard most surely was no lustier when I knew him than now."

And I also thought I heard a green-clad man, like Robin Hood, say in some mixed Norman French, "But I saw the man dying."

"I have felt like this a long time," said Father Christmas, in his feeble way again.

Mr. Charles Dickens suddenly leant across to him.

"Since when?" he asked. "Since you were born?"

"Yes," said the old man, and sank shaking into a chair. "I have been always dying."

Mr. Dickens took off his hat with a flourish like a man calling a mob to rise.

"I understand it now," he cried, "you will never die."

Chapter 38
The Ballade of a Strange Town

y friend and I, in fooling about Flanders, fell into a fixed affection for the town of Mechlin or Malines. Our rest there was so restful that we almost felt it as a home, and hardly strayed out of it.

We sat day after day in the market-place, under little trees growing in wooden tubs, and looked up at the noble converging lines of the Cathedral tower, from which the three riders from Ghent, in the poem, heard the bell which told them they were not too late. But we took as much pleasure in the people, in the little boys with open, flat Flemish faces and fur collars round their necks, making them look like burgomasters; or the women, whose prim, oval faces, hair strained tightly off the temples, and mouths at once hard, meek, and humorous, exactly reproduced the late mediaeval faces in Memling and Van Eyck.

But one afternoon, as it happened, my friend rose from under his little tree, and pointing to a sort of toy train that was puffing smoke in one corner of the clear square, suggested that we should go by it. We got into the little train, which was meant really to take the peasants and their vegetables to and fro from their fields beyond the town, and the official came round to give us tickets. We asked him what place we should get to if we paid fivepence. The Belgians are not a romantic people, and he asked us (with a lamentable mixture of Flemish coarseness and French rationalism) where we wanted to go.

We explained that we wanted to go to fairyland, and the only question was whether we could get there for fivepence. At last, after a great deal of international misunderstanding (for he spoke French in the Flemish and we in the English manner), he told us that fivepence would take us to a place which I have never seen written down, but which when spoken sounded like the word "Waterloo" pronounced by an intoxicated patriot; I think it was Waerlowe.

We clasped our hands and said it was the place we had been seeking from boyhood, and when we had got there we descended with promptitude.

For a moment I had a horrible fear that it really was the field of Waterloo; but I was comforted by remembering that it was in quite a different part of Belgium. It was a cross-roads, with one cottage at the corner, a perspective of tall trees like Hobbema's "Avenue," and beyond only the infinite flat chess-board of the little fields. It was the scene of peace and prosperity; but I must confess that my friend's first action was to ask the man when there would be another train back to Mechlin. The man stated that there would be a train back in exactly one hour. We walked up the avenue, and when we were nearly half an hour's walk away it began to rain.

We arrived back at the cross-roads sodden and dripping, and, finding the train waiting, climbed into it with some relief. The officer on this train could speak nothing but Flemish, but he understood the name Mechlin, and indicated that when we came to Mechlin Station he would put us down, which, after the right interval of time, he did.

We got down, under a steady downpour, evidently on the edge of Mechlin, though the features could not easily be recognised through the grey screen of the rain. I do not generally agree with those who find rain depressing. A shower-bath is not depressing; it is rather startling. And if it is exciting when a man throws a pail of water over you, why should it not also be exciting when the gods throw many pails? But on this soaking afternoon, whether it was the dull sky-line of the Netherlands or the fact that we were returning home without any adventure, I really did think things a trifle dreary. As soon as we could creep under the shelter of a street we turned into a little café, kept by one woman. She was incredibly old, and she spoke no French. There we drank black coffee and what was called "cognac fine." "Cognac fine" were the only two French words used in the establishment, and they were not true. At least, the fineness (perhaps by its very ethereal delicacy) escaped me. After a little my friend, who was more restless than I, got up and went out, to see if the rain had stopped and if we could at once stroll back to our hotel by the station. I sat finishing my coffee in a colourless mood, and listening to the unremitting rain.

Suddenly the door burst open, and my friend appeared, transfigured and frantic.

"Get up!" he cried, waving his hands wildly. "Get up! We're in the wrong town! We're not in Mechlin at all. Mechlin is ten miles, twenty miles off—God knows what! We're somewhere near Antwerp."

"What!" I cried, leaping from my seat, and sending the furniture flying. "Then all is well, after all! Poetry only hid her face for an instant behind a cloud. Positively for a moment I was feeling depressed because we were in the right town. But if we are in the wrong town—why, we have our adventure after all! If we are in the wrong town, we are in the right place."

I rushed out into the rain, and my friend followed me somewhat more grimly. We discovered we were in a town called Lierre, which seemed to consist chiefly of bankrupt pastry cooks, who sold lemonade.

"This is the peak of our whole poetic progress!" I cried enthusiastically. "We must do something, something sacramental and commemorative! We cannot sacrifice an ox, and it would be a bore to build a temple. Let us write a poem."

With but slight encouragement, I took out an old envelope and one of those pencils that turn bright violet in water. There was plenty of water about, and the violet ran down the paper, symbolising the rich purple of that romantic hour. I began, choosing the form of an old French ballade; it is the easiest because it is the most restricted—

> "Can Man to Mount Olympus rise,
> And fancy Primrose Hill the scene?
> Can a man walk in Paradise
> And think he is in Turnham Green?
> And could I take you for Malines,
> Not knowing the nobler thing you were?
> O Pearl of all the plain, and queen,
> The lovely city of Lierre.
>
> "Through memory's mist in glimmering guise
> Shall shine your streets of sloppy sheen.
> And wet shall grow my dreaming eyes,
> To think how wet my boots have been
> Now if I die or shoot a Dean—— "

Here I broke off to ask my friend whether he thought it expressed a more wild calamity to shoot a Dean or to be a Dean. But he only turned up his coat collar, and I felt that for him the muse had folded her wings. I rewrote—

> "Now if I die a Rural Dean,
> Or rob a bank I do not care,
> Or turn a Tory. I have seen
> The lovely city of Lierre."

"The next line," I resumed, warming to it; but my friend interrupted me.

"The next line," he said somewhat harshly, "will be a railway line. We can get back to Mechlin from here, I find, though we have to change twice. I dare say I should think this jolly romantic but for the weather. Adventure is the champagne of life, but I prefer my champagne and my adventures dry. Here is the station."

We did not speak again until we had left Lierre, in its sacred cloud of rain, and were coming to Mechlin, under a clearer sky, that even made one think of stars. Then I leant forward and said to my friend in a low voice—"I have found out everything. We have come to the wrong star."

He stared his query, and I went on eagerly: "That is what makes life at once so splendid and so strange. We are in the wrong world. When I thought that was the right town, it bored me; when I knew it was wrong, I was happy. So the false optimism, the modern happiness, tires us because it tells us we fit into this world.

The true happiness is that we don't fit. We come from somewhere else. We have lost our way."

He silently nodded, staring out of the window, but whether I had impressed or only fatigued him I could not tell. "This," I added, "is suggested in the last verse of a fine poem you have grossly neglected–

" 'Happy is he and more than wise
Who sees with wondering eyes and clean
The world through all the grey disguise
Of sleep and custom in between.
Yes; we may pass the heavenly screen,
But shall we know when we are there?
Who know not what these dead stones mean,
The lovely city of Lierre.' "

Here the train stopped abruptly. And from Mechlin church steeple we heard the half-chime: and Joris broke silence with "No bally HORS D'OEUVRES for me: I shall get on to something solid at once."

L'Envoy
Prince, wide your Empire spreads, I ween,
Yet happier is that moistened Mayor,
Who drinks her cognac far from fine,
The lovely city of Lierre.

Chapter 39
The Mystery of a Pageant

nce upon a time, it seems centuries ago, I was prevailed on to take a small part in one of those historical processions or pageants which happened to be fashionable in or about the year 1909. And since I tend, like all who are growing old, to re-enter the remote past as a paradise or playground, I disinter a memory which may serve to stand among those memories of small but strange incidents with which I have sometimes filled this column. The thing has really some of the dark qualities of a detective-story; though I suppose that Sherlock Holmes himself could hardly unravel it now, when the scent is so old and cold and most of the actors, doubtless, long dead.

This old pageant included a series of figures from the eighteenth century, and I was told that I was just like Dr. Johnson. Seeing that Dr. Johnson was heavily seamed with small-pox, had a waistcoat all over gravy, snorted and rolled as he walked, and was probably the ugliest man in London, I mention this identification as a fact and not as a vaunt. I had nothing to do with the arrangement; and such fleeting suggestions as I made were not taken so seriously as they might have been. I requested that a row of posts be erected across the lawn, so that I might touch all of them but one, and then go back and touch that. Failing this, I felt that the least they could do was to have twenty-five cups of tea stationed at regular intervals along the course, each held by a Mrs. Thrale in full costume. My best constructive suggestion was the most harshly rejected of all. In front of me in the procession walked the great Bishop Berkeley, the man who turned the tables on the early materialists by maintaining that matter itself possibly does not exist. Dr. Johnson, you will remember, did not like such bottomless fancies as Berkeley's, and kicked a stone with his foot, saying, "I refute him so!" Now (as I pointed out) kicking a stone would not make the metaphysical quarrel quite clear; besides, it would hurt. But how picturesque and perfect it would be if I moved across the ground in the symbolic attitude of kicking Bishop Berkeley! How complete an allegoric group; the great transcendentalist walking with his head among the stars, but behind him the avenging realist pede claudo, with uplifted foot. But I must not take up space with these forgotten frivolities; we old men grow too garrulous in talking of the distant past.

This story scarcely concerns me either in my real or my assumed character. Suffice it to say that the procession took place at night in a large garden and by torchlight (so remote is the date), that the garden was crowded with Puritans, monks, and men-at-arms, and especially with early Celtic saints smoking pipes, and with elegant Renaissance gentlemen talking Cockney. Suffice it to say, or rather it is needless to say, that I got lost. I wandered away into some dim corner of that dim shrubbery, where there was nothing to do except tumbling over tent ropes, and I began almost to feel like my prototype, and to share his horror of solitude and hatred of a country life.

In this detachment and dilemma I saw another man in a white wig advancing across this forsaken stretch of lawn; a tall, lean man, who stooped in his long black robes like a stooping eagle. When I thought he would pass me, he stopped before my face, and said, "Dr. Johnson, I think. I am Paley."

"Sir," I said, "you used to guide men to the beginnings of Christianity. If you can guide me now to wherever this infernal thing begins you will perform a yet higher and harder function."

His costume and style were so perfect that for the instant I really thought he was a ghost. He took no notice of my flippancy, but, turning his black-robed back on me, led me through verdurous glooms and winding mossy ways, until we came out into the glare of gaslight and laughing men in masquerade, and I could easily laugh at myself.

And there, you will say, was an end of the matter. I am (you will say) naturally obtuse, cowardly, and mentally deficient. I was, moreover, unused to pageants; I felt frightened in the dark and took a man for a spectre whom, in the light, I could recognise as a modern gentleman in a masquerade dress. No; far from it. That spectral person was my first introduction to a special incident which has never been explained and which still lays its finger on my nerve.

I mixed with the men of the eighteenth century; and we fooled as one does at a fancy-dress ball. There was Burke as large as life and a great deal better looking. There was Cowper much larger than life; he ought to have been a little man in a night-cap, with a cat under one arm and a spaniel under the other. As it was, he was a magnificent person, and looked more like the Master of Ballantrae than Cowper. I persuaded him at last to the night-cap, but never, alas, to the cat and dog. When I came the next night Burke was still the same beautiful improvement upon himself; Cowper was still weeping for his dog and cat and would not be comforted; Bishop Berkeley was still waiting to be kicked in the interests of philosophy. In short, I met all my old friends but one. Where was Paley? I had been mystically moved by the man's presence; I was moved more by his absence. At last I saw advancing towards us across the twilight garden a little man with a large book and a bright attractive face. When he came near enough he said, in a small, clear voice, "I'm Paley." The thing was quite natural, of course; the man was ill and had sent a substitute. Yet somehow the contrast was a shock.

By the next night I had grown quite friendly with my four or five colleagues; I had discovered what is called a mutual friend with Berkeley and several points of difference with Burke. Cowper, I think it was, who introduced me to a friend of his, a fresh face, square and sturdy, framed in a white wig. "This," he explained, "is my friend So-and-So. He's Paley." I looked round at all the faces by this time fixed and familiar; I studied them; I counted them; then I bowed to the third Paley as one bows to necessity. So far the thing was all within the limits of coincidence. It certainly seemed odd that this one particular cleric should be so varying and elusive. It was singular that Paley, alone among men, should swell and shrink and alter like a phantom, while all else remained solid. But the thing was explicable; two men had been ill and there was an end of it; only I went again the next night, and a clear-coloured elegant youth with powdered hair bounded up to me, and told me with boyish excitement that he was Paley.

For the next twenty-four hours I remained in the mental condition of the modern world. I mean the condition in which all natural explanations have broken down and no supernatural explanation has been established. My bewilderment had reached to boredom when I found myself once more in the colour and clatter of the pageant, and I was all the more pleased because I met an old school-fellow, and we mutually recognised each other under our heavy clothes and hoary wigs. We talked about all those great things for which literature is too small and only life large enough; red-hot memories and those gigantic details which make up the characters of men. I heard all about the friends he had lost sight of and those he had kept in sight; I heard about his profession, and asked at last how he came into the pageant.

"The fact is," he said, "a friend of mine asked me, just for to-night, to act a chap called Paley; I don't know who he was . . . "

"No, by thunder!" I said, "nor does anyone."

This was the last blow, and the next night passed like a dream. I scarcely noticed the slender, sprightly, and entirely new figure which fell into the ranks in the place of Paley, so many times deceased. What could it mean? Why was the giddy Paley unfaithful among the faithful found? Did these perpetual changes prove the popularity or the unpopularity of being Paley? Was it that no human being could support being Paley for one night and live till morning? Or was it that the gates were crowded with eager throngs of the British public thirsting to be Paley, who could only be let in one at a time? Or is there some ancient vendetta against Paley? Does some secret society of Deists still assassinate any one who adopts the name?

I cannot conjecture further about this true tale of mystery; and that for two reasons. First, the story is so true that I have had to put a lie into it. Every word of this narrative is veracious, except the one word Paley. And second, because I have got to go into the next room and dress up as Dr. Johnson.

Orthodoxy

Preface

his book is meant to be a companion to "Heretics," and to put the positive side in addition to the negative. Many critics complained of the book called "Heretics" because it merely criticised current philosophies without offering any alternative philosophy. This book is an attempt to answer the challenge. It is unavoidably affirmative and therefore unavoidably autobiographical. The writer has been driven back upon somewhat the same difficulty as that which beset Newman in writing his Apologia; he has been forced to be egotistical only in order to be sincere. While everything else may be different the motive in both cases is the same. It is the purpose of the writer to attempt an explanation, not of whether the Christian Faith can be believed, but of how he personally has come to believe it. The book is therefore arranged upon the positive principle of a riddle and its answer. It deals first with all the writer's own solitary and sincere speculations and then with all the startling style in which they were all suddenly satisfied by the Christian Theology. The writer regards it as amounting to a convincing creed. But if it is not that it is at least a repeated and surprising coincidence.

Introduction in Defence of Everything Else

he only possible excuse for this book is that it is an answer to a challenge. Even a bad shot is dignified when he accepts a duel. When some time ago I published a series of hasty but sincere papers, under the name of "Heretics," several critics for whose intellect I have a warm respect (I may mention specially Mr. G.S.Street) said that it was all very well for me to tell everybody to affirm his cosmic theory, but that I had carefully avoided supporting my precepts with example. "I will begin to worry about my philosophy," said Mr. Street, "when Mr. Chesterton has given us his." It was perhaps an incautious suggestion to make to a person only too ready to write books upon the feeblest provocation. But after all, though Mr. Street has inspired and created this book, he need not read it. If he does read it, he will find that in its pages I have attempted in a vague and personal way, in a set of mental pictures rather than in a series of deductions, to state the philosophy in which I have come to believe. I will not call it my philosophy; for I did not make it. God and humanity made it; and it made me.

I have often had a fancy for writing a romance about an English yachtsman who slightly miscalculated his course and discovered England under the impression that it was a new island in the South Seas. I always find, however, that I am either too busy or too lazy to write this fine work, so I may as well give it away for the purposes of philosophical illustration. There will probably be a general impression that the man who landed (armed to the teeth and talking by signs) to plant the British flag on that barbaric temple which turned out to be the Pavilion at Brighton, felt rather a fool. I am not here concerned to deny that he looked a fool. But if you imagine that he felt a fool, or at any rate that the sense of folly was his sole or his dominant emotion, then you have not studied with sufficient delicacy the rich romantic nature of the hero of this tale. His mistake was really a most enviable mistake; and he knew it, if he was the man I take him for. What could be more delightful than to have in the same few minutes all the fascinating terrors of going abroad combined with all the humane security of coming home again? What could be better than to have all the fun of discovering South Africa without the disgusting necessity of landing there? What could be more glorious than to brace one's self up to discover New South Wales and then realize, with a gush of happy tears, that it was really old South Wales. This at least seems to me the main problem for philosophers, and is in a manner the main problem of this book. How can we contrive to be at once astonished at the world and yet at home in it? How can this queer cosmic town, with its many-legged citizens, with its monstrous and ancient lamps, how can this world give us at once the fascination of a strange town and the comfort and honour of being our own town?

To show that a faith or a philosophy is true from every standpoint would be too big an undertaking even for a much bigger book than this; it is necessary to follow one path of argument; and this is the path that I here propose to follow. I wish to set forth my faith as particularly answering this double spiritual need, the need for that mixture of the familiar and the unfamiliar which Christendom has rightly named romance. For the very word "romance" has in it the mystery and ancient meaning of Rome. Any one setting out to dispute anything ought always to begin by saying what he does not dispute. Beyond stating what he proposes to prove he should always state what he does not propose to prove. The thing I do not propose to prove, the thing I propose to take as common ground between myself and any average reader, is this desirability of an active and imaginative life, picturesque and full of a poetical curiosity, a life such as western man at any rate always seems to have desired. If a man says that extinction is better than existence or blank existence better than variety and adventure, then he is not one of the ordinary people to whom I am talking. If a man prefers nothing I can give him nothing. But nearly all people I have ever met in this western society in which I live would agree to the general proposition that we need this life of practical romance; the combination of something that is strange with something that is secure. We need so to view the world as to combine an idea of wonder and an idea of welcome. We need to be happy in this wonderland without once being merely comfortable. It is THIS achievement of my creed that I shall chiefly pursue in these pages.

But I have a peculiar reason for mentioning the man in a yacht, who discovered England. For I am that man in a yacht. I discovered England. I do not see how this book can avoid being egotistical; and I do not quite see (to tell the truth) how it can avoid being dull. Dulness will, however, free me from the charge which I most lament; the charge of being flippant. Mere light sophistry is the thing that I happen to despise most of all things, and it is perhaps a wholesome fact that this is the thing of which I am generally accused. I know nothing so contemptible as a mere paradox; a mere ingenious defence of the indefensible. If it were true (as has been said) that Mr. Bernard Shaw lived upon paradox, then he ought to be a mere common millionaire; for a man of his mental activity could invent a sophistry every six minutes. It is as easy as lying; because it is lying. The truth is, of course, that Mr. Shaw is cruelly hampered by the fact that he cannot tell any lie unless he thinks it is the truth. I find myself under the same intolerable bondage. I never in my life said anything merely because I thought it funny; though of course, I have had ordinary human vainglory, and may have thought it funny because I had said it. It is one thing to describe an interview with a gorgon or a griffin, a creature who does not exist. It is another thing to discover that the rhinoceros does exist and then take pleasure in the fact that he looks as if he didn't. One searches for truth, but it may be that one pursues instinctively the more extraordinary truths. And I offer this book with the heartiest sentiments to all the jolly people who hate what I write, and regard it (very justly, for all I know), as a piece of poor clowning or a single tiresome joke.

For if this book is a joke it is a joke against me. I am the man who with the utmost daring discovered what had been discovered before. If there is an element of farce in what follows, the farce is at my own expense; for this book explains how I fancied I was the first to set foot in Brighton and then found I was the last. It recounts my elephantine adventures in pursuit of the obvious. No one can think my case more ludicrous than I think it myself; no reader can accuse me here of trying to make a fool of him: I am the fool of this story, and no rebel shall hurl me from my throne. I freely confess all the idiotic ambitions of the end of the nineteenth century. I did, like all other solemn little boys, try to be in advance of the age. Like them I tried to be some ten minutes in advance of the truth. And I found that I was eighteen hundred years behind it. I did strain my voice with a painfully juvenile exaggeration in uttering my truths. And I was punished in the fittest and funniest way, for I have kept my truths: but I have discovered, not that they were not truths, but simply that they were not mine. When I fancied that I stood alone I was really in the ridiculous position of being backed up by all Christendom. It may be, Heaven forgive me, that I did try to be original; but I only succeeded in inventing all by myself an inferior copy of the existing traditions of civilized religion. The man from the yacht thought he was the first to find England; I thought I was the first to find Europe. I did try to found a heresy of my own; and when I had put the last touches to it, I discovered that it was orthodoxy.

It may be that somebody will be entertained by the account of this happy fiasco. It might amuse a friend or an enemy to read how I gradually learnt from the truth of some stray legend or from the falsehood of some dominant philosophy, things that I might have learnt from my catechism—if I had ever learnt it. There may or may not be some entertainment in reading how I found at last in an anarchist club or a Babylonian temple what I might have found in the nearest parish church. If any one is entertained by learning how the flowers of the field or the phrases in an omnibus, the accidents of politics or the pains of youth came together in a certain order to produce a certain conviction of Christian orthodoxy, he may possibly read this book. But there is in everything a reasonable division of labour. I have written the book, and nothing on earth would induce me to read it.

I add one purely pedantic note which comes, as a note naturally should, at the beginning of the book. These essays are concerned only to discuss the actual fact that the central Christian theology (sufficiently summarized in the Apostles' Creed) is the best root of energy and sound ethics. They are not intended to discuss the very fascinating but quite different question of what is the present seat of authority for the proclamation of that creed. When the word "orthodoxy" is used here it means the Apostles' Creed, as understood by everybody calling himself Christian until a very short time ago and the general historic conduct of those who held such a creed. I have been forced by mere space to confine myself to what I have got from this creed; I do not touch the matter much disputed among modern Christians, of where we ourselves got it. This is not an ecclesiastical treatise but a sort of slovenly autobiography. But if any one wants my opinions about the actual nature of the authority, Mr. G.S.Street has only to throw me another challenge, and I will write him another book.

Chapter 1
The Maniac

horoughly worldly people never understand even the world; they rely altogether on a few cynical maxims which are not true. Once I remember walking with a prosperous publisher, who made a remark which I had often heard before; it is, indeed, almost a motto of the modern world. Yet I had heard it once too often, and I saw suddenly that there was nothing in it. The publisher said of somebody, "That man will get on; he believes in himself." And I remember that as I lifted my head to listen, my eye caught an omnibus on which was written "Hanwell." I said to him, "Shall I tell you where the men are who believe most in themselves? For I can tell you. I know of men who believe in themselves more colossally than Napoleon or Caesar. I know where flames the fixed star of certainty and success. I can guide you to the thrones of the Super-men. The men who really believe in themselves are all in lunatic asylums." He said mildly that there were a good many men after all who believed in themselves and who were not in lunatic asylums. "Yes, there are," I retorted, "and you of all men ought to know them. That drunken poet from whom you would not take a dreary tragedy, he believed in himself. That elderly minister with an epic from whom you were hiding in a back room, he believed in himself. If you consulted your business experience instead of your ugly individualistic philosophy, you would know that believing in himself is one of the commonest signs of a rotter. Actors who can't act believe in themselves; and debtors who won't pay. It would be much truer to say that a man will certainly fail, because he believes in himself. Complete self-confidence is not merely a sin; complete self-confidence is a weakness. Believing utterly in one's self is a hysterical and superstitious belief like believing in Joanna Southcote: the man who has it has 'Hanwell' written on his face as plain as it is written on that omnibus." And to all this my friend the publisher made this very deep and effective reply, "Well, if a man is not to believe in himself, in what is he to believe?" After a long pause I replied, "I will go home and write a book in answer to that question." This is the book that I have written in answer to it.

But I think this book may well start where our argument started— in the neighbourhood of the mad-house. Modern masters of science are much impressed with the need of beginning all inquiry with a fact. The ancient masters of religion were quite equally impressed with that necessity. They began with the fact of sin—a fact as practical as potatoes. Whether or no man could be washed in miraculous waters, there was no doubt at any rate that he wanted washing. But certain religious leaders in London, not mere materialists, have begun in our day not to deny the highly disputable water, but to deny the indisputable dirt. Certain new theologians dispute original sin, which is the only part of Christian theology which can really be proved. Some followers of the Reverend R.J.Campbell, in their almost too fastidious spirituality, admit divine sinlessness, which they cannot see even in their dreams. But they essentially deny human sin, which they can see in the street. The strongest saints and the strongest sceptics alike took positive evil as the starting-point of their argument. If it be true (as it certainly is) that a man can feel exquisite happiness in skinning a cat, then the religious philosopher can only draw one of two deductions. He must either deny the existence of God, as all atheists do; or he must deny the present union between God and man, as all Christians do. The new theologians seem to think it a highly rationalistic solution to deny the cat.

In this remarkable situation it is plainly not now possible (with any hope of a universal appeal) to start, as our fathers did, with the fact of sin. This very fact which was to them (and is to me) as plain as a pikestaff, is the very fact that has been specially diluted or denied. But though moderns deny the existence of sin, I do not think that they have yet denied the existence of a lunatic asylum. We all agree still that there is a collapse of the intellect as unmistakable as a falling house. Men deny hell, but not, as yet, Hanwell. For the purpose of our primary argument the one may very well stand where the other stood. I mean that as all thoughts and theories were once judged by whether they tended to make a man lose his soul, so for our present purpose all modern thoughts and theories may be judged by whether they tend to make a man lose his wits.

It is true that some speak lightly and loosely of insanity as in itself attractive. But a moment's thought will show that if disease is beautiful, it is generally some one else's disease. A blind man may be picturesque; but it requires two eyes to see the picture. And similarly even the wildest poetry of insanity can only be enjoyed by the sane. To the insane man his insanity is quite prosaic, because it is quite true. A man who thinks himself a chicken is to himself as ordinary as a chicken. A man who thinks he is a bit of glass is to himself as dull as a bit of glass. It is the homogeneity of his mind which makes him dull, and which makes him mad. It is only because we see the irony of his idea that we think him even amusing; it is only because he does not see the irony of his idea that he is put in Hanwell at all. In short, oddities only strike ordinary people. Oddities do not strike odd people. This is why ordinary people have a much more exciting time; while odd people are always complaining of the dulness of life. This is also why the new novels die so quickly, and why the old fairy tales endure for ever. The old fairy tale makes the hero a normal human boy; it is his adventures that are startling; they startle him because he is normal. But in the modern psychological novel the hero is abnormal; the centre is not central. Hence the fiercest adventures fail to affect him adequately, and the book is monotonous. You can make a story out of a hero among dragons; but not out of a dragon among dragons. The fairy tale discusses what a sane man will do in a mad world. The sober realistic novel of to-day discusses what an essential lunatic will do in a dull world.

Let us begin, then, with the mad-house; from this evil and fantastic inn let us set forth on our intellectual journey. Now, if we are to glance at the philosophy of sanity, the first thing to do in the matter is to blot out one big and common mistake. There is a notion adrift everywhere that imagination, especially mystical imagination, is dangerous to man's mental balance. Poets are commonly spoken of as psychologically unreliable; and generally there is a vague association between wreathing laurels in your hair and sticking straws in it. Facts and history utterly contradict this view. Most of the very great poets have been not only sane, but extremely business-like; and if Shakespeare ever really held horses, it was because he was much the safest man to hold them. Imagination does not breed insanity. Exactly what does breed insanity is reason. Poets do not go mad; but chess-players do. Mathematicians go mad, and cashiers; but creative artists very seldom. I am not, as will be seen, in any sense attacking logic: I only say that this danger does lie in logic, not in imagination. Artistic paternity is as wholesome as physical paternity. Moreover, it is worthy of remark that when a poet really was morbid it was commonly because he had some weak spot of rationality on his brain. Poe, for instance, really was morbid; not because he was poetical, but because he was specially analytical. Even chess was too poetical for him; he disliked chess because it was full of knights and castles, like a poem. He avowedly preferred the black discs of draughts, because they were more like the mere black dots on a diagram. Perhaps the strongest case of all is this: that only one great English poet went mad, Cowper. And he was definitely driven mad by logic, by the ugly and alien logic of predestination. Poetry was not the disease, but the medicine; poetry partly kept him in health. He could sometimes forget the red and thirsty hell to which his hideous necessitarianism dragged him among the wide waters and the white flat lilies of the Ouse. He was damned by John Calvin; he was almost saved by John Gilpin. Everywhere we see that men do not go mad by dreaming. Critics are much madder than poets. Homer is complete and calm enough; it is his critics who tear him into extravagant tatters. Shakespeare is quite himself; it is only some of his critics who have discovered that he was somebody else. And though St. John the Evangelist saw many strange monsters in his vision, he saw no creature so wild as one of his own commentators. The general fact is simple. Poetry is sane because it floats easily in an infinite sea; reason seeks to cross the infinite sea, and so make it finite. The result is mental exhaustion, like the physical exhaustion of Mr. Holbein. To accept everything is an exercise, to understand everything a strain. The poet only desires exaltation and expansion, a world to stretch himself in. The poet only asks to get his head into the heavens. It is the logician who seeks to get the heavens into his head. And it is his head that splits.

It is a small matter, but not irrelevant, that this striking mistake is commonly supported by a striking misquotation. We have all heard people cite the celebrated line of Dryden as "Great genius is to madness near allied." But Dryden did not say that great genius was to madness near allied. Dryden was a great genius himself, and knew better. It would have been hard to find a man more romantic than he, or more sensible. What Dryden said was this, "Great wits are oft to madness near allied"; and that is true. It is the pure promptitude of the intellect that is in peril of a breakdown. Also people might remember of what sort of man Dryden was talking. He was not talking of any unworldly visionary like Vaughan or George Herbert. He was talking of a cynical man of the world, a sceptic, a diplomatist, a great practical politician. Such men are indeed to madness near allied. Their incessant calculation of their own brains and other people's brains is a dangerous trade. It is always perilous to the mind to reckon up the mind. A flippant person has asked why we say, "As mad as a hatter." A more flippant person might answer that a hatter is mad because he has to measure the human head.

And if great reasoners are often maniacal, it is equally true that maniacs are commonly great reasoners. When I was engaged in a controversy with the CLAR-ION on the matter of free will, that able writer Mr. R.B.Suthers said that free will was lunacy, because it meant causeless actions, and the actions of a lunatic would be causeless. I do not dwell here upon the disastrous lapse in determinist logic. Obviously if any actions, even a lunatic's, can be causeless, determinism is done for. If the chain of causation can be broken for a madman, it can be broken for a man. But my purpose is to point out something more practical. It was natural, perhaps, that a modern Marxian Socialist should not know anything about free will. But it was certainly remarkable that a modern Marxian Socialist should not know anything about lunatics. Mr. Suthers evidently did not know anything about lunatics. The last thing that can be said of a lunatic is that his actions are causeless. If any human acts may loosely be called causeless, they are the minor acts of a healthy man; whistling as he walks; slashing the grass with a stick; kicking his heels or rubbing his hands. It is the happy man who does the useless things; the sick man is not strong enough to be idle. It is exactly such careless and causeless actions that the madman could never understand; for the madman (like the determinist) generally sees too much cause in everything. The madman would read a conspiratorial significance into those empty activities. He would think that the lopping of the grass was an attack on private property. He would think that the kicking of the heels was a signal to an accomplice. If the madman could for an instant become careless, he would become sane. Every one who has had the misfortune to talk with people in the heart or on the edge of mental disorder, knows that their most sinister quality is a horrible clarity of detail; a connecting of one thing with another in a map more elaborate than a maze. If you argue with a madman, it is extremely probable that you will get the worst of it; for in many ways his mind moves all the quicker for not being delayed by the things that go with good judgment. He is not hampered by a sense of humour or by charity, or by the dumb certainties of experience. He is the more logical for losing certain sane affections. Indeed, the common phrase for insanity is in this respect a misleading one. The madman is not the man who has lost his reason. The madman is the man who has lost everything except his reason.

The madman's explanation of a thing is always complete, and often in a purely rational sense satisfactory. Or, to speak more strictly, the insane explanation, if not conclusive, is at least unanswerable; this may be observed specially in the two or three commonest kinds of madness. If a man says (for instance) that men have a conspiracy against him, you cannot dispute it except by saying that all the men deny that they are conspirators; which is exactly what conspirators would do. His explanation covers the facts as much as yours. Or if a man says that he is the rightful King of England, it is no complete answer to say that the existing authorities call him mad; for if he were King of England that might be the wisest thing for the existing authorities to do. Or if a man says that he is Jesus Christ, it is no answer to tell him that the world denies his divinity; for the world denied Christ's.

Nevertheless he is wrong. But if we attempt to trace his error in exact terms, we shall not find it quite so easy as we had supposed. Perhaps the nearest we can get to expressing it is to say this: that his mind moves in a perfect but narrow circle. A small circle is quite as infinite as a large circle; but, though it is quite as infinite, it is not so large. In the same way the insane explanation is quite as complete as the sane one, but it is not so large. A bullet is quite as round as the world, but it is not the world. There is such a thing as a narrow universality; there is such a thing as a small and cramped eternity; you may see it in many modern religions. Now, speaking quite externally and empirically, we may say that the strongest and most unmistakable MARK of madness is this combination between a logical completeness and a spiritual contraction. The lunatic's theory explains a large number of things, but it does not explain them in a large way. I mean that if you or I were dealing with a mind that was growing morbid, we should be chiefly concerned not so much to give it arguments as to give it air, to convince it that there was something cleaner and cooler outside the suffocation of a single argument. Suppose, for instance, it were the first case that I took as typical; suppose it were the case of a man who accused everybody of conspiring against him. If we could express our deepest feelings of protest and appeal against this obsession, I suppose we should say something like this: "Oh, I admit that you have your case and have it by heart, and that many things do fit into other things as you say. I admit that your explanation explains a great deal; but what a great deal it leaves out! Are there no other stories in the world except yours; and are all men busy with your business? Suppose we grant the details; perhaps when the man in the street did not seem to see you it was only his cunning; perhaps when the policeman asked you your name it was only because he knew it already. But how much happier you would be if you only knew that these people cared nothing about you! How much larger your life would be if your self could become smaller in it; if you could really look at other men with common curiosity and pleasure; if you could see them walking as they are in their sunny selfishness and their virile indifference! You would begin to be interested in them, because they were not interested in you. You would break out of this tiny and tawdry theatre in which your own little plot is always being played, and you would find yourself under a freer sky, in a street full of splendid strangers." Or suppose it were the second case of madness, that of a man who claims the crown, your impulse would be to answer, "All right! Perhaps you know that you are the King of England; but why do you care? Make one magnificent effort and you will be a human being and look down on all the kings of the earth." Or it might be the third case, of the madman who called himself Christ. If we said what we felt, we should say, "So you are the Creator and Redeemer of the world: but what a small world it must be! What a little heaven you must inhabit, with angels no bigger than butterflies! How sad it must be to be God; and an inadequate God! Is there really no life fuller and no love more marvellous than yours; and is it really in your small and painful pity that all flesh must put its faith? How much happier you would be, how much more of you there would be, if the hammer of a higher God could smash your small cosmos, scattering the stars like spangles, and leave you in the open, free like other men to look up as well as down!"

And it must be remembered that the most purely practical science does take this view of mental evil; it does not seek to argue with it like a heresy but simply to snap it like a spell. Neither modern science nor ancient religion believes in complete free thought. Theology rebukes certain thoughts by calling them blasphemous. Science rebukes certain thoughts by calling them morbid. For example, some religious societies discouraged men more or less from thinking about sex. The new scientific society definitely discourages men from thinking about death; it is a fact, but it is considered a morbid fact. And in dealing with those whose morbidity has a touch of mania, modern science cares far less for pure logic than a dancing Dervish. In these cases it is not enough that the unhappy man should desire truth; he must desire health. Nothing can save him but a blind hunger for normality, like that of a beast. A man cannot think himself out of mental evil; for it is actually the organ of thought that has become diseased, ungovernable, and, as it were, independent. He can only be saved by will or faith. The moment his mere reason moves, it moves in the old circular rut; he will go round and round his logical circle, just as a man in a third-class carriage on the Inner Circle will go round and round the Inner Circle unless he performs the voluntary, vigorous, and mystical act of getting out at Gower Street. Decision is the whole business here; a door must be shut for ever. Every remedy is a desperate remedy. Every cure is a miraculous cure. Curing a madman is not arguing with a philosopher; it is casting out a devil. And however quietly doctors and psychologists may go to work in the matter, their attitude is profoundly intolerant— as intolerant as Bloody Mary. Their attitude is really this: that the man must stop thinking, if he is to go on living. Their counsel is one of intellectual amputation. If thy HEAD offend thee, cut it off; for it is better, not merely to enter the Kingdom of Heaven as a child, but to enter it as an imbecile, rather than with your whole intellect to be cast into hell— or into

Hanwell.

Such is the madman of experience; he is commonly a reasoner, frequently a successful reasoner. Doubtless he could be vanquished in mere reason, and the case against him put logically. But it can be put much more precisely in more general and even aesthetic terms. He is in the clean and well-lit prison of one idea: he is sharpened to one painful point. He is without healthy hesitation and healthy complexity. Now, as I explain in the introduction, I have determined in these early chapters to give not so much a diagram of a doctrine as some pictures of a point of view. And I have described at length my vision of the maniac for this reason: that just as I am affected by the maniac, so I am affected by most modern thinkers. That unmistakable mood or note that I hear from Hanwell, I hear also from half the chairs of science and seats of learning to-day; and most of the mad doctors are mad doctors in more senses than one. They all have exactly that combination we have noted: the combination of an expansive and exhaustive reason with a contracted common sense. They are universal only in the sense that they take one thin explanation and carry it very far. But a pattern can stretch for ever and still be a small pattern. They see a chess-board white on black, and if the universe is paved with it, it is still white on black. Like the lunatic, they cannot alter their standpoint; they cannot make a mental effort and suddenly see it black on white.

Take first the more obvious case of materialism. As an explanation of the world, materialism has a sort of insane simplicity. It has just the quality of the madman's argument; we have at once the sense of it covering everything and the sense of it leaving everything out. Contemplate some able and sincere materialist, as, for instance, Mr. McCabe, and you will have exactly this unique sensation. He understands everything, and everything does not seem worth understanding. His cosmos may be complete in every rivet and cog-wheel, but still his cosmos is smaller than our world. Somehow his scheme, like the lucid scheme of the madman, seems unconscious of the alien energies and the large indifference of the earth; it is not thinking of the real things of the earth, of fighting peoples or proud mothers, or first love or fear upon the sea. The earth is so very large, and the cosmos is so very small. The cosmos is about the smallest hole that a man can hide his head in.

It must be understood that I am not now discussing the relation of these creeds to truth; but, for the present, solely their relation to health. Later in the argument I hope to attack the question of objective verity; here I speak only of a phenomenon of psychology. I do not for the present attempt to prove to Haeckel that materialism is untrue, any more than I attempted to prove to the man who thought he was Christ that he was labouring under an error. I merely remark here on the fact that both cases have the same kind of completeness and the same kind of incompleteness. You can explain a man's detention at Hanwell by an indifferent public by saying that it is the crucifixion of a god of whom the world is not worthy.

The explanation does explain. Similarly you may explain the order in the universe by saying that all things, even the souls of men, are leaves inevitably unfolding on an utterly unconscious tree— the blind destiny of matter. The explanation does explain, though not, of course, so completely as the madman's. But the point here is that the normal human mind not only objects to both, but feels to both the same objection. Its approximate statement is that if the man in Hanwell is the real God, he is not much of a god. And, similarly, if the cosmos of the materialist is the real cosmos, it is not much of a cosmos. The thing has shrunk. The deity is less divine than many men; and (according to Haeckel) the whole of life is something much more grey, narrow, and trivial than many separate aspects of it. The parts seem greater than the whole.

For we must remember that the materialist philosophy (whether true or not) is certainly much more limiting than any religion. In one sense, of course, all intelligent ideas are narrow. They cannot be broader than themselves. A Christian is only restricted in the same sense that an atheist is restricted. He cannot think Christianity false and continue to be a Christian; and the atheist cannot think atheism false and continue to be an atheist. But as it happens, there is a very special sense in which materialism has more restrictions than spiritualism. Mr. McCabe thinks me a slave because I am not allowed to believe in determinism. I think Mr. McCabe a slave because he is not allowed to believe in fairies. But if we examine the two vetoes we shall see that his is really much more of a pure veto than mine. The Christian is quite free to believe that there is a considerable amount of settled order and inevitable development in the universe. But the materialist is not allowed to admit into his spotless machine the slightest speck of spiritualism or miracle. Poor Mr. McCabe is not allowed to retain even the tiniest imp, though it might be hiding in a pimpernel. The Christian admits that the universe is manifold and even miscellaneous, just as a sane man knows that he is complex. The sane man knows that he has a touch of the beast, a touch of the devil, a touch of the saint, a touch of the citizen. Nay, the really sane man knows that he has a touch of the madman. But the materialist's world is quite simple and solid, just as the madman is quite sure he is sane. The materialist is sure that history has been simply and solely a chain of causation, just as the interesting person before mentioned is quite sure that he is simply and solely a chicken. Materialists and madmen never have doubts.

Spiritual doctrines do not actually limit the mind as do materialistic denials. Even if I believe in immortality I need not think about it. But if I disbelieve in immortality I must not think about it. In the first case the road is open and I can go as far as I like; in the second the road is shut. But the case is even stronger, and the parallel with madness is yet more strange. For it was our case against the exhaustive and logical theory of the lunatic that, right or wrong, it gradually destroyed his humanity. Now it is the charge against the main deductions of the materialist that, right or wrong, they gradually destroy his humanity; I do not mean only kindness, I mean hope, courage, poetry, initiative, all that is human. For instance, when materialism leads men to complete fatalism (as it generally does), it is quite idle to pretend that it is in any sense a liberating force. It is absurd to say that you are especially advancing freedom when you only use free thought to destroy free will. The determinists come to bind, not to loose. They may well call their law the "chain" of causation. It is the worst chain that ever fettered a human being. You may use the language of liberty, if you like, about materialistic teaching, but it is obvious that this is just as inapplicable to it as a whole as the same language when applied to a man locked up in a mad-house. You may say, if you like, that the man is free to think himself a poached egg. But it is surely a more massive and important fact that if he is a poached egg he is not free to eat, drink, sleep, walk, or smoke a cigarette. Similarly you may say, if you like, that the bold determinist speculator is free to disbelieve in the reality of the will. But it is a much more massive and important fact that he is not free to raise, to curse, to thank, to justify, to urge, to punish, to resist temptations, to incite mobs, to make New Year resolutions, to pardon sinners, to rebuke tyrants, or even to say "thank you" for the mustard.

In passing from this subject I may note that there is a queer fallacy to the effect that materialistic fatalism is in some way favourable to mercy, to the abolition of cruel punishments or punishments of any kind. This is startlingly the reverse of the truth. It is quite tenable that the doctrine of necessity makes no difference at all; that it leaves the flogger flogging and the kind friend exhorting as before. But obviously if it stops either of them it stops the kind exhortation. That the sins are inevitable does not prevent punishment; if it prevents anything it prevents persuasion. Determinism is quite as likely to lead to cruelty as it is certain to lead to cowardice. Determinism is not inconsistent with the cruel treatment of criminals. What it is (perhaps) inconsistent with is the generous treatment of criminals; with any appeal to their better feelings or encouragement in their moral struggle. The determinist does not believe in appealing to the will, but he does believe in changing the environment. He must not say to the sinner, "Go and sin no more," because the sinner cannot help it. But he can put him in boiling oil; for boiling oil is an environment. Considered as a figure, therefore, the materialist has the fantastic outline of the figure of the madman. Both take up a position at once unanswerable and intolerable.

Of course it is not only of the materialist that all this is true. The same would apply to the other extreme of speculative logic. There is a sceptic far more terrible than he who believes that everything began in matter. It is possible to meet the sceptic who believes that everything began in himself. He doubts not the existence of angels or devils, but the existence of men and cows. For him his own friends are a mythology made up by himself. He created his own father and his own mother. This horrible fancy has in it something decidedly attractive to the somewhat mystical egoism of our day. That publisher who thought that men would get on if they believed in themselves, those seekers after the Superman who are always looking for him in the looking-glass, those writers who talk about impressing their personalities instead of creating life for the world, all these people have really only an inch between them and this awful emptiness. Then when this kindly world all round the man has been blackened out like a lie; when friends fade into ghosts, and the foundations of the world fail; then when the man, believing in nothing and in no man, is alone in his own nightmare, then the great individualistic motto shall be written over him in avenging irony. The stars will be only dots in the blackness of his own brain; his mother's face will be only a sketch from his own insane pencil on the walls of his cell. But over his cell shall be written, with dreadful truth, "He believes in himself."

All that concerns us here, however, is to note that this panegoistic extreme of thought exhibits the same paradox as the other extreme of materialism. It is equally complete in theory and equally crippling in practice. For the sake of simplicity, it is easier to state the notion by saying that a man can believe that he is always in a dream. Now, obviously there can be no positive proof given to him that he is not in a dream, for the simple reason that no proof can be offered that might not be offered in a dream. But if the man began to burn down London and say that his housekeeper would soon call him to breakfast, we should take him and put him with other logicians in a place which has often been alluded to in the course of this chapter. The man who cannot believe his senses, and the man who cannot believe anything else, are both insane, but their insanity is proved not by any error in their argument, but by the manifest mistake of their whole lives. They have both locked themselves up in two boxes, painted inside with the sun and stars; they are both unable to get out, the one into the health and happiness of heaven, the other even into the health and happiness of the earth. Their position is quite reasonable; nay, in a sense it is infinitely reasonable, just as a threepenny bit is infinitely circular. But there is such a thing as a mean infinity, a base and slavish eternity. It is amusing to notice that many of the moderns, whether sceptics or mystics, have taken as their sign a certain eastern symbol, which is the very symbol of this ultimate nullity. When they wish to represent eternity, they represent it by a serpent with his tail in his mouth. There is a startling sarcasm in the image of that very unsatisfactory meal. The eternity of the material fatalists, the eternity of the eastern pessimists, the eternity of the supercilious theosophists and higher scientists of to-day is, indeed, very well presented by a serpent eating his tail, a degraded animal who destroys even himself.

This chapter is purely practical and is concerned with what actually is the chief mark and element of insanity; we may say in summary that it is reason used without root, reason in the void. The man who begins to think without the proper first principles goes mad; he begins to think at the wrong end. And for the rest of these pages we have to try and discover what is the right end. But we may ask in conclusion, if this be what drives men mad, what is it that keeps them sane? By the end of this book I hope to give a definite, some will think a far too definite, answer. But for the moment it is possible in the same solely practical manner to give a general answer touching what in actual human history keeps men sane. Mysticism keeps men sane. As long as you have mystery you have health; when you destroy mystery you create morbidity. The ordinary man has always been sane because the ordinary man has always been a mystic. He has permitted the twilight. He has always had one foot in earth and the other in fairyland. He has always left himself free to doubt his gods; but (unlike the agnostic of to-day) free also to believe in them. He has always cared more for truth than for consistency. If he saw two truths that seemed to contradict each other, he would take the two truths and the contradiction along with them. His spiritual sight is stereoscopic, like his physical sight: he sees two different pictures at once and yet sees all the better for that. Thus he has always believed that there was such a thing as fate, but such a thing as free will also. Thus he believed that children were indeed the kingdom of heaven, but nevertheless ought to be obedient to the kingdom of earth. He admired youth because it was young and age because it was not. It is exactly this balance of apparent contradictions that has been the whole buoyancy of the healthy man. The whole secret of mysticism is this: that man can understand everything by the help of what he does not understand. The morbid logician seeks to make everything lucid, and succeeds in making everything mysterious. The mystic allows one thing to be mysterious, and everything else becomes lucid. The determinist makes the theory of causation quite clear, and then finds that he cannot say "if you please" to the housemaid. The Christian permits free will to remain a sacred mystery; but because of this his relations with the housemaid become of a sparkling and crystal clearness. He puts the seed of dogma in a central darkness; but it branches forth in all directions with abounding natural health. As we have taken the circle as the symbol of reason and madness, we may very well take the cross as the symbol at once of mystery and of health. Buddhism is centripetal, but Christianity is centrifugal: it breaks out. For the circle is perfect and infinite in its nature; but it is fixed for ever in its size; it can never be larger or smaller. But the cross, though it has at its heart a collision and a contradiction, can extend its four arms for ever without altering its shape. Because it has a paradox in its centre it can grow without changing. The circle returns upon itself and is bound. The cross opens its arms to the four winds; it is a signpost for free travellers.

Symbols alone are of even a cloudy value in speaking of this deep matter; and another symbol from physical nature will express sufficiently well the real place of mysticism before mankind. The one created thing which we cannot look at is the one thing in the light of which we look at everything. Like the sun at noonday, mysticism explains everything else by the blaze of its own victorious invisibility. Detached intellectualism is (in the exact sense of a popular phrase) all moonshine; for it is light without heat, and it is secondary light, reflected from a dead world. But the Greeks were right when they made Apollo the god both of imagination and of sanity; for he was both the patron of poetry and the patron of healing. Of necessary dogmas and a special creed I shall speak later. But that transcendentalism by which all men live has primarily much the position of the sun in the sky. We are conscious of it as of a kind of splendid confusion; it is something both shining and shapeless, at once a blaze and a blur. But the circle of the moon is as clear and unmistakable, as recurrent and inevitable, as the circle of Euclid on a blackboard. For the moon is utterly reasonable; and the moon is the mother of lunatics and has given to them all her name.

Chapter 2
The Suicide of Thought

he phrases of the street are not only forcible but subtle: for a figure of speech can often get into a crack too small for a definition. Phrases like "put out" or "off colour" might have been coined by Mr. Henry James in an agony of verbal precision. And there is no more subtle truth than that of the everyday phrase about a man having "his heart in the right place." It involves the idea of normal proportion; not only does a certain function exist, but it is rightly related to other functions. Indeed, the negation of this phrase would describe with peculiar accuracy the somewhat morbid mercy and perverse tenderness of the most representative moderns. If, for instance, I had to describe with fairness the character of Mr. Bernard Shaw, I could not express myself more exactly than by saying that he has a heroically large and generous heart; but not a heart in the right place. And this is so of the typical society of our time.

The modern world is not evil; in some ways the modern world is far too good. It is full of wild and wasted virtues. When a religious scheme is shattered (as Christianity was shattered at the Reformation), it is not merely the vices that are let loose. The vices are, indeed, let loose, and they wander and do damage. But the virtues are let loose also; and the virtues wander more wildly, and the virtues do more terrible damage. The modern world is full of the old Christian virtues gone mad. The virtues have gone mad because they have been isolated from each other and are wandering alone. Thus some scientists care for truth; and their truth is pitiless. Thus some humanitarians only care for pity; and their pity (I am sorry to say) is often untruthful. For example, Mr. Blatchford attacks Christianity because he is mad on one Christian virtue: the merely mystical and almost irrational virtue of charity. He has a strange idea that he will make it easier to forgive sins by saying that there are no sins to forgive. Mr. Blatchford is not only an early Christian, he is the only early Christian who ought really to have been eaten by lions. For in his case the pagan accusation is really true: his mercy would mean mere anarchy. He really is the enemy of the human race— because he is so human. As the other extreme, we may take the acrid realist, who has deliberately killed in himself all human pleasure in happy tales or in the healing of the heart. Torquemada tortured people physically for the sake of moral truth. Zola tortured people morally for the sake of physical truth. But in Torquemada's time there was at least a system that could to some extent make righteousness and peace kiss each other. Now they do not even bow. But a much stronger case than these two of truth and pity can be found in the remarkable case of the dislocation of humility.

It is only with one aspect of humility that we are here concerned. Humility was largely meant as a restraint upon the arrogance and infinity of the appetite of man.

He was always outstripping his mercies with his own newly invented needs. His very power of enjoyment destroyed half his joys. By asking for pleasure, he lost the chief pleasure; for the chief pleasure is surprise. Hence it became evident that if a man would make his world large, he must be always making himself small. Even the haughty visions, the tall cities, and the toppling pinnacles are the creations of humility. Giants that tread down forests like grass are the creations of humility. Towers that vanish upwards above the loneliest star are the creations of humility. For towers are not tall unless we look up at them; and giants are not giants unless they are larger than we. All this gigantesque imagination, which is, perhaps, the mightiest of the pleasures of man, is at bottom entirely humble. It is impossible without humility to enjoy anything— even pride.

But what we suffer from to-day is humility in the wrong place. Modesty has moved from the organ of ambition. Modesty has settled upon the organ of conviction; where it was never meant to be. A man was meant to be doubtful about himself, but undoubting about the truth; this has been exactly reversed. Nowadays the part of a man that a man does assert is exactly the part he ought not to assert—himself. The part he doubts is exactly the part he ought not to doubt—the Divine Reason. Huxley preached a humility content to learn from Nature. But the new sceptic is so humble that he doubts if he can even learn. Thus we should be wrong if we had said hastily that there is no humility typical of our time. The truth is that there is a real humility typical of our time; but it so happens that it is practically a more poisonous humility than the wildest prostrations of the ascetic. The old humility was a spur that prevented a man from stopping; not a nail in his boot that prevented him from going on. For the old humility made a man doubtful about his efforts, which might make him work harder. But the new humility makes a man doubtful about his aims, which will make him stop working altogether.

At any street corner we may meet a man who utters the frantic and blasphemous statement that he may be wrong. Every day one comes across somebody who says that of course his view may not be the right one. Of course his view must be the right one, or it is not his view. We are on the road to producing a race of men too mentally modest to believe in the multiplication table. We are in danger of seeing philosophers who doubt the law of gravity as being a mere fancy of their own. Scoffers of old time were too proud to be convinced; but these are too humble to be convinced. The meek do inherit the earth; but the modern sceptics are too meek even to claim their inheritance. It is exactly this intellectual helplessness which is our second problem.

The last chapter has been concerned only with a fact of observation: that what peril of morbidity there is for man comes rather from his reason than his imagination. It was not meant to attack the authority of reason; rather it is the ultimate purpose to defend it. For it needs defence. The whole modern world is at war with reason; and the tower already reels.

The sages, it is often said, can see no answer to the riddle of religion. But the trouble with our sages is not that they cannot see the answer; it is that they cannot even see the riddle. They are like children so stupid as to notice nothing paradoxical in the playful assertion that a door is not a door. The modern latitudinarians speak, for instance, about authority in religion not only as if there were no reason in it, but as if there had never been any reason for it. Apart from seeing its philosophical basis, they cannot even see its historical cause. Religious authority has often, doubtless, been oppressive or unreasonable; just as every legal system (and especially our present one) has been callous and full of a cruel apathy. It is rational to attack the police; nay, it is glorious. But the modern critics of religious authority are like men who should attack the police without ever having heard of burglars. For there is a great and possible peril to the human mind: a peril as practical as burglary. Against it religious authority was reared, rightly or wrongly, as a barrier. And against it something certainly must be reared as a barrier, if our race is to avoid ruin.

That peril is that the human intellect is free to destroy itself. Just as one generation could prevent the very existence of the next generation, by all entering a monastery or jumping into the sea, so one set of thinkers can in some degree prevent further thinking by teaching the next generation that there is no validity in any human thought. It is idle to talk always of the alternative of reason and faith. Reason is itself a matter of faith. It is an act of faith to assert that our thoughts have any relation to reality at all. If you are merely a sceptic, you must sooner or later ask yourself the question, "Why should ANYTHING go right; even observation and deduction? Why should not good logic be as misleading as bad logic? They are both movements in the brain of a bewildered ape?" The young sceptic says, "I have a right to think for myself." But the old sceptic, the complete sceptic, says, "I have no right to think for myself. I have no right to think at all."

There is a thought that stops thought. That is the only thought that ought to be stopped. That is the ultimate evil against which all religious authority was aimed. It only appears at the end of decadent ages like our own: and already Mr. H.G.Wells has raised its ruinous banner; he has written a delicate piece of scepticism called "Doubts of the Instrument." In this he questions the brain itself, and endeavours to remove all reality from all his own assertions, past, present, and to come. But it was against this remote ruin that all the military systems in religion were originally ranked and ruled. The creeds and the crusades, the hierarchies and the horrible persecutions were not organized, as is ignorantly said, for the suppression of reason. They were organized for the difficult defence of reason. Man, by a blind instinct, knew that if once things were wildly questioned, reason could be questioned first. The authority of priests to absolve, the authority of popes to define the authority, even of inquisitors to terrify: these were all only dark defences erected round one central authority, more undemonstrable, more supernatural than all—the authority of a man to think. We know now that this is so; we have no excuse for not knowing it. For we can hear scepticism crashing through the old ring of authorities, and at the same moment we can see reason swaying upon her throne. In so far as religion is gone, reason is going. For they are both of the same primary and authoritative kind. They are both methods of proof which cannot themselves be proved. And in the act of destroying the idea of Divine authority we have largely destroyed the idea of that human authority by which we do a long-division sum. With a long and sustained tug we have attempted to pull the mitre off pontifical man; and his head has come off with it.

Lest this should be called loose assertion, it is perhaps desirable, though dull, to run rapidly through the chief modern fashions of thought which have this effect of stopping thought itself. Materialism and the view of everything as a personal illusion have some such effect; for if the mind is mechanical, thought cannot be very exciting, and if the cosmos is unreal, there is nothing to think about. But in these cases the effect is indirect and doubtful. In some cases it is direct and clear; notably in the case of what is generally called evolution.

Evolution is a good example of that modern intelligence which, if it destroys anything, destroys itself. Evolution is either an innocent scientific description of how certain earthly things came about; or, if it is anything more than this, it is an attack upon thought itself. If evolution destroys anything, it does not destroy religion but rationalism. If evolution simply means that a positive thing called an ape turned very slowly into a positive thing called a man, then it is stingless for the most orthodox; for a personal God might just as well do things slowly as quickly, especially if, like the Christian God, he were outside time. But if it means anything more, it means that there is no such thing as an ape to change, and no such thing as a man for him to change into. It means that there is no such thing as a thing. At best, there is only one thing, and that is a flux of everything and anything. This is an attack not upon the faith, but upon the mind; you cannot think if there are no things to think about. You cannot think if you are not separate from the subject of thought. Descartes said, "I think; therefore I am." The philosophic evolutionist reverses and negatives the epigram. He says, "I am not; therefore I cannot think."

Then there is the opposite attack on thought: that urged by Mr. H.G.Wells when he insists that every separate thing is "unique," and there are no categories at all. This also is merely destructive. Thinking means connecting things, and stops if they cannot be connected. It need hardly be said that this scepticism forbidding thought necessarily forbids speech; a man cannot open his mouth without contradicting it. Thus when Mr. Wells says (as he did somewhere), "All chairs are quite different," he utters not merely a misstatement, but a contradiction in terms. If all chairs were quite different, you could not call them "all chairs."

Akin to these is the false theory of progress, which maintains that we alter the test instead of trying to pass the test. We often hear it said, for instance, "What is right in one age is wrong in another." This is quite reasonable, if it means that there is a fixed aim, and that certain methods attain at certain times and not at other times. If women, say, desire to be elegant, it may be that they are improved at one time by growing fatter and at another time by growing thinner. But you cannot say that they are improved by ceasing to wish to be elegant and beginning to wish to be oblong. If the standard changes, how can there be improvement, which implies a standard? Nietzsche started a nonsensical idea that men had once sought as good what we now call evil; if it were so, we could not talk of surpassing or even falling short of them. How can you overtake Jones if you walk in the other direction? You cannot discuss whether one people has succeeded more in being miserable than another succeeded in being happy. It would be like discussing whether Milton was more puritanical than a pig is fat.

It is true that a man (a silly man) might make change itself his object or ideal. But as an ideal, change itself becomes unchangeable. If the change-worshipper wishes to estimate his own progress, he must be sternly loyal to the ideal of change; he must not begin to flirt gaily with the ideal of monotony. Progress itself cannot progress. It is worth remark, in passing, that when Tennyson, in a wild and rather weak manner, welcomed the idea of infinite alteration in society, he instinctively took a metaphor which suggests an imprisoned tedium. He wrote—

"Let the great world spin for ever down the ringing grooves of change."

He thought of change itself as an unchangeable groove; and so it is. Change is about the narrowest and hardest groove that a man can get into.

The main point here, however, is that this idea of a fundamental alteration in the standard is one of the things that make thought about the past or future simply impossible. The theory of a complete change of standards in human history does not merely deprive us of the pleasure of honouring our fathers; it deprives us even of the more modern and aristocratic pleasure of despising them.

This bald summary of the thought-destroying forces of our time would not be complete without some reference to pragmatism; for though I have here used and should everywhere defend the pragmatist method as a preliminary guide to truth, there is an extreme application of it which involves the absence of all truth whatever. My meaning can be put shortly thus. I agree with the pragmatists that apparent objective truth is not the whole matter; that there is an authoritative need to believe the things that are necessary to the human mind. But I say that one of those necessities precisely is a belief in objective truth. The pragmatist tells a man to think what he must think and never mind the Absolute. But precisely one of the things that he must think is the Absolute. This philosophy, indeed, is a kind of verbal paradox. Pragmatism is a matter of human needs; and one of the first of human needs is to be something more than a pragmatist. Extreme pragmatism is just as inhuman as the determinism it so powerfully attacks. The determinist (who, to do him justice, does not pretend to be a human being) makes nonsense of the human sense of actual choice. The pragmatist, who professes to be specially human, makes nonsense of the human sense of actual fact.

To sum up our contention so far, we may say that the most characteristic current philosophies have not only a touch of mania, but a touch of suicidal mania. The mere questioner has knocked his head against the limits of human thought; and cracked it. This is what makes so futile the warnings of the orthodox and the boasts of the advanced about the dangerous boyhood of free thought. What we are looking at is not the boyhood of free thought; it is the old age and ultimate dissolution of free thought. It is vain for bishops and pious bigwigs to discuss what dreadful things will happen if wild scepticism runs its course. It has run its course. It is vain for eloquent atheists to talk of the great truths that will be revealed if once we see free thought begin. We have seen it end. It has no more questions to ask; it has questioned itself. You cannot call up any wilder vision than a city in which men ask themselves if they have any selves. You cannot fancy a more sceptical world than that in which men doubt if there is a world. It might certainly have reached its bankruptcy more quickly and cleanly if it had not been feebly hampered by the application of indefensible laws of blasphemy or by the absurd pretence that modern England is Christian. But it would have reached the bankruptcy anyhow. Militant atheists are still unjustly persecuted; but rather because they are an old minority than because they are a new one. Free thought has exhausted its own freedom. It is weary of its own success. If any eager freethinker now hails philosophic freedom as the dawn, he is only like the man in Mark Twain who came out wrapped in blankets to see the sun rise and was just in time to see it set. If any frightened curate still says that it will be awful if the darkness of free thought should spread, we can only answer him in the high and powerful words of Mr. Belloc, "Do not, I beseech you, be troubled about the increase of forces already in dissolution. You have mistaken the hour of the night: it is already morning." We have no more questions left to ask. We have looked for questions in the darkest corners and on the wildest peaks. We have found all the questions that can be found. It is time we gave up looking for questions and began looking for answers.

But one more word must be added. At the beginning of this preliminary negative sketch I said that our mental ruin has been wrought by wild reason, not by wild imagination. A man does not go mad because he makes a statue a mile high, but he may go mad by thinking it out in square inches. Now, one school of thinkers has seen this and jumped at it as a way of renewing the pagan health of the world. They see that reason destroys; but Will, they say, creates. The ultimate authority, they say, is in will, not in reason. The supreme point is not why a man demands a thing, but the fact that he does demand it. I have no space to trace or expound this philosophy of Will. It came, I suppose, through Nietzsche, who preached something that is called egoism. That, indeed, was simpleminded enough; for Nietzsche denied egoism simply by preaching it. To preach anything is to give it away. First, the egoist calls life a war without mercy, and then he takes the greatest possible trouble to drill his enemies in war. To preach egoism is to practise altruism. But however it began, the view is common enough in current literature. The main defence of these thinkers is that they are not thinkers; they are makers. They say that choice is itself the divine thing. Thus Mr. Bernard Shaw has attacked the old idea that men's acts are to be judged by the standard of the desire of happiness. He says that a man does not act for his happiness, but from his will. He does not say, "Jam will make me happy," but "I want jam." And in all this others follow him with yet greater enthusiasm. Mr. John Davidson, a remarkable poet, is so passionately excited about it that he is obliged to write prose. He publishes a short play with several long prefaces. This is natural enough in Mr. Shaw, for all his plays are prefaces: Mr. Shaw is (I suspect) the only man on earth who has never written any poetry. But that Mr. Davidson (who can write excellent poetry) should write instead laborious metaphysics in defence of this doctrine of will, does show that the doctrine of will has taken hold of men. Even Mr. H.G.Wells has half spoken in its language; saying that one should test acts not like a thinker, but like an artist, saying, "I FEEL this curve is right," or "that line SHALL go thus." They are all excited; and well they may be. For by this doctrine of the divine authority of will, they think they can break out of the doomed fortress of rationalism. They think they can escape.

But they cannot escape. This pure praise of volition ends in the same break up and blank as the mere pursuit of logic. Exactly as complete free thought involves the doubting of thought itself, so the acceptation of mere "willing" really paralyzes the will. Mr. Bernard Shaw has not perceived the real difference between the old utilitarian test of pleasure (clumsy, of course, and easily misstated) and that which he propounds. The real difference between the test of happiness and the test of will is simply that the test of happiness is a test and the other isn't. You can discuss whether a man's act in jumping over a cliff was directed towards happiness; you cannot discuss whether it was derived from will. Of course it was. You can praise an action by saying that it is calculated to bring pleasure or pain to discover truth or to save the soul. But you cannot praise an action because it shows will; for to say that is merely to say that it is an action. By this praise of will you cannot really choose one course as better than another. And yet choosing one course as better than another is the very definition of the will you are praising.

The worship of will is the negation of will. To admire mere choice is to refuse to choose. If Mr. Bernard Shaw comes up to me and says, "Will something," that is tantamount to saying, "I do not mind what you will," and that is tantamount to saying, "I have no will in the matter." You cannot admire will in general, because the essence of will is that it is particular. A brilliant anarchist like Mr. John Davidson feels an irritation against ordinary morality, and therefore he invokes will—will to anything. He only wants humanity to want something. But humanity does want something. It wants ordinary morality. He rebels against the law and tells us to will something or anything. But we have willed something. We have willed the law against which he rebels.

All the will-worshippers, from Nietzsche to Mr. Davidson, are really quite empty of volition. They cannot will, they can hardly wish. And if any one wants a proof of this, it can be found quite easily. It can be found in this fact: that they always talk of will as something that expands and breaks out. But it is quite the opposite. Every act of will is an act of self-limitation. To desire action is to desire limitation. In that sense every act is an act of self-sacrifice. When you choose anything, you reject everything else. That objection, which men of this school used to make to the act of marriage, is really an objection to every act. Every act is an irrevocable selection and exclusion. Just as when you marry one woman you give up all the others, so when you take one course of action you give up all the other courses. If you become King of England, you give up the post of Beadle in Brompton. If you go to Rome, you sacrifice a rich suggestive life in Wimbledon. It is the existence of this negative or limiting side of will that makes most of the talk of the anarchic will-worshippers little better than nonsense. For instance, Mr. John Davidson tells us to have nothing to do with "Thou shalt not"; but it is surely obvious that "Thou shalt not" is only one of the necessary corollaries of "I will." "I will go to the Lord Mayor's Show, and thou shalt not stop me." Anarchism adjures us to be bold creative artists, and care for no laws or limits. But it is impossible to be an artist and not care for laws and limits. Art is limitation; the essence of every picture is the frame. If you draw a giraffe, you must draw him with a long neck. If, in your bold creative way, you hold yourself free to draw a giraffe with a short neck, you will really find that you are not free to draw a giraffe. The moment you step into the world of facts, you step into a world of limits. You can free things from alien or accidental laws, but not from the laws of their own nature. You may, if you like, free a tiger from his bars; but do not free him from his stripes. Do not free a camel of the burden of his hump: you may be freeing him from being a camel. Do not go about as a demagogue, encouraging triangles to break out of the prison of their three sides. If a triangle breaks out of its three sides, its life comes to a lamentable end. Somebody wrote a work called "The Loves of the Triangles"; I never read it, but I am sure that if triangles ever were loved, they were loved for being triangular. This is certainly the case with all artistic creation, which is in some ways the most decisive example of pure will. The artist loves his limitations: they constitute the THING he is doing. The painter is glad that the canvas is flat. The sculptor is glad that the clay is colourless.

In case the point is not clear, an historic example may illustrate it. The French Revolution was really an heroic and decisive thing, because the Jacobins willed something definite and limited. They desired the freedoms of democracy, but also all the vetoes of democracy. They wished to have votes and NOT to have titles. Republicanism had an ascetic side in Franklin or Robespierre as well as an expansive side in Danton or Wilkes. Therefore they have created something with a solid substance and shape, the square social equality and peasant wealth of France. But since then the revolutionary or speculative mind of Europe has been weakened by shrinking from any proposal because of the limits of that proposal. Liberalism has been degraded into liberality. Men have tried to turn "revolutionise" from a transitive to an intransitive verb. The Jacobin could tell you not only the system he would rebel against, but (what was more important) the system he would NOT rebel against, the system he would trust. But the new rebel is a Sceptic, and will not entirely trust anything. He has no loyalty; therefore he can never be really a revolutionist. And the fact that he doubts everything really gets in his way when he wants to denounce anything. For all denunciation implies a moral doctrine of some kind; and the modern revolutionist doubts not only the institution he denounces, but the doctrine by which he denounces it. Thus he writes one book complaining that imperial oppression insults the purity of women, and then he writes another book (about the sex problem) in which he insults it himself. He curses the Sultan because Christian girls lose their virginity, and then curses Mrs. Grundy because they keep it. As a politician, he will cry out that war is a waste of life, and then, as a philosopher, that all life is waste of time. A Russian pessimist will denounce a policeman for killing a peasant, and then prove by the highest philosophical principles that the peasant ought to have killed himself. A man denounces marriage as a lie, and then denounces aristocratic profligates for treating it as a lie. He calls a flag a bauble, and then blames the oppressors of Poland or Ireland because they take away that bauble. The man of this school goes first to a political meeting, where he complains that savages are treated as if they were beasts; then he takes his hat and umbrella and goes on to a scientific meeting, where he proves that they practically are beasts. In short, the modern revolutionist, being an infinite sceptic, is always engaged in undermining his own mines. In his book on politics he attacks men for trampling on morality; in his book on ethics he attacks morality for trampling on men. Therefore the modern man in revolt has become practically useless for all purposes of revolt. By rebelling against everything he has lost his right to rebel against anything.

It may be added that the same blank and bankruptcy can be observed in all fierce and terrible types of literature, especially in satire. Satire may be mad and anarchic, but it presupposes an admitted superiority in certain things over others; it presupposes a standard. When little boys in the street laugh at the fatness of some distinguished journalist, they are unconsciously assuming a standard of Greek sculpture. They are appealing to the marble Apollo. And the curious disappearance of satire from our literature is an instance of the fierce things fading for want of any principle to be fierce about. Nietzsche had some natural talent for sarcasm: he could sneer, though he could not laugh; but there is always something bodiless and without weight in his satire, simply because it has not any mass of common morality behind it. He is himself more preposterous than anything he denounces. But, indeed, Nietzsche will stand very well as the type of the whole of this failure of abstract violence. The softening of the brain which ultimately overtook him was not a physical accident. If Nietzsche had not ended in imbecility, Nietzscheism would end in imbecility. Thinking in isolation and with pride ends in being an idiot. Every man who will not have softening of the heart must at last have softening of the brain.

This last attempt to evade intellectualism ends in intellectualism, and therefore in death. The sortie has failed. The wild worship of lawlessness and the materialist worship of law end in the same void. Nietzsche scales staggering mountains, but he turns up ultimately in Tibet. He sits down beside Tolstoy in the land of nothing and Nirvana. They are both helpless—one because he must not grasp anything, and the other because he must not let go of anything. The Tolstoyan's will is frozen by a Buddhist instinct that all special actions are evil. But the Nietzscheite's will is quite equally frozen by his view that all special actions are good; for if all special actions are good, none of them are special. They stand at the crossroads, and one hates all the roads and the other likes all the roads. The result is—well, some things are not hard to calculate. They stand at the cross-roads.

Here I end (thank God) the first and dullest business of this book—the rough review of recent thought. After this I begin to sketch a view of life which may not interest my reader, but which, at any rate, interests me. In front of me, as I close this page, is a pile of modern books that I have been turning over for the purpose—a pile of ingenuity, a pile of futility. By the accident of my present detachment, I can see the inevitable smash of the philosophies of Schopenhauer and Tolstoy, Nietzsche and Shaw, as clearly as an inevitable railway smash could be seen from a balloon. They are all on the road to the emptiness of the asylum. For madness may be defined as using mental activity so as to reach mental helplessness; and they have nearly reached it. He who thinks he is made of glass, thinks to the destruction of thought; for glass cannot think. So he who wills to reject nothing, wills the destruction of will; for will is not only the choice of something, but the rejection of almost everything. And as I turn and tumble over the clever, wonderful, tiresome, and useless modern books, the title of one of them rivets my eye. It is called "Jeanne d'Arc," by Anatole France. I have only glanced at it, but a glance was enough to remind me of Renan's "Vie de Jesus." It has the same strange method of the reverent sceptic. It discredits supernatural stories that have some foundation, simply by telling natural stories that have no foundation. Because we cannot believe in what a saint did, we are to pretend that we know exactly what he felt. But I do not mention either book in order to criticise it, but because the accidental combination of the names called up two startling images of Sanity which blasted all the books before me. Joan of Arc was not stuck at the cross-roads, either by rejecting all the paths like Tolstoy, or by accepting them all like Nietzsche. She chose a path, and went down it like a thunderbolt. Yet Joan, when I came to think of her, had in her all that was true either in Tolstoy or Nietzsche, all that was even tolerable in either of them. I thought of all that is noble in Tolstoy, the pleasure in plain things, especially in plain pity, the actualities of the earth, the reverence for the poor, the dignity of the bowed back. Joan of Arc had all that and with this great addition, that she endured poverty as well as admiring it; whereas Tolstoy is only a typical aristocrat trying to find out its secret. And then I thought of all that was brave and proud and pathetic in poor Nietzsche, and his mutiny against the emptiness and timidity of our time. I thought of his cry for the ecstatic equilibrium of danger, his hunger for the rush of great horses, his cry to arms. Well, Joan of Arc had all that, and again with this difference, that she did not praise fighting, but fought. We KNOW that she was not afraid of an army, while Nietzsche, for all we know, was afraid of a cow. Tolstoy only praised the peasant; she was the peasant. Nietzsche only praised the warrior; she was the warrior. She beat them both at their own antagonistic ideals; she was more gentle than the one, more violent than the other. Yet she was a perfectly practical person who did something, while they are wild speculators who do nothing. It was impossible that the thought should not cross my mind that she and her faith had perhaps some secret of moral unity and utility that has been lost. And with that thought came a larger one, and the colossal figure of her Master had also crossed the theatre of my thoughts. The same modern difficulty which darkened the subject-matter of Anatole France also darkened that of Ernest Renan. Renan also divided his hero's pity from his hero's pugnacity. Renan even represented the righteous anger at Jerusalem as a mere nervous breakdown after the idyllic expectations of Galilee. As if there were any inconsistency between having a love for humanity and having a hatred for inhumanity! Altruists, with thin, weak voices, denounce Christ as an egoist. Egoists (with even thinner and weaker voices) denounce Him as an altruist. In our present atmosphere such cavils are comprehensible enough. The love of a hero is more terrible than the hatred of a tyrant. The hatred of a hero is more generous than the love of a philanthropist. There is a huge and heroic sanity of which moderns can only collect the fragments. There is a giant of whom we see only the lopped arms and legs walking about. They have torn the soul of Christ into silly strips, labelled egoism and altruism, and they are equally puzzled by His insane magnificence and His insane meekness. They have parted His garments among them, and for His vesture they have cast lots; though the coat was without seam woven from the top throughout.

Chapter 3
The Ethics of Elfland

hen the business man rebukes the idealism of his office-boy, it is commonly in some such speech as this: "Ah, yes, when one is young, one has these ideals in the abstract and these castles in the air; but in middle age they all break up like clouds, and one comes down to a belief in practical politics, to using the machinery one has and getting on with the world as it is." Thus, at least, venerable and philanthropic old men now in their honoured graves used to talk to me when I was a boy. But since then I have grown up and have discovered that these philanthropic old men were telling lies. What has really happened is exactly the opposite of what they said would happen. They said that I should lose my ideals and begin to believe in the methods of practical politicians. Now, I have not lost my ideals in the least; my faith in fundamentals is exactly what it always was. What I have lost is my old childlike faith in practical politics. I am still as much concerned as ever about the Battle of Armageddon; but I am not so much concerned about the General Election. As a babe I leapt up on my mother's knee at the mere mention of it. No; the vision is always solid and reliable. The vision is always a fact. It is the reality that is often a fraud. As much as I ever did, more than I ever did, I believe in Liberalism. But there was a rosy time of innocence when I believed in Liberals.

I take this instance of one of the enduring faiths because, having now to trace the roots of my personal speculation, this may be counted, I think, as the only positive bias. I was brought up a Liberal, and have always believed in democracy, in the elementary liberal doctrine of a self-governing humanity. If any one finds the phrase vague or threadbare, I can only pause for a moment to explain that the principle of democracy, as I mean it, can be stated in two propositions. The first is this: that the things common to all men are more important than the things peculiar to any men. Ordinary things are more valuable than extraordinary things; nay, they are more extraordinary. Man is something more awful than men; something more strange. The sense of the miracle of humanity itself should be always more vivid to us than any marvels of power, intellect, art, or civilization. The mere man on two legs, as such, should be felt as something more heartbreaking than any music and more startling than any caricature. Death is more tragic even than death by starvation. Having a nose is more comic even than having a Norman nose.

This is the first principle of democracy: that the essential things in men are the things they hold in common, not the things they hold separately. And the second principle is merely this: that the political instinct or desire is one of these things which they hold in common. Falling in love is more poetical than dropping into poetry. The democratic contention is that government (helping to rule the tribe) is a thing like falling in love, and not a thing like dropping into poetry. It is not something analogous to playing the church organ, painting on vellum, discovering the North Pole (that insidious habit), looping the loop, being Astronomer Royal, and so on. For these things we do not wish a man to do at all unless he does them well. It is, on the contrary, a thing analogous to writing one's own love-letters or blowing one's own nose. These things we want a man to do for himself, even if he does them badly. I am not here arguing the truth of any of these conceptions; I know that some moderns are asking to have their wives chosen by scientists, and they may soon be asking, for all I know, to have their noses blown by nurses. I merely say that mankind does recognize these universal human functions, and that democracy classes government among them. In short, the democratic faith is this: that the most terribly important things must be left to ordinary men themselves—the mating of the sexes, the rearing of the young, the laws of the state. This is democracy; and in this I have always believed.

But there is one thing that I have never from my youth up been able to understand. I have never been able to understand where people got the idea that democracy was in some way opposed to tradition. It is obvious that tradition is only democracy extended through time. It is trusting to a consensus of common human voices rather than to some isolated or arbitrary record. The man who quotes some German historian against the tradition of the Catholic Church, for instance, is strictly appealing to aristocracy. He is appealing to the superiority of one expert against the awful authority of a mob. It is quite easy to see why a legend is treated, and ought to be treated, more respectfully than a book of history. The legend is generally made by the majority of people in the village, who are sane. The book is generally written by the one man in the village who is mad. Those who urge against tradition that men in the past were ignorant may go and urge it at the Carlton Club, along with the statement that voters in the slums are ignorant. It will not do for us. If we attach great importance to the opinion of ordinary men in great unanimity when we are dealing with daily matters, there is no reason why we should disregard it when we are dealing with history or fable. Tradition may be defined as an extension of the franchise. Tradition means giving votes to the most obscure of all classes, our ancestors. It is the democracy of the dead. Tradition refuses to submit to the small and arrogant oligarchy of those who merely happen to be walking about. All democrats object to men being disqualified by the accident of birth; tradition objects to their being disqualified by the accident of death. Democracy tells us not to neglect a good man's opinion, even if he is our groom; tradition asks us not to neglect a good man's opinion, even if he is our father. I, at any rate, cannot separate the two ideas of democracy and tradition; it seems evident to me that they are the same idea. We will have the dead at our councils. The ancient Greeks voted by stones; these shall vote by tombstones. It is all quite regular and official, for most tombstones, like most ballot papers, are marked with a cross.

I have first to say, therefore, that if I have had a bias, it was always a bias in favour of democracy, and therefore of tradition. Before we come to any theoretic or logical beginnings I am content to allow for that personal equation; I have always been more inclined to believe the ruck of hard-working people than to believe that special and troublesome literary class to which I belong. I prefer even the fancies and prejudices of the people who see life from the inside to the clearest demonstrations of the people who see life from the outside. I would always trust the old wives' fables against the old maids' facts. As long as wit is mother wit it can be as wild as it pleases.

Now, I have to put together a general position, and I pretend to no training in such things. I propose to do it, therefore, by writing down one after another the three or four fundamental ideas which I have found for myself, pretty much in the way that I found them. Then I shall roughly synthesise them, summing up my personal philosophy or natural religion; then I shall describe my startling discovery that the whole thing had been discovered before. It had been discovered by Christianity. But of these profound persuasions which I have to recount in order, the earliest was concerned with this element of popular tradition. And without the foregoing explanation touching tradition and democracy I could hardly make my mental experience clear. As it is, I do not know whether I can make it clear, but I now propose to try.

My first and last philosophy, that which I believe in with unbroken certainty, I learnt in the nursery. I generally learnt it from a nurse; that is, from the solemn and star-appointed priestess at once of democracy and tradition. The things I believed most then, the things I believe most now, are the things called fairy tales. They seem to me to be the entirely reasonable things. They are not fantasies: compared with them other things are fantastic. Compared with them religion and rationalism are both abnormal, though religion is abnormally right and rationalism abnormally wrong. Fairyland is nothing but the sunny country of common sense. It is not earth that judges heaven, but heaven that judges earth; so for me at least it was not earth that criticised elfland, but elfland that criticised the earth. I knew the magic beanstalk before I had tasted beans; I was sure of the Man in the Moon before I was certain of the moon. This was at one with all popular tradition. Modern minor poets are naturalists, and talk about the bush or the brook; but the singers of the old epics and fables were supernaturalists, and talked about the gods of brook and bush. That is what the moderns mean when they say that the ancients did not "appreciate Nature," because they said that Nature was divine. Old nurses do not tell children about the grass, but about the fairies that dance on the grass; and the old Greeks could not see the trees for the dryads.

But I deal here with what ethic and philosophy come from being fed on fairy tales. If I were describing them in detail I could note many noble and healthy principles that arise from them. There is the chivalrous lesson of "Jack the Giant Killer"; that giants should be killed because they are gigantic. It is a manly mutiny against pride as such. For the rebel is older than all the kingdoms, and the Jacobin has more tradition than the Jacobite. There is the lesson of "Cinderella," which is the same as that of the Magnificat— EXALTAVIT HUMILES. There is the great lesson of "Beauty and the Beast"; that a thing must be loved BEFORE it is loveable. There is the terrible allegory of the "Sleeping Beauty," which tells how the human creature was blessed with all birthday gifts, yet cursed with death; and how death also may perhaps be softened to a sleep. But I am not concerned with any of the separate statutes of elfland, but with the whole spirit of its law, which I learnt before I could speak, and shall retain when I cannot write. I am concerned with a certain way of looking at life, which was created in me by the fairy tales, but has since been meekly ratified by the mere facts.

It might be stated this way. There are certain sequences or developments (cases of one thing following another), which are, in the true sense of the word, reasonable. They are, in the true sense of the word, necessary. Such are mathematical and merely logical sequences. We in fairyland (who are the most reasonable of all creatures) admit that reason and that necessity. For instance, if the Ugly Sisters are older than Cinderella, it is (in an iron and awful sense) NECESSARY that Cinderella is younger than the Ugly Sisters. There is no getting out of it. Haeckel may talk as much fatalism about that fact as he pleases: it really must be. If Jack is the son of a miller, a miller is the father of Jack. Cold reason decrees it from her awful throne: and we in fairyland submit. If the three brothers all ride horses, there are six animals and eighteen legs involved: that is true rationalism, and fairyland is full of it. But as I put my head over the hedge of the elves and began to take notice of the natural world, I observed an extraordinary thing. I observed that learned men in spectacles were talking of the actual things that happened— dawn and death and so on—as if THEY were rational and inevitable. They talked as if the fact that trees bear fruit were just as NECESSARY as the fact that two and one trees make three. But it is not. There is an enormous difference by the test of fairyland; which is the test of the imagination. You cannot IMAGINE two and one not making three. But you can easily imagine trees not growing fruit; you can imagine them growing golden candlesticks or tigers hanging on by the tail. These men in spectacles spoke much of a man named Newton, who was hit by an apple, and who discovered a law. But they could not be got to see the distinction between a true law, a law of reason, and the mere fact of apples falling. If the apple hit Newton's nose, Newton's nose hit the apple. That is a true necessity: because we cannot conceive the one occurring without the other. But we can quite well conceive the apple not falling on his nose; we can fancy it flying ardently through the air to hit some other nose, of which it had a more definite dislike. We have always in our fairy tales kept this sharp distinction between the science of mental relations, in which there really are laws, and the science of physical facts, in which there are no laws, but only weird repetitions. We believe in bodily miracles, but not in mental impossibilities. We believe that a Bean-stalk climbed up to Heaven;

but that does not at all confuse our convictions on the philosophical question of how many beans make five.

Here is the peculiar perfection of tone and truth in the nursery tales. The man of science says, "Cut the stalk, and the apple will fall"; but he says it calmly, as if the one idea really led up to the other. The witch in the fairy tale says, "Blow the horn, and the ogre's castle will fall"; but she does not say it as if it were something in which the effect obviously arose out of the cause. Doubtless she has given the advice to many champions, and has seen many castles fall, but she does not lose either her wonder or her reason. She does not muddle her head until it imagines a necessary mental connection between a horn and a falling tower. But the scientific men do muddle their heads, until they imagine a necessary mental connection between an apple leaving the tree and an apple reaching the ground. They do really talk as if they had found not only a set of marvellous facts, but a truth connecting those facts. They do talk as if the connection of two strange things physically connected them philosophically. They feel that because one incomprehensible thing constantly follows another incomprehensible thing the two together somehow make up a comprehensible thing. Two black riddles make a white answer.

In fairyland we avoid the word "law"; but in the land of science they are singularly fond of it. Thus they will call some interesting conjecture about how forgotten folks pronounced the alphabet, Grimm's Law. But Grimm's Law is far less intellectual than Grimm's Fairy Tales. The tales are, at any rate, certainly tales; while the law is not a law. A law implies that we know the nature of the generalisation and enactment; not merely that we have noticed some of the effects. If there is a law that pick-pockets shall go to prison, it implies that there is an imaginable mental connection between the idea of prison and the idea of picking pockets. And we know what the idea is. We can say why we take liberty from a man who takes liberties. But we cannot say why an egg can turn into a chicken any more than we can say why a bear could turn into a fairy prince. As IDEAS, the egg and the chicken are further off from each other than the bear and the prince; for no egg in itself suggests a chicken, whereas some princes do suggest bears. Granted, then, that certain transformations do happen, it is essential that we should regard them in the philosophic manner of fairy tales, not in the unphilosophic manner of science and the "Laws of Nature." When we are asked why eggs turn to birds or fruits fall in autumn, we must answer exactly as the fairy godmother would answer if Cinderella asked her why mice turned to horses or her clothes fell from her at twelve o'clock. We must answer that it is MAGIC. It is not a "law," for we do not understand its general formula. It is not a necessity, for though we can count on it happening practically, we have no right to say that it must always happen. It is no argument for unalterable law (as Huxley fancied) that we count on the ordinary course of things. We do not count on it; we bet on it. We risk the remote possibility of a miracle as we do that of a poisoned pancake or a world-destroying comet. We leave it out of account, not because it is a miracle, and therefore an impossibility, but because it is a miracle, and therefore an exception. All the terms used in the science books, "law," "necessity," "order," "tendency," and so on, are really unintellectual, because they assume an inner synthesis, which we do not possess. The only words that ever satisfied me as describing Nature are the terms used in the fairy books, "charm," "spell," "enchantment." They express the arbitrariness of the fact and its mystery. A tree grows fruit because it is a MAGIC tree. Water runs downhill because it is bewitched. The sun shines because it is bewitched.

I deny altogether that this is fantastic or even mystical. We may have some mysticism later on; but this fairy-tale language about things is simply rational and agnostic. It is the only way I can express in words my clear and definite perception that one thing is quite distinct from another; that there is no logical connection between flying and laying eggs. It is the man who talks about "a law" that he has never seen who is the mystic. Nay, the ordinary scientific man is strictly a sentimentalist. He is a sentimentalist in this essential sense, that he is soaked and swept away by mere associations. He has so often seen birds fly and lay eggs that he feels as if there must be some dreamy, tender connection between the two ideas, whereas there is none. A forlorn lover might be unable to dissociate the moon from lost love; so the materialist is unable to dissociate the moon from the tide. In both cases there is no connection, except that one has seen them together. A sentimentalist might shed tears at the smell of apple-blossom, because, by a dark association of his own, it reminded him of his boyhood. So the materialist professor (though he conceals his tears) is yet a sentimentalist, because, by a dark association of his own, apple-blossoms remind him of apples. But the cool rationalist from fairyland does not see why, in the abstract, the apple tree should not grow crimson tulips; it sometimes does in his country.

This elementary wonder, however, is not a mere fancy derived from the fairy tales; on the contrary, all the fire of the fairy tales is derived from this. Just as we all like love tales because there is an instinct of sex, we all like astonishing tales because they touch the nerve of the ancient instinct of astonishment. This is proved by the fact that when we are very young children we do not need fairy tales: we only need tales. Mere life is interesting enough. A child of seven is excited by being told that Tommy opened a door and saw a dragon. But a child of three is excited by being told that Tommy opened a door. Boys like romantic tales; but babies like realistic tales—because they find them romantic. In fact, a baby is about the only person, I should think, to whom a modern realistic novel could be read without boring him. This proves that even nursery tales only echo an almost pre-natal leap of interest and amazement. These tales say that apples were golden only to refresh the forgotten moment when we found that they were green. They make rivers run with wine only to make us remember, for one wild moment, that they run with water. I have said that this is wholly reasonable and even agnostic. And, indeed, on this point I am all for the higher agnosticism; its better name is Ignorance. We have all read in scientific books, and, indeed, in all romances, the story of the man who has forgotten his name. This man walks about the streets and can see and appreciate everything; only he cannot remember who he is. Well, every man is that man in the story. Every man has forgotten who he is. One may understand the cosmos, but never the ego; the self is more distant than any star. Thou shalt love the Lord thy God; but thou shalt not know thyself. We are all under the same mental calamity; we have all forgotten our names. We have all forgotten what we really are. All that we call common sense and rationality and practicality and positivism only means that for certain dead levels of our life we forget that we have forgotten. All that we call spirit and art and ecstasy only means that for one awful instant we remember that we forget.

But though (like the man without memory in the novel) we walk the streets with a sort of half-witted admiration, still it is admiration. It is admiration in English and not only admiration in Latin. The wonder has a positive element of praise. This is the next milestone to be definitely marked on our road through fairyland. I shall speak in the next chapter about optimists and pessimists in their intellectual aspect, so far as they have one. Here I am only trying to describe the enormous emotions which cannot be described. And the strongest emotion was that life was as precious as it was puzzling. It was an ecstasy because it was an adventure; it was an adventure because it was an opportunity. The goodness of the fairy tale was not affected by the fact that there might be more dragons than princesses; it was good to be in a fairy tale. The test of all happiness is gratitude; and I felt grateful, though I hardly knew to whom. Children are grateful when Santa Claus puts in their stockings gifts of toys or sweets. Could I not be grateful to Santa Claus when he put in my stockings the gift of two miraculous legs? We thank people for birthday presents of cigars and slippers. Can I thank no one for the birthday present of birth?

There were, then, these two first feelings, indefensible and indisputable. The world was a shock, but it was not merely shocking; existence was a surprise, but it was a pleasant surprise. In fact, all my first views were exactly uttered in a riddle that stuck in my brain from boyhood. The question was, "What did the first frog say?" And the answer was, "Lord, how you made me jump!" That says succinctly all that I am saying. God made the frog jump; but the frog prefers jumping. But when these things are settled there enters the second great principle of the fairy philosophy.

Any one can see it who will simply read "Grimm's Fairy Tales" or the fine collections of Mr. Andrew Lang. For the pleasure of pedantry I will call it the Doctrine of Conditional Joy. Touchstone talked of much virtue in an "if"; according to elfin ethics all virtue is in an "if." The note of the fairy utterance always is, "You may live in a palace of gold and sapphire, if you do not say the word 'cow'"; or "You may live happily with the King's daughter, if you do not show her an onion." The vision always hangs upon a veto. All the dizzy and colossal things conceded depend upon one small thing withheld. All the wild and whirling things that are let loose depend upon one thing that is forbidden. Mr. W.B.Yeats, in his exquisite and piercing elfin poetry, describes the elves as lawless; they plunge in innocent anarchy on the unbridled horses of the air—

"Ride on the crest of the dishevelled tide, And dance upon the mountains like a flame."

It is a dreadful thing to say that Mr. W.B.Yeats does not understand fairyland. But I do say it. He is an ironical Irishman, full of intellectual reactions. He is not stupid enough to understand fairyland. Fairies prefer people of the yokel type like myself; people who gape and grin and do as they are told. Mr. Yeats reads into elfland all the righteous insurrection of his own race. But the lawlessness of Ireland is a Christian lawlessness, founded on reason and justice. The Fenian is rebelling against something he understands only too well; but the true citizen of fairyland is obeying something that he does not understand at all. In the fairy tale an incomprehensible happiness rests upon an incomprehensible condition. A box is opened, and all evils fly out. A word is forgotten, and cities perish. A lamp is lit, and love flies away. A flower is plucked, and human lives are forfeited. An apple is eaten, and the hope of God is gone.

This is the tone of fairy tales, and it is certainly not lawlessness or even liberty, though men under a mean modern tyranny may think it liberty by comparison. People out of Portland Gaol might think Fleet Street free; but closer study will prove that both fairies and journalists are the slaves of duty. Fairy godmothers seem at least as strict as other godmothers. Cinderella received a coach out of Wonderland and a coachman out of nowhere, but she received a command—which might have come out of Brixton—that she should be back by twelve. Also, she had a glass slipper; and it cannot be a coincidence that glass is so common a substance in folk-lore. This princess lives in a glass castle, that princess on a glass hill; this one sees all things in a mirror; they may all live in glass houses if they will not throw stones. For this thin glitter of glass everywhere is the expression of the fact that the happiness is bright but brittle, like the substance most easily smashed by a housemaid or a cat. And this fairy-tale sentiment also sank into me and became my sentiment towards the whole world. I felt and feel that life itself is as bright as the diamond, but as brittle as the window-pane; and when the heavens were compared to the terrible crystal I can remember a shudder. I was afraid that God would drop the cosmos with a crash.

Remember, however, that to be breakable is not the same as to be perishable. Strike a glass, and it will not endure an instant; simply do not strike it, and it will endure a thousand years. Such, it seemed, was the joy of man, either in elfland or on earth; the happiness depended on NOT DOING SOMETHING which you could at any moment do and which, very often, it was not obvious why you should not do. Now, the point here is that to ME this did not seem unjust. If the miller's third son said to the fairy, "Explain why I must not stand on my head in the fairy palace," the other might fairly reply, "Well, if it comes to that, explain the fairy palace." If Cinderella says, "How is it that I must leave the ball at twelve?" her godmother might answer, "How is it that you are going there till twelve?" If I leave a man in my will ten talking elephants and a hundred winged horses, he cannot complain if the conditions partake of the slight eccentricity of the gift. He must not look a winged horse in the mouth. And it seemed to me that existence was itself so very eccentric a legacy that I could not complain of not understanding the limitations of the vision when I did not understand the vision they limited. The frame was no stranger than the picture. The veto might well be as wild as the vision; it might be as startling as the sun, as elusive as the waters, as fantastic and terrible as the towering trees.

For this reason (we may call it the fairy godmother philosophy) I never could join the young men of my time in feeling what they called the general sentiment of REVOLT. I should have resisted, let us hope, any rules that were evil, and with these and their definition I shall deal in another chapter. But I did not feel disposed to resist any rule merely because it was mysterious. Estates are sometimes held by foolish forms, the breaking of a stick or the payment of a peppercorn: I was willing to hold the huge estate of earth and heaven by any such feudal fantasy. It could not well be wilder than the fact that I was allowed to hold it at all. At this stage I give only one ethical instance to show my meaning. I could never mix in the common murmur of that rising generation against monogamy, because no restriction on sex seemed so odd and unexpected as sex itself. To be allowed, like Endymion, to make love to the moon and then to complain that Jupiter kept his own moons in a harem seemed to me (bred on fairy tales like Endymion's) a vulgar anti-climax. Keeping to one woman is a small price for so much as seeing one woman. To complain that I could only be married once was like complaining that I had only been born once. It was incommensurate with the terrible excitement of which one was talking. It showed, not an exaggerated sensibility to sex, but a curious insensibility to it. A man is a fool who complains that he cannot enter Eden by five gates at once. Polygamy is a lack of the realization of sex; it is like a man plucking five pears in mere absence of mind. The aesthetes touched the last insane limits of language in their eulogy on lovely things. The thistledown made them weep; a burnished beetle brought them to their knees. Yet their emotion never impressed me for an instant, for this reason, that it never occurred to them to pay for their pleasure in any sort of symbolic sacrifice. Men (I felt) might fast forty days for the sake of hearing a blackbird sing. Men might go through fire to find a cowslip. Yet these lovers of beauty could not even keep sober for the blackbird. They would not go through common Christian marriage by way of recompense to the cowslip. Surely one might pay for extraordinary joy in ordinary morals. Oscar Wilde said that sunsets were not valued because we could not pay for sunsets. But Oscar Wilde was wrong; we can pay for sunsets. We can pay for them by not being Oscar Wilde.

Well, I left the fairy tales lying on the floor of the nursery, and I have not found any books so sensible since. I left the nurse guardian of tradition and democracy, and I have not found any modern type so sanely radical or so sanely conservative. But the matter for important comment was here: that when I first went out into the mental atmosphere of the modern world, I found that the modern world was positively opposed on two points to my nurse and to the nursery tales. It has taken me a long time to find out that the modern world is wrong and my nurse was right. The really curious thing was this: that modern thought contradicted this basic creed of my boyhood on its two most essential doctrines. I have explained that the fairy tales founded in me two convictions; first, that this world is a wild and startling place, which might have been quite different, but which is quite delightful; second, that before this wildness and delight one may well be modest and submit to the queerest limitations of so queer a kindness. But I found the whole modern world running like a high tide against both my tendernesses; and the shock of that collision created two sudden and spontaneous sentiments, which I have had ever since and which, crude as they were, have since hardened into convictions.

First, I found the whole modern world talking scientific fatalism; saying that everything is as it must always have been, being unfolded without fault from the beginning. The leaf on the tree is green because it could never have been anything else. Now, the fairy-tale philosopher is glad that the leaf is green precisely because it might have been scarlet. He feels as if it had turned green an instant before he looked at it. He is pleased that snow is white on the strictly reasonable ground that it might have been black. Every colour has in it a bold quality as of choice; the red of garden roses is not only decisive but dramatic, like suddenly spilt blood. He feels that something has been DONE. But the great determinists of the nineteenth century were strongly against this native feeling that something had happened an instant before. In fact, according to them, nothing ever really had happened since the beginning of the world. Nothing ever had happened since existence had happened; and even about the date of that they were not very sure.

The modern world as I found it was solid for modern Calvinism, for the necessity of things being as they are. But when I came to ask them I found they had really no proof of this unavoidable repetition in things except the fact that the things were repeated. Now, the mere repetition made the things to me rather more weird than more rational. It was as if, having seen a curiously shaped nose in the street and dismissed it as an accident, I had then seen six other noses of the same astonishing shape. I should have fancied for a moment that it must be some local secret society. So one elephant having a trunk was odd; but all elephants having trunks looked like a plot. I speak here only of an emotion, and of an emotion at once stubborn and subtle. But the repetition in Nature seemed sometimes to be an excited repetition, like that of an angry schoolmaster saying the same thing over and over again. The grass seemed signalling to me with all its fingers at once; the crowded stars seemed bent upon being understood. The sun would make me see him if he rose a thousand times. The recurrences of the universe rose to the maddening rhythm of an incantation, and I began to see an idea.

All the towering materialism which dominates the modern mind rests ultimately upon one assumption; a false assumption. It is supposed that if a thing goes on repeating itself it is probably dead; a piece of clockwork. People feel that if the universe was personal it would vary; if the sun were alive it would dance. This is a fallacy even in relation to known fact. For the variation in human affairs is generally brought into them, not by life, but by death; by the dying down or breaking off of their strength or desire. A man varies his movements because of some slight element of failure or fatigue. He gets into an omnibus because he is tired of walking; or he walks because he is tired of sitting still. But if his life and joy were so gigantic that he never tired of going to Islington, he might go to Islington as regularly as the Thames goes to Sheerness. The very speed and ecstasy of his life would have the stillness of death. The sun rises every morning. I do not rise every morning; but the variation is due not to my activity, but to my inaction. Now, to put the matter in a popular phrase, it might be true that the sun rises regularly because he never gets tired of rising. His routine might be due, not to a lifelessness, but to a rush of life. The thing I mean can be seen, for instance, in children, when they find some game or joke that they specially enjoy. A child kicks his legs rhythmically through excess, not absence, of life. Because children have abounding vitality, because they are in spirit fierce and free, therefore they want things repeated and unchanged. They always say, "Do it again"; and the grown-up person does it again until he is nearly dead. For grown-up people are not strong enough to exult in monotony. But perhaps God is strong enough to exult in monotony. It is possible that God says every morning, "Do it again" to the sun; and every evening, "Do it again" to the moon. It may not be automatic necessity that makes all daisies alike; it may be that God makes every daisy separately, but has never got tired of making them. It may be that He has the eternal appetite of infancy; for we have sinned and grown old, and our Father is younger than we. The repetition in Nature may not be a mere recurrence; it may be a theatrical ENCORE. Heaven may ENCORE the bird who laid an egg. If the human being conceives and brings forth a human child instead of bringing forth a fish, or a bat, or a griffin, the reason may not be that we are fixed in an animal fate without life or purpose. It may be that our little tragedy has touched the gods, that they admire it from their starry galleries, and that at the end of every human drama man is called again and again before the curtain. Repetition may go on for millions of years, by mere choice, and at any instant it may stop. Man may stand on the earth generation after generation, and yet each birth be his positively last appearance.

This was my first conviction; made by the shock of my childish emotions meeting the modern creed in mid-career. I had always vaguely felt facts to be miracles in the sense that they are wonderful: now I began to think them miracles in the stricter sense that they were WILFUL. I mean that they were, or might be, repeated exercises of some will. In short, I had always believed that the world involved magic: now I thought that perhaps it involved a magician. And this pointed a profound emotion always present and sub-conscious; that this world of ours has some purpose; and if there is a purpose, there is a person. I had always felt life first as a story: and if there is a story there is a story-teller.

But modern thought also hit my second human tradition. It went against the fairy feeling about strict limits and conditions. The one thing it loved to talk about was expansion and largeness. Herbert Spencer would have been greatly annoyed if any one had called him an imperialist, and therefore it is highly regrettable that nobody did. But he was an imperialist of the lowest type. He popularized this contemptible notion that the size of the solar system ought to over-awe the spiritual dogma of man. Why should a man surrender his dignity to the solar system any more than to a whale? If mere size proves that man is not the image of God, then a whale may be the image of God; a somewhat formless image; what one might call an impressionist portrait. It is quite futile to argue that man is small compared to the cosmos; for man was always small compared to the nearest tree. But Herbert Spencer, in his headlong imperialism, would insist that we had in some way been conquered and annexed by the astronomical universe. He spoke about men and their ideals exactly as the most insolent Unionist talks about the Irish and their ideals. He turned mankind into a small nationality. And his evil influence can be seen even in the most spirited and honourable of later scientific authors; notably in the early romances of Mr. H.G.Wells. Many moralists have in an exaggerated way represented the earth as wicked. But Mr. Wells and his school made the heavens wicked. We should lift up our eyes to the stars from whence would come our ruin.

But the expansion of which I speak was much more evil than all this. I have remarked that the materialist, like the madman, is in prison; in the prison of one thought. These people seemed to think it singularly inspiring to keep on saying that the prison was very large. The size of this scientific universe gave one no novelty, no relief. The cosmos went on for ever, but not in its wildest constellation could there be anything really interesting; anything, for instance, such as forgiveness or free will. The grandeur or infinity of the secret of its cosmos added nothing to it. It was like telling a prisoner in Reading gaol that he would be glad to hear that the gaol now covered half the county. The warder would have nothing to show the man except more and more long corridors of stone lit by ghastly lights and empty of all that is human. So these expanders of the universe had nothing to show us except more and more infinite corridors of space lit by ghastly suns and empty of all that is divine.

In fairyland there had been a real law; a law that could be broken, for the definition of a law is something that can be broken. But the machinery of this cosmic prison was something that could not be broken; for we ourselves were only a part of its machinery. We were either unable to do things or we were destined to do them. The idea of the mystical condition quite disappeared; one can neither have the firmness of keeping laws nor the fun of breaking them. The largeness of this universe had nothing of that freshness and airy outbreak which we have praised in the universe of the poet. This modern universe is literally an empire; that is, it was vast, but it is not free. One went into larger and larger windowless rooms, rooms big with Babylonian perspective; but one never found the smallest window or a whisper of outer air.

Their infernal parallels seemed to expand with distance; but for me all good things come to a point, swords for instance. So finding the boast of the big cosmos so unsatisfactory to my emotions I began to argue about it a little; and I soon found that the whole attitude was even shallower than could have been expected. According to these people the cosmos was one thing since it had one unbroken rule. Only (they would say) while it is one thing, it is also the only thing there is. Why, then, should one worry particularly to call it large? There is nothing to compare it with. It would be just as sensible to call it small. A man may say, "I like this vast cosmos, with its throng of stars and its crowd of varied creatures." But if it comes to that why should not a man say, "I like this cosy little cosmos, with its decent number of stars and as neat a provision of live stock as I wish to see"? One is as good as the other; they are both mere sentiments. It is mere sentiment to rejoice that the sun is larger than the earth; it is quite as sane a sentiment to rejoice that the sun is no larger than it is. A man chooses to have an emotion about the largeness of the world; why should he not choose to have an emotion about its smallness?

It happened that I had that emotion. When one is fond of anything one addresses it by diminutives, even if it is an elephant or a life-guardsman. The reason is, that anything, however huge, that can be conceived of as complete, can be conceived of as small. If military moustaches did not suggest a sword or tusks a tail, then the object would be vast because it would be immeasurable. But the moment you can imagine a guardsman you can imagine a small guardsman. The moment you really see an elephant you can call it "Tiny." If you can make a statue of a thing you can make a statuette of it. These people professed that the universe was one coherent thing; but they were not fond of the universe. But I was frightfully fond of the universe and wanted to address it by a diminutive. I often did so; and it never seemed to mind. Actually and in truth I did feel that these dim dogmas of vitality were better expressed by calling the world small than by calling it large. For about infinity there was a sort of carelessness which was the reverse of the fierce and pious care which I felt touching the pricelessness and the peril of life. They showed only a dreary waste; but I felt a sort of sacred thrift. For economy is far more romantic than extravagance. To them stars were an unending income of halfpence; but I felt about the golden sun and the silver moon as a schoolboy feels if he has one sovereign and one shilling.

These subconscious convictions are best hit off by the colour and tone of certain tales. Thus I have said that stories of magic alone can express my sense that life is not only a pleasure but a kind of eccentric privilege. I may express this other feeling of cosmic cosiness by allusion to another book always read in boyhood, "Robinson Crusoe," which I read about this time, and which owes its eternal vivacity to the fact that it celebrates the poetry of limits, nay, even the wild romance of prudence. Crusoe is a man on a small rock with a few comforts just snatched from the sea: the best thing in the book is simply the list of things saved from the wreck. The greatest of poems is an inventory. Every kitchen tool becomes ideal because Crusoe might have dropped it in the sea. It is a good exercise, in empty or ugly hours of the day, to look at anything, the coal-scuttle or the book-case, and think how happy one could be to have brought it out of the sinking ship on to the solitary island. But it is a better exercise still to remember how all things have had this hair-breadth escape: everything has been saved from a wreck. Every man has had one horrible adventure: as a hidden untimely birth he had not been, as infants that never see the light. Men spoke much in my boyhood of restricted or ruined men of genius: and it was common to say that many a man was a Great Might-Have-Been. To me it is a more solid and startling fact that any man in the street is a Great Might-Not-Have-Been.

But I really felt (the fancy may seem foolish) as if all the order and number of things were the romantic remnant of Crusoe's ship. That there are two sexes and one sun, was like the fact that there were two guns and one axe. It was poignantly urgent that none should be lost; but somehow, it was rather fun that none could be added. The trees and the planets seemed like things saved from the wreck: and when I saw the Matterhorn I was glad that it had not been overlooked in the confusion. I felt economical about the stars as if they were sapphires (they are called so in Milton's Eden): I hoarded the hills. For the universe is a single jewel, and while it is a natural cant to talk of a jewel as peerless and priceless, of this jewel it is literally true. This cosmos is indeed without peer and without price: for there cannot be another one.

Thus ends, in unavoidable inadequacy, the attempt to utter the unutterable things. These are my ultimate attitudes towards life; the soils for the seeds of doctrine. These in some dark way I thought before I could write, and felt before I could think: that we may proceed more easily afterwards, I will roughly recapitulate them now. I felt in my bones; first, that this world does not explain itself. It may be a miracle with a supernatural explanation; it may be a conjuring trick, with a natural explanation. But the explanation of the conjuring trick, if it is to satisfy me, will have to be better than the natural explanations I have heard. The thing is magic, true or false. Second, I came to feel as if magic must have a meaning, and meaning must have some one to mean it. There was something personal in the world, as in a work of art; whatever it meant it meant violently. Third, I thought this purpose beautiful in its old design, in spite of its defects, such as dragons. Fourth, that the proper form of thanks to it is some form of humility and restraint: we should thank God for beer and Burgundy by not drinking too much of them. We owed, also, an obedience to whatever made us. And last, and strangest, there had come into my mind a vague and vast impression that in some way all good was a remnant to be stored and held sacred out of some primordial ruin. Man had saved his good as Crusoe saved his goods: he had saved them from a wreck. All this I felt and the age gave me no encouragement to feel it. And all this time I had not even thought of Christian theology.

Chapter 4
The Flag of the World

hen I was a boy there were two curious men running about who were called the optimist and the pessimist. I constantly used the words myself, but I cheerfully confess that I never had any very special idea of what they meant. The only thing which might be considered evident was that they could not mean what they said; for the ordinary verbal explanation was that the optimist thought this world as good as it could be, while the pessimist thought it as bad as it could be. Both these statements being obviously raving nonsense, one had to cast about for other explanations. An optimist could not mean a man who thought everything right and nothing wrong. For that is meaningless; it is like calling everything right and nothing left. Upon the whole, I came to the conclusion that the optimist thought everything good except the pessimist, and that the pessimist thought everything bad, except himself. It would be unfair to omit altogether from the list the mysterious but suggestive definition said to have been given by a little girl, "An optimist is a man who looks after your eyes, and a pessimist is a man who looks after your feet." I am not sure that this is not the best definition of all. There is even a sort of allegorical truth in it. For there might, perhaps, be a profitable distinction drawn between that more dreary thinker who thinks merely of our contact with the earth from moment to moment, and that happier thinker who considers rather our primary power of vision and of choice of road.

But this is a deep mistake in this alternative of the optimist and the pessimist. The assumption of it is that a man criticises this world as if he were house-hunting, as if he were being shown over a new suite of apartments. If a man came to this world from some other world in full possession of his powers he might discuss whether the advantage of midsummer woods made up for the disadvantage of mad dogs, just as a man looking for lodgings might balance the presence of a telephone against the absence of a sea view. But no man is in that position. A man belongs to this world before he begins to ask if it is nice to belong to it. He has fought for the flag, and often won heroic victories for the flag long before he has ever enlisted. To put shortly what seems the essential matter, he has a loyalty long before he has any admiration.

In the last chapter it has been said that the primary feeling that this world is strange and yet attractive is best expressed in fairy tales. The reader may, if he likes, put down the next stage to that bellicose and even jingo literature which commonly comes next in the history of a boy. We all owe much sound morality to the penny dreadfuls. Whatever the reason, it seemed and still seems to me that our attitude towards life can be better expressed in terms of a kind of military loyalty than in terms of criticism and approval. My acceptance of the universe is not optimism, it is more like patriotism. It is a matter of primary loyalty. The world is not a lodging-house at Brighton, which we are to leave because it is miserable. It is the fortress of our family, with the flag flying on the turret, and the more miserable it is the less we should leave it. The point is not that this world is too sad to love or too glad not to love; the point is that when you do love a thing, its gladness is a reason for loving it, and its sadness a reason for loving it more. All optimistic thoughts about England and all pessimistic thoughts about her are alike reasons for the English patriot. Similarly, optimism and pessimism are alike arguments for the cosmic patriot.

Let us suppose we are confronted with a desperate thing—say Pimlico. If we think what is really best for Pimlico we shall find the thread of thought leads to the throne or the mystic and the arbitrary. It is not enough for a man to disapprove of Pimlico: in that case he will merely cut his throat or move to Chelsea. Nor, certainly, is it enough for a man to approve of Pimlico: for then it will remain Pimlico, which would be awful. The only way out of it seems to be for somebody to love Pimlico: to love it with a transcendental tie and without any earthly reason. If there arose a man who loved Pimlico, then Pimlico would rise into ivory towers and golden pinnacles; Pimlico would attire herself as a woman does when she is loved. For decoration is not given to hide horrible things: but to decorate things already adorable. A mother does not give her child a blue bow because he is so ugly without it. A lover does not give a girl a necklace to hide her neck. If men loved Pimlico as mothers love children, arbitrarily, because it is THEIRS, Pimlico in a year or two might be fairer than Florence. Some readers will say that this is a mere fantasy. I answer that this is the actual history of mankind. This, as a fact, is how cities did grow great. Go back to the darkest roots of civilization and you will find them knotted round some sacred stone or encircling some sacred well. People first paid honour to a spot and afterwards gained glory for it. Men did not love Rome because she was great. She was great because they had loved her.

The eighteenth-century theories of the social contract have been exposed to much clumsy criticism in our time; in so far as they meant that there is at the back of all historic government an idea of content and co-operation, they were demonstrably right. But they really were wrong, in so far as they suggested that men had ever aimed at order or ethics directly by a conscious exchange of interests. Morality did not begin by one man saying to another, "I will not hit you if you do not hit me"; there is no trace of such a transaction. There IS a trace of both men having said, "We must not hit each other in the holy place." They gained their morality by guarding their religion. They did not cultivate courage. They fought for the shrine, and found they had become courageous. They did not cultivate cleanliness. They purified themselves for the altar, and found that they were clean. The history of the Jews is the only early document known to most Englishmen, and the facts can be judged sufficiently from that. The Ten Commandments which have been found substantially common to mankind were merely military commands; a code of regimental orders, issued to protect a certain ark across a certain desert. Anarchy was evil because it endangered the sanctity. And only when they made a holy day for God did they find they had made a holiday for men.

If it be granted that this primary devotion to a place or thing is a source of creative energy, we can pass on to a very peculiar fact. Let us reiterate for an instant that the only right optimism is a sort of universal patriotism. What is the matter with the pessimist? I think it can be stated by saying that he is the cosmic anti-patriot. And what is the matter with the anti-patriot? I think it can be stated, without undue bitterness, by saying that he is the candid friend. And what is the matter with the candid friend? There we strike the rock of real life and immutable human nature.

I venture to say that what is bad in the candid friend is simply that he is not candid. He is keeping something back— his own gloomy pleasure in saying unpleasant things. He has a secret desire to hurt, not merely to help. This is certainly, I think, what makes a certain sort of anti-patriot irritating to healthy citizens. I do not speak (of course) of the anti-patriotism which only irritates feverish stockbrokers and gushing actresses; that is only patriotism speaking plainly. A man who says that no patriot should attack the Boer War until it is over is not worth answering intelligently; he is saying that no good son should warn his mother off a cliff until she has fallen over it. But there is an anti-patriot who honestly angers honest men, and the explanation of him is, I think, what I have suggested: he is the uncandid candid friend; the man who says, "I am sorry to say we are ruined," and is not sorry at all. And he may be said, without rhetoric, to be a traitor; for he is using that ugly knowledge which was allowed him to strengthen the army, to discourage people from joining it. Because he is allowed to be pessimistic as a military adviser he is being pessimistic as a recruiting sergeant. Just in the same way the pessimist (who is the cosmic anti-patriot) uses the freedom that life allows to her counsellors to lure away the people from her flag. Granted that he states only facts, it is still essential to know what are his emotions, what is his motive. It may be that twelve hundred men in Tottenham are down with smallpox; but we want to know whether this is stated by some great philosopher who wants to curse the gods, or only by some common clergyman who wants to help the men.

The evil of the pessimist is, then, not that he chastises gods and men, but that he does not love what he chastises—he has not this primary and supernatural loyalty to things. What is the evil of the man commonly called an optimist? Obviously, it is felt that the optimist, wishing to defend the honour of this world, will defend the indefensible. He is the jingo of the universe; he will say, "My cosmos, right or wrong." He will be less inclined to the reform of things; more inclined to a sort of front-bench official answer to all attacks, soothing every one with assurances. He will not wash the world, but whitewash the world. All this (which is true of a type of optimist) leads us to the one really interesting point of psychology, which could not be explained without it.

We say there must be a primal loyalty to life: the only question is, shall it be a natural or a supernatural loyalty? If you like to put it so, shall it be a reasonable or an unreasonable loyalty? Now, the extraordinary thing is that the bad optimism (the whitewashing, the weak defence of everything) comes in with the reasonable optimism. Rational optimism leads to stagnation: it is irrational optimism that leads to reform. Let me explain by using once more the parallel of patriotism. The man who is most likely to ruin the place he loves is exactly the man who loves it with a reason. The man who will improve the place is the man who loves it without a reason. If a man loves some feature of Pimlico (which seems unlikely), he may find himself defending that feature against Pimlico itself. But if he simply loves Pimlico itself, he may lay it waste and turn it into the New Jerusalem. I do not deny that reform may be excessive; I only say that it is the mystic patriot who reforms. Mere jingo self-contentment is commonest among those who have some pedantic reason for their patriotism. The worst jingoes do not love England, but a theory of England. If we love England for being an empire, we may overrate the success with which we rule the Hindoos. But if we love it only for being a nation, we can face all events: for it would be a nation even if the Hindoos ruled us. Thus also only those will permit their patriotism to falsify history whose patriotism depends on history. A man who loves England for being English will not mind how she arose. But a man who loves England for being Anglo-Saxon may go against all facts for his fancy. He may end (like Carlyle and Freeman) by maintaining that the Norman Conquest was a Saxon Conquest. He may end in utter unreason—because he has a reason. A man who loves France for being military will palliate the army of 1870. But a man who loves France for being France will improve the army of 1870. This is exactly what the French have done, and France is a good instance of the working paradox. Nowhere else is patriotism more purely abstract and arbitrary; and nowhere else is reform more drastic and sweeping. The more transcendental is your patriotism, the more practical are your politics.

Perhaps the most everyday instance of this point is in the case of women; and their strange and strong loyalty. Some stupid people started the idea that because women obviously back up their own people through everything, therefore women are blind and do not see anything. They can hardly have known any women. The same women who are ready to defend their men through thick and thin are (in their personal intercourse with the man) almost morbidly lucid about the thinness of his excuses or the thickness of his head. A man's friend likes him but leaves him as he is: his wife loves him and is always trying to turn him into somebody else. Women who are utter mystics in their creed are utter cynics in their criticism. Thackeray expressed this well when he made Pendennis' mother, who worshipped her son as a god, yet assume that he would go wrong as a man. She underrated his virtue, though she overrated his value. The devotee is entirely free to criticise;

the fanatic can safely be a sceptic. Love is not blind; that is the last thing that it is. Love is bound; and the more it is bound the less it is blind.

This at least had come to be my position about all that was called optimism, pessimism, and improvement. Before any cosmic act of reform we must have a cosmic oath of allegiance. A man must be interested in life, then he could be disinterested in his views of it. "My son give me thy heart"; the heart must be fixed on the right thing: the moment we have a fixed heart we have a free hand. I must pause to anticipate an obvious criticism. It will be said that a rational person accepts the world as mixed of good and evil with a decent satisfaction and a decent endurance. But this is exactly the attitude which I maintain to be defective. It is, I know, very common in this age; it was perfectly put in those quiet lines of Matthew Arnold which are more piercingly blasphemous than the shrieks of Schopenhauer—

"Enough we live:—and if a life, With large results so little rife, Though bearable, seem hardly worth This pomp of worlds, this pain of birth."

I know this feeling fills our epoch, and I think it freezes our epoch. For our Titanic purposes of faith and revolution, what we need is not the cold acceptance of the world as a compromise, but some way in which we can heartily hate and heartily love it. We do not want joy and anger to neutralize each other and produce a surly contentment; we want a fiercer delight and a fiercer discontent. We have to feel the universe at once as an ogre's castle, to be stormed, and yet as our own cottage, to which we can return at evening.

No one doubts that an ordinary man can get on with this world: but we demand not strength enough to get on with it, but strength enough to get it on. Can he hate it enough to change it, and yet love it enough to think it worth changing? Can he look up at its colossal good without once feeling acquiescence? Can he look up at its colossal evil without once feeling despair? Can he, in short, be at once not only a pessimist and an optimist, but a fanatical pessimist and a fanatical optimist? Is he enough of a pagan to die for the world, and enough of a Christian to die to it? In this combination, I maintain, it is the rational optimist who fails, the irrational optimist who succeeds. He is ready to smash the whole universe for the sake of itself.

I put these things not in their mature logical sequence, but as they came: and this view was cleared and sharpened by an accident of the time. Under the lengthening shadow of Ibsen, an argument arose whether it was not a very nice thing to murder one's self. Grave moderns told us that we must not even say "poor fellow," of a man who had blown his brains out, since he was an enviable person, and had only blown them out because of their exceptional excellence. Mr. William Archer even suggested that in the golden age there would be penny-in-the-slot machines, by which a man could kill himself for a penny. In all this I found myself utterly hostile to many who called themselves liberal and humane. Not only is suicide a sin, it is *the* sin. It is the ultimate and absolute evil, the refusal to take an interest in existence; the refusal to take the oath of loyalty to life. The man who kills a man, kills a man. The man who kills himself, kills all men; as far as he is concerned he wipes out the world. His act is worse (symbolically considered) than any rape or dynamite outrage. For it destroys all buildings: it insults all women. The thief is satisfied with diamonds; but the suicide is not: that is his crime. He cannot be bribed, even by the blazing stones of the Celestial City. The thief compliments the things he steals, if not the owner of them. But the suicide insults everything on earth by not stealing it. He defiles every flower by refusing to live for its sake. There is not a tiny creature in the cosmos at whom his death is not a sneer. When a man hangs himself on a tree, the leaves might fall off in anger and the birds fly away in fury: for each has received a personal affront. Of course there may be pathetic emotional excuses for the act. There often are for rape, and there almost always are for dynamite. But if it comes to clear ideas and the intelligent meaning of things, then there is much more rational and philosophic truth in the burial at the cross-roads and the stake driven through the body, than in Mr. Archer's suicidal automatic machines. There is a meaning in burying the suicide apart. The man's crime is different from other crimes—for it makes even crimes impossible.

About the same time I read a solemn flippancy by some free thinker: he said that a suicide was only the same as a martyr. The open fallacy of this helped to clear the question. Obviously a suicide is the opposite of a martyr. A martyr is a man who cares so much for something outside him, that he forgets his own personal life. A suicide is a man who cares so little for anything outside him, that he wants to see the last of everything. One wants something to begin: the other wants everything to end. In other words, the martyr is noble, exactly because (however he renounces the world or execrates all humanity) he confesses this ultimate link with life; he sets his heart outside himself: he dies that something may live. The suicide is ignoble because he has not this link with being: he is a mere destroyer; spiritually, he destroys the universe. And then I remembered the stake and the cross-roads, and the queer fact that Christianity had shown this weird harshness to the suicide. For Christianity had shown a wild encouragement of the martyr. Historic Christianity was accused, not entirely without reason, of carrying martyrdom and asceticism to a point, desolate and pessimistic. The early Christian martyrs talked of death with a horrible happiness. They blasphemed the beautiful duties of the body: they smelt the grave afar off like a field of flowers. All this has seemed to many the very poetry of pessimism. Yet there is the stake at the crossroads to show what Christianity thought of the pessimist.

This was the first of the long train of enigmas with which Christianity entered the discussion. And there went with it a peculiarity of which I shall have to speak more markedly, as a note of all Christian notions, but which distinctly began in this one. The Christian attitude to the martyr and the suicide was not what is so often affirmed in modern morals. It was not a matter of degree. It was not that a line must be drawn somewhere, and that the self-slayer in exaltation fell within the line, the self-slayer in sadness just beyond it. The Christian feeling evidently was not merely that the suicide was carrying martyrdom too far. The Christian feeling was furiously for one and furiously against the other: these two things that looked so much alike were at opposite ends of heaven and hell. One man flung away his life; he was so good that his dry bones could heal cities in pestilence. Another man flung away life; he was so bad that his bones would pollute his brethren's. I am not saying this fierceness was right; but why was it so fierce?

Here it was that I first found that my wandering feet were in some beaten track. Christianity had also felt this opposition of the martyr to the suicide: had it perhaps felt it for the same reason? Had Christianity felt what I felt, but could not (and cannot) express—this need for a first loyalty to things, and then for a ruinous reform of things? Then I remembered that it was actually the charge against Christianity that it combined these two things which I was wildly trying to combine. Christianity was accused, at one and the same time, of being too optimistic about the universe and of being too pessimistic about the world. The coincidence made me suddenly stand still.

An imbecile habit has arisen in modern controversy of saying that such and such a creed can be held in one age but cannot be held in another. Some dogma, we are told, was credible in the twelfth century, but is not credible in the twentieth. You might as well say that a certain philosophy can be believed on Mondays, but cannot be believed on Tuesdays. You might as well say of a view of the cosmos that it was suitable to half-past three, but not suitable to half-past four. What a man can believe depends upon his philosophy, not upon the clock or the century. If a man believes in unalterable natural law, he cannot believe in any miracle in any age. If a man believes in a will behind law, he can believe in any miracle in any age. Suppose, for the sake of argument, we are concerned with a case of thaumaturgic healing. A materialist of the twelfth century could not believe it any more than a materialist of the twentieth century. But a Christian Scientist of the twentieth century can believe it as much as a Christian of the twelfth century. It is simply a matter of a man's theory of things. Therefore in dealing with any historical answer, the point is not whether it was given in our time, but whether it was given in answer to our question. And the more I thought about when and how Christianity had come into the world, the more I felt that it had actually come to answer this question.

It is commonly the loose and latitudinarian Christians who pay quite indefensible compliments to Christianity. They talk as if there had never been any piety or pity until Christianity came, a point on which any mediaeval would have been eager to correct them. They represent that the remarkable thing about Christianity was that it was the first to preach simplicity or self-restraint, or inwardness and sincerity. They will think me very narrow (whatever that means) if I say that the remarkable thing about Christianity was that it was the first to preach Christianity.

Its peculiarity was that it was peculiar, and simplicity and sincerity are not peculiar, but obvious ideals for all mankind. Christianity was the answer to a riddle, not the last truism uttered after a long talk. Only the other day I saw in an excellent weekly paper of Puritan tone this remark, that Christianity when stripped of its armour of dogma (as who should speak of a man stripped of his armour of bones), turned out to be nothing but the Quaker doctrine of the Inner Light. Now, if I were to say that Christianity came into the world specially to destroy the doctrine of the Inner Light, that would be an exaggeration. But it would be very much nearer to the truth. The last Stoics, like Marcus Aurelius, were exactly the people who did believe in the Inner Light. Their dignity, their weariness, their sad external care for others, their incurable internal care for themselves, were all due to the Inner Light, and existed only by that dismal illumination. Notice that Marcus Aurelius insists, as such introspective moralists always do, upon small things done or undone; it is because he has not hate or love enough to make a moral revolution. He gets up early in the morning, just as our own aristocrats living the Simple Life get up early in the morning; because such altruism is much easier than stopping the games of the amphitheatre or giving the English people back their land. Marcus Aurelius is the most intolerable of human types. He is an unselfish egoist. An unselfish egoist is a man who has pride without the excuse of passion. Of all conceivable forms of enlightenment the worst is what these people call the Inner Light. Of all horrible religions the most horrible is the worship of the god within. Any one who knows any body knows how it would work; any one who knows any one from the Higher Thought Centre knows how it does work. That Jones shall worship the god within him turns out ultimately to mean that Jones shall worship Jones. Let Jones worship the sun or moon, anything rather than the Inner Light; let Jones worship cats or crocodiles, if he can find any in his street, but not the god within. Christianity came into the world firstly in order to assert with violence that a man had not only to look inwards, but to look outwards, to behold with astonishment and enthusiasm a divine company and a divine captain. The only fun of being a Christian was that a man was not left alone with the Inner Light, but definitely recognized an outer light, fair as the sun, clear as the moon, terrible as an army with banners.

All the same, it will be as well if Jones does not worship the sun and moon. If he does, there is a tendency for him to imitate them; to say, that because the sun burns insects alive, he may burn insects alive. He thinks that because the sun gives people sun-stroke, he may give his neighbour measles. He thinks that because the moon is said to drive men mad, he may drive his wife mad. This ugly side of mere external optimism had also shown itself in the ancient world. About the time when the Stoic idealism had begun to show the weaknesses of pessimism, the old nature worship of the ancients had begun to show the enormous weaknesses of optimism. Nature worship is natural enough while the society is young, or, in other words, Pantheism is all right as long as it is the worship of Pan. But Nature has another side which experience and sin are not slow in finding out, and it is no flippancy to say of the god Pan that he soon showed the cloven hoof. The only objection to Natural Religion is that somehow it always becomes unnatural. A man loves Nature in the morning for her innocence and amiability, and at nightfall, if he is loving her still, it is for her darkness and her cruelty. He washes at dawn in clear water as did the Wise Man of the Stoics, yet, somehow at the dark end of the day, he is bathing in hot bull's blood, as did Julian the Apostate. The mere pursuit of health always leads to something unhealthy. Physical nature must not be made the direct object of obedience; it must be enjoyed, not worshipped. Stars and mountains must not be taken seriously. If they are, we end where the pagan nature worship ended. Because the earth is kind, we can imitate all her cruelties. Because sexuality is sane, we can all go mad about sexuality. Mere optimism had reached its insane and appropriate termination. The theory that everything was good had become an orgy of everything that was bad.

On the other side our idealist pessimists were represented by the old remnant of the Stoics. Marcus Aurelius and his friends had really given up the idea of any god in the universe and looked only to the god within. They had no hope of any virtue in nature, and hardly any hope of any virtue in society. They had not enough interest in the outer world really to wreck or revolutionise it. They did not love the city enough to set fire to it. Thus the ancient world was exactly in our own desolate dilemma. The only people who really enjoyed this world were busy breaking it up; and the virtuous people did not care enough about them to knock them down. In this dilemma (the same as ours) Christianity suddenly stepped in and offered a singular answer, which the world eventually accepted as THE answer. It was the answer then, and I think it is the answer now.

This answer was like the slash of a sword; it sundered; it did not in any sense sentimentally unite. Briefly, it divided God from the cosmos. That transcendence and distinctness of the deity which some Christians now want to remove from Christianity, was really the only reason why any one wanted to be a Christian. It was the whole point of the Christian answer to the unhappy pessimist and the still more unhappy optimist. As I am here only concerned with their particular problem, I shall indicate only briefly this great metaphysical suggestion. All descriptions of the creating or sustaining principle in things must be metaphorical, because they must be verbal. Thus the pantheist is forced to speak of God in all things as if he were in a box. Thus the evolutionist has, in his very name, the idea of being unrolled like a carpet. All terms, religious and irreligious, are open to this charge. The only question is whether all terms are useless, or whether one can, with such a phrase, cover a distinct IDEA about the origin of things. I think one can, and so evidently does the evolutionist, or he would not talk about evolution. And the root phrase for all Christian theism was this, that God was a creator, as an artist is a creator. A poet is so separate from his poem that he himself speaks of it as a little thing he has "thrown off." Even in giving it forth he has flung it away. This principle that all creation and procreation is a breaking off is at least as consistent through the cosmos as the evolutionary principle that all growth is a branching out. A woman loses a child even in having a child. All creation is separation. Birth is as solemn a parting as death.

It was the prime philosophic principle of Christianity that this divorce in the divine act of making (such as severs the poet from the poem or the mother from the new-born child) was the true description of the act whereby the absolute energy made the world. According to most philosophers, God in making the world enslaved it. According to Christianity, in making it, He set it free. God had written, not so much a poem, but rather a play; a play he had planned as perfect, but which had necessarily been left to human actors and stage-managers, who had since made a great mess of it. I will discuss the truth of this theorem later. Here I have only to point out with what a startling smoothness it passed the dilemma we have discussed in this chapter. In this way at least one could be both happy and indignant without degrading one's self to be either a pessimist or an optimist. On this system one could fight all the forces of existence without deserting the flag of existence. One could be at peace with the universe and yet be at war with the world. St. George could still fight the dragon, however big the monster bulked in the cosmos, though he were bigger than the mighty cities or bigger than the everlasting hills. If he were as big as the world he could yet be killed in the name of the world. St. George had not to consider any obvious odds or proportions in the scale of things, but only the original secret of their design. He can shake his sword at the dragon, even if it is everything; even if the empty heavens over his head are only the huge arch of its open jaws.

And then followed an experience impossible to describe. It was as if I had been blundering about since my birth with two huge and unmanageable machines, of different shapes and without apparent connection—the world and the Christian tradition. I had found this hole in the world: the fact that one must somehow find a way of loving the world without trusting it; somehow one must love the world without being worldly. I found this projecting feature of Christian theology, like a sort of hard spike, the dogmatic insistence that God was personal, and had made a world separate from Himself. The spike of dogma fitted exactly into the hole in the world—it had evidently been meant to go there— and then the strange thing began to happen. When once these two parts of the two machines had come together, one after another, all the other parts fitted and fell in with an eerie exactitude. I could hear bolt after bolt over all the machinery falling into its place with a kind of click of relief. Having got one part right, all the other parts were repeating that rectitude, as clock after clock strikes noon. Instinct after instinct was answered by doctrine after doctrine. Or, to vary the metaphor, I was like one who had advanced into a hostile country to take one high fortress. And when that fort had fallen the whole country surrendered and turned solid behind me. The whole land was lit up, as it were, back to the first fields of my childhood. All those blind fancies of boyhood which in the fourth chapter I have tried in vain to trace on the darkness, became suddenly transparent and sane. I was right when I felt that roses were red by some sort of choice: it was the divine choice. I was right when I felt that I would almost rather say that grass was the wrong colour than say it must by necessity have been that colour: it might verily have been any other. My sense that happiness hung on the crazy thread of a condition did mean something when all was said: it meant the whole doctrine of the Fall. Even those dim and shapeless monsters of notions which I have not been able to describe, much less defend, stepped quietly into their places like colossal caryatides of the creed. The fancy that the cosmos was not vast and void, but small and cosy, had a fulfilled significance now, for anything that is a work of art must be small in the sight of the artist; to God the stars might be only small and dear, like diamonds. And my haunting instinct that somehow good was not merely a tool to be used, but a relic to be guarded, like the goods from Crusoe's ship— even that had been the wild whisper of something originally wise, for, according to Christianity, we were indeed the survivors of a wreck, the crew of a golden ship that had gone down before the beginning of the world.

But the important matter was this, that it entirely reversed the reason for optimism. And the instant the reversal was made it felt like the abrupt ease when a bone is put back in the socket. I had often called myself an optimist, to avoid the too evident blasphemy of pessimism. But all the optimism of the age had been false and disheartening for this reason, that it had always been trying to prove that we fit in to the world. The Christian optimism is based on the fact that we do NOT fit in to the world. I had tried to be happy by telling myself that man is an animal, like any other which sought its meat from God. But now I really was happy, for I had learnt that man is a monstrosity. I had been right in feeling all things as odd, for I myself was at once worse and better than all things. The optimist's pleasure was prosaic, for it dwelt on the naturalness of everything; the Christian pleasure was poetic, for it dwelt on the unnaturalness of everything in the light of the supernatural. The modern philosopher had told me again and again that I was in the right place, and I had still felt depressed even in acquiescence. But I had heard that I was in the WRONG place, and my soul sang for joy, like a bird in spring. The knowledge found out and illuminated forgotten chambers in the dark house of infancy. I knew now why grass had always seemed to me as queer as the green beard of a giant, and why I could feel homesick at home.

Chapter 5
The Paradoxes of Christianity

he real trouble with this world of ours is not that it is an unreasonable world, nor even that it is a reasonable one. The commonest
kind of trouble is that it is nearly reasonable, but not quite. Life is
not an illogicality; yet it is a trap for logicians. It looks just a little
more mathematical and regular than it is; its exactitude is obvious,
but its inexactitude is hidden; its wildness lies in wait. I give one coarse instance of
what I mean. Suppose some mathematical creature from the moon were to reckon
up the human body; he would at once see that the essential thing about it was that
it was duplicate. A man is two men, he on the right exactly resembling him on the
left. Having noted that there was an arm on the right and one on the left, a leg
on the right and one on the left, he might go further and still find on each side
the same number of fingers, the same number of toes, twin eyes, twin ears, twin
nostrils, and even twin lobes of the brain. At last he would take it as a law; and
then, where he found a heart on one side, would deduce that there was another
heart on the other. And just then, where he most felt he was right, he would be
wrong.

It is this silent swerving from accuracy by an inch that is the uncanny element
in everything. It seems a sort of secret treason in the universe. An apple or an
orange is round enough to get itself called round, and yet is not round after all.
The earth itself is shaped like an orange in order to lure some simple astronomer
into calling it a globe. A blade of grass is called after the blade of a sword, because
it comes to a point; but it doesn't. Everywhere in things there is this element of
the quiet and incalculable. It escapes the rationalists, but it never escapes till the
last moment. From the grand curve of our earth it could easily be inferred that
every inch of it was thus curved. It would seem rational that as a man has a brain
on both sides, he should have a heart on both sides. Yet scientific men are still
organizing expeditions to find the North Pole, because they are so fond of flat
country. Scientific men are also still organizing expeditions to find a man's heart;
and when they try to find it, they generally get on the wrong side of him.

Now, actual insight or inspiration is best tested by whether it guesses these
hidden malformations or surprises. If our mathematician from the moon saw the
two arms and the two ears, he might deduce the two shoulder-blades and the
two halves of the brain. But if he guessed that the man's heart was in the right
place, then I should call him something more than a mathematician. Now, this
is exactly the claim which I have since come to propound for Christianity. Not
merely that it deduces logical truths, but that when it suddenly becomes illogical,
it has found, so to speak, an illogical truth. It not only goes right about things,
but it goes wrong (if one may say so) exactly where the things go wrong. Its plan

suits the secret irregularities, and expects the unexpected. It is simple about the simple truth; but it is stubborn about the subtle truth. It will admit that a man has two hands, it will not admit (though all the Modernists wail to it) the obvious deduction that he has two hearts. It is my only purpose in this chapter to point this out; to show that whenever we feel there is something odd in Christian theology, we shall generally find that there is something odd in the truth.

I have alluded to an unmeaning phrase to the effect that such and such a creed cannot be believed in our age. Of course, anything can be believed in any age. But, oddly enough, there really is a sense in which a creed, if it is believed at all, can be believed more fixedly in a complex society than in a simple one. If a man finds Christianity true in Birmingham, he has actually clearer reasons for faith than if he had found it true in Mercia. For the more complicated seems the coincidence, the less it can be a coincidence. If snowflakes fell in the shape, say, of the heart of Midlothian, it might be an accident. But if snowflakes fell in the exact shape of the maze at Hampton Court, I think one might call it a miracle. It is exactly as of such a miracle that I have since come to feel of the philosophy of Christianity. The complication of our modern world proves the truth of the creed more perfectly than any of the plain problems of the ages of faith. It was in Notting Hill and Battersea that I began to see that Christianity was true. This is why the faith has that elaboration of doctrines and details which so much distresses those who admire Christianity without believing in it. When once one believes in a creed, one is proud of its complexity, as scientists are proud of the complexity of science. It shows how rich it is in discoveries. If it is right at all, it is a compliment to say that it's elaborately right. A stick might fit a hole or a stone a hollow by accident. But a key and a lock are both complex. And if a key fits a lock, you know it is the right key.

But this involved accuracy of the thing makes it very difficult to do what I now have to do, to describe this accumulation of truth. It is very hard for a man to defend anything of which he is entirely convinced. It is comparatively easy when he is only partially convinced. He is partially convinced because he has found this or that proof of the thing, and he can expound it. But a man is not really convinced of a philosophic theory when he finds that something proves it. He is only really convinced when he finds that everything proves it. And the more converging reasons he finds pointing to this conviction, the more bewildered he is if asked suddenly to sum them up. Thus, if one asked an ordinary intelligent man, on the spur of the moment, "Why do you prefer civilization to savagery?" he would look wildly round at object after object, and would only be able to answer vaguely, "Why, there is that bookcase ... and the coals in the coal-scuttle ... and pianos ... and policemen." The whole case for civilization is that the case for it is complex. It has done so many things. But that very multiplicity of proof which ought to make reply overwhelming makes reply impossible.

There is, therefore, about all complete conviction a kind of huge helplessness.

The belief is so big that it takes a long time to get it into action. And this hesitation chiefly arises, oddly enough, from an indifference about where one should begin. All roads lead to Rome; which is one reason why many people never get there. In the case of this defence of the Christian conviction I confess that I would as soon begin the argument with one thing as another; I would begin it with a turnip or a taximeter cab. But if I am to be at all careful about making my meaning clear, it will, I think, be wiser to continue the current arguments of the last chapter, which was concerned to urge the first of these mystical coincidences, or rather ratifications. All I had hitherto heard of Christian theology had alienated me from it. I was a pagan at the age of twelve, and a complete agnostic by the age of sixteen; and I cannot understand any one passing the age of seventeen without having asked himself so simple a question. I did, indeed, retain a cloudy reverence for a cosmic deity and a great historical interest in the Founder of Christianity. But I certainly regarded Him as a man; though perhaps I thought that, even in that point, He had an advantage over some of His modern critics. I read the scientific and sceptical literature of my time—all of it, at least, that I could find written in English and lying about; and I read nothing else; I mean I read nothing else on any other note of philosophy. The penny dreadfuls which I also read were indeed in a healthy and heroic tradition of Christianity; but I did not know this at the time. I never read a line of Christian apologetics. I read as little as I can of them now. It was Huxley and Herbert Spencer and Bradlaugh who brought me back to orthodox theology. They sowed in my mind my first wild doubts of doubt. Our grandmothers were quite right when they said that Tom Paine and the free-thinkers unsettled the mind. They do. They unsettled mine horribly. The rationalist made me question whether reason was of any use whatever; and when I had finished Herbert Spencer I had got as far as doubting (for the first time) whether evolution had occurred at all. As I laid down the last of Colonel Ingersoll's atheistic lectures the dreadful thought broke across my mind, "Almost thou persuadest me to be a Christian." I was in a desperate way.

This odd effect of the great agnostics in arousing doubts deeper than their own might be illustrated in many ways. I take only one. As I read and re-read all the non-Christian or anti-Christian accounts of the faith, from Huxley to Bradlaugh, a slow and awful impression grew gradually but graphically upon my mind—the impression that Christianity must be a most extraordinary thing. For not only (as I understood) had Christianity the most flaming vices, but it had apparently a mystical talent for combining vices which seemed inconsistent with each other. It was attacked on all sides and for all contradictory reasons. No sooner had one rationalist demonstrated that it was too far to the east than another demonstrated with equal clearness that it was much too far to the west. No sooner had my indignation died down at its angular and aggressive squareness than I was called up again to notice and condemn its enervating and sensual roundness. In case any reader has not come across the thing I mean, I will give such instances as I remember at random of this self-contradiction in the sceptical attack. I give four or five of them; there are fifty more.

Thus, for instance, I was much moved by the eloquent attack on Christianity as a thing of inhuman gloom; for I thought (and still think) sincere pessimism the unpardonable sin. Insincere pessimism is a social accomplishment, rather agreeable than otherwise; and fortunately nearly all pessimism is insincere. But if Christianity was, as these people said, a thing purely pessimistic and opposed to life, then I was quite prepared to blow up St. Paul's Cathedral. But the extraordinary thing is this. They did prove to me in Chapter I. (to my complete satisfaction) that Christianity was too pessimistic; and then, in Chapter II., they began to prove to me that it was a great deal too optimistic. One accusation against Christianity was that it prevented men, by morbid tears and terrors, from seeking joy and liberty in the bosom of Nature. But another accusation was that it comforted men with a fictitious providence, and put them in a pink-and-white nursery. One great agnostic asked why Nature was not beautiful enough, and why it was hard to be free. Another great agnostic objected that Christian optimism, "the garment of make-believe woven by pious hands," hid from us the fact that Nature was ugly, and that it was impossible to be free. One rationalist had hardly done calling Christianity a nightmare before another began to call it a fool's paradise. This puzzled me; the charges seemed inconsistent. Christianity could not at once be the black mask on a white world, and also the white mask on a black world. The state of the Christian could not be at once so comfortable that he was a coward to cling to it, and so uncomfortable that he was a fool to stand it. If it falsified human vision it must falsify it one way or another; it could not wear both green and rose-coloured spectacles. I rolled on my tongue with a terrible joy, as did all young men of that time, the taunts which Swinburne hurled at the dreariness of the creed—

"Thou hast conquered, O pale Galilaean, the world has grown gray with Thy breath."

But when I read the same poet's accounts of paganism (as in "Atalanta"), I gathered that the world was, if possible, more gray before the Galilean breathed on it than afterwards. The poet maintained, indeed, in the abstract, that life itself was pitch dark. And yet, somehow, Christianity had darkened it. The very man who denounced Christianity for pessimism was himself a pessimist. I thought there must be something wrong. And it did for one wild moment cross my mind that, perhaps, those might not be the very best judges of the relation of religion to happiness who, by their own account, had neither one nor the other.

It must be understood that I did not conclude hastily that the accusations were false or the accusers fools. I simply deduced that Christianity must be something even weirder and wickeder than they made out. A thing might have these two opposite vices; but it must be a rather queer thing if it did. A man might be too fat in one place and too thin in another; but he would be an odd shape. At this point my thoughts were only of the odd shape of the Christian religion; I did not allege any odd shape in the rationalistic mind.

Here is another case of the same kind. I felt that a strong case against Christianity lay in the charge that there is something timid, monkish, and unmanly about all that is called "Christian," especially in its attitude towards resistance and fighting. The great sceptics of the nineteenth century were largely virile. Bradlaugh in an expansive way, Huxley, in a reticent way, were decidedly men. In comparison, it did seem tenable that there was something weak and over patient about Christian counsels. The Gospel paradox about the other cheek, the fact that priests never fought, a hundred things made plausible the accusation that Christianity was an attempt to make a man too like a sheep. I read it and believed it, and if I had read nothing different, I should have gone on believing it. But I read something very different. I turned the next page in my agnostic manual, and my brain turned up-side down. Now I found that I was to hate Christianity not for fighting too little, but for fighting too much. Christianity, it seemed, was the mother of wars. Christianity had deluged the world with blood. I had got thoroughly angry with the Christian, because he never was angry. And now I was told to be angry with him because his anger had been the most huge and horrible thing in human history; because his anger had soaked the earth and smoked to the sun. The very people who reproached Christianity with the meekness and non-resistance of the monasteries were the very people who reproached it also with the violence and valour of the Crusades. It was the fault of poor old Christianity (somehow or other) both that Edward the Confessor did not fight and that Richard Coeur de Leon did. The Quakers (we were told) were the only characteristic Christians; and yet the massacres of Cromwell and Alva were characteristic Christian crimes. What could it all mean? What was this Christianity which always forbade war and always produced wars? What could be the nature of the thing which one could abuse first because it would not fight, and second because it was always fighting? In what world of riddles was born this monstrous murder and this monstrous meekness? The shape of Christianity grew a queerer shape every instant.

I take a third case; the strangest of all, because it involves the one real objection to the faith. The one real objection to the Christian religion is simply that it is one religion. The world is a big place, full of very different kinds of people. Christianity (it may reasonably be said) is one thing confined to one kind of people; it began in Palestine, it has practically stopped with Europe. I was duly impressed with this argument in my youth, and I was much drawn towards the doctrine often preached in Ethical Societies— I mean the doctrine that there is one great unconscious church of all humanity founded on the omnipresence of the human conscience. Creeds, it was said, divided men; but at least morals united them. The soul might seek the strangest and most remote lands and ages and still find essential ethical common sense. It might find Confucius under

Eastern trees, and he would be writing "Thou shalt not steal." It might decipher the darkest hieroglyphic on the most primeval desert, and the meaning when deciphered would be "Little boys should tell the truth." I believed this doctrine of the brotherhood of all men in the possession of a moral sense, and I believe it still—with other things. And I was thoroughly annoyed with Christianity for suggesting (as I supposed) that whole ages and empires of men had utterly escaped this light of justice and reason. But then I found an astonishing thing. I found that the very people who said that mankind was one church from Plato to Emerson were the very people who said that morality had changed altogether, and that what was right in one age was wrong in another. If I asked, say, for an altar, I was told that we needed none, for men our brothers gave us clear oracles and one creed in their universal customs and ideals. But if I mildly pointed out that one of men's universal customs was to have an altar, then my agnostic teachers turned clean round and told me that men had always been in darkness and the superstitions of savages. I found it was their daily taunt against Christianity that it was the light of one people and had left all others to die in the dark. But I also found that it was their special boast for themselves that science and progress were the discovery of one people, and that all other peoples had died in the dark. Their chief insult to Christianity was actually their chief compliment to themselves, and there seemed to be a strange unfairness about all their relative insistence on the two things. When considering some pagan or agnostic, we were to remember that all men had one religion; when considering some mystic or spiritualist, we were only to consider what absurd religions some men had. We could trust the ethics of Epictetus, because ethics had never changed. We must not trust the ethics of Bossuet, because ethics had changed. They changed in two hundred years, but not in two thousand.

This began to be alarming. It looked not so much as if Christianity was bad enough to include any vices, but rather as if any stick was good enough to beat Christianity with. What again could this astonishing thing be like which people were so anxious to contradict, that in doing so they did not mind contradicting themselves? I saw the same thing on every side. I can give no further space to this discussion of it in detail; but lest any one supposes that I have unfairly selected three accidental cases I will run briefly through a few others. Thus, certain sceptics wrote that the great crime of Christianity had been its attack on the family; it had dragged women to the loneliness and contemplation of the cloister, away from their homes and their children. But, then, other sceptics (slightly more advanced) said that the great crime of Christianity was forcing the family and marriage upon us; that it doomed women to the drudgery of their homes and children, and forbade them loneliness and contemplation. The charge was actually reversed. Or, again, certain phrases in the Epistles or the marriage service, were said by the anti-Christians to show contempt for woman's intellect. But I found that the anti-Christians themselves had a contempt for woman's intellect; for it was their great sneer at the Church on the Continent that "only women" went to it. Or again, Christianity was reproached with its naked and hungry habits; with its sackcloth and dried peas. But the next minute Christianity was being reproached with its pomp and its ritualism; its shrines of porphyry and its robes of gold. It was abused for being too plain and for being too coloured. Again Christianity had always been accused of restraining sexuality too much, when Bradlaugh the Malthusian discovered that it restrained it too little. It is often accused in the same breath of prim respectability and of religious extravagance. Between the covers of the same atheistic pamphlet I have found the faith rebuked for its disunion, "One thinks one thing, and one another," and rebuked also for its union, "It is difference of opinion that prevents the world from going to the dogs." In the same conversation a free-thinker, a friend of mine, blamed Christianity for despising Jews, and then despised it himself for being Jewish.

I wished to be quite fair then, and I wish to be quite fair now; and I did not conclude that the attack on Christianity was all wrong. I only concluded that if Christianity was wrong, it was very wrong indeed. Such hostile horrors might be combined in one thing, but that thing must be very strange and solitary. There are men who are misers, and also spendthrifts; but they are rare. There are men sensual and also ascetic; but they are rare. But if this mass of mad contradictions really existed, quakerish and bloodthirsty, too gorgeous and too thread-bare, austere, yet pandering preposterously to the lust of the eye, the enemy of women and their foolish refuge, a solemn pessimist and a silly optimist, if this evil existed, then there was in this evil something quite supreme and unique. For I found in my rationalist teachers no explanation of such exceptional corruption. Christianity (theoretically speaking) was in their eyes only one of the ordinary myths and errors of mortals. THEY gave me no key to this twisted and unnatural badness. Such a paradox of evil rose to the stature of the supernatural. It was, indeed, almost as supernatural as the infallibility of the Pope. An historic institution, which never went right, is really quite as much of a miracle as an institution that cannot go wrong. The only explanation which immediately occurred to my mind was that Christianity did not come from heaven, but from hell. Really, if Jesus of Nazareth was not Christ, He must have been Antichrist.

And then in a quiet hour a strange thought struck me like a still thunderbolt. There had suddenly come into my mind another explanation. Suppose we heard an unknown man spoken of by many men. Suppose we were puzzled to hear that some men said he was too tall and some too short; some objected to his fatness, some lamented his leanness; some thought him too dark, and some too fair. One explanation (as has been already admitted) would be that he might be an odd shape. But there is another explanation. He might be the right shape. Outrageously tall men might feel him to be short. Very short men might feel him to be tall. Old bucks who are growing stout might consider him insufficiently filled out; old beaux who were growing thin might feel that he expanded beyond the narrow lines of elegance. Perhaps Swedes (who have pale hair like tow) called him a dark man, while negroes considered him distinctly blonde. Perhaps (in short) this extraordinary thing is really the ordinary thing; at least the normal thing, the centre. Perhaps, after all, it is Christianity that is sane and all its critics that are mad—in various ways. I tested this idea by asking myself whether there was about any of the accusers anything morbid that might explain the accusation. I was startled to find that this key fitted a lock. For instance, it was certainly odd that the modern world charged Christianity at once with bodily austerity and with artistic pomp. But then it was also odd, very odd, that the modern world itself combined extreme bodily luxury with an extreme absence of artistic pomp. The modern man thought Becket's robes too rich and his meals too poor. But then the modern man was really exceptional in history; no man before ever ate such elaborate dinners in such ugly clothes. The modern man found the church too simple exactly where modern life is too complex; he found the church too gorgeous exactly where modern life is too dingy. The man who disliked the plain fasts and feasts was mad on entrees. The man who disliked vestments wore a pair of preposterous trousers. And surely if there was any insanity involved in the matter at all it was in the trousers, not in the simply falling robe. If there was any insanity at all, it was in the extravagant entrees, not in the bread and wine.

I went over all the cases, and I found the key fitted so far. The fact that Swinburne was irritated at the unhappiness of Christians and yet more irritated at their happiness was easily explained. It was no longer a complication of diseases in Christianity, but a complication of diseases in Swinburne. The restraints of Christians saddened him simply because he was more hedonist than a healthy man should be. The faith of Christians angered him because he was more pessimist than a healthy man should be. In the same way the Malthusians by instinct attacked Christianity; not because there is anything especially anti-Malthusian about Christianity, but because there is something a little anti-human about Malthusianism.

Nevertheless it could not, I felt, be quite true that Christianity was merely sensible and stood in the middle. There was really an element in it of emphasis and even frenzy which had justified the secularists in their superficial criticism. It might be wise, I began more and more to think that it was wise, but it was not merely worldly wise; it was not merely temperate and respectable. Its fierce crusaders and meek saints might balance each other; still, the crusaders were very fierce and the saints were very meek, meek beyond all decency. Now, it was just at this point of the speculation that I remembered my thoughts about the martyr and the suicide. In that matter there had been this combination between two almost insane positions which yet somehow amounted to sanity. This was just such another contradiction; and this I had already found to be true. This was exactly one of the paradoxes in which sceptics found the creed wrong; and in this I had found it right. Madly as Christians might love the martyr or hate the suicide, they never felt these passions more madly than I had felt them long before I dreamed of Christianity. Then the most difficult and interesting part of the mental process opened, and I began to trace this idea darkly through all the enormous thoughts of our theology. The idea was that which I had outlined touching the optimist and the pessimist; that we want not an amalgam or compromise, but both things at the top of their energy; love and wrath both burning. Here I shall only trace it in relation to ethics. But I need not remind the reader that the idea of this combination is indeed central in orthodox theology. For orthodox theology has specially insisted that Christ was not a being apart from God and man, like an elf, nor yet a being half human and half not, like a centaur, but both things at once and both things thoroughly, very man and very God. Now let me trace this notion as I found it.

All sane men can see that sanity is some kind of equilibrium; that one may be mad and eat too much, or mad and eat too little. Some moderns have indeed appeared with vague versions of progress and evolution which seeks to destroy the MESON or balance of Aristotle. They seem to suggest that we are meant to starve progressively, or to go on eating larger and larger breakfasts every morning for ever. But the great truism of the MESON remains for all thinking men, and these people have not upset any balance except their own. But granted that we have all to keep a balance, the real interest comes in with the question of how that balance can be kept. That was the problem which Paganism tried to solve: that was the problem which I think Christianity solved and solved in a very strange way.

Paganism declared that virtue was in a balance; Christianity declared it was in a conflict: the collision of two passions apparently opposite. Of course they were not really inconsistent; but they were such that it was hard to hold simultaneously. Let us follow for a moment the clue of the martyr and the suicide; and take the case of courage. No quality has ever so much addled the brains and tangled the definitions of merely rational sages. Courage is almost a contradiction in terms. It means a strong desire to live taking the form of a readiness to die. "He that will lose his life, the same shall save it," is not a piece of mysticism for saints and heroes. It is a piece of everyday advice for sailors or mountaineers. It might be printed in an Alpine guide or a drill book. This paradox is the whole principle of courage; even of quite earthly or quite brutal courage. A man cut off by the sea may save his life if he will risk it on the precipice.

He can only get away from death by continually stepping within an inch of it. A soldier surrounded by enemies, if he is to cut his way out, needs to combine a strong desire for living with a strange carelessness about dying. He must not merely cling to life, for then he will be a coward, and will not escape. He must not merely wait for death, for then he will be a suicide, and will not escape. He must seek his life in a spirit of furious indifference to it; he must desire life like water and yet drink death like wine. No philosopher, I fancy, has ever expressed this romantic riddle with adequate lucidity, and I certainly have not done so. But Christianity has done more: it has marked the limits of it in the awful graves of the suicide and the hero, showing the distance between him who dies for the sake of living and him who dies for the sake of dying. And it has held up ever since above the European lances the banner of the mystery of chivalry: the Christian courage, which is a disdain of death; not the Chinese courage, which is a disdain of life.

And now I began to find that this duplex passion was the Christian key to ethics everywhere. Everywhere the creed made a moderation out of the still crash of two impetuous emotions. Take, for instance, the matter of modesty, of the balance between mere pride and mere prostration. The average pagan, like the average agnostic, would merely say that he was content with himself, but not insolently self-satisfied, that there were many better and many worse, that his deserts were limited, but he would see that he got them. In short, he would walk with his head in the air; but not necessarily with his nose in the air. This is a manly and rational position, but it is open to the objection we noted against the compromise between optimism and pessimism—the "resignation" of Matthew Arnold. Being a mixture of two things, it is a dilution of two things; neither is present in its full strength or contributes its full colour. This proper pride does not lift the heart like the tongue of trumpets; you cannot go clad in crimson and gold for this. On the other hand, this mild rationalist modesty does not cleanse the soul with fire and make it clear like crystal; it does not (like a strict and searching humility) make a man as a little child, who can sit at the feet of the grass. It does not make him look up and see marvels; for Alice must grow small if she is to be Alice in Wonderland. Thus it loses both the poetry of being proud and the poetry of being humble. Christianity sought by this same strange expedient to save both of them.

It separated the two ideas and then exaggerated them both. In one way Man was to be haughtier than he had ever been before; in another way he was to be humbler than he had ever been before. In so far as I am Man I am the chief of creatures. In so far as I am a man I am the chief of sinners. All humility that had meant pessimism, that had meant man taking a vague or mean view of his whole destiny—all that was to go. We were to hear no more the wail of Ecclesiastes that humanity had no pre-eminence over the brute, or the awful cry of Homer that man was only the saddest of all the beasts of the field. Man was a statue of God walking about the garden. Man had pre-eminence over all the brutes; man was only sad because he was not a beast, but a broken god. The Greek had spoken of men creeping on the earth, as if clinging to it. Now Man was to tread on the earth as if to subdue it. Christianity thus held a thought of the dignity of man that could only be expressed in crowns rayed like the sun and fans of peacock plumage. Yet at the same time it could hold a thought about the abject smallness of man that could only be expressed in fasting and fantastic submission, in the gray ashes of St. Dominic and the white snows of St. Bernard. When one came to think of ONE'S SELF, there was vista and void enough for any amount of bleak abnegation and bitter truth. There the realistic gentleman could let himself go—as long as he let himself go at himself. There was an open playground for the happy pessimist. Let him say anything against himself short of blaspheming the original aim of his being; let him call himself a fool and even a damned fool (though that is Calvinistic); but he must not say that fools are not worth saving. He must not say that a man, QUA man, can be valueless. Here, again in short, Christianity got over the difficulty of combining furious opposites, by keeping them both, and keeping them both furious. The Church was positive on both points. One can hardly think too little of one's self. One can hardly think too much of one's soul.

Take another case: the complicated question of charity, which some highly uncharitable idealists seem to think quite easy. Charity is a paradox, like modesty and courage. Stated baldly, charity certainly means one of two things—pardoning unpardonable acts, or loving unlovable people. But if we ask ourselves (as we did in the case of pride) what a sensible pagan would feel about such a subject, we shall probably be beginning at the bottom of it. A sensible pagan would say that there were some people one could forgive, and some one couldn't: a slave who stole wine could be laughed at; a slave who betrayed his benefactor could be killed, and cursed even after he was killed. In so far as the act was pardonable, the man was pardonable. That again is rational, and even refreshing; but it is a dilution. It leaves no place for a pure horror of injustice, such as that which is a great beauty in the innocent. And it leaves no place for a mere tenderness for men as men, such as is the whole fascination of the charitable. Christianity came in here as before. It came in startlingly with a sword, and clove one thing from another. It divided the crime from the criminal. The criminal we must forgive unto seventy times seven. The crime we must not forgive at all. It was not enough that slaves who stole wine inspired partly anger and partly kindness. We must be much more angry with theft than before, and yet much kinder to thieves than before. There was room for wrath and love to run wild. And the more I considered Christianity, the more I found that while it had established a rule and order, the chief aim of that order was to give room for good things to run wild.

Mental and emotional liberty are not so simple as they look. Really they require almost as careful a balance of laws and conditions as do social and political liberty. The ordinary aesthetic anarchist who sets out to feel everything freely gets knotted at last in a paradox that prevents him feeling at all. He breaks away from home limits to follow poetry. But in ceasing to feel home limits he has ceased to feel the "Odyssey." He is free from national prejudices and outside patriotism. But being outside patriotism he is outside "Henry V." Such a literary man is simply outside all literature: he is more of a prisoner than any bigot. For if there is a wall between you and the world, it makes little difference whether you describe yourself as locked in or as locked out. What we want is not the universality that is outside all normal sentiments; we want the universality that is inside all normal sentiments. It is all the difference between being free from them, as a man is free from a prison, and being free of them as a man is free of a city. I am free from Windsor Castle (that is, I am not forcibly detained there), but I am by no means free of that building. How can man be approximately free of fine emotions, able to swing them in a clear space without breakage or wrong? THIS was the achievement of this Christian paradox of the parallel passions. Granted the primary dogma of the war between divine and diabolic, the revolt and ruin of the world, their optimism and pessimism, as pure poetry, could be loosened like cataracts.

St. Francis, in praising all good, could be a more shouting optimist than Walt Whitman. St. Jerome, in denouncing all evil, could paint the world blacker than Schopenhauer. Both passions were free because both were kept in their place. The optimist could pour out all the praise he liked on the gay music of the march, the golden trumpets, and the purple banners going into battle. But he must not call the fight needless. The pessimist might draw as darkly as he chose the sickening marches or the sanguine wounds. But he must not call the fight hopeless. So it was with all the other moral problems, with pride, with protest, and with compassion. By defining its main doctrine, the Church not only kept seemingly inconsistent things side by side, but, what was more, allowed them to break out in a sort of artistic violence otherwise possible only to anarchists. Meekness grew more dramatic than madness. Historic Christianity rose into a high and strange COUP DE THEATRE of morality—things that are to virtue what the crimes of Nero are to vice. The spirits of indignation and of charity took terrible and attractive forms, ranging from that monkish fierceness that scourged like a dog the first and greatest of the Plantagenets, to the sublime pity of St. Catherine, who, in the official shambles, kissed the bloody head of the criminal. Poetry could be acted as well as composed. This heroic and monumental manner in ethics has entirely vanished with supernatural religion. They, being humble, could parade themselves: but we are too proud to be prominent. Our ethical teachers write reasonably for prison reform; but we are not likely to see Mr. Cadbury, or any eminent philanthropist, go into Reading Gaol and embrace the strangled corpse before it is cast into the quicklime. Our ethical teachers write mildly against the power of millionaires; but we are not likely to see Mr. Rockefeller, or any modern tyrant, publicly whipped in Westminster Abbey.

Thus, the double charges of the secularists, though throwing nothing but darkness and confusion on themselves, throw a real light on the faith. It is true that the historic Church has at once emphasised celibacy and emphasised the family; has at once (if one may put it so) been fiercely for having children and fiercely for not having children. It has kept them side by side like two strong colours, red and white, like the red and white upon the shield of St. George. It has always had a healthy hatred of pink. It hates that combination of two colours which is the feeble expedient of the philosophers. It hates that evolution of black into white which is tantamount to a dirty gray. In fact, the whole theory of the Church on virginity might be symbolized in the statement that white is a colour: not merely the absence of a colour. All that I am urging here can be expressed by saying that Christianity sought in most of these cases to keep two colours coexistent but pure. It is not a mixture like russet or purple; it is rather like a shot silk, for a shot silk is always at right angles, and is in the pattern of the cross.

So it is also, of course, with the contradictory charges of the anti-Christians about submission and slaughter. It IS true that the Church told some men to fight and others not to fight; and it IS true that those who fought were like thunderbolts and those who did not fight were like statues. All this simply means that the Church preferred to use its Supermen and to use its Tolstoyans. There must be SOME good in the life of battle, for so many good men have enjoyed being soldiers. There must be SOME good in the idea of non-resistance, for so many good men seem to enjoy being Quakers. All that the Church did (so far as that goes) was to prevent either of these good things from ousting the other. They existed side by side. The Tolstoyans, having all the scruples of monks, simply became monks. The Quakers became a club instead of becoming a sect. Monks said all that Tolstoy says; they poured out lucid lamentations about the cruelty of battles and the vanity of revenge. But the Tolstoyans are not quite right enough to run the whole world; and in the ages of faith they were not allowed to run it. The world did not lose the last charge of Sir James Douglas or the banner of Joan the Maid. And sometimes this pure gentleness and this pure fierceness met and justified their juncture; the paradox of all the prophets was fulfilled, and, in the soul of St. Louis, the lion lay down with the lamb. But remember that this text is too lightly interpreted. It is constantly assured, especially in our Tolstoyan tendencies, that when the lion lies down with the lamb the lion becomes lamb-like. But that is brutal annexation and imperialism on the part of the lamb. That is simply the lamb absorbing the lion instead of the lion eating the lamb. The real problem is—Can the lion lie down with the lamb and still retain his royal ferocity? THAT is the problem the Church attempted; THAT is the miracle she achieved.

This is what I have called guessing the hidden eccentricities of life. This is knowing that a man's heart is to the left and not in the middle. This is knowing not only that the earth is round, but knowing exactly where it is flat. Christian doctrine detected the oddities of life. It not only discovered the law, but it foresaw the exceptions. Those underrate Christianity who say that it discovered mercy; any one might discover mercy. In fact every one did. But to discover a plan for being merciful and also severe— THAT was to anticipate a strange need of human nature. For no one wants to be forgiven for a big sin as if it were a little one. Any one might say that we should be neither quite miserable nor quite happy. But to find out how far one MAY be quite miserable without making it impossible to be quite happy—that was a discovery in psychology. Any one might say, "Neither swagger nor grovel"; and it would have been a limit. But to say, "Here you can swagger and there you can grovel"—that was an emancipation.

This was the big fact about Christian ethics; the discovery of the new balance. Paganism had been like a pillar of marble, upright because proportioned with symmetry. Christianity was like a huge and ragged and romantic rock, which, though it sways on its pedestal at a touch, yet, because its exaggerated excrescences exactly balance each other, is enthroned there for a thousand years. In a Gothic cathedral the columns were all different, but they were all necessary. Every support seemed an accidental and fantastic support; every buttress was a flying buttress. So in Christendom apparent accidents balanced. Becket wore a hair shirt under his gold and crimson, and there is much to be said for the combination; for Becket got the benefit of the hair shirt while the people in the street got the benefit of the crimson and gold. It is at least better than the manner of the modern millionaire, who has the black and the drab outwardly for others, and the gold next his heart. But the balance was not always in one man's body as in Becket's; the balance was often distributed over the whole body of Christendom. Because a man prayed and fasted on the Northern snows, flowers could be flung at his festival in the Southern cities; and because fanatics drank water on the sands of Syria, men could still drink cider in the orchards of England. This is what makes Christendom at once so much more perplexing and so much more interesting than the Pagan empire; just as Amiens Cathedral is not better but more interesting than the Parthenon. If any one wants a modern proof of all this, let him consider the curious fact that, under Christianity, Europe (while remaining a unity) has broken up into individual nations. Patriotism is a perfect example of this deliberate balancing of one emphasis against another emphasis. The instinct of the Pagan empire would have said, "You shall all be Roman citizens, and grow alike; let the German grow less slow and reverent; the Frenchmen less experimental and swift." But the instinct of Christian Europe says, "Let the German remain slow and reverent, that the Frenchman may the more safely be swift and experimental. We will make an equipoise out of these excesses. The absurdity called Germany shall correct the insanity called France."

Last and most important, it is exactly this which explains what is so inexplicable to all the modern critics of the history of Christianity. I mean the monstrous wars about small points of theology, the earthquakes of emotion about a gesture or a word. It was only a matter of an inch; but an inch is everything when you are balancing. The Church could not afford to swerve a hair's breadth on some things if she was to continue her great and daring experiment of the irregular equilibrium. Once let one idea become less powerful and some other idea would become too powerful. It was no flock of sheep the Christian shepherd was leading, but a herd of bulls and tigers, of terrible ideals and devouring doctrines, each one of them strong enough to turn to a false religion and lay waste the world. Remember that the Church went in specifically for dangerous ideas; she was a lion tamer.

The idea of birth through a Holy Spirit, of the death of a divine being, of the forgiveness of sins, or the fulfilment of prophecies, are ideas which, any one can see, need but a touch to turn them into something blasphemous or ferocious. The smallest link was let drop by the artificers of the Mediterranean, and the lion of ancestral pessimism burst his chain in the forgotten forests of the north. Of these theological equalisations I have to speak afterwards. Here it is enough to notice that if some small mistake were made in doctrine, huge blunders might be made in human happiness. A sentence phrased wrong about the nature of symbolism would have broken all the best statues in Europe. A slip in the definitions might stop all the dances; might wither all the Christmas trees or break all the Easter eggs. Doctrines had to be defined within strict limits, even in order that man might enjoy general human liberties. The Church had to be careful, if only that the world might be careless.

This is the thrilling romance of Orthodoxy. People have fallen into a foolish habit of speaking of orthodoxy as something heavy, humdrum, and safe. There never was anything so perilous or so exciting as orthodoxy. It was sanity: and to be sane is more dramatic than to be mad. It was the equilibrium of a man behind madly rushing horses, seeming to stoop this way and to sway that, yet in every attitude having the grace of statuary and the accuracy of arithmetic. The Church in its early days went fierce and fast with any warhorse; yet it is utterly unhistoric to say that she merely went mad along one idea, like a vulgar fanaticism. She swerved to left and right, so exactly as to avoid enormous obstacles. She left on one hand the huge bulk of Arianism, buttressed by all the worldly powers to make Christianity too worldly. The next instant she was swerving to avoid an orientalism, which would have made it too unworldly. The orthodox Church never took the tame course or accepted the conventions; the orthodox Church was never respectable. It would have been easier to have accepted the earthly power of the Arians. It would have been easy, in the Calvinistic seventeenth century, to fall into the bottomless pit of predestination. It is easy to be a madman: it is easy to be a heretic. It is always easy to let the age have its head; the difficult thing is to keep one's own. It is always easy to be a modernist; as it is easy to be a snob. To have fallen into any of those open traps of error and exaggeration which fashion after fashion and sect after sect set along the historic path of Christendom—that would indeed have been simple. It is always simple to fall; there are an infinity of angles at which one falls, only one at which one stands. To have fallen into any one of the fads from Gnosticism to Christian Science would indeed have been obvious and tame. But to have avoided them all has been one whirling adventure; and in my vision the heavenly chariot flies thundering through the ages, the dull heresies sprawling and prostrate, the wild truth reeling but erect.

Chapter 6
The Eternal Revolution

he following propositions have been urged: First, that some faith in our life is required even to improve it; second, that some dissatisfaction with things as they are is necessary even in order to be satisfied; third, that to have this necessary content and necessary discontent it is not sufficient to have the obvious equilibrium of the Stoic. For mere resignation has neither the gigantic levity of pleasure nor the superb intolerance of pain. There is a vital objection to the advice merely to grin and bear it. The objection is that if you merely bear it, you do not grin. Greek heroes do not grin: but gargoyles do—because they are Christian. And when a Christian is pleased, he is (in the most exact sense) frightfully pleased; his pleasure is frightful. Christ prophesied the whole of Gothic architecture in that hour when nervous and respectable people (such people as now object to barrel organs) objected to the shouting of the gutter-snipes of Jerusalem. He said, "If these were silent, the very stones would cry out." Under the impulse of His spirit arose like a clamorous chorus the facades of the mediaeval cathedrals, thronged with shouting faces and open mouths. The prophecy has fulfilled itself: the very stones cry out.

If these things be conceded, though only for argument, we may take up where we left it the thread of the thought of the natural man, called by the Scotch (with regrettable familiarity), "The Old Man." We can ask the next question so obviously in front of us. Some satisfaction is needed even to make things better. But what do we mean by making things better? Most modern talk on this matter is a mere argument in a circle—that circle which we have already made the symbol of madness and of mere rationalism. Evolution is only good if it produces good; good is only good if it helps evolution. The elephant stands on the tortoise, and the tortoise on the elephant.

Obviously, it will not do to take our ideal from the principle in nature; for the simple reason that (except for some human or divine theory), there is no principle in nature. For instance, the cheap anti-democrat of to-day will tell you solemnly that there is no equality in nature. He is right, but he does not see the logical addendum. There is no equality in nature; also there is no inequality in nature. Inequality, as much as equality, implies a standard of value. To read aristocracy into the anarchy of animals is just as sentimental as to read democracy into it. Both aristocracy and democracy are human ideals: the one saying that all men are valuable, the other that some men are more valuable. But nature does not say that cats are more valuable than mice; nature makes no remark on the subject. She does not even say that the cat is enviable or the mouse pitiable. We think the cat superior because we have (or most of us have) a particular philosophy to the effect that life is better than death. But if the mouse were a German pessimist mouse, he might not think that the cat had beaten him at all. He might think he had beaten the cat by getting to the grave first. Or he might feel that he had actually inflicted frightful punishment on the cat by keeping him alive. Just as a microbe might feel proud of spreading a pestilence, so the pessimistic mouse might exult to think that he was renewing in the cat the torture of conscious existence. It all depends on the philosophy of the mouse. You cannot even say that there is victory or superiority in nature unless you have some doctrine about what things are superior. You cannot even say that the cat scores unless there is a system of scoring. You cannot even say that the cat gets the best of it unless there is some best to be got.

We cannot, then, get the ideal itself from nature, and as we follow here the first and natural speculation, we will leave out (for the present) the idea of getting it from God. We must have our own vision. But the attempts of most moderns to express it are highly vague.

Some fall back simply on the clock: they talk as if mere passage through time brought some superiority; so that even a man of the first mental calibre carelessly uses the phrase that human morality is never up to date. How can anything be up to date?— a date has no character. How can one say that Christmas celebrations are not suitable to the twenty-fifth of a month? What the writer meant, of course, was that the majority is behind his favourite minority—or in front of it. Other vague modern people take refuge in material metaphors; in fact, this is the chief mark of vague modern people. Not daring to define their doctrine of what is good, they use physical figures of speech without stint or shame, and, what is worst of all, seem to think these cheap analogies are exquisitely spiritual and superior to the old morality. Thus they think it intellectual to talk about things being "high." It is at least the reverse of intellectual; it is a mere phrase from a steeple or a weathercock. "Tommy was a good boy" is a pure philosophical statement, worthy of Plato or Aquinas. "Tommy lived the higher life" is a gross metaphor from a ten-foot rule.

This, incidentally, is almost the whole weakness of Nietzsche, whom some are representing as a bold and strong thinker. No one will deny that he was a poetical and suggestive thinker; but he was quite the reverse of strong. He was not at all bold. He never put his own meaning before himself in bald abstract words: as did Aristotle and Calvin, and even Karl Marx, the hard, fearless men of thought. Nietzsche always escaped a question by a physical metaphor, like a cheery minor poet. He said, "beyond good and evil," because he had not the courage to say, "more good than good and evil," or, "more evil than good and evil." Had he faced his thought without metaphors, he would have seen that it was nonsense. So, when he describes his hero, he does not dare to say, "the purer man," or "the happier man," or "the sadder man," for all these are ideas; and ideas are alarming. He says "the upper man," or "over man," a physical metaphor from acrobats or alpine climbers. Nietzsche is truly a very timid thinker. He does not really know in the least what sort of man he wants evolution to produce. And if he does not know, certainly the ordinary evolutionists, who talk about things being "higher," do not know either.

Then again, some people fall back on sheer submission and sitting still. Nature is going to do something some day; nobody knows what, and nobody knows when. We have no reason for acting, and no reason for not acting. If anything happens it is right: if anything is prevented it was wrong. Again, some people try to anticipate nature by doing something, by doing anything. Because we may possibly grow wings they cut off their legs. Yet nature may be trying to make them centipedes for all they know.

Lastly, there is a fourth class of people who take whatever it is that they happen to want, and say that that is the ultimate aim of evolution. And these are the only sensible people. This is the only really healthy way with the word evolution, to work for what you want, and to call THAT evolution. The only intelligible sense that progress or advance can have among men, is that we have a definite vision, and that we wish to make the whole world like that vision. If you like to put it so, the essence of the doctrine is that what we have around us is the mere method and preparation for something that we have to create. This is not a world, but rather the material for a world. God has given us not so much the colours of a picture as the colours of a palette. But he has also given us a subject, a model, a fixed vision. We must be clear about what we want to paint. This adds a further principle to our previous list of principles. We have said we must be fond of this world, even in order to change it. We now add that we must be fond of another world (real or imaginary) in order to have something to change it to.

We need not debate about the mere words evolution or progress: personally I prefer to call it reform. For reform implies form. It implies that we are trying to shape the world in a particular image; to make it something that we see already in our minds. Evolution is a metaphor from mere automatic unrolling. Progress is a metaphor from merely walking along a road—very likely the wrong road. But reform is a metaphor for reasonable and determined men: it means that we see a certain thing out of shape and we mean to put it into shape. And we know what shape.

Now here comes in the whole collapse and huge blunder of our age. We have mixed up two different things, two opposite things. Progress should mean that we are always changing the world to suit the vision. Progress does mean (just now) that we are always changing the vision. It should mean that we are slow but sure in bringing justice and mercy among men: it does mean that we are very swift in doubting the desirability of justice and mercy: a wild page from any Prussian sophist makes men doubt it. Progress should mean that we are always walking towards the New Jerusalem. It does mean that the New Jerusalem is always walking away from us. We are not altering the real to suit the ideal. We are altering the ideal: it is easier.

Silly examples are always simpler; let us suppose a man wanted a particular kind of world; say, a blue world. He would have no cause to complain of the slightness or swiftness of his task; he might toil for a long time at the transformation; he could work away (in every sense) until all was blue. He could have heroic adventures; the putting of the last touches to a blue tiger. He could have fairy dreams; the dawn of a blue moon. But if he worked hard, that high-minded reformer would certainly (from his own point of view) leave the world better and bluer than he found it. If he altered a blade of grass to his favourite colour every day, he would get on slowly. But if he altered his favourite colour every day, he would not get on at all. If, after reading a fresh philosopher, he started to paint everything red or yellow, his work would be thrown away: there would be nothing to show except a few blue tigers walking about, specimens of his early bad manner. This is exactly the position of the average modern thinker. It will be said that this is avowedly a preposterous example. But it is literally the fact of recent history. The great and grave changes in our political civilization all belonged to the early nineteenth century, not to the later. They belonged to the black and white epoch when men believed fixedly in Toryism, in Protestantism, in Calvinism, in Reform, and not unfrequently in Revolution. And whatever each man believed in he hammered at steadily, without scepticism: and there was a time when the Established Church might have fallen, and the House of Lords nearly fell. It was because Radicals were wise enough to be constant and consistent; it was because Radicals were wise enough to be Conservative. But in the existing atmosphere there is not enough time and tradition in Radicalism to pull anything down. There is a great deal of truth in Lord Hugh Cecil's suggestion (made in a fine speech) that the era of change is over, and that ours is an era of conservation and repose. But probably it would pain Lord Hugh Cecil if he realized (what is certainly the case) that ours is only an age of conservation because it is an age of complete unbelief. Let beliefs fade fast and frequently, if you wish institutions to remain the same. The more the life of the mind is unhinged, the more the machinery of matter will be left to itself. The net result of all our political suggestions, Collectivism, Tolstoyanism, Neo-Feudalism, Communism, Anarchy, Scientific Bureaucracy—the plain fruit of all of them is that the Monarchy and the House of Lords will remain. The net result of all the new religions will be that the Church of England will not (for heaven knows how long) be disestablished. It was Karl Marx, Nietzsche, Tolstoy, Cunninghame Grahame, Bernard Shaw and Auberon Herbert, who between them, with bowed gigantic backs, bore up the throne of the Archbishop of Canterbury.

We may say broadly that free thought is the best of all the safeguards against freedom. Managed in a modern style the emancipation of the slave's mind is the best way of preventing the emancipation of the slave. Teach him to worry about whether he wants to be free, and he will not free himself. Again, it may be said that this instance is remote or extreme. But, again, it is exactly true of the men in the streets around us. It is true that the negro slave, being a debased barbarian, will probably have either a human affection of loyalty, or a human affection for liberty. But the man we see every day—the worker in Mr. Gradgrind's factory, the little clerk in Mr. Gradgrind's office—he is too mentally worried to believe in freedom. He is kept quiet with revolutionary literature. He is calmed and kept in his place by a constant succession of wild philosophies. He is a Marxian one day, a Nietzscheite the next day, a Superman (probably) the next day; and a slave every day. The only thing that remains after all the philosophies is the factory. The only man who gains by all the philosophies is Gradgrind. It would be worth his while to keep his commercial helotry supplied with sceptical literature. And now I come to think of it, of course, Gradgrind is famous for giving libraries. He shows his sense. All modern books are on his side. As long as the vision of heaven is always changing, the vision of earth will be exactly the same. No ideal will remain long enough to be realized, or even partly realized. The modern young man will never change his environment; for he will always change his mind.

This, therefore, is our first requirement about the ideal towards which progress is directed; it must be fixed. Whistler used to make many rapid studies of a sitter; it did not matter if he tore up twenty portraits. But it would matter if he looked up twenty times, and each time saw a new person sitting placidly for his portrait. So it does not matter (comparatively speaking) how often humanity fails to imitate its ideal; for then all its old failures are fruitful. But it does frightfully matter how often humanity changes its ideal; for then all its old failures are fruitless. The question therefore becomes this: How can we keep the artist discontented with his pictures while preventing him from being vitally discontented with his art? How can we make a man always dissatisfied with his work, yet always satisfied with working? How can we make sure that the portrait painter will throw the portrait out of window instead of taking the natural and more human course of throwing the sitter out of window?

A strict rule is not only necessary for ruling; it is also necessary for rebelling. This fixed and familiar ideal is necessary to any sort of revolution. Man will sometimes act slowly upon new ideas; but he will only act swiftly upon old ideas. If I am merely to float or fade or evolve, it may be towards something anarchic; but if I am to riot, it must be for something respectable. This is the whole weakness of certain schools of progress and moral evolution. They suggest that there has been a slow movement towards morality, with an imperceptible ethical change in every year or at every instant. There is only one great disadvantage in this theory. It talks of a slow movement towards justice; but it does not permit a swift movement. A man is not allowed to leap up and declare a certain state of things to be intrinsically intolerable. To make the matter clear, it is better to take a specific example. Certain of the idealistic vegetarians, such as Mr. Salt, say that the time has now come for eating no meat; by implication they assume that at one time it was right to eat meat, and they suggest (in words that could be quoted) that some day it may be wrong to eat milk and eggs. I do not discuss here the question of what is justice to animals. I only say that whatever is justice ought, under given conditions, to be prompt justice. If an animal is wronged, we ought to be able to rush to his rescue. But how can we rush if we are, perhaps, in advance of our time? How can we rush to catch a train which may not arrive for a few centuries? How can I denounce a man for skinning cats, if he is only now what I may possibly become in drinking a glass of milk? A splendid and insane Russian sect ran about taking all the cattle out of all the carts. How can I pluck up courage to take the horse out of my hansom-cab, when I do not know whether my evolutionary watch is only a little fast or the cabman's a little slow? Suppose I say to a sweater, "Slavery suited one stage of evolution." And suppose he answers, "And sweating suits this stage of evolution." How can I answer if there is no eternal test? If sweaters can be behind the current morality, why should not philanthropists be in front of it? What on earth is the current morality, except in its literal sense—the morality that is always running away?

Thus we may say that a permanent ideal is as necessary to the innovator as to the conservative; it is necessary whether we wish the king's orders to be promptly executed or whether we only wish the king to be promptly executed. The guillotine has many sins, but to do it justice there is nothing evolutionary about it. The favourite evolutionary argument finds its best answer in the axe. The Evolutionist says, "Where do you draw the line?" the Revolutionist answers, "I draw it HERE: exactly between your head and body." There must at any given moment be an abstract right and wrong if any blow is to be struck; there must be something eternal if there is to be anything sudden. Therefore for all intelligible human purposes, for altering things or for keeping things as they are, for founding a system for ever, as in China, or for altering it every month as in the early French Revolution, it is equally necessary that the vision should be a fixed vision. This is our first requirement.

When I had written this down, I felt once again the presence of something else in the discussion: as a man hears a church bell above the sound of the street. Something seemed to be saying, "My ideal at least is fixed; for it was fixed before the foundations of the world. My vision of perfection assuredly cannot be altered; for it is called Eden. You may alter the place to which you are going; but you cannot alter the place from which you have come. To the orthodox there must always be a case for revolution; for in the hearts of men God has been put under the feet of Satan. In the upper world hell once rebelled against heaven. But in this world heaven is rebelling against hell. For the orthodox there can always be a revolution; for a revolution is a restoration. At any instant you may strike a blow for the perfection which no man has seen since Adam. No unchanging custom, no changing evolution can make the original good any thing but good. Man may have had concubines as long as cows have had horns: still they are not a part of him if they are sinful. Men may have been under oppression ever since fish were under water; still they ought not to be, if oppression is sinful. The chain may seem as natural to the slave, or the paint to the harlot, as does the plume to the bird or the burrow to the fox; still they are not, if they are sinful. I lift my prehistoric legend to defy all your history. Your vision is not merely a fixture: it is a fact." I paused to note the new coincidence of Christianity: but I passed on.

I passed on to the next necessity of any ideal of progress. Some people (as we have said) seem to believe in an automatic and impersonal progress in the nature of things. But it is clear that no political activity can be encouraged by saying that progress is natural and inevitable; that is not a reason for being active, but rather a reason for being lazy. If we are bound to improve, we need not trouble to improve. The pure doctrine of progress is the best of all reasons for not being a progressive. But it is to none of these obvious comments that I wish primarily to call attention.

The only arresting point is this: that if we suppose improvement to be natural, it must be fairly simple. The world might conceivably be working towards one consummation, but hardly towards any particular arrangement of many qualities. To take our original simile: Nature by herself may be growing more blue; that is, a process so simple that it might be impersonal. But Nature cannot be making a careful picture made of many picked colours, unless Nature is personal. If the end of the world were mere darkness or mere light it might come as slowly and inevitably as dusk or dawn. But if the end of the world is to be a piece of elaborate and artistic chiaroscuro, then there must be design in it, either human or divine. The world, through mere time, might grow black like an old picture, or white like an old coat; but if it is turned into a particular piece of black and white art— then there is an artist.

If the distinction be not evident, I give an ordinary instance. We constantly hear a particularly cosmic creed from the modern humanitarians;

I use the word humanitarian in the ordinary sense, as meaning one who upholds the claims of all creatures against those of humanity. They suggest that through the ages we have been growing more and more humane, that is to say, that one after another, groups or sections of beings, slaves, children, women, cows, or what not, have been gradually admitted to mercy or to justice. They say that we once thought it right to eat men (we didn't); but I am not here concerned with their history, which is highly unhistorical. As a fact, anthropophagy is certainly a decadent thing, not a primitive one. It is much more likely that modern men will eat human flesh out of affectation than that primitive man ever ate it out of ignorance. I am here only following the outlines of their argument, which consists in maintaining that man has been progressively more lenient, first to citizens, then to slaves, then to animals, and then (presumably) to plants. I think it wrong to sit on a man. Soon, I shall think it wrong to sit on a horse. Eventually (I suppose) I shall think it wrong to sit on a chair. That is the drive of the argument. And for this argument it can be said that it is possible to talk of it in terms of evolution or inevitable progress. A perpetual tendency to touch fewer and fewer things might—one feels, be a mere brute unconscious tendency, like that of a species to produce fewer and fewer children. This drift may be really evolutionary, because it is stupid.

Darwinism can be used to back up two mad moralities, but it cannot be used to back up a single sane one. The kinship and competition of all living creatures can be used as a reason for being insanely cruel or insanely sentimental; but not for a healthy love of animals. On the evolutionary basis you may be inhumane, or you may be absurdly humane; but you cannot be human. That you and a tiger are one may be a reason for being tender to a tiger. Or it may be a reason for being as cruel as the tiger. It is one way to train the tiger to imitate you, it is a shorter way to imitate the tiger. But in neither case does evolution tell you how to treat a tiger reasonably, that is, to admire his stripes while avoiding his claws.

If you want to treat a tiger reasonably, you must go back to the garden of Eden. For the obstinate reminder continued to recur: only the supernatural has taken a sane view of Nature. The essence of all pantheism, evolutionism, and modern cosmic religion is really in this proposition: that Nature is our mother. Unfortunately, if you regard Nature as a mother, you discover that she is a step-mother. The main point of Christianity was this: that Nature is not our mother: Nature is our sister. We can be proud of her beauty, since we have the same father; but she has no authority over us; we have to admire, but not to imitate. This gives to the typically Christian pleasure in this earth a strange touch of lightness that is almost frivolity. Nature was a solemn mother to the worshippers of Isis and Cybele. Nature was a solemn mother to Wordsworth or to Emerson. But Nature is not solemn to Francis of Assisi or to George Herbert. To St. Francis, Nature is a sister, and even a younger sister: a little, dancing sister, to be laughed at as well as loved.

This, however, is hardly our main point at present; I have admitted it only in order to show how constantly, and as it were accidentally, the key would fit the smallest doors. Our main point is here, that if there be a mere trend of impersonal improvement in Nature, it must presumably be a simple trend towards some simple triumph. One can imagine that some automatic tendency in biology might work for giving us longer and longer noses. But the question is, do we want to have longer and longer noses? I fancy not; I believe that we most of us want to say to our noses, "thus far, and no farther; and here shall thy proud point be stayed:" we require a nose of such length as may ensure an interesting face. But we cannot imagine a mere biological trend towards producing interesting faces; because an interesting face is one particular arrangement of eyes, nose, and mouth, in a most complex relation to each other. Proportion cannot be a drift: it is either an accident or a design. So with the ideal of human morality and its relation to the humanitarians and the anti-humanitarians. It is conceivable that we are going more and more to keep our hands off things: not to drive horses; not to pick flowers. We may eventually be bound not to disturb a man's mind even by argument; not to disturb the sleep of birds even by coughing. The ultimate apotheosis would appear to be that of a man sitting quite still, nor daring to stir for fear of disturbing a fly, nor to eat for fear of incommoding a microbe. To so crude a consummation as that we might perhaps unconsciously drift. But do we want so crude a consummation? Similarly, we might unconsciously evolve along the opposite or Nietzschian line of development—superman crushing superman in one tower of tyrants until the universe is smashed up for fun. But do we want the universe smashed up for fun? Is it not quite clear that what we really hope for is one particular management and proposition of these two things; a certain amount of restraint and respect, a certain amount of energy and mastery? If our life is ever really as beautiful as a fairy-tale, we shall have to remember that all the beauty of a fairy-tale lies in this: that the prince has a wonder which just stops short of being fear. If he is afraid of the giant, there is an end of him; but also if he is not astonished at the giant, there is an end of the fairy-tale. The whole point depends upon his being at once humble enough to wonder, and haughty enough to defy. So our attitude to the giant of the world must not merely be increasing delicacy or increasing contempt: it must be one particular proportion of the two—which is exactly right. We must have in us enough reverence for all things outside us to make us tread fearfully on the grass. We must also have enough disdain for all things outside us, to make us, on due occasion, spit at the stars. Yet these two things (if we are to be good or happy) must be combined, not in any combination, but in one particular combination. The perfect happiness of men on the earth (if it ever comes) will not be a flat and solid thing, like the satisfaction of animals. It will be an exact and perilous balance; like that of a desperate romance. Man must have just enough faith in himself to have adventures, and just enough doubt of himself to enjoy them.

This, then, is our second requirement for the ideal of progress. First, it must be fixed; second, it must be composite. It must not (if it is to satisfy our souls) be the mere victory of some one thing swallowing up everything else, love or pride or peace or adventure; it must be a definite picture composed of these elements in their best proportion and relation. I am not concerned at this moment to deny that some such good culmination may be, by the constitution of things, reserved for the human race. I only point out that if this composite happiness is fixed for us it must be fixed by some mind; for only a mind can place the exact proportions of a composite happiness. If the beatification of the world is a mere work of nature, then it must be as simple as the freezing of the world, or the burning up of the world. But if the beatification of the world is not a work of nature but a work of art, then it involves an artist. And here again my contemplation was cloven by the ancient voice which said, "I could have told you all this a long time ago. If there is any certain progress it can only be my kind of progress, the progress towards a complete city of virtues and dominations where righteousness and peace contrive to kiss each other. An impersonal force might be leading you to a wilderness of perfect flatness or a peak of perfect height. But only a personal God can possibly be leading you (if, indeed, you are being led) to a city with just streets and architectural proportions, a city in which each of you can contribute exactly the right amount of your own colour to the many coloured coat of Joseph."

Twice again, therefore, Christianity had come in with the exact answer that I required. I had said, "The ideal must be fixed," and the Church had answered, "Mine is literally fixed, for it existed before anything else." I said secondly, "It must be artistically combined, like a picture"; and the Church answered, "Mine is quite literally a picture, for I know who painted it." Then I went on to the third thing, which, as it seemed to me, was needed for an Utopia or goal of progress. And of all the three it is infinitely the hardest to express. Perhaps it might be put thus: that we need watchfulness even in Utopia, lest we fall from Utopia as we fell from Eden.

We have remarked that one reason offered for being a progressive is that things naturally tend to grow better. But the only real reason for being a progressive is that things naturally tend to grow worse. The corruption in things is not only the best argument for being progressive; it is also the only argument against being conservative. The conservative theory would really be quite sweeping and unanswerable if it were not for this one fact. But all conservatism is based upon the idea that if you leave things alone you leave them as they are. But you do not. If you leave a thing alone you leave it to a torrent of change. If you leave a white post alone it will soon be a black post. If you particularly want it to be white you must be always painting it again; that is, you must be always having a revolution. Briefly, if you want the old white post you must have a new white post. But this which is true even of inanimate things is in a quite special and terrible sense true of all human things. An almost unnatural vigilance is really required of the citizen because of the horrible rapidity with which human institutions grow old. It is the custom in passing romance and journalism to talk of men suffering under old tyrannies. But, as a fact, men have almost always suffered under new tyrannies; under tyrannies that had been public liberties hardly twenty years before. Thus England went mad with joy over the patriotic monarchy of Elizabeth; and then (almost immediately afterwards) went mad with rage in the trap of the tyranny of Charles the First. So, again, in France the monarchy became intolerable, not just after it had been tolerated, but just after it had been adored. The son of Louis the well-beloved was Louis the guillotined. So in the same way in England in the nineteenth century the Radical manufacturer was entirely trusted as a mere tribune of the people, until suddenly we heard the cry of the Socialist that he was a tyrant eating the people like bread. So again, we have almost up to the last instant trusted the newspapers as organs of public opinion. Just recently some of us have seen (not slowly, but with a start) that they are obviously nothing of the kind. They are, by the nature of the case, the hobbies of a few rich men. We have not any need to rebel against antiquity; we have to rebel against novelty. It is the new rulers, the capitalist or the editor, who really hold up the modern world. There is no fear that a modern king will attempt to override the constitution; it is more likely that he will ignore the constitution and work behind its back; he will take no advantage of his kingly power; it is more likely that he will take advantage of his kingly powerlessness, of the fact that he is free from criticism and publicity. For the king is the most private person of our time. It will not be necessary for any one to fight again against the proposal of a censorship of the press. We do not need a censorship of the press. We have a censorship by the press.

This startling swiftness with which popular systems turn oppressive is the third fact for which we shall ask our perfect theory of progress to allow. It must always be on the look out for every privilege being abused, for every working right becoming a wrong. In this matter I am entirely on the side of the revolutionists. They are really right to be always suspecting human institutions; they are right not to put their trust in princes nor in any child of man. The chieftain chosen to be the friend of the people becomes the enemy of the people; the newspaper started to tell the truth now exists to prevent the truth being told. Here, I say, I felt that I was really at last on the side of the revolutionary. And then I caught my breath again: for I remembered that I was once again on the side of the orthodox.

Christianity spoke again and said: "I have always maintained that men were naturally backsliders; that human virtue tended of its own nature to rust or to rot; I have always said that human beings as such go wrong, especially happy human beings, especially proud and prosperous human beings. This eternal revolution, this suspicion sustained through centuries, you (being a vague modern) call the doctrine of progress. If you were a philosopher you would call it, as I do, the doctrine of original sin. You may call it the cosmic advance as much as you like; I call it what it is—the Fall."

I have spoken of orthodoxy coming in like a sword; here I confess it came in like a battle-axe. For really (when I came to think of it) Christianity is the only thing left that has any real right to question the power of the well-nurtured or the well-bred. I have listened often enough to Socialists, or even to democrats, saying that the physical conditions of the poor must of necessity make them mentally and morally degraded. I have listened to scientific men (and there are still scientific men not opposed to democracy) saying that if we give the poor healthier conditions vice and wrong will disappear. I have listened to them with a horrible attention, with a hideous fascination. For it was like watching a man energetically sawing from the tree the branch he is sitting on. If these happy democrats could prove their case, they would strike democracy dead. If the poor are thus utterly demoralized, it may or may not be practical to raise them. But it is certainly quite practical to disfranchise them. If the man with a bad bedroom cannot give a good vote, then the first and swiftest deduction is that he shall give no vote. The governing class may not unreasonably say: "It may take us some time to reform his bedroom. But if he is the brute you say, it will take him very little time to ruin our country. Therefore we will take your hint and not give him the chance." It fills me with horrible amusement to observe the way in which the earnest Socialist industriously lays the foundation of all aristocracy, expatiating blandly upon the evident unfitness of the poor to rule. It is like listening to somebody at an evening party apologising for entering without evening dress, and explaining that he had recently been intoxicated, had a personal habit of taking off his clothes in the street, and had, moreover, only just changed from prison uniform. At any moment, one feels, the host might say that really, if it was as bad as that, he need not come in at all. So it is when the ordinary Socialist, with a beaming face, proves that the poor, after their smashing experiences, cannot be really trustworthy. At any moment the rich may say, "Very well, then, we won't trust them," and bang the door in his face. On the basis of Mr. Blatchford's view of heredity and environment, the case for the aristocracy is quite overwhelming. If clean homes and clean air make clean souls, why not give the power (for the present at any rate) to those who undoubtedly have the clean air? If better conditions will make the poor more fit to govern themselves, why should not better conditions already make the rich more fit to govern them? On the ordinary environment argument the matter is fairly manifest. The comfortable class must be merely our vanguard in Utopia.

Is there any answer to the proposition that those who have had the best opportunities will probably be our best guides? Is there any answer to the argument that those who have breathed clean air had better decide for those who have breathed foul? As far as I know, there is only one answer, and that answer is Christianity. Only the Christian Church can offer any rational objection to a complete confidence in the rich. For she has maintained from the beginning that the danger was not in man's environment, but in man. Further, she has maintained that if we come to talk of a dangerous environment, the most dangerous environment of all is the commodious environment. I know that the most modern manufacture has been really occupied in trying to produce an abnormally large needle. I know that the most recent biologists have been chiefly anxious to discover a very small camel. But if we diminish the camel to his smallest, or open the eye of the needle to its largest—if, in short, we assume the words of Christ to have meant the very least that they could mean, His words must at the very least mean this— that rich men are not very likely to be morally trustworthy. Christianity even when watered down is hot enough to boil all modern society to rags. The mere minimum of the Church would be a deadly ultimatum to the world. For the whole modern world is absolutely based on the assumption, not that the rich are necessary (which is tenable), but that the rich are trustworthy, which (for a Christian) is not tenable. You will hear everlastingly, in all discussions about newspapers, companies, aristocracies, or party politics, this argument that the rich man cannot be bribed. The fact is, of course, that the rich man is bribed; he has been bribed already. That is why he is a rich man. The whole case for Christianity is that a man who is dependent upon the luxuries of this life is a corrupt man, spiritually corrupt, politically corrupt, financially corrupt. There is one thing that Christ and all the Christian saints have said with a sort of savage monotony. They have said simply that to be rich is to be in peculiar danger of moral wreck. It is not demonstrably un-Christian to kill the rich as violators of definable justice. It is not demonstrably un-Christian to crown the rich as convenient rulers of society. It is not certainly un-Christian to rebel against the rich or to submit to the rich. But it is quite certainly un-Christian to trust the rich, to regard the rich as more morally safe than the poor. A Christian may consistently say, "I respect that man's rank, although he takes bribes." But a Christian cannot say, as all modern men are saying at lunch and breakfast, "a man of that rank would not take bribes." For it is a part of Christian dogma that any man in any rank may take bribes. It is a part of Christian dogma; it also happens by a curious coincidence that it is a part of obvious human history. When people say that a man "in that position" would be incorruptible, there is no need to bring Christianity into the discussion. Was Lord Bacon a bootblack? Was the Duke of Marlborough a crossing sweeper? In the best Utopia, I must be prepared for the moral fall of any man in any position at any moment; especially for my fall from my position at this moment.

Much vague and sentimental journalism has been poured out to the effect that Christianity is akin to democracy, and most of it is scarcely strong or clear enough to refute the fact that the two things have often quarrelled. The real ground upon which Christianity and democracy are one is very much deeper. The one specially and peculiarly un-Christian idea is the idea of Carlyle— the idea that the man should rule who feels that he can rule. Whatever else is Christian, this is heathen. If our faith comments on government at all, its comment must be this—that the man should rule who does NOT think that he can rule. Carlyle's hero may say, "I will be king"; but the Christian saint must say "Nolo episcopari." If the great paradox of Christianity means anything, it means this— that we must take the crown in our hands, and go hunting in dry places and dark corners of the earth until we find the one man who feels himself unfit to wear it. Carlyle was quite wrong; we have not got to crown the exceptional man who knows he can rule. Rather we must crown the much more exceptional man who knows he can't.

Now, this is one of the two or three vital defences of working democracy. The mere machinery of voting is not democracy, though at present it is not easy to effect any simpler democratic method. But even the machinery of voting is profoundly Christian in this practical sense—that it is an attempt to get at the opinion of those who would be too modest to offer it. It is a mystical adventure; it is specially trusting those who do not trust themselves. That enigma is strictly peculiar to Christendom. There is nothing really humble about the abnegation of the Buddhist; the mild Hindoo is mild, but he is not meek. But there is something psychologically Christian about the idea of seeking for the opinion of the obscure rather than taking the obvious course of accepting the opinion of the prominent. To say that voting is particularly Christian may seem somewhat curious. To say that canvassing is Christian may seem quite crazy. But canvassing is very Christian in its primary idea. It is encouraging the humble; it is saying to the modest man, "Friend, go up higher." Or if there is some slight defect in canvassing, that is in its perfect and rounded piety, it is only because it may possibly neglect to encourage the modesty of the canvasser.

Aristocracy is not an institution: aristocracy is a sin; generally a very venial one. It is merely the drift or slide of men into a sort of natural pomposity and praise of the powerful, which is the most easy and obvious affair in the world.

It is one of the hundred answers to the fugitive perversion of modern "force" that the promptest and boldest agencies are also the most fragile or full of sensibility. The swiftest things are the softest things. A bird is active, because a bird is soft. A stone is helpless, because a stone is hard. The stone must by its own nature go downwards, because hardness is weakness. The bird can of its nature go upwards, because fragility is force. In perfect force there is a kind of frivolity, an airiness that can maintain itself in the air. Modern investigators of miraculous history have solemnly admitted that a characteristic of the great saints is their power of "levitation." They might go further; a characteristic of the great saints is their power of levity. Angels can fly because they can take themselves lightly. This has been always the instinct of Christendom, and especially the instinct of Christian art. Remember how Fra Angelico represented all his angels, not only as birds, but almost as butterflies. Remember how the most earnest mediaeval art was full of light and fluttering draperies, of quick and capering feet. It was the one thing that the modern Pre-raphaelites could not imitate in the real Pre-raphaelites. Burne-Jones could never recover the deep levity of the Middle Ages. In the old Christian pictures the sky over every figure is like a blue or gold parachute. Every figure seems ready to fly up and float about in the heavens. The tattered cloak of the beggar will bear him up like the rayed plumes of the angels. But the kings in their heavy gold and the proud in their robes of purple will all of their nature sink downwards, for pride cannot rise to levity or levitation. Pride is the downward drag of all things into an easy solemnity. One "settles down" into a sort of selfish seriousness; but one has to rise to a gay self-forgetfulness. A man "falls" into a brown study; he reaches up at a blue sky. Seriousness is not a virtue. It would be a heresy, but a much more sensible heresy, to say that seriousness is a vice. It is really a natural trend or lapse into taking one's self gravely, because it is the easiest thing to do. It is much easier to write a good TIMES leading article than a good joke in PUNCH. For solemnity flows out of men naturally; but laughter is a leap. It is easy to be heavy: hard to be light. Satan fell by the force of gravity.

Now, it is the peculiar honour of Europe since it has been Christian that while it has had aristocracy it has always at the back of its heart treated aristocracy as a weakness—generally as a weakness that must be allowed for. If any one wishes to appreciate this point, let him go outside Christianity into some other philosophical atmosphere. Let him, for instance, compare the classes of Europe with the castes of India. There aristocracy is far more awful, because it is far more intellectual. It is seriously felt that the scale of classes is a scale of spiritual values; that the baker is better than the butcher in an invisible and sacred sense. But no Christianity, not even the most ignorant or perverse, ever suggested that a baronet was better than a butcher in that sacred sense. No Christianity, however ignorant or extravagant, ever suggested that a duke would not be damned. In pagan society there may have been (I do not know) some such serious division between the free man and the slave. But in Christian society we have always thought the gentleman a sort of joke, though I admit that in some great crusades and councils he earned the right to be called a practical joke. But we in Europe never really and at the root of our souls took aristocracy seriously. It is only an occasional non-European alien (such as Dr. Oscar Levy, the only intelligent Nietzscheite) who can even manage for a moment to take aristocracy seriously. It may be a mere patriotic bias, though I do not think so, but it seems to me that the English aristocracy is not only the type, but is the crown and flower of all actual aristocracies; it has all the oligarchical virtues as well as all the defects. It is casual, it is kind, it is courageous in obvious matters; but it has one great merit that overlaps even these. The great and very obvious merit of the English aristocracy is that nobody could possibly take it seriously.

In short, I had spelled out slowly, as usual, the need for an equal law in Utopia; and, as usual, I found that Christianity had been there before me. The whole history of my Utopia has the same amusing sadness. I was always rushing out of my architectural study with plans for a new turret only to find it sitting up there in the sunlight, shining, and a thousand years old. For me, in the ancient and partly in the modern sense, God answered the prayer, "Prevent us, O Lord, in all our doings." Without vanity, I really think there was a moment when I could have invented the marriage vow (as an institution) out of my own head; but I discovered, with a sigh, that it had been invented already. But, since it would be too long a business to show how, fact by fact and inch by inch, my own conception of Utopia was only answered in the New Jerusalem, I will take this one case of the matter of marriage as indicating the converging drift, I may say the converging crash of all the rest.

When the ordinary opponents of Socialism talk about impossibilities and alterations in human nature they always miss an important distinction. In modern ideal conceptions of society there are some desires that are possibly not attainable: but there are some desires that are not desirable. That all men should live in equally beautiful houses is a dream that may or may not be attained. But that all men should live in the same beautiful house is not a dream at all; it is a nightmare. That a man should love all old women is an ideal that may not be attainable. But that a man should regard all old women exactly as he regards his mother is not

only an unattainable ideal, but an ideal which ought not to be attained. I do not
know if the reader agrees with me in these examples; but I will add the example
which has always affected me most. I could never conceive or tolerate any Utopia
which did not leave to me the liberty for which I chiefly care, the liberty to bind
myself. Complete anarchy would not merely make it impossible to have any
discipline or fidelity; it would also make it impossible to have any fun. To take
an obvious instance, it would not be worth while to bet if a bet were not binding.
The dissolution of all contracts would not only ruin morality but spoil sport. Now
betting and such sports are only the stunted and twisted shapes of the original
instinct of man for adventure and romance, of which much has been said in these
pages. And the perils, rewards, punishments, and fulfilments of an adventure must
be real, or the adventure is only a shifting and heartless nightmare. If I bet I must
be made to pay, or there is no poetry in betting. If I challenge I must be made to
fight, or there is no poetry in challenging. If I vow to be faithful I must be cursed
when I am unfaithful, or there is no fun in vowing. You could not even make a
fairy tale from the experiences of a man who, when he was swallowed by a whale,
might find himself at the top of the Eiffel Tower, or when he was turned into a
frog might begin to behave like a flamingo. For the purpose even of the wildest
romance results must be real; results must be irrevocable. Christian marriage is
the great example of a real and irrevocable result; and that is why it is the chief
subject and centre of all our romantic writing. And this is my last instance of the
things that I should ask, and ask imperatively, of any social paradise; I should ask
to be kept to my bargain, to have my oaths and engagements taken seriously; I
should ask Utopia to avenge my honour on myself.

All my modern Utopian friends look at each other rather doubtfully, for
their ultimate hope is the dissolution of all special ties. But again I seem to
hear, like a kind of echo, an answer from beyond the world. "You will have real
obligations, and therefore real adventures when you get to my Utopia. But the
hardest obligation and the steepest adventure is to get there."

Chapter 7
The Romance of Orthodoxy

t is customary to complain of the bustle and strenuousness of our epoch. But in truth the chief mark of our epoch is a profound laziness and fatigue; and the fact is that the real laziness is the cause of the apparent bustle. Take one quite external case; the streets are noisy with taxicabs and motorcars; but this is not due to human activity but to human repose. There would be less bustle if there were more activity, if people were simply walking about. Our world would be more silent if it were more strenuous. And this which is true of the apparent physical bustle is true also of the apparent bustle of the intellect. Most of the machinery of modern language is labour-saving machinery; and it saves mental labour very much more than it ought. Scientific phrases are used like scientific wheels and piston-rods to make swifter and smoother yet the path of the comfortable. Long words go rattling by us like long railway trains. We know they are carrying thousands who are too tired or too indolent to walk and think for themselves. It is a good exercise to try for once in a way to express any opinion one holds in words of one syllable. If you say "The social utility of the indeterminate sentence is recognized by all criminologists as a part of our sociological evolution towards a more humane and scientific view of punishment," you can go on talking like that for hours with hardly a movement of the gray matter inside your skull. But if you begin "I wish Jones to go to gaol and Brown to say when Jones shall come out," you will discover, with a thrill of horror, that you are obliged to think. The long words are not the hard words, it is the short words that are hard. There is much more metaphysical subtlety in the word "damn" than in the word "degeneration."

But these long comfortable words that save modern people the toil of reasoning have one particular aspect in which they are especially ruinous and confusing. This difficulty occurs when the same long word is used in different connections to mean quite different things. Thus, to take a well-known instance, the word "idealist" has one meaning as a piece of philosophy and quite another as a piece of moral rhetoric. In the same way the scientific materialists have had just reason to complain of people mixing up "materialist" as a term of cosmology with "materialist" as a moral taunt. So, to take a cheaper instance, the man who hates "progressives" in London always calls himself a "progressive" in South Africa.

A confusion quite as unmeaning as this has arisen in connection with the word "liberal" as applied to religion and as applied to politics and society. It is often suggested that all Liberals ought to be freethinkers, because they ought to love everything that is free. You might just as well say that all idealists ought to be High Churchmen, because they ought to love everything that is high. You might as well say that Low Churchmen ought to like Low Mass, or that Broad Churchmen ought to like broad jokes. The thing is a mere accident of words. In actual modern Europe a freethinker does not mean a man who thinks for himself. It means a man who, having thought for himself, has come to one particular class of conclusions, the material origin of phenomena, the impossibility of miracles, the improbability of personal immortality and so on. And none of these ideas are particularly liberal. Nay, indeed almost all these ideas are definitely illiberal, as it is the purpose of this chapter to show.

In the few following pages I propose to point out as rapidly as possible that on every single one of the matters most strongly insisted on by liberalisers of theology their effect upon social practice would be definitely illiberal. Almost every contemporary proposal to bring freedom into the church is simply a proposal to bring tyranny into the world. For freeing the church now does not even mean freeing it in all directions. It means freeing that peculiar set of dogmas loosely called scientific, dogmas of monism, of pantheism, or of Arianism, or of necessity. And every one of these (and we will take them one by one) can be shown to be the natural ally of oppression. In fact, it is a remarkable circumstance (indeed not so very remarkable when one comes to think of it) that most things are the allies of oppression. There is only one thing that can never go past a certain point in its alliance with oppression—and that is orthodoxy. I may, it is true, twist orthodoxy so as partly to justify a tyrant. But I can easily make up a German philosophy to justify him entirely.

Now let us take in order the innovations that are the notes of the new theology or the modernist church. We concluded the last chapter with the discovery of one of them. The very doctrine which is called the most old-fashioned was found to be the only safeguard of the new democracies of the earth. The doctrine seemingly most unpopular was found to be the only strength of the people. In short, we found that the only logical negation of oligarchy was in the affirmation of original sin. So it is, I maintain, in all the other cases.

I take the most obvious instance first, the case of miracles. For some extraordinary reason, there is a fixed notion that it is more liberal to disbelieve in miracles than to believe in them. Why, I cannot imagine, nor can anybody tell me. For some inconceivable cause a "broad" or "liberal" clergyman always means a man who wishes at least to diminish the number of miracles; it never means a man who wishes to increase that number. It always means a man who is free to disbelieve that Christ came out of His grave; it never means a man who is free to believe that his own aunt came out of her grave. It is common to find trouble in a parish because the parish priest cannot admit that St. Peter walked on water; yet how rarely do we find trouble in a parish because the clergyman says that his father walked on the Serpentine? And this is not because (as the swift secularist debater would immediately retort) miracles cannot be believed in our experience. It is not because "miracles do not happen," as in the dogma which Matthew Arnold recited with simple faith. More supernatural things are

ALLEGED to have happened in our time than would have been possible eighty years ago. Men of science believe in such marvels much more than they did: the most perplexing, and even horrible, prodigies of mind and spirit are always being unveiled in modern psychology. Things that the old science at least would frankly have rejected as miracles are hourly being asserted by the new science. The only thing which is still old-fashioned enough to reject miracles is the New Theology. But in truth this notion that it is "free" to deny miracles has nothing to do with the evidence for or against them. It is a lifeless verbal prejudice of which the original life and beginning was not in the freedom of thought, but simply in the dogma of materialism. The man of the nineteenth century did not disbelieve in the Resurrection because his liberal Christianity allowed him to doubt it. He disbelieved in it because his very strict materialism did not allow him to believe it. Tennyson, a very typical nineteenth century man, uttered one of the instinctive truisms of his contemporaries when he said that there was faith in their honest doubt. There was indeed. Those words have a profound and even a horrible truth. In their doubt of miracles there was a faith in a fixed and godless fate; a deep and sincere faith in the incurable routine of the cosmos. The doubts of the agnostic were only the dogmas of the monist.

Of the fact and evidence of the supernatural I will speak afterwards. Here we are only concerned with this clear point; that in so far as the liberal idea of freedom can be said to be on either side in the discussion about miracles, it is obviously on the side of miracles. Reform or (in the only tolerable sense) progress means simply the gradual control of matter by mind. A miracle simply means the swift control of matter by mind. If you wish to feed the people, you may think that feeding them miraculously in the wilderness is impossible—but you cannot think it illiberal. If you really want poor children to go to the seaside, you cannot think it illiberal that they should go there on flying dragons; you can only think it unlikely. A holiday, like Liberalism, only means the liberty of man. A miracle only means the liberty of God. You may conscientiously deny either of them, but you cannot call your denial a triumph of the liberal idea. The Catholic Church believed that man and God both had a sort of spiritual freedom. Calvinism took away the freedom from man, but left it to God. Scientific materialism binds the Creator Himself; it chains up God as the Apocalypse chained the devil. It leaves nothing free in the universe. And those who assist this process are called the "liberal theologians."

This, as I say, is the lightest and most evident case. The assumption that there is something in the doubt of miracles akin to liberality or reform is literally the opposite of the truth. If a man cannot believe in miracles there is an end of the matter; he is not particularly liberal, but he is perfectly honourable and logical, which are much better things. But if he can believe in miracles, he is certainly the more liberal for doing so; because they mean first, the freedom of the soul, and secondly, its control over the tyranny of circumstance. Sometimes this truth

is ignored in a singularly naive way, even by the ablest men. For instance, Mr.
Bernard Shaw speaks with hearty old-fashioned contempt for the idea of miracles,
as if they were a sort of breach of faith on the part of nature: he seems strangely
unconscious that miracles are only the final flowers of his own favourite tree, the
doctrine of the omnipotence of will. Just in the same way he calls the desire for
immortality a paltry selfishness, forgetting that he has just called the desire for
life a healthy and heroic selfishness. How can it be noble to wish to make one's life
infinite and yet mean to wish to make it immortal? No, if it is desirable that man
should triumph over the cruelty of nature or custom, then miracles are certainly
desirable; we will discuss afterwards whether they are possible.

But I must pass on to the larger cases of this curious error; the notion that
the "liberalising" of religion in some way helps the liberation of the world. The
second example of it can be found in the question of pantheism—or rather of a
certain modern attitude which is often called immanentism, and which often is
Buddhism. But this is so much more difficult a matter that I must approach it with
rather more preparation.

The things said most confidently by advanced persons to crowded audiences
are generally those quite opposite to the fact; it is actually our truisms that are
untrue. Here is a case. There is a phrase of facile liberality uttered again and
again at ethical societies and parliaments of religion: "the religions of the earth
differ in rites and forms, but they are the same in what they teach." It is false;
it is the opposite of the fact. The religions of the earth do not greatly differ
in rites and forms; they do greatly differ in what they teach. It is as if a man
were to say, "Do not be misled by the fact that the CHURCH TIMES and the
FREETHINKER look utterly different, that one is painted on vellum and the
other carved on marble, that one is triangular and the other hectagonal; read them
and you will see that they say the same thing." The truth is, of course, that they
are alike in everything except in the fact that they don't say the same thing. An
atheist stockbroker in Surbiton looks exactly like a Swedenborgian stockbroker
in Wimbledon. You may walk round and round them and subject them to the most
personal and offensive study without seeing anything Swedenborgian in the hat or
anything particularly godless in the umbrella. It is exactly in their souls that they
are divided. So the truth is that the difficulty of all the creeds of the earth is not as
alleged in this cheap maxim: that they agree in meaning, but differ in machinery.
It is exactly the opposite. They agree in machinery; almost every great religion
on earth works with the same external methods, with priests, scriptures, altars,
sworn brotherhoods, special feasts. They agree in the mode of teaching; what
they differ about is the thing to be taught. Pagan optimists and Eastern pessimists
would both have temples, just as Liberals and Tories would both have newspapers.
Creeds that exist to destroy each other both have scriptures, just as armies that
exist to destroy each other both have guns.

The great example of this alleged identity of all human religions is the alleged spiritual identity of Buddhism and Christianity. Those who adopt this theory generally avoid the ethics of most other creeds, except, indeed, Confucianism, which they like because it is not a creed. But they are cautious in their praises of Mahommedanism, generally confining themselves to imposing its morality only upon the refreshment of the lower classes. They seldom suggest the Mahommedan view of marriage (for which there is a great deal to be said), and towards Thugs and fetish worshippers their attitude may even be called cold. But in the case of the great religion of Gautama they feel sincerely a similarity.

Students of popular science, like Mr. Blatchford, are always insisting that Christianity and Buddhism are very much alike, especially Buddhism. This is generally believed, and I believed it myself until I read a book giving the reasons for it. The reasons were of two kinds: resemblances that meant nothing because they were common to all humanity, and resemblances which were not resemblances at all. The author solemnly explained that the two creeds were alike in things in which all creeds are alike, or else he described them as alike in some point in which they are quite obviously different. Thus, as a case of the first class, he said that both Christ and Buddha were called by the divine voice coming out of the sky, as if you would expect the divine voice to come out of the coal-cellar. Or, again, it was gravely urged that these two Eastern teachers, by a singular coincidence, both had to do with the washing of feet. You might as well say that it was a remarkable coincidence that they both had feet to wash. And the other class of similarities were those which simply were not similar. Thus this reconciler of the two religions draws earnest attention to the fact that at certain religious feasts the robe of the Lama is rent in pieces out of respect, and the remnants highly valued. But this is the reverse of a resemblance, for the garments of Christ were not rent in pieces out of respect, but out of derision; and the remnants were not highly valued except for what they would fetch in the rag shops. It is rather like alluding to the obvious connection between the two ceremonies of the sword: when it taps a man's shoulder, and when it cuts off his head. It is not at all similar for the man. These scraps of puerile pedantry would indeed matter little if it were not also true that the alleged philosophical resemblances are also of these two kinds, either proving too much or not proving anything. That Buddhism approves of mercy or of self-restraint is not to say that it is specially like Christianity; it is only to say that it is not utterly unlike all human existence. Buddhists disapprove in theory of cruelty or excess because all sane human beings disapprove in theory of cruelty or excess. But to say that Buddhism and Christianity give the same philosophy of these things is simply false. All humanity does agree that we are in a net of sin. Most of humanity agrees that there is some way out. But as to what is the way out, I do not think that there are two institutions in the universe which contradict each other so flatly as Buddhism and Christianity.

Even when I thought, with most other well-informed, though unscholarly, people, that Buddhism and Christianity were alike, there was one thing about them that always perplexed me; I mean the startling difference in their type of religious art. I do not mean in its technical style of representation, but in the things that it was manifestly meant to represent. No two ideals could be more opposite than a Christian saint in a Gothic cathedral and a Buddhist saint in a Chinese temple. The opposition exists at every point; but perhaps the shortest statement of it is that the Buddhist saint always has his eyes shut, while the Christian saint always has them very wide open. The Buddhist saint has a sleek and harmonious body, but his eyes are heavy and sealed with sleep. The mediaeval saint's body is wasted to its crazy bones, but his eyes are frightfully alive. There cannot be any real community of spirit between forces that produced symbols so different as that. Granted that both images are extravagances, are perversions of the pure creed, it must be a real divergence which could produce such opposite extravagances. The Buddhist is looking with a peculiar intentness inwards. The Christian is staring with a frantic intentness outwards. If we follow that clue steadily we shall find some interesting things.

A short time ago Mrs. Besant, in an interesting essay, announced that there was only one religion in the world, that all faiths were only versions or perversions of it, and that she was quite prepared to say what it was. According to Mrs. Besant this universal Church is simply the universal self. It is the doctrine that we are really all one person; that there are no real walls of individuality between man and man. If I may put it so, she does not tell us to love our neighbours; she tells us to be our neighbours. That is Mrs. Besant's thoughtful and suggestive description of the religion in which all men must find themselves in agreement. And I never heard of any suggestion in my life with which I more violently disagree. I want to love my neighbour not because he is I, but precisely because he is not I. I want to adore the world, not as one likes a looking-glass, because it is one's self, but as one loves a woman, because she is entirely different. If souls are separate love is possible. If souls are united love is obviously impossible. A man may be said loosely to love himself, but he can hardly fall in love with himself, or, if he does, it must be a monotonous courtship. If the world is full of real selves, they can be really unselfish selves. But upon Mrs. Besant's principle the whole cosmos is only one enormously selfish person.

It is just here that Buddhism is on the side of modern pantheism and immanence. And it is just here that Christianity is on the side of humanity and liberty and love. Love desires personality; therefore love desires division. It is the instinct of Christianity to be glad that God has broken the universe into little pieces, because they are living pieces. It is her instinct to say "little children love one another" rather than to tell one large person to love himself. This is the intellectual abyss between Buddhism and Christianity; that for the Buddhist or Theosophist personality is the fall of man, for the Christian it is the purpose of God, the whole point of his cosmic idea. The world-soul of the Theosophists asks man to love it only in order that man may throw himself into it. But the divine centre of Christianity actually threw man out of it in order that he might love it. The oriental deity is like a giant who should have lost his leg or hand and be always seeking to find it; but the Christian power is like some giant who in a strange generosity should cut off his right hand, so that it might of its own accord shake hands with him. We come back to the same tireless note touching the nature of Christianity; all modern philosophies are chains which connect and fetter; Christianity is a sword which separates and sets free. No other philosophy makes God actually rejoice in the separation of the universe into living souls. But according to orthodox Christianity this separation between God and man is sacred, because this is eternal. That a man may love God it is necessary that there should be not only a God to be loved, but a man to love him. All those vague theosophical minds for whom the universe is an immense melting-pot are exactly the minds which shrink instinctively from that earthquake saying of our Gospels, which declare that the Son of God came not with peace but with a sundering sword. The saying rings entirely true even considered as what it obviously is; the statement that any man who preaches real love is bound to beget hate. It is as true of democratic fraternity as a divine love; sham love ends in compromise and common philosophy; but real love has always ended in bloodshed. Yet there is another and yet more awful truth behind the obvious meaning of this utterance of our Lord. According to Himself the Son was a sword separating brother and brother that they should for an aeon hate each other. But the Father also was a sword, which in the black beginning separated brother and brother, so that they should love each other at last.

This is the meaning of that almost insane happiness in the eyes of the mediaeval saint in the picture. This is the meaning of the sealed eyes of the superb Buddhist image. The Christian saint is happy because he has verily been cut off from the world; he is separate from things and is staring at them in astonishment. But why should the Buddhist saint be astonished at things?— since there is really only one thing, and that being impersonal can hardly be astonished at itself. There have been many pantheist poems suggesting wonder, but no really successful ones. The pantheist cannot wonder, for he cannot praise God or praise anything as really distinct from himself. Our immediate business here, however, is with the effect of this Christian admiration (which strikes outwards, towards a deity distinct from the worshipper) upon the general need for ethical activity and social reform. And surely its effect is sufficiently obvious. There is no real possibility of getting out of pantheism, any special impulse to moral action. For pantheism implies in its nature that one thing is as good as another; whereas action implies in its nature that one thing is greatly preferable to another. Swinburne in the high summer of his scepticism tried in vain to wrestle with this difficulty. In "Songs before Sunrise," written under the inspiration of Garibaldi and the revolt of Italy he proclaimed the newer religion and the purer God which should wither up all the priests of the world:

"What doest thou now Looking Godward to cry I am I, thou art thou, I am low, thou art high, I am thou that thou seekest to find him, find thou but thyself, thou art I."

Of which the immediate and evident deduction is that tyrants are as much the sons of God as Garibaldis; and that King Bomba of Naples having, with the utmost success, "found himself" is identical with the ultimate good in all things. The truth is that the western energy that dethrones tyrants has been directly due to the western theology that says "I am I, thou art thou." The same spiritual separation which looked up and saw a good king in the universe looked up and saw a bad king in Naples. The worshippers of Bomba's god dethroned Bomba. The worshippers of Swinburne's god have covered Asia for centuries and have never dethroned a tyrant. The Indian saint may reasonably shut his eyes because he is looking at that which is I and Thou and We and They and It. It is a rational occupation: but it is not true in theory and not true in fact that it helps the Indian to keep an eye on Lord Curzon. That external vigilance which has always been the mark of Christianity (the command that we should WATCH and pray) has expressed itself both in typical western orthodoxy and in typical western politics: but both depend on the idea of a divinity transcendent, different from ourselves, a deity that disappears. Certainly the most sagacious creeds may suggest that we should pursue God into deeper and deeper rings of the labyrinth of our own ego. But only we of Christendom have said that we should hunt God like an eagle upon the mountains: and we have killed all monsters in the chase.

Here again, therefore, we find that in so far as we value democracy and the self-renewing energies of the west, we are much more likely to find them in the old theology than the new. If we want reform, we must adhere to orthodoxy: especially in this matter (so much disputed in the counsels of Mr. R.J.Campbell), the matter of insisting on the immanent or the transcendent deity. By insisting specially on the immanence of God we get introspection, self-isolation, quietism, social indifference—Tibet. By insisting specially on the transcendence of God we get wonder, curiosity, moral and political adventure, righteous indignation— Christendom. Insisting that God is inside man, man is always inside himself. By insisting that God transcends man, man has transcended himself.

If we take any other doctrine that has been called old-fashioned we shall find the case the same. It is the same, for instance, in the deep matter of the Trinity. Unitarians (a sect never to be mentioned without a special respect for their distinguished intellectual dignity and high intellectual honour) are often reformers by the accident that throws so many small sects into such an attitude. But there is nothing in the least liberal or akin to reform in the substitution of pure monotheism for the Trinity. The complex God of the Athanasian Creed may be an enigma for the intellect; but He is far less likely to gather the mystery and cruelty of a Sultan than the lonely god of Omar or Mahomet. The god who is a mere awful unity is not only a king but an Eastern king. The HEART of humanity, especially of European humanity, is certainly much more satisfied by the strange hints and symbols that gather round the Trinitarian idea, the image of a council at which mercy pleads as well as justice, the conception of a sort of liberty and variety existing even in the inmost chamber of the world. For Western religion has always felt keenly the idea "it is not well for man to be alone." The social instinct asserted itself everywhere as when the Eastern idea of hermits was practically expelled by the Western idea of monks. So even asceticism became brotherly; and the Trappists were sociable even when they were silent. If this love of a living complexity be our test, it is certainly healthier to have the Trinitarian religion than the Unitarian. For to us Trinitarians (if I may say it with reverence)–to us God Himself is a society. It is indeed a fathomless mystery of theology, and even if I were theologian enough to deal with it directly, it would not be relevant to do so here. Suffice it to say here that this triple enigma is as comforting as wine and open as an English fireside; that this thing that bewilders the intellect utterly quiets the heart: but out of the desert, from the dry places and the dreadful suns, come the cruel children of the lonely God; the real Unitarians who with scimitar in hand have laid waste the world. For it is not well for God to be alone.

Again, the same is true of that difficult matter of the danger of the soul, which has unsettled so many just minds. To hope for all souls is imperative; and it is quite tenable that their salvation is inevitable. It is tenable, but it is not specially favourable to activity or progress. Our fighting and creative society ought rather to insist on the danger of everybody, on the fact that every man is hanging by a thread or clinging to a precipice. To say that all will be well anyhow is a comprehensible remark: but it cannot be called the blast of a trumpet. Europe ought rather to emphasize possible perdition; and Europe always has emphasized it. Here its highest religion is at one with all its cheapest romances. To the Buddhist or the eastern fatalist existence is a science or a plan, which must end up in a certain way. But to a Christian existence is a STORY, which may end up in any way. In a thrilling novel (that purely Christian product) the hero is not eaten by cannibals; but it is essential to the existence of the thrill that he MIGHT be eaten by cannibals. The hero must (so to speak) be an eatable hero. So Christian morals have always said to the man, not that he would lose his soul, but that he must take care that he didn't. In Christian morals, in short, it is wicked to call a man "damned": but it is strictly religious and philosophic to call him damnable.

All Christianity concentrates on the man at the cross-roads. The vast and shallow philosophies, the huge syntheses of humbug, all talk about ages and evolution and ultimate developments. The true philosophy is concerned with the instant. Will a man take this road or that?–that is the only thing to think about, if you enjoy thinking. The aeons are easy enough to think about, any one can think about them. The instant is really awful: and it is because our religion has intensely felt the instant, that it has in literature dealt much with battle and in theology dealt much with hell. It is full of DANGER, like a boy's book: it is at an immortal crisis. There is a great deal of real similarity between popular fiction and the religion of the western people. If you say that popular fiction is vulgar and tawdry, you only say what the dreary and well-informed say also about the images in the Catholic churches. Life (according to the faith) is very like a serial story in a magazine: life ends with the promise (or menace) "to be continued in our next." Also, with a noble vulgarity, life imitates the serial and leaves off at the exciting moment. For death is distinctly an exciting moment.

But the point is that a story is exciting because it has in it so strong an element of will, of what theology calls free-will. You cannot finish a sum how you like. But you can finish a story how you like. When somebody discovered the Differential Calculus there was only one Differential Calculus he could discover. But when Shakespeare killed Romeo he might have married him to Juliet's old nurse if he had felt inclined. And Christendom has excelled in the narrative romance exactly because it has insisted on the theological free-will. It is a large matter and too much to one side of the road to be discussed adequately here; but this is the real objection to that torrent of modern talk about treating crime as disease, about making a prison merely a hygienic environment like a hospital, of healing sin by slow scientific methods. The fallacy of the whole thing is that evil is a matter of active choice whereas disease is not. If you say that you are going to cure a profligate as you cure an asthmatic, my cheap and obvious answer is, "Produce the people who want to be asthmatics as many people want to be profligates." A man may lie still and be cured of a malady. But he must not lie still if he wants to be cured of a sin; on the contrary, he must get up and jump about violently. The whole point indeed is perfectly expressed in the very word which we use for a man in hospital; "patient" is in the passive mood; "sinner" is in the active. If a man is to be saved from influenza, he may be a patient. But if he is to be saved from forging, he must be not a patient but an IMPATIENT. He must be personally impatient with forgery. All moral reform must start in the active not the passive will.

Here again we reach the same substantial conclusion. In so far as we desire the definite reconstructions and the dangerous revolutions which have distinguished European civilization, we shall not discourage the thought of possible ruin; we shall rather encourage it. If we want, like the Eastern saints, merely to contemplate how right things are, of course we shall only say that they must go right. But if we particularly want to MAKE them go right, we must insist that they may go wrong.

Lastly, this truth is yet again true in the case of the common modern attempts to diminish or to explain away the divinity of Christ. The thing may be true or not; that I shall deal with before I end. But if the divinity is true it is certainly terribly revolutionary. That a good man may have his back to the wall is no more than we knew already; but that God could have his back to the wall is a boast for all insurgents for ever. Christianity is the only religion on earth that has felt that omnipotence made God incomplete. Christianity alone has felt that God, to be wholly God, must have been a rebel as well as a king. Alone of all creeds, Christianity has added courage to the virtues of the Creator. For the only courage worth calling courage must necessarily mean that the soul passes a breaking point— and does not break. In this indeed I approach a matter more dark and awful than it is easy to discuss; and I apologise in advance if any of my phrases fall wrong or seem irreverent touching a matter which the greatest saints and thinkers have justly feared to approach. But in that terrific tale of the Passion there is a distinct emotional suggestion that the author of all things (in some unthinkable way) went not only through agony, but through doubt. It is written, "Thou shalt not tempt the Lord thy God." No; but the Lord thy God may tempt Himself; and it seems as if this was what happened in Gethsemane. In a garden Satan tempted man: and in a garden God tempted God. He passed in some superhuman manner through our human horror of pessimism. When the world shook and the sun was wiped out of heaven, it was not at the crucifixion, but at the cry from the cross: the cry which confessed that God was forsaken of God. And now let the revolutionists choose a creed from all the creeds and a god from all the gods of the world, carefully weighing all the gods of inevitable recurrence and of unalterable power. They will not find another god who has himself been in revolt. Nay, (the matter grows too difficult for human speech,) but let the atheists themselves choose a god. They will find only one divinity who ever uttered their isolation; only one religion in which God seemed for an instant to be an atheist.

These can be called the essentials of the old orthodoxy, of which the chief merit is that it is the natural fountain of revolution and reform; and of which the chief defect is that it is obviously only an abstract assertion. Its main advantage is that it is the most adventurous and manly of all theologies. Its chief disadvantage is simply that it is a theology. It can always be urged against it that it is in its nature arbitrary and in the air. But it is not so high in the air but that great archers spend their whole lives in shooting arrows at it—yes, and their last arrows; there are men who will ruin themselves and ruin their civilization if they may ruin also this old fantastic tale. This is the last and most astounding fact about this faith; that its enemies will use any weapon against it, the swords that cut their own fingers, and the firebrands that burn their own homes. Men who begin to fight the Church for the sake of freedom and humanity end by flinging away freedom and humanity if only they may fight the Church. This is no exaggeration; I could fill a book with the instances of it. Mr. Blatchford set out, as an ordinary Bible-smasher, to prove that Adam was guiltless of sin against God; in manoeuvring so as to maintain this he admitted, as a mere side issue, that all the tyrants, from Nero to King Leopold, were guiltless of any sin against humanity. I know a man who has such a passion for proving that he will have no personal existence after death that he falls back on the position that he has no personal existence now. He invokes Buddhism and says that all souls fade into each other; in order to prove that he cannot go to heaven he proves that he cannot go to Hartlepool. I have known people who protested against religious education with arguments against any education, saying that the child's mind must grow freely or that the old must not teach the young. I have known people who showed that there could be no divine judgment by showing that there can be no human judgment, even for practical purposes. They burned their own corn to set fire to the church; they smashed their own tools to smash it; any stick was good enough to beat it with, though it were the last stick of their own dismembered furniture. We do not admire, we hardly excuse, the fanatic who wrecks this world for love of the other. But what are we to say of the fanatic who wrecks this world out of hatred of the other? He sacrifices the very existence of humanity to the non-existence of God. He offers his victims not to the altar, but merely to assert the idleness of the altar and the emptiness of the throne. He is ready to ruin even that primary ethic by which all things live, for his strange and eternal vengeance upon some one who never lived at all.

And yet the thing hangs in the heavens unhurt. Its opponents only succeed in destroying all that they themselves justly hold dear. They do not destroy orthodoxy; they only destroy political and common courage sense. They do not prove that Adam was not responsible to God; how could they prove it? They only prove (from their premises) that the Czar is not responsible to Russia. They do not prove that Adam should not have been punished by God; they only prove that the nearest sweater should not be punished by men. With their oriental doubts about personality they do not make certain that we shall have no personal life hereafter; they only make certain that we shall not have a very jolly or complete one here. With their paralysing hints of all conclusions coming out wrong they do not tear the book of the Recording Angel; they only make it a little harder to keep the books of Marshall & Snelgrove. Not only is the faith the mother of all worldly energies, but its foes are the fathers of all worldly confusion. The secularists have not wrecked divine things; but the secularists have wrecked secular things, if that is any comfort to them. The Titans did not scale heaven; but they laid waste the world.

Chapter 8
Authority and the Adventurer

he last chapter has been concerned with the contention that orthodoxy is not only (as is often urged) the only safe guardian of morality or order, but is also the only logical guardian of liberty, innovation and advance. If we wish to pull down the prosperous oppressor we cannot do it with the new doctrine of human perfectibility; we can do it with the old doctrine of Original Sin. If we want to uproot inherent cruelties or lift up lost populations we cannot do it with the scientific theory that matter precedes mind; we can do it with the supernatural theory that mind precedes matter. If we wish specially to awaken people to social vigilance and tireless pursuit of practise, we cannot help it much by insisting on the Immanent God and the Inner Light: for these are at best reasons for contentment; we can help it much by insisting on the transcendent God and the flying and escaping gleam; for that means divine discontent. If we wish particularly to assert the idea of a generous balance against that of a dreadful autocracy we shall instinctively be Trinitarian rather than Unitarian. If we desire European civilization to be a raid and a rescue, we shall insist rather that souls are in real peril than that their peril is ultimately unreal. And if we wish to exalt the outcast and the crucified, we shall rather wish to think that a veritable God was crucified, rather than a mere sage or hero. Above all, if we wish to protect the poor we shall be in favour of fixed rules and clear dogmas. The RULES of a club are occasionally in favour of the poor member. The drift of a club is always in favour of the rich one.

And now we come to the crucial question which truly concludes the whole matter. A reasonable agnostic, if he has happened to agree with me so far, may justly turn round and say, "You have found a practical philosophy in the doctrine of the Fall; very well. You have found a side of democracy now dangerously neglected wisely asserted in Original Sin; all right. You have found a truth in the doctrine of hell; I congratulate you. You are convinced that worshippers of a personal God look outwards and are progressive; I congratulate them. But even supposing that those doctrines do include those truths, why cannot you take the truths and leave the doctrines? Granted that all modern society is trusting the rich too much because it does not allow for human weakness; granted that orthodox ages have had a great advantage because (believing in the Fall) they did allow for human weakness, why cannot you simply allow for human weakness without believing in the Fall? If you have discovered that the idea of damnation represents a healthy idea of danger, why can you not simply take the idea of danger and leave the idea of damnation? If you see clearly the kernel of common-sense in the nut of Christian orthodoxy, why cannot you simply take the kernel and leave the nut? Why cannot you (to use that cant phrase of the newspapers which I, as a highly scholarly agnostic, am a little ashamed of using) why cannot you simply take what is good in Christianity, what you can define as valuable, what you can comprehend, and leave all the rest, all the absolute dogmas that are in their nature incomprehensible?" This is the real question; this is the last question; and it is a pleasure to try to answer it.

The first answer is simply to say that I am a rationalist. I like to have some intellectual justification for my intuitions. If I am treating man as a fallen being it is an intellectual convenience to me to believe that he fell; and I find, for some odd psychological reason, that I can deal better with a man's exercise of freewill if I believe that he has got it. But I am in this matter yet more definitely a rationalist. I do not propose to turn this book into one of ordinary Christian apologetics; I should be glad to meet at any other time the enemies of Christianity in that more obvious arena. Here I am only giving an account of my own growth in spiritual certainty. But I may pause to remark that the more I saw of the merely abstract arguments against the Christian cosmology the less I thought of them. I mean that having found the moral atmosphere of the Incarnation to be common sense, I then looked at the established intellectual arguments against the Incarnation and found them to be common nonsense. In case the argument should be thought to suffer from the absence of the ordinary apologetic I will here very briefly summarise my own arguments and conclusions on the purely objective or scientific truth of the matter.

If I am asked, as a purely intellectual question, why I believe in Christianity, I can only answer, "For the same reason that an intelligent agnostic disbelieves in Christianity." I believe in it quite rationally upon the evidence. But the evidence in my case, as in that of the intelligent agnostic, is not really in this or that alleged demonstration; it is in an enormous accumulation of small but unanimous facts. The secularist is not to be blamed because his objections to Christianity are miscellaneous and even scrappy; it is precisely such scrappy evidence that does convince the mind. I mean that a man may well be less convinced of a philosophy from four books, than from one book, one battle, one landscape, and one old friend. The very fact that the things are of different kinds increases the importance of the fact that they all point to one conclusion. Now, the non-Christianity of the average educated man to-day is almost always, to do him justice, made up of these loose but living experiences. I can only say that my evidences for Christianity are of the same vivid but varied kind as his evidences against it. For when I look at these various anti-Christian truths, I simply discover that none of them are true. I discover that the true tide and force of all the facts flows the other way. Let us take cases. Many a sensible modern man must have abandoned Christianity under the pressure of three such converging convictions as these: first, that men, with their shape, structure, and sexuality, are, after all, very much like beasts, a mere variety of the animal kingdom; second, that primeval religion arose in ignorance and fear; third, that priests have blighted societies with bitterness and gloom. Those three anti-Christian arguments are very different; but they are all quite logical and legitimate; and they all converge. The only objection to them (I discover) is that they are all untrue. If you leave off looking at books about beasts and men, if you begin to look at beasts and men then (if you have any humour or imagination, any sense of the frantic or the farcical) you will observe that the startling thing is not how like man is to the brutes, but how unlike he is. It is the monstrous scale of his divergence that requires an explanation. That man and brute are like is, in a sense, a truism; but that being so like they should then be so insanely unlike, that is the shock and the enigma. That an ape has hands is far less interesting to the philosopher than the fact that having hands he does next to nothing with them; does not play knuckle-bones or the violin; does not carve marble or carve mutton. People talk of barbaric architecture and debased art. But elephants do not build colossal temples of ivory even in a roccoco style; camels do not paint even bad pictures, though equipped with the material of many camel's-hair brushes. Certain modern dreamers say that ants and bees have a society superior to ours. They have, indeed, a civilization; but that very truth only reminds us that it is an inferior civilization. Who ever found an ant-hill decorated with the statues of celebrated ants? Who has seen a bee-hive carved with the images of gorgeous queens of old? No; the chasm between man and other creatures may have a natural explanation, but it is a chasm. We talk of wild animals; but man is the only wild animal. It is man that has broken out. All other animals are tame animals; following the rugged respectability of the tribe or type. All other animals are domestic animals; man alone is ever undomestic, either as a profligate or a monk. So that this first superficial reason for materialism is, if anything, a reason for its opposite; it is exactly where biology leaves off that all religion begins.

It would be the same if I examined the second of the three chance rationalist arguments; the argument that all that we call divine began in some darkness and terror. When I did attempt to examine the foundations of this modern idea I simply found that there were none. Science knows nothing whatever about pre-historic man; for the excellent reason that he is pre-historic. A few professors choose to conjecture that such things as human sacrifice were once innocent and general and that they gradually dwindled; but there is no direct evidence of it, and the small amount of indirect evidence is very much the other way. In the earliest legends we have, such as the tales of Isaac and of Iphigenia, human sacrifice is not introduced as something old, but rather as something new; as a strange and frightful exception darkly demanded by the gods. History says nothing; and legends all say that the earth was kinder in its earliest time. There is no tradition of progress; but the whole human race has a tradition of the Fall. Amusingly enough, indeed, the very dissemination of this idea is used against its authenticity. Learned men literally say that this pre-historic calamity cannot be true because every race of mankind remembers it. I cannot keep pace with these paradoxes.

And if we took the third chance instance, it would be the same; the view that priests darken and embitter the world. I look at the world and simply discover that they don't. Those countries in Europe which are still influenced by priests, are exactly the countries where there is still singing and dancing and coloured dresses and art in the open-air. Catholic doctrine and discipline may be walls; but they are the walls of a playground. Christianity is the only frame which has preserved the pleasure of Paganism. We might fancy some children playing on the flat grassy top of some tall island in the sea. So long as there was a wall round the cliff's edge they could fling themselves into every frantic game and make the place the noisiest of nurseries. But the walls were knocked down, leaving the naked peril of the precipice. They did not fall over; but when their friends returned to them they were all huddled in terror in the centre of the island; and their song had ceased.

Thus these three facts of experience, such facts as go to make an agnostic, are, in this view, turned totally round. I am left saying, "Give me an explanation, first, of the towering eccentricity of man among the brutes; second, of the vast human tradition of some ancient happiness; third, of the partial perpetuation of such pagan joy in the countries of the Catholic Church." One explanation, at any rate, covers all three: the theory that twice was the natural order interrupted by some explosion or revelation such as people now call "psychic." Once Heaven came upon the earth with a power or seal called the image of God, whereby man took command of Nature; and once again (when in empire after empire men had been found wanting) Heaven came to save mankind in the awful shape of a man. This would explain why the mass of men always look backwards; and why the only corner where they in any sense look forwards is the little continent where Christ has His Church. I know it will be said that Japan has become progressive. But how can this be an answer when even in saying "Japan has become progressive," we really only mean, "Japan has become European"? But I wish here not so much to insist on my own explanation as to insist on my original remark. I agree with the ordinary unbelieving man in the street in being guided by three or four odd facts all pointing to something; only when I came to look at the facts I always found they pointed to something else.

I have given an imaginary triad of such ordinary anti-Christian arguments; if that be too narrow a basis I will give on the spur of the moment another. These are the kind of thoughts which in combination create the impression that Christianity is something weak and diseased. First, for instance, that Jesus was a gentle creature, sheepish and unworldly, a mere ineffectual appeal to the world; second, that Christianity arose and flourished in the dark ages of ignorance, and that to these the Church would drag us back; third, that the people still strongly religious or (if you will) superstitious—such people as the Irish—are weak, unpractical, and behind the times. I only mention these ideas to affirm the same thing: that when I looked into them independently I found, not that the conclusions were unphilosophical, but simply that the facts were not facts. Instead of looking at books and pictures about the New Testament I looked at the New Testament. There I found an account, not in the least of a person with his hair parted in the middle or his hands clasped in appeal, but of an extraordinary being with lips of thunder and acts of lurid decision, flinging down tables, casting out devils, passing with the wild secrecy of the wind from mountain isolation to a sort of dreadful demagogy; a being who often acted like an angry god— and always like a god. Christ had even a literary style of his own, not to be found, I think, elsewhere; it consists of an almost furious use of the A FORTIORI. His "how much more" is piled one upon another like castle upon castle in the clouds. The diction used ABOUT Christ has been, and perhaps wisely, sweet and submissive. But the diction used by Christ is quite curiously gigantesque; it is full of camels leaping through needles and mountains hurled into the sea. Morally it is equally terrific; he called himself a sword of slaughter, and told men to buy swords if they sold their coats for them. That he used other even wilder words on the side of non-resistance greatly increases the mystery; but it also, if anything, rather increases the violence. We cannot even explain it by calling such a being insane; for insanity is usually along one consistent channel. The maniac is generally a monomaniac. Here we must remember the difficult definition of Christianity already given; Christianity is a superhuman paradox whereby two opposite passions may blaze beside each other. The one explanation of the Gospel language that does explain it, is that it is the survey of one who from some supernatural height beholds some more startling synthesis.

I take in order the next instance offered: the idea that Christianity belongs to the Dark Ages. Here I did not satisfy myself with reading modern generalisations; I read a little history. And in history I found that Christianity, so far from belonging to the Dark Ages, was the one path across the Dark Ages that was not dark. It was a shining bridge connecting two shining civilizations. If any one says that the faith arose in ignorance and savagery the answer is simple: it didn't. It arose in the Mediterranean civilization in the full summer of the Roman Empire. The world was swarming with sceptics, and pantheism was as plain as the sun, when Constantine nailed the cross to the mast. It is perfectly true that afterwards the ship sank; but it is far more extraordinary that the ship came up again: repainted and glittering, with the cross still at the top. This is the amazing thing the religion did: it turned a sunken ship into a submarine. The ark lived under the load of waters; after being buried under the debris of dynasties and clans, we arose and remembered Rome. If our faith had been a mere fad of the fading empire, fad would have followed fad in the twilight, and if the civilization ever re-emerged (and many such have never re-emerged) it would have been under some new barbaric flag. But the Christian Church was the last life of the old society and was also the first life of the new. She took the people who were forgetting how to make an arch and she taught them to invent the Gothic arch. In a word, the most absurd thing that could be said of the Church is the thing we have all heard said of it. How can we say that the Church wishes to bring us back into the Dark Ages? The Church was the only thing that ever brought us out of them.

I added in this second trinity of objections an idle instance taken from those who feel such people as the Irish to be weakened or made stagnant by superstition. I only added it because this is a peculiar case of a statement of fact that turns out to be a statement of falsehood. It is constantly said of the Irish that they are impractical. But if we refrain for a moment from looking at what is said about them and look at what is DONE about them, we shall see that the Irish are not only practical, but quite painfully successful. The poverty of their country, the minority of their members are simply the conditions under which they were asked to work; but no other group in the British Empire has done so much with such conditions. The Nationalists were the only minority that ever succeeded in twisting the whole British Parliament sharply out of its path. The Irish peasants are the only poor men in these islands who have forced their masters to disgorge. These people, whom we call priest-ridden, are the only Britons who will not be squire-ridden. And when I came to look at the actual Irish character, the case was the same. Irishmen are best at the specially HARD professions—the trades of iron, the lawyer, and the soldier. In all these cases, therefore, I came back to the same conclusion: the sceptic was quite right to go by the facts, only he had not looked at the facts. The sceptic is too credulous; he believes in newspapers or even in encyclopedias. Again the three questions left me with three very antagonistic questions. The average sceptic wanted to know how I explained the namby-pamby note in the Gospel, the connection of the creed with mediaeval darkness and the political impracticability of the Celtic Christians. But I wanted to ask, and to ask with an earnestness amounting to urgency, "What is this incomparable energy which appears first in one walking the earth like a living judgment and this energy which can die with a dying civilization and yet force it to a resurrection from the dead; this energy which last of all can inflame a bankrupt peasantry with so fixed a faith in justice that they get what they ask, while others go empty away; so that the most helpless island of the Empire can actually help itself?"

There is an answer: it is an answer to say that the energy is truly from out-side the world; that it is psychic, or at least one of the results of a real psychical disturbance. The highest gratitude and respect are due to the great human civi-lizations such as the old Egyptian or the existing Chinese. Nevertheless it is no injustice for them to say that only modern Europe has exhibited incessantly a power of self-renewal recurring often at the shortest intervals and descending to the smallest facts of building or costume. All other societies die finally and with dignity. We die daily. We are always being born again with almost indecent obstetrics. It is hardly an exaggeration to say that there is in historic Christendom a sort of unnatural life: it could be explained as a supernatural life. It could be explained as an awful galvanic life working in what would have been a corpse.

For our civilization OUGHT to have died, by all parallels, by all sociological probability, in the Ragnorak of the end of Rome. That is the weird inspiration of our estate: you and I have no business to be here at all. We are all REVENANTS; all living Christians are dead pagans walking about. Just as Europe was about to be gathered in silence to Assyria and Babylon, something entered into its body. And Europe has had a strange life—it is not too much to say that it has had the JUMPS— ever since.

I have dealt at length with such typical triads of doubt in order to convey the main contention—that my own case for Christianity is rational; but it is not simple. It is an accumulation of varied facts, like the attitude of the ordinary agnostic. But the ordinary agnostic has got his facts all wrong. He is a non-believer for a multitude of reasons; but they are untrue reasons. He doubts because the Middle Ages were barbaric, but they weren't; because Darwinism is demonstrated, but it isn't; because miracles do not happen, but they do; because monks were lazy, but they were very industrious; because nuns are unhappy, but they are particularly cheerful; because Christian art was sad and pale, but it was picked out in peculiarly bright colours and gay with gold; because modern science is moving away from the supernatural, but it isn't, it is moving towards the supernatural with the rapidity of a railway train.

But among these million facts all flowing one way there is, of course, one question sufficiently solid and separate to be treated briefly, but by itself; I mean the objective occurrence of the supernatural. In another chapter I have indicated the fallacy of the ordinary supposition that the world must be impersonal because it is orderly. A person is just as likely to desire an orderly thing as a disorderly thing. But my own positive conviction that personal creation is more conceivable than material fate, is, I admit, in a sense, undiscussable. I will not call it a faith or an intuition, for those words are mixed up with mere emotion, it is strictly an intellectual conviction; but it is a PRIMARY intellectual conviction like the certainty of self of the good of living. Any one who likes, therefore, may call my belief in God merely mystical; the phrase is not worth fighting about. But my belief that miracles have happened in human history is not a mystical belief at all; I believe in them upon human evidences as I do in the discovery of America. Upon this point there is a simple logical fact that only requires to be stated and cleared up. Somehow or other an extraordinary idea has arisen that the disbelievers in miracles consider them coldly and fairly, while believers in miracles accept them only in connection with some dogma. The fact is quite the other way. The believers in miracles accept them (rightly or wrongly) because they have evidence for them. The disbelievers in miracles deny them (rightly or wrongly) because they have a doctrine against them. The open, obvious, democratic thing is to believe an old apple-woman when she bears testimony to a miracle, just as you believe an old apple-woman when she bears testimony to a murder. The plain, popular course is to trust the peasant's word about the ghost exactly as far as you trust the peasant's word about the landlord. Being a peasant he will probably have a great deal of healthy agnosticism about both. Still you could fill the British Museum with evidence uttered by the peasant, and given in favour of the ghost. If it comes to human testimony there is a choking cataract of human testimony in favour of the supernatural. If you reject it, you can only mean one of two things. You reject the peasant's story about the ghost either because the man is a peasant or because the story is a ghost story. That is, you either deny the main principle of democracy, or you affirm the main principle of materialism— the abstract impossibility of miracle. You have a perfect right to do so; but in that case you are the dogmatist. It is we Christians who accept all actual evidence—it is you rationalists who refuse actual evidence being constrained to do so by your creed. But I am not constrained by any creed in the matter, and looking impartially into certain miracles of mediaeval and modern times, I have come to the conclusion that they occurred. All argument against these plain facts is always argument in a circle. If I say, "Mediaeval documents attest certain miracles as much as they attest certain battles," they answer, "But mediaevals were superstitious"; if I want to know in what they were superstitious, the only ultimate answer is that they believed in the miracles. If I say "a peasant saw a ghost," I am told, "But peasants are so credulous." If I ask, "Why credulous?" the only answer is—that they see ghosts. Iceland is impossible because only stupid sailors have seen it; and the sailors are only stupid because they say they have seen Iceland. It is only fair to add that there is another argument that the unbeliever may rationally use against miracles, though he himself generally forgets to use it.

He may say that there has been in many miraculous stories a notion of spiritual preparation and acceptance: in short, that the miracle could only come to him who believed in it. It may be so, and if it is so how are we to test it? If we are inquiring whether certain results follow faith, it is useless to repeat wearily that (if they happen) they do follow faith. If faith is one of the conditions, those without faith have a most healthy right to laugh. But they have no right to judge. Being a believer may be, if you like, as bad as being drunk; still if we were extracting psychological facts from drunkards, it would be absurd to be always taunting them with having been drunk. Suppose we were investigating whether angry men really saw a red mist before their eyes. Suppose sixty excellent householders swore that when angry they had seen this crimson cloud: surely it would be absurd to answer "Oh, but you admit you were angry at the time." They might reasonably rejoin (in a stentorian chorus), "How the blazes could we discover, without being angry, whether angry people see red?" So the saints and ascetics might rationally reply, "Suppose that the question is whether believers can see visions—even then, if you are interested in visions it is no point to object to believers." You are still arguing in a circle—in that old mad circle with which this book began.

The question of whether miracles ever occur is a question of common sense and of ordinary historical imagination: not of any final physical experiment. One may here surely dismiss that quite brainless piece of pedantry which talks about the need for "scientific conditions" in connection with alleged spiritual phenomena. If we are asking whether a dead soul can communicate with a living it is ludicrous to insist that it shall be under conditions in which no two living souls in their senses would seriously communicate with each other. The fact that ghosts prefer darkness no more disproves the existence of ghosts than the fact that lovers prefer darkness disproves the existence of love. If you choose to say, "I will believe that Miss Brown called her fiance a periwinkle or, any other endearing term, if she will repeat the word before seventeen psychologists," then I shall reply, "Very well, if those are your conditions, you will never get the truth, for she certainly will not say it." It is just as unscientific as it is unphilosophical to be surprised that in an unsympathetic atmosphere certain extraordinary sympathies do not arise. It is as if I said that I could not tell if there was a fog because the air was not clear enough; or as if I insisted on perfect sunlight in order to see a solar eclipse.

As a common-sense conclusion, such as those to which we come about sex or about midnight (well knowing that many details must in their own nature be concealed) I conclude that miracles do happen. I am forced to it by a conspiracy of facts: the fact that the men who encounter elves or angels are not the mystics and the morbid dreamers, but fishermen, farmers, and all men at once coarse and cautious; the fact that we all know men who testify to spiritualistic incidents but are not spiritualists, the fact that science itself admits such things more and more every day. Science will even admit the Ascension if you call it Levitation, and will very likely admit the Resurrection when it has thought of another word for it. I suggest the Regalvanisation. But the strongest of all is the dilemma above mentioned, that these supernatural things are never denied except on the basis either of anti-democracy or of materialist dogmatism—I may say materialist mysticism. The sceptic always takes one of the two positions; either an ordinary man need not be believed, or an extraordinary event must not be believed. For I hope we may dismiss the argument against wonders attempted in the mere recapitulation of frauds, of swindling mediums or trick miracles. That is not an argument at all, good or bad. A false ghost disproves the reality of ghosts exactly as much as a forged banknote disproves the existence of the Bank of England— if anything, it proves its existence.

Given this conviction that the spiritual phenomena do occur (my evidence for which is complex but rational), we then collide with one of the worst mental evils of the age. The greatest disaster of the nineteenth century was this: that men began to use the word "spiritual" as the same as the word "good." They thought that to grow in refinement and uncorporeality was to grow in virtue. When scientific evolution was announced, some feared that it would encourage mere animality. It did worse: it encouraged mere spirituality. It taught men to think that so long as they were passing from the ape they were going to the angel. But you can pass from the ape and go to the devil. A man of genius, very typical of that time of bewilderment, expressed it perfectly. Benjamin Disraeli was right when he said he was on the side of the angels. He was indeed; he was on the side of the fallen angels. He was not on the side of any mere appetite or animal brutality; but he was on the side of all the imperialism of the princes of the abyss; he was on the side of arrogance and mystery, and contempt of all obvious good. Between this sunken pride and the towering humilities of heaven there are, one must suppose, spirits of shapes and sizes. Man, in encountering them, must make much the same mistakes that he makes in encountering any other varied types in any other distant continent. It must be hard at first to know who is supreme and who is subordinate. If a shade arose from the under world, and stared at Piccadilly, that shade would not quite understand the idea of an ordinary closed carriage. He would suppose that the coachman on the box was a triumphant conqueror, dragging behind him a kicking and imprisoned captive. So, if we see spiritual facts for the first time, we may mistake who is uppermost. It is not enough to find the gods; they are obvious; we must find God, the real chief of the gods. We must have a long historic experience in supernatural phenomena— in order to discover which are really natural. In this light I find the history of Christianity, and even of its Hebrew origins, quite practical and clear. It does not trouble me to be told that the Hebrew god was one among many. I know he was, without any research to tell me so. Jehovah and Baal looked equally important, just as the sun and the moon looked the same size. It is only slowly that we learn that the sun is immeasurably our master, and the small moon only our satellite. Believing that there is a world of spirits, I shall walk in it as I do in the world of men, looking for the thing that I like and think good. Just as I should seek in a desert for clean water, or toil at the North Pole to make a comfortable fire, so I shall search the land of void and vision until I find something fresh like water, and comforting like fire; until I find some place in eternity, where I am literally at home. And there is only one such place to be found.

I have now said enough to show (to any one to whom such an explanation is essential) that I have in the ordinary arena of apologetics, a ground of belief. In pure records of experiment (if these be taken democratically without contempt or favour) there is evidence first, that miracles happen, and second that the nobler miracles belong to our tradition. But I will not pretend that this curt discussion is my real reason for accepting Christianity instead of taking the moral good of Christianity as I should take it out of Confucianism.

I have another far more solid and central ground for submitting to it as a faith, instead of merely picking up hints from it as a scheme. And that is this: that the Christian Church in its practical relation to my soul is a living teacher, not a dead one. It not only certainly taught me yesterday, but will almost certainly teach me to-morrow. Once I saw suddenly the meaning of the shape of the cross; some day I may see suddenly the meaning of the shape of the mitre. One fine morning I saw why windows were pointed; some fine morning I may see why priests were shaven. Plato has told you a truth; but Plato is dead. Shakespeare has startled you with an image; but Shakespeare will not startle you with any more. But imagine what it would be to live with such men still living, to know that Plato might break out with an original lecture to-morrow, or that at any moment Shakespeare might shatter everything with a single song. The man who lives in contact with what he believes to be a living Church is a man always expecting to meet Plato and Shakespeare to-morrow at breakfast. He is always expecting to see some truth that he has never seen before. There is one only other parallel to this position; and that is the parallel of the life in which we all began. When your father told you, walking about the garden, that bees stung or that roses smelt sweet, you did not talk of taking the best out of his philosophy. When the bees stung you, you did not call it an entertaining coincidence. When the rose smelt sweet you did not say "My father is a rude, barbaric symbol, enshrining (perhaps unconsciously) the deep delicate truths that flowers smell." No: you believed your father, because you had found him to be a living fountain of facts, a thing that really knew more than you; a thing that would tell you truth to-morrow, as well as to-day. And if this was true of your father, it was even truer of your mother; at least it was true of mine, to whom this book is dedicated. Now, when society is in a rather futile fuss about the subjection of women, will no one say how much every man owes to the tyranny and privilege of women, to the fact that they alone rule education until education becomes futile: for a boy is only sent to be taught at school when it is too late to teach him anything. The real thing has been done already, and thank God it is nearly always done by women. Every man is womanised, merely by being born. They talk of the masculine woman; but every man is a feminised man. And if ever men walk to Westminster to protest against this female privilege, I shall not join their procession.

For I remember with certainty this fixed psychological fact; that the very time when I was most under a woman's authority, I was most full of flame and adventure. Exactly because when my mother said that ants bit they did bite, and because snow did come in winter (as she said); therefore the whole world was to me a fairyland of wonderful fulfilments, and it was like living in some Hebraic age, when prophecy after prophecy came true. I went out as a child into the garden, and it was a terrible place to me, precisely because I had a clue to it: if I had held no clue it would not have been terrible, but tame. A mere unmeaning wilderness is not even impressive. But the garden of childhood was fascinating, exactly because everything had a fixed meaning which could be found out in its turn. Inch by inch I might discover what was the object of the ugly shape called a rake; or form some shadowy conjecture as to why my parents kept a cat.

So, since I have accepted Christendom as a mother and not merely as a chance example, I have found Europe and the world once more like the little garden where I stared at the symbolic shapes of cat and rake; I look at everything with the old elvish ignorance and expectancy. This or that rite or doctrine may look as

ugly and extraordinary as a rake; but I have found by experience that such things
end somehow in grass and flowers. A clergyman may be apparently as useless as
a cat, but he is also as fascinating, for there must be some strange reason for his
existence. I give one instance out of a hundred; I have not myself any instinctive
kinship with that enthusiasm for physical virginity, which has certainly been a note
of historic Christianity. But when I look not at myself but at the world, I perceive
that this enthusiasm is not only a note of Christianity, but a note of Paganism, a
note of high human nature in many spheres. The Greeks felt virginity when they
carved Artemis, the Romans when they robed the vestals, the worst and wildest
of the great Elizabethan playwrights clung to the literal purity of a woman as to
the central pillar of the world. Above all, the modern world (even while mocking
sexual innocence) has flung itself into a generous idolatry of sexual innocence—
the great modern worship of children. For any man who loves children will agree
that their peculiar beauty is hurt by a hint of physical sex. With all this human
experience, allied with the Christian authority, I simply conclude that I am wrong,
and the church right; or rather that I am defective, while the church is universal.
It takes all sorts to make a church; she does not ask me to be celibate. But the fact
that I have no appreciation of the celibates, I accept like the fact that I have no
ear for music. The best human experience is against me, as it is on the subject of
Bach. Celibacy is one flower in my father's garden, of which I have not been told
the sweet or terrible name. But I may be told it any day.

This, therefore, is, in conclusion, my reason for accepting the religion and
not merely the scattered and secular truths out of the religion. I do it because
the thing has not merely told this truth or that truth, but has revealed itself as a
truth-telling thing. All other philosophies say the things that plainly seem to be
true; only this philosophy has again and again said the thing that does not seem to
be true, but is true. Alone of all creeds it is convincing where it is not attractive;
it turns out to be right, like my father in the garden. Theosophists for instance
will preach an obviously attractive idea like re-incarnation; but if we wait for its
logical results, they are spiritual superciliousness and the cruelty of caste. For if a
man is a beggar by his own pre-natal sins, people will tend to despise the beggar.
But Christianity preaches an obviously unattractive idea, such as original sin; but
when we wait for its results, they are pathos and brotherhood, and a thunder
of laughter and pity; for only with original sin we can at once pity the beggar
and distrust the king. Men of science offer us health, an obvious benefit; it is
only afterwards that we discover that by health, they mean bodily slavery and
spiritual tedium. Orthodoxy makes us jump by the sudden brink of hell; it is only
afterwards that we realise that jumping was an athletic exercise highly beneficial
to our health. It is only afterwards that we realise that this danger is the root of
all drama and romance. The strongest argument for the divine grace is simply its
ungraciousness. The unpopular parts of Christianity turn out when examined to
be the very props of the people. The outer ring of Christianity is a rigid guard of

ethical abnegations and professional priests; but inside that inhuman guard you will find the old human life dancing like children, and drinking wine like men; for Christianity is the only frame for pagan freedom. But in the modern philosophy the case is opposite; it is its outer ring that is obviously artistic and emancipated; its despair is within.

And its despair is this, that it does not really believe that there is any meaning in the universe; therefore it cannot hope to find any romance; its romances will have no plots. A man cannot expect any adventures in the land of anarchy. But a man can expect any number of adventures if he goes travelling in the land of authority. One can find no meanings in a jungle of scepticism; but the man will find more and more meanings who walks through a forest of doctrine and design. Here everything has a story tied to its tail, like the tools or pictures in my father's house; for it is my father's house. I end where I began—at the right end. I have entered at last the gate of all good philosophy. I have come into my second childhood.

But this larger and more adventurous Christian universe has one final mark difficult to express; yet as a conclusion of the whole matter I will attempt to express it. All the real argument about religion turns on the question of whether a man who was born upside down can tell when he comes right way up. The primary paradox of Christianity is that the ordinary condition of man is not his sane or sensible condition; that the normal itself is an abnormality. That is the inmost philosophy of the Fall. In Sir Oliver Lodge's interesting new Catechism, the first two questions were: "What are you?" and "What, then, is the meaning of the Fall of Man?" I remember amusing myself by writing my own answers to the questions; but I soon found that they were very broken and agnostic answers. To the question, "What are you?" I could only answer, "God knows." And to the question, "What is meant by the Fall?" I could answer with complete sincerity, "That whatever I am, I am not myself." This is the prime paradox of our religion; something that we have never in any full sense known, is not only better than ourselves, but even more natural to us than ourselves. And there is really no test of this except the merely experimental one with which these pages began, the test of the padded cell and the open door. It is only since I have known orthodoxy that I have known mental emancipation. But, in conclusion, it has one special application to the ultimate idea of joy.

It is said that Paganism is a religion of joy and Christianity of sorrow; it would be just as easy to prove that Paganism is pure sorrow and Christianity pure joy. Such conflicts mean nothing and lead nowhere. Everything human must have in it both joy and sorrow; the only matter of interest is the manner in which the two things are balanced or divided. And the really interesting thing is this, that the pagan was (in the main) happier and happier as he approached the earth, but sadder and sadder as he approached the heavens. The gaiety of the best Paganism, as in the playfulness of Catullus or Theocritus, is, indeed, an eternal gaiety never to be forgotten by a grateful humanity. But it is all a gaiety about the facts of life, not about its origin. To the pagan the small things are as sweet as the small brooks breaking out of the mountain; but the broad things are as bitter as the sea. When the pagan looks at the very core of the cosmos he is struck cold. Behind the gods, who are merely despotic, sit the fates, who are deadly. Nay, the fates are worse than deadly; they are dead. And when rationalists say that the ancient world was more enlightened than the Christian, from their point of view they are right. For when they say "enlightened" they mean darkened with incurable despair. It is profoundly true that the ancient world was more modern than the Christian. The common bond is in the fact that ancients and moderns have both been miserable about existence, about everything, while mediaevals were happy about that at least. I freely grant that the pagans, like the moderns, were only miserable about everything—they were quite jolly about everything else. I concede that the Christians of the Middle Ages were only at peace about everything—they were at war about everything else. But if the question turn on the primary pivot of the cosmos, then there was more cosmic contentment in the narrow and bloody streets of Florence than in the theatre of Athens or the open garden of Epicurus. Giotto lived in a gloomier town than Euripides, but he lived in a gayer universe.

The mass of men have been forced to be gay about the little things, but sad about the big ones. Nevertheless (I offer my last dogma defiantly) it is not native to man to be so. Man is more himself, man is more manlike, when joy is the fundamental thing in him, and grief the superficial. Melancholy should be an innocent interlude, a tender and fugitive frame of mind; praise should be the permanent pulsation of the soul. Pessimism is at best an emotional half-holiday; joy is the uproarious labour by which all things live. Yet, according to the apparent estate of man as seen by the pagan or the agnostic, this primary need of human nature can never be fulfilled. Joy ought to be expansive; but for the agnostic it must be contracted, it must cling to one corner of the world. Grief ought to be a concentration; but for the agnostic its desolation is spread through an unthinkable eternity. This is what I call being born upside down. The sceptic may truly be said to be topsy-turvy; for his feet are dancing upwards in idle ecstasies, while his brain is in the abyss. To the modern man the heavens are actually below the earth. The explanation is simple; he is standing on his head; which is a very weak pedestal to stand on. But when he has found his feet again he knows it. Christianity satisfies suddenly and perfectly man's ancestral instinct for being the right way up; satisfies it supremely in this; that by its creed joy becomes something gigantic and sadness something special and small. The vault above us is not deaf because the universe is an idiot; the silence is not the heartless silence of an endless and aimless world. Rather the silence around us is a small and pitiful stillness like the prompt stillness in a sick-room. We are perhaps permitted tragedy as a sort of merciful comedy: because the frantic energy of divine things would knock us down like a drunken farce. We can take our own tears more lightly than we could take the tremendous levities of the angels. So we sit perhaps in a starry chamber of silence, while the laughter of the heavens is too loud for us to hear.

Joy, which was the small publicity of the pagan, is the gigantic secret of the Christian. And as I close this chaotic volume I open again the strange small book from which all Christianity came; and I am again haunted by a kind of confirmation. The tremendous figure which fills the Gospels towers in this respect, as in every other, above all the thinkers who ever thought themselves tall. His pathos was natural, almost casual. The Stoics, ancient and modern, were proud of concealing their tears. He never concealed His tears; He showed them plainly on His open face at any daily sight, such as the far sight of His native city. Yet He concealed something. Solemn supermen and imperial diplomatists are proud of restraining their anger. He never restrained His anger. He flung furniture down the front steps of the Temple, and asked men how they expected to escape the damnation of Hell. Yet He restrained something. I say it with reverence; there was in that shattering personality a thread that must be called shyness. There was something that He hid from all men when He went up a mountain to pray. There was something that He covered constantly by abrupt silence or impetuous isolation. There was some one thing that was too great for God to show us when He walked upon our earth; and I have sometimes fancied that it was His mirth.

What's Wrong with the World

Dedication

To C. F G. Masterman, M. P.
My Dear Charles,

 originally called this book "What is Wrong," and it would have satisfied your sardonic temper to note the number of social misunderstandings that arose from the use of the title. Many a mild lady visitor opened her eyes when I remarked casually, "I have been doing 'What is Wrong' all this morning." And one minister of religion moved quite sharply in his chair when I told him (as he understood it) that I had to run upstairs and do what was wrong, but should be down again in a minute. Exactly of what occult vice they silently accused me I cannot conjecture, but I know of what I accuse myself; and that is, of having written a very shapeless and inadequate book, and one quite unworthy to be dedicated to you. As far as literature goes, this book is what is wrong and no mistake.

It may seem a refinement of insolence to present so wild a composition to one who has recorded two or three of the really impressive visions of the moving millions of England. You are the only man alive who can make the map of England crawl with life; a most creepy and enviable accomplishment. Why then should I trouble you with a book which, even if it achieves its object (which is monstrously unlikely) can only be a thundering gallop of theory?

Well, I do it partly because I think you politicians are none the worse for a few inconvenient ideals; but more because you will recognise the many arguments we have had, those arguments which the most wonderful ladies in the world can never endure for very long. And, perhaps, you will agree with me that the thread of comradeship and conversation must be protected because it is so frivolous. It must be held sacred, it must not be snapped, because it is not worth tying together again. It is exactly because argument is idle that men (I mean males) must take it seriously; for when (we feel), until the crack of doom, shall we have so delightful a difference again? But most of all I offer it to you because there exists not only comradeship, but a very different thing, called friendship; an agreement under all the arguments and a thread which, please God, will never break.

Yours always,

G. K. Chesterton.

Part 1: The Homelessness of Man

Chapter 1
The Medical Mistake

book of modern social inquiry has a shape that is somewhat sharply defined. It begins as a rule with an analysis, with statistics, tables of population, decrease of crime among Congregationalists, growth of hysteria among policemen, and similar ascertained facts; it ends with a chapter that is generally called "The Remedy." It is almost wholly due to this careful, solid, and scientific method that "The Remedy" is never found. For this scheme of medical question and answer is a blunder; the first great blunder of sociology. It is always called stating the disease before we find the cure. But it is the whole definition and dignity of man that in social matters we must actually find the cure before we find the disease.

The fallacy is one of the fifty fallacies that come from the modern madness for biological or bodily metaphors. It is convenient to speak of the Social Organism, just as it is convenient to speak of the British Lion. But Britain is no more an organism than Britain is a lion. The moment we begin to give a nation the unity and simplicity of an animal, we begin to think wildly. Because every man is a biped, fifty men are not a centipede. This has produced, for instance, the gaping absurdity of perpetually talking about "young nations" and "dying nations," as if a nation had a fixed and physical span of life. Thus people will say that Spain has entered a final senility; they might as well say that Spain is losing all her teeth. Or people will say that Canada should soon produce a literature; which is like saying that Canada must soon grow a new moustache. Nations consist of people; the first generation may be decrepit, or the ten thousandth may be vigorous. Similar applications of the fallacy are made by those who see in the increasing size of national possessions, a simple increase in wisdom and stature, and in favor with God and man. These people, indeed, even fall short in subtlety of the parallel of a human body. They do not even ask whether an empire is growing taller in its youth, or only growing fatter in its old age. But of all the instances of error arising from this physical fancy, the worst is that we have before us: the habit of exhaustively describing a social sickness, and then propounding a social drug.

Now we do talk first about the disease in cases of bodily breakdown; and that for an excellent reason. Because, though there may be doubt about the way in which the body broke down, there is no doubt at all about the shape in which it should be built up again. No doctor proposes to produce a new kind of man, with a new arrangement of eyes or limbs. The hospital, by necessity, may send a man home with one leg less: but it will not (in a creative rapture) send him home with one leg extra. Medical science is content with the normal human body, and only seeks to restore it.

But social science is by no means always content with the normal human soul; it has all sorts of fancy souls for sale. Man as a social idealist will say "I am tired of being a Puritan; I want to be a Pagan," or "Beyond this dark probation of Individualism I see the shining paradise of Collectivism." Now in bodily ills there is none of this difference about the ultimate ideal. The patient may or may not want quinine; but he certainly wants health. No one says "I am tired of this headache; I want some toothache," or "The only thing for this Russian influenza is a few German measles," or "Through this dark probation of catarrh I see the shining paradise of rheumatism." But exactly the whole difficulty in our public problems is that some men are aiming at cures which other men would regard as worse maladies; are offering ultimate conditions as states of health which others would uncompromisingly call states of disease. Mr. Belloc once said that he would no more part with the idea of property than with his teeth; yet to Mr. Bernard Shaw property is not a tooth, but a toothache. Lord Milner has sincerely attempted to introduce German efficiency; and many of us would as soon welcome German measles. Dr. Saleeby would honestly like to have Eugenics; but I would rather have rheumatics.

This is the arresting and dominant fact about modern social discussion; that the quarrel is not merely about the difficulties, but about the aim. We agree about the evil; it is about the good that we should tear each other's eyes out. We all admit that a lazy aristocracy is a bad thing. We should not by any means all admit that an active aristocracy would be a good thing. We all feel angry with an irreligious priesthood; but some of us would go mad with disgust at a really religious one. Everyone is indignant if our army is weak, including the people who would be even more indignant if it were strong. The social case is exactly the opposite of the medical case. We do not disagree, like doctors, about the precise nature of the illness, while agreeing about the nature of health. On the contrary, we all agree that England is unhealthy, but half of us would not look at her in what the other half would call blooming health. Public abuses are so prominent and pestilent that they sweep all generous people into a sort of fictitious unanimity. We forget that, while we agree about the abuses of things, we should differ very much about the uses of them. Mr. Cadbury and I would agree about the bad public house. It would be precisely in front of the good public-house that our painful personal fracas would occur.

I maintain, therefore, that the common sociological method is quite useless: that of first dissecting abject poverty or cataloguing prostitution. We all dislike abject poverty; but it might be another business if we began to discuss independent and dignified poverty. We all disapprove of prostitution; but we do not all approve of purity. The only way to discuss the social evil is to get at once to the social ideal. We can all see the national madness; but what is national sanity? I have called this book "What Is Wrong with the World?" and the upshot of the title can be easily and clearly stated. What is wrong is that we do not ask what is right.

Chapter 2
Wanted, an Unpractical Man

here is a popular philosophical joke intended to typify the endless and useless arguments of philosophers; I mean the joke about which came first, the chicken or the egg? I am not sure that properly understood, it is so futile an inquiry after all. I am not concerned here to enter on those deep metaphysical and theological differences of which the chicken and egg debate is a frivolous, but a very felicitous, type. The evolutionary materialists are appropriately enough represented in the vision of all things coming from an egg, a dim and monstrous oval germ that had laid itself by accident. That other supernatural school of thought (to which I personally adhere) would be not unworthily typified in the fancy that this round world of ours is but an egg brooded upon by a sacred unbegotten bird; the mystic dove of the prophets. But it is to much humbler functions that I here call the awful power of such a distinction. Whether or no the living bird is at the beginning of our mental chain, it is absolutely necessary that it should be at the end of our mental chain. The bird is the thing to be aimed at—not with a gun, but a life-bestowing wand. What is essential to our right thinking is this: that the egg and the bird must not be thought of as equal cosmic occurrences recurring alternatively forever. They must not become a mere egg and bird pattern, like the egg and dart pattern. One is a means and the other an end; they are in different mental worlds. Leaving the complications of the human breakfast-table out of account, in an elemental sense, the egg only exists to produce the chicken. But the chicken does not exist only in order to produce another egg. He may also exist to amuse himself, to praise God, and even to suggest ideas to a French dramatist. Being a conscious life, he is, or may be, valuable in himself. Now our modern politics are full of a noisy forgetfulness; forgetfulness that the production of this happy and conscious life is after all the aim of all complexities and compromises. We talk of nothing but useful men and working institutions; that is, we only think of the chickens as things that will lay more eggs. Instead of seeking to breed our ideal bird, the eagle of Zeus or the Swan of Avon, or whatever we happen to want, we talk entirely in terms of the process and the embryo. The process itself, divorced from its divine object, becomes doubtful and even morbid; poison enters the embryo of everything; and our politics are rotten eggs.

Idealism is only considering everything in its practical essence. Idealism only means that we should consider a poker in reference to poking before we discuss its suitability for wife-beating; that we should ask if an egg is good enough for practical poultry-rearing before we decide that the egg is bad enough for practical politics. But I know that this primary pursuit of the theory (which is but pursuit of the aim) exposes one to the cheap charge of fiddling while Rome is burning. A school, of which Lord Rosebery is representative, has endeavored to substitute for the moral or social ideals which have hitherto been the motive of politics a general coherency or completeness in the social system which has gained the nick-name of "efficiency." I am not very certain of the secret doctrine of this sect in the matter. But, as far as I can make out, "efficiency" means that we ought to discover everything about a machine except what it is for. There has arisen in our time a most singular fancy: the fancy that when things go very wrong we need a practical man. It would be far truer to say, that when things go very wrong we need an unpractical man. Certainly, at least, we need a theorist. A practical man means a man accustomed to mere daily practice, to the way things commonly work. When things will not work, you must have the thinker, the man who has some doctrine about why they work at all. It is wrong to fiddle while Rome is burning; but it is quite right to study the theory of hydraulics while Rome is burning.

It is then necessary to drop one's daily agnosticism and attempt rerum cognoscere causas. If your aeroplane has a slight indisposition, a handy man may mend it. But, if it is seriously ill, it is all the more likely that some absent-minded old professor with wild white hair will have to be dragged out of a college or laboratory to analyze the evil. The more complicated the smash, the whiter-haired and more absent-minded will be the theorist who is needed to deal with it; and in some extreme cases, no one but the man (probably insane) who invented your flying-ship could possibly say what was the matter with it.

"Efficiency," of course, is futile for the same reason that strong men, will-power and the superman are futile. That is, it is futile because it only deals with actions after they have been performed. It has no philosophy for incidents before they happen; therefore it has no power of choice. An act can only be successful or unsuccessful when it is over; if it is to begin, it must be, in the abstract, right or wrong. There is no such thing as backing a winner; for he cannot be a winner when he is backed. There is no such thing as fighting on the winning side; one fights to find out which is the winning side. If any operation has occurred, that operation was efficient. If a man is murdered, the murder was efficient. A tropical sun is as efficient in making people lazy as a Lancashire foreman bully in making them energetic. Maeterlinck is as efficient in filling a man with strange spiritual tremors as Messrs. Crosse and Blackwell are in filling a man with jam. But it all depends on what you want to be filled with. Lord Rosebery, being a modern skeptic, probably prefers the spiritual tremors. I, being an orthodox Christian, prefer the jam. But both are efficient when they have been effected; and inefficient until they are effected. A man who thinks much about success must be the drowsiest sentimentalist; for he must be always looking back. If he only likes victory he must always come late for the battle. For the man of action there is nothing but idealism.

This definite ideal is a far more urgent and practical matter in our existing

English trouble than any immediate plans or proposals. For the present chaos is due to a sort of general oblivion of all that men were originally aiming at. No man demands what he desires; each man demands what he fancies he can get. Soon people forget what the man really wanted first; and after a successful and vigorous political life, he forgets it himself. The whole is an extravagant riot of second bests, a pandemonium of pis-aller. Now this sort of pliability does not merely prevent any heroic consistency, it also prevents any really practical compromise. One can only find the middle distance between two points if the two points will stand still. We may make an arrangement between two litigants who cannot both get what they want; but not if they will not even tell us what they want. The keeper of a restaurant would much prefer that each customer should give his order smartly, though it were for stewed ibis or boiled elephant, rather than that each customer should sit holding his head in his hands, plunged in arithmetical calculations about how much food there can be on the premises. Most of us have suffered from a certain sort of ladies who, by their perverse unselfishness, give more trouble than the selfish; who almost clamor for the unpopular dish and scramble for the worst seat. Most of us have known parties or expeditions full of this seething fuss of self-effacement. From much meaner motives than those of such admirable women, our practical politicians keep things in the same confusion through the same doubt about their real demands. There is nothing that so much prevents a settlement as a tangle of small surrenders. We are bewildered on every side by politicians who are in favor of secular education, but think it hopeless to work for it; who desire total prohibition, but are certain they should not demand it; who regret compulsory education, but resignedly continue it; or who want peasant proprietorship and therefore vote for something else. It is this dazed and floundering opportunism that gets in the way of everything. If our statesmen were visionaries something practical might be done. If we ask for something in the abstract we might get something in the concrete. As it is, it is not only impossible to get what one wants, but it is impossible to get any part of it, because nobody can mark it out plainly like a map. That clear and even hard quality that there was in the old bargaining has wholly vanished. We forget that the word "compromise" contains, among other things, the rigid and ringing word "promise." Moderation is not vague; it is as definite as perfection. The middle point is as fixed as the extreme point.

If I am made to walk the plank by a pirate, it is vain for me to offer, as a common-sense compromise, to walk along the plank for a reasonable distance. It is exactly about the reasonable distance that the pirate and I differ. There is an exquisite mathematical split second at which the plank tips up. My common-sense ends just before that instant; the pirate's common-sense begins just beyond it. But the point itself is as hard as any geometrical diagram; as abstract as any theological dogma.

Chapter 3
The New Hypocrite

ut this new cloudy political cowardice has rendered useless the old English compromise. People have begun to be terrified of an improvement merely because it is complete. They call it utopian and revolutionary that anyone should really have his own way, or anything be really done, and done with. Compromise used to mean that half a loaf was better than no bread. Among modern statesmen it really seems to mean that half a loaf is better than a whole loaf.

As an instance to sharpen the argument, I take the one case of our everlasting education bills. We have actually contrived to invent a new kind of hypocrite. The old hypocrite, Tartuffe or Pecksniff, was a man whose aims were really worldly and practical, while he pretended that they were religious. The new hypocrite is one whose aims are really religious, while he pretends that they are worldly and practical. The Rev. Brown, the Wesleyan minister, sturdily declares that he cares nothing for creeds, but only for education; meanwhile, in truth, the wildest Wesleyanism is tearing his soul. The Rev. Smith, of the Church of England, explains gracefully, with the Oxford manner, that the only question for him is the prosperity and efficiency of the schools; while in truth all the evil passions of a curate are roaring within him. It is a fight of creeds masquerading as policies. I think these reverend gentlemen do themselves wrong; I think they are more pious than they will admit. Theology is not (as some suppose) expunged as an error. It is merely concealed, like a sin. Dr. Clifford really wants a theological atmosphere as much as Lord Halifax; only it is a different one. If Dr. Clifford would ask plainly for Puritanism and Lord Halifax ask plainly for Catholicism, something might be done for them. We are all, one hopes, imaginative enough to recognize the dignity and distinctness of another religion, like Islam or the cult of Apollo. I am quite ready to respect another man's faith; but it is too much to ask that I should respect his doubt, his worldly hesitations and fictions, his political bargain and make-believe. Most Nonconformists with an instinct for English history could see something poetic and national about the Archbishop of Canterbury as an Archbishop of Canterbury. It is when he does the rational British statesman that they very justifiably get annoyed. Most Anglicans with an eye for pluck and simplicity could admire Dr. Clifford as a Baptist minister. It is when he says that he is simply a citizen that nobody can possibly believe him.

But indeed the case is yet more curious than this. The one argument that used to be urged for our creedless vagueness was that at least it saved us from fanaticism. But it does not even do that. On the contrary, it creates and renews fanaticism with a force quite peculiar to itself. This is at once so strange and so true that I will ask the reader's attention to it with a little more precision.

Some people do not like the word "dogma." Fortunately they are free, and there is an alternative for them. There are two things, and two things only, for the human mind, a dogma and a prejudice. The Middle Ages were a rational epoch, an age of doctrine. Our age is, at its best, a poetical epoch, an age of prejudice. A doctrine is a definite point; a prejudice is a direction. That an ox may be eaten, while a man should not be eaten, is a doctrine. That as little as possible of anything should be eaten is a prejudice; which is also sometimes called an ideal. Now a direction is always far more fantastic than a plan. I would rather have the most archaic map of the road to Brighton than a general recommendation to turn to the left. Straight lines that are not parallel must meet at last; but curves may recoil forever. A pair of lovers might walk along the frontier of France and Germany, one on the one side and one on the other, so long as they were not vaguely told to keep away from each other. And this is a strictly true parable of the effect of our modern vagueness in losing and separating men as in a mist.

It is not merely true that a creed unites men. Nay, a difference of creed unites men—so long as it is a clear difference. A boundary unites. Many a magnanimous Moslem and chivalrous Crusader must have been nearer to each other, because they were both dogmatists, than any two homeless agnostics in a pew of Mr. Campbell's chapel. "I say God is One," and "I say God is One but also Three," that is the beginning of a good quarrelsome, manly friendship. But our age would turn these creeds into tendencies. It would tell the Trinitarian to follow multiplicity as such (because it was his "temperament"), and he would turn up later with three hundred and thirty-three persons in the Trinity. Meanwhile, it would turn the Moslem into a Monist: a frightful intellectual fall. It would force that previously healthy person not only to admit that there was one God, but to admit that there was nobody else. When each had, for a long enough period, followed the gleam of his own nose (like the Dong) they would appear again; the Christian a Polytheist, and the Moslem a Panegoist, both quite mad, and far more unfit to understand each other than before.

It is exactly the same with politics. Our political vagueness divides men, it does not fuse them. Men will walk along the edge of a chasm in clear weather, but they will edge miles away from it in a fog. So a Tory can walk up to the very edge of Socialism, if he knows what is Socialism. But if he is told that Socialism is a spirit, a sublime atmosphere, a noble, indefinable tendency, why, then he keeps out of its way; and quite right too. One can meet an assertion with argument; but healthy bigotry is the only way in which one can meet a tendency. I am told that the Japanese method of wrestling consists not of suddenly pressing, but of suddenly giving way. This is one of my many reasons for disliking the Japanese civilization. To use surrender as a weapon is the very worst spirit of the East. But certainly there is no force so hard to fight as the force which it is easy to conquer; the force that always yields and then returns. Such is the force of a great impersonal prejudice, such as possesses the modern world on so many points. Against this there is no weapon at all except a rigid and steely sanity, a resolution not to listen to fads, and not to be infected by diseases.

In short, the rational human faith must armor itself with prejudice in an age of prejudices, just as it armoured itself with logic in an age of logic. But the difference between the two mental methods is marked and unmistakable. The essential of the difference is this: that prejudices are divergent, whereas creeds are always in collision. Believers bump into each other; whereas bigots keep out of each other's way. A creed is a collective thing, and even its sins are sociable. A prejudice is a private thing, and even its tolerance is misanthropic. So it is with our existing divisions. They keep out of each other's way; the Tory paper and the Radical paper do not answer each other; they ignore each other. Genuine controversy, fair cut and thrust before a common audience, has become in our special epoch very rare. For the sincere controversialist is above all things a good listener. The really burning enthusiast never interrupts; he listens to the enemy's arguments as eagerly as a spy would listen to the enemy's arrangements. But if you attempt an actual argument with a modern paper of opposite politics, you will find that no medium is admitted between violence and evasion. You will have no answer except slanging or silence. A modern editor must not have that eager ear that goes with the honest tongue. He may be deaf and silent; and that is called dignity. Or he may be deaf and noisy; and that is called slashing journalism. In neither case is there any controversy; for the whole object of modern party combatants is to charge out of earshot.

The only logical cure for all this is the assertion of a human ideal. In dealing with this, I will try to be as little transcendental as is consistent with reason; it is enough to say that unless we have some doctrine of a divine man, all abuses may be excused, since evolution may turn them into uses. It will be easy for the scientific plutocrat to maintain that humanity will adapt itself to any conditions which we now consider evil. The old tyrants invoked the past; the new tyrants will invoke the future evolution has produced the snail and the owl; evolution can produce a workman who wants no more space than a snail, and no more light than an owl. The employer need not mind sending a Kaffir to work underground; he will soon become an underground animal, like a mole. He need not mind sending a diver to hold his breath in the deep seas; he will soon be a deep-sea animal. Men need not trouble to alter conditions, conditions will so soon alter men. The head can be beaten small enough to fit the hat. Do not knock the fetters off the slave; knock the slave until he forgets the fetters. To all this plausible modern argument for oppression, the only adequate answer is, that there is a permanent human ideal that must not be either confused or destroyed. The most important man on earth is the perfect man who is not there. The Christian religion has specially uttered the ultimate sanity of Man, says Scripture, who shall judge the incarnate and human truth. Our lives and laws are not judged by divine superiority, but simply by human perfection. It is man, says Aristotle, who is the measure. It is the

Son of Man, says Scripture, who shall judge the quick and the dead.

Doctrine, therefore, does not cause dissensions; rather a doctrine alone can cure our dissensions. It is necessary to ask, however, roughly, what abstract and ideal shape in state or family would fulfil the human hunger; and this apart from whether we can completely obtain it or not. But when we come to ask what is the need of normal men, what is the desire of all nations, what is the ideal house, or road, or rule, or republic, or king, or priesthood, then we are confronted with a strange and irritating difficulty peculiar to the present time; and we must call a temporary halt and examine that obstacle.

Chapter 4
The Fear of the Past

he last few decades have been marked by a special cultivation of the romance of the future. We seem to have made up our minds to misunderstand what has happened; and we turn, with a sort of relief, to stating what will happen—which is (apparently) much easier. The modern man no longer presents the memoirs of his great grandfather; but is engaged in writing a detailed and authoritative biography of his great-grandson. Instead of trembling before the specters of the dead, we shudder abjectly under the shadow of the babe unborn. This spirit is apparent everywhere, even to the creation of a form of futurist romance. Sir Walter Scott stands at the dawn of the nineteenth century for the novel of the past; Mr. H. G. Wells stands at the dawn of the twentieth century for the novel of the future. The old story, we know, was supposed to begin: "Late on a winter's evening two horsemen might have been seen—." The new story has to begin: "Late on a winter's evening two aviators will be seen—." The movement is not without its elements of charm; there is something spirited, if eccentric, in the sight of so many people fighting over again the fights that have not yet happened; of people still glowing with the memory of tomorrow morning. A man in advance of the age is a familiar phrase enough. An age in advance of the age is really rather odd.

But when full allowance has been made for this harmless element of poetry and pretty human perversity in the thing, I shall not hesitate to maintain here that this cult of the future is not only a weakness but a cowardice of the age. It is the peculiar evil of this epoch that even its pugnacity is fundamentally frightened; and the Jingo is contemptible not because he is impudent, but because he is timid. The reason why modern armaments do not inflame the imagination like the arms and emblazonments of the Crusades is a reason quite apart from optical ugliness or beauty. Some battleships are as beautiful as the sea; and many Norman nosepieces were as ugly as Norman noses. The atmospheric ugliness that surrounds our scientific war is an emanation from that evil panic which is at the heart of it. The charge of the Crusades was a charge; it was charging towards God, the wild consolation of the braver. The charge of the modern armaments is not a charge at all. It is a rout, a retreat, a flight from the devil, who will catch the hindmost. It is impossible to imagine a mediaeval knight talking of longer and longer French lances, with precisely the quivering employed about larger and larger German ships The man who called the Blue Water School the "Blue Funk School" uttered a psychological truth which that school itself would scarcely essentially deny. Even the two-power standard, if it be a necessity, is in a sense a degrading necessity. Nothing has more alienated many magnanimous minds from Imperial enterprises than the fact that they are always exhibited as stealthy or sudden defenses against a world of cold rapacity and fear. The Boer War, for instance, was colored not so much by the creed that we were doing something right, as by the creed that Boers and Germans were probably doing something wrong; driving us (as it was said) to the sea. Mr. Chamberlain, I think, said that the war was a feather in his cap and so it was: a white feather.

Now this same primary panic that I feel in our rush towards patriotic armaments I feel also in our rush towards future visions of society. The modern mind is forced towards the future by a certain sense of fatigue, not unmixed with terror, with which it regards the past. It is propelled towards the coming time; it is, in the exact words of the popular phrase, knocked into the middle of next week. And the goad which drives it on thus eagerly is not an affectation for futurity Futurity does not exist, because it is still future. Rather it is a fear of the past; a fear not merely of the evil in the past, but of the good in the past also. The brain breaks down under the unbearable virtue of mankind. There have been so many flaming faiths that we cannot hold; so many harsh heroisms that we cannot imitate; so many great efforts of monumental building or of military glory which seem to us at once sublime and pathetic. The future is a refuge from the fierce competition of our forefathers. The older generation, not the younger, is knocking at our door. It is agreeable to escape, as Henley said, into the Street of By-and-Bye, where stands the Hostelry of Never. It is pleasant to play with children, especially unborn children. The future is a blank wall on which every man can write his own name as large as he likes; the past I find already covered with illegible scribbles, such as Plato, Isaiah, Shakespeare, Michael Angelo, Napoleon. I can make the future as narrow as myself; the past is obliged to be as broad and turbulent as humanity. And the upshot of this modern attitude is really this: that men invent new ideals because they dare not attempt old ideals. They look forward with enthusiasm, because they are afraid to look back.

Now in history there is no Revolution that is not a Restoration. Among the many things that leave me doubtful about the modern habit of fixing eyes on the future, none is stronger than this: that all the men in history who have really done anything with the future have had their eyes fixed upon the past. I need not mention the Renaissance, the very word proves my case. The originality of Michael Angelo and Shakespeare began with the digging up of old vases and manuscripts. The mildness of poets absolutely arose out of the mildness of antiquaries. So the great mediaeval revival was a memory of the Roman Empire. So the Reformation looked back to the Bible and Bible times. So the modern Catholic movement has looked back to patristic times. But that modern movement which many would count the most anarchic of all is in this sense the most conservative of all. Never was the past more venerated by men than it was by the French Revolutionists. They invoked the little republics of antiquity with the complete confidence of one who invokes the gods. The Sans-culottes believed (as their name might imply) in a return to simplicity. They believed most piously in a remote past; some might call it a mythical past. For some strange reason man must always thus plant his fruit trees in a graveyard. Man can only find life among the dead. Man is a misshapen monster, with his feet set forward and his face turned back. He can make the future luxuriant and gigantic, so long as he is thinking about the past. When he tries to think about the future itself, his mind diminishes to a pin point with imbecility, which some call Nirvana. To-morrow is the Gorgon; a man must only see it mirrored in the shining shield of yesterday. If he sees it directly he is turned to stone. This has been the fate of all those who have really seen fate and futurity as clear and inevitable. The Calvinists, with their perfect creed of predestination, were turned to stone. The modern sociological scientists (with their excruciating Eugenics) are turned to stone. The only difference is that the Puritans make dignified, and the Eugenists somewhat amusing, statues.

But there is one feature in the past which more than all the rest defies and depresses the moderns and drives them towards this featureless future. I mean the presence in the past of huge ideals, unfulfilled and sometimes abandoned. The sight of these splendid failures is melancholy to a restless and rather morbid generation; and they maintain a strange silence about them—sometimes amounting to an unscrupulous silence. They keep them entirely out of their newspapers and almost entirely out of their history books. For example, they will often tell you (in their praises of the coming age) that we are moving on towards a United States of Europe. But they carefully omit to tell you that we are moving away from a United States of Europe, that such a thing existed literally in Roman and essentially in mediaeval times. They never admit that the international hatreds (which they call barbaric) are really very recent, the mere breakdown of the ideal of the Holy Roman Empire. Or again, they will tell you that there is going to be a social revolution, a great rising of the poor against the rich; but they never rub it in that France made that magnificent attempt, unaided, and that we and all the world allowed it to be trampled out and forgotten. I say decisively that nothing is so marked in modern writing as the prediction of such ideals in the future combined with the ignoring of them in the past. Anyone can test this for himself. Read any thirty or forty pages of pamphlets advocating peace in Europe and see how many of them praise the old Popes or Emperors for keeping the peace in Europe. Read any armful of essays and poems in praise of social democracy, and see how many of them praise the old Jacobins who created democracy and died for it. These colossal ruins are to the modern only enormous eyesores. He looks back along the valley of the past and sees a perspective of splendid but unfinished cities. They are unfinished, not always through enmity or accident, but often through fickleness, mental fatigue, and the lust for alien philosophies. We have not only left undone those things that we ought to have done, but we have even left undone those things that we wanted to do

It is very currently suggested that the modern man is the heir of all the ages, that he has got the good out of these successive human experiments. I know not what to say in answer to this, except to ask the reader to look at the modern man, as I have just looked at the modern man—in the looking-glass. Is it really true that you and I are two starry towers built up of all the most towering visions of the past? Have we really fulfilled all the great historic ideals one after the other, from our naked ancestor who was brave enough to kill a mammoth with a stone knife, through the Greek citizen and the Christian saint to our own grandfather or great-grandfather, who may have been sabred by the Manchester Yeomanry or shot in the '48? Are we still strong enough to spear mammoths, but now tender enough to spare them? Does the cosmos contain any mammoth that we have either speared or spared? When we decline (in a marked manner) to fly the red flag and fire across a barricade like our grandfathers, are we really declining in deference to sociologists—or to soldiers? Have we indeed outstripped the warrior and passed the ascetical saint? I fear we only outstrip the warrior in the sense that we should probably run away from him. And if we have passed the saint, I fear we have passed him without bowing.

This is, first and foremost, what I mean by the narrowness of the new ideas, the limiting effect of the future. Our modern prophetic idealism is narrow because it has undergone a persistent process of elimination. We must ask for new things because we are not allowed to ask for old things. The whole position is based on this idea that we have got all the good that can be got out of the ideas of the past. But we have not got all the good out of them, perhaps at this moment not any of the good out of them. And the need here is a need of complete freedom for restoration as well as revolution.

We often read nowadays of the valor or audacity with which some rebel attacks a hoary tyranny or an antiquated superstition. There is not really any courage at all in attacking hoary or antiquated things, any more than in offering to fight one's grandmother. The really courageous man is he who defies tyrannies young as the morning and superstitions fresh as the first flowers. The only true free-thinker is he whose intellect is as much free from the future as from the past. He cares as little for what will be as for what has been; he cares only for what ought to be. And for my present purpose I specially insist on this abstract independence. If I am to discuss what is wrong, one of the first things that are wrong is this: the deep and silent modern assumption that past things have become impossible. There is one metaphor of which the moderns are very fond; they are always saying, "You can't put the clock back." The simple and obvious answer is "You can." A clock, being a piece of human construction, can be restored by the human finger to any figure or hour. In the same way society, being a piece of human construction, can be reconstructed upon any plan that has ever existed.

There is another proverb, "As you have made your bed, so you must lie on it"; which again is simply a lie. If I have made my bed uncomfortable, please God I will make it again. We could restore the Heptarchy or the stage coaches if we chose. It might take some time to do, and it might be very inadvisable to do it; but certainly it is not impossible as bringing back last Friday is impossible. This is, as I say, the first freedom that I claim: the freedom to restore. I claim a right to propose as a solution the old patriarchal system of a Highland clan, if that should seem to eliminate the largest number of evils. It certainly would eliminate some evils; for instance, the unnatural sense of obeying cold and harsh strangers, mere bureaucrats and policemen. I claim the right to propose the complete independence of the small Greek or Italian towns, a sovereign city of Brixton or Brompton, if that seems the best way out of our troubles. It would be a way out of some of our troubles; we could not have in a small state, for instance, those enormous illusions about men or measures which are nourished by the great national or international newspapers. You could not persuade a city state that Mr. Beit was an Englishman, or Mr. Dillon a desperado, any more than you could persuade a Hampshire Village that the village drunkard was a teetotaller or the village idiot a statesman. Nevertheless, I do not as a fact propose that the Browns and the Smiths should be collected under separate tartans. Nor do I even propose that Clapham should declare its independence. I merely declare my independence. I merely claim my choice of all the tools in the universe; and I shall not admit that any of them are blunted merely because they have been used.

Chapter 5
The Unfinished Temple

he task of modern idealists indeed is made much too easy for them by the fact that they are always taught that if a thing has been defeated it has been disproved. Logically, the case is quite clearly the other way. The lost causes are exactly those which might have saved the world. If a man says that the Young Pretender would have made England happy, it is hard to answer him. If anyone says that the Georges made England happy, I hope we all know what to answer. That which was prevented is always impregnable; and the only perfect King of England was he who was smothered. Exactly be cause Jacobitism failed we cannot call it a failure. Precisely because the Commune collapsed as a rebellion we cannot say that it collapsed as a system. But such outbursts were brief or incidental. Few people realize how many of the largest efforts, the facts that will fill history, were frustrated in their full design and come down to us as gigantic cripples. I have only space to allude to the two largest facts of modern history: the Catholic Church and that modern growth rooted in the French Revolution.

When four knights scattered the blood and brains of St. Thomas of Canterbury, it was not only a sign of anger but of a sort of black admiration. They wished for his blood, but they wished even more for his brains. Such a blow will remain forever unintelligible unless we realise what the brains of St. Thomas were thinking about just before they were distributed over the floor. They were thinking about the great mediaeval conception that the church is the judge of the world. Becket objected to a priest being tried even by the Lord Chief Justice. And his reason was simple: because the Lord Chief Justice was being tried by the priest. The judiciary was itself sub judice. The kings were themselves in the dock. The idea was to create an invisible kingdom, without armies or prisons, but with complete freedom to condemn publicly all the kingdoms of the earth. Whether such a supreme church would have cured society we cannot affirm definitely; because the church never was a supreme church. We only know that in England at any rate the princes conquered the saints. What the world wanted we see before us; and some of us call it a failure. But we cannot call what the church wanted a failure, simply because the church failed. Tracy struck a little too soon. England had not yet made the great Protestant discovery that the king can do no wrong. The king was whipped in the cathedral; a performance which I recommend to those who regret the unpopularity of church-going. But the discovery was made; and Henry VIII scattered Becket's bones as easily as Tracy had scattered his brains.

Of course, I mean that Catholicism was not tried; plenty of Catholics were tried, and found guilty. My point is that the world did not tire of the church's ideal, but of its reality. Monasteries were impugned not for the chastity of monks, but for the unchastity of monks. Christianity was unpopular not because of the humility, but of the arrogance of Christians. Certainly, if the church failed it was largely through the churchmen. But at the same time hostile elements had certainly begun to end it long before it could have done its work. In the nature of things it needed a common scheme of life and thought in Europe. Yet the mediaeval system began to be broken to pieces intellectually, long before it showed the slightest hint of falling to pieces morally. The huge early heresies, like the Albigenses, had not the faintest excuse in moral superiority. And it is actually true that the Reformation began to tear Europe apart before the Catholic Church had had time to pull it together. The Prussians, for instance, were not converted to Christianity at all until quite close to the Reformation. The poor creatures hardly had time to become Catholics before they were told to become Protestants. This explains a great deal of their subsequent conduct. But I have only taken this as the first and most evident case of the general truth: that the great ideals of the past failed not by being outlived (which must mean over-lived), but by not being lived enough. Mankind has not passed through the Middle Ages. Rather mankind has retreated from the Middle Ages in reaction and rout. The Christian ideal has not been tried and found wanting. It has been found difficult; and left untried.

It is, of course, the same in the case of the French Revolution. A great part of our present perplexity arises from the fact that the French Revolution has half succeeded and half failed. In one sense, Valmy was the decisive battle of the West, and in another Trafalgar. We have, indeed, destroyed the largest territorial tyrannies, and created a free peasantry in almost all Christian countries except England; of which we shall say more anon. But representative government, the one universal relic, is a very poor fragment of the full republican idea. The theory of the French Revolution presupposed two things in government, things which it achieved at the time, but which it has certainly not bequeathed to its imitators in England, Germany, and America. The first of these was the idea of honorable poverty; that a statesman must be something of a stoic; the second was the idea of extreme publicity. Many imaginative English writers, including Carlyle, seem quite unable to imagine how it was that men like Robespierre and Marat were ardently admired. The best answer is that they were admired for being poor—poor when they might have been rich.

No one will pretend that this ideal exists at all in the haute politique of this country. Our national claim to political incorruptibility is actually based on exactly the opposite argument; it is based on the theory that wealthy men in assured positions will have no temptation to financial trickery. Whether the history of the English aristocracy, from the spoliation of the monasteries to the annexation of the mines, entirely supports this theory I am not now inquiring; but certainly it is our theory, that wealth will be a protection against political corruption. The English statesman is bribed not to be bribed. He is born with a silver spoon in his mouth, so that he may never afterwards be found with the silver spoons in his pocket. So strong is our faith in this protection by plutocracy, that we are more and more trusting our empire in the hands of families which inherit wealth without either blood or manners. Some of our political houses are parvenue by pedigree; they hand on vulgarity like a coat of-arms. In the case of many a modern statesman to say that he is born with a silver spoon in his mouth, is at once inadequate and excessive. He is born with a silver knife in his mouth. But all this only illustrates the English theory that poverty is perilous for a politician.

It will be the same if we compare the conditions that have come about with the Revolution legend touching publicity. The old democratic doctrine was that the more light that was let in to all departments of State, the easier it was for a righteous indignation to move promptly against wrong. In other words, monarchs were to live in glass houses, that mobs might throw stones. Again, no admirer of existing English politics (if there is any admirer of existing English politics) will really pretend that this ideal of publicity is exhausted, or even attempted. Obviously public life grows more private every day. The French have, indeed, continued the tradition of revealing secrets and making scandals; hence they are more flagrant and palpable than we, not in sin but in the confession of sin. The first trial of Dreyfus might have happened in England; it is exactly the second trial that would have been legally impossible. But, indeed, if we wish to realise how far we fall short of the original republican outline, the sharpest way to test it is to note how far we fall short even of the republican element in the older regime. Not only are we less democratic than Danton and Condorcet, but we are in many ways less democratic than Choiseul and Marie Antoinette. The richest nobles before the revolt were needy middle-class people compared with our Rothschilds and Roseberys. And in the matter of publicity the old French monarchy was infinitely more democratic than any of the monarchies of today. Practically anybody who chose could walk into the palace and see the king playing with his children, or paring his nails. The people possessed the monarch, as the people possess Primrose Hill; that is, they cannot move it, but they can sprawl all over it. The old French monarchy was founded on the excellent principle that a cat may look at a king. But nowadays a cat may not look at a king; unless it is a very tame cat. Even where the press is free for criticism it is only used for adulation. The substantial difference comes to something uncommonly like this: Eighteenth century tyranny meant that you could say "The K__ of Br__rd is a profligate." Twentieth century liberty really means that you are allowed to say "The King of Brentford is a model family man."

But we have delayed the main argument too long for the parenthetical purpose of showing that the great democratic dream, like the great mediaeval dream, has in a strict and practical sense been a dream unfulfilled. Whatever is the matter with modern England it is not that we have carried out too literally, or achieved with disappointing completeness, either the Catholicism of Becket or the equality of Marat. Now I have taken these two cases merely because they are typical of ten thousand other cases; the world is full of these unfulfilled ideas, these uncompleted temples. History does not consist of completed and crumbling ruins; rather it consists of half-built villas abandoned by a bankrupt-builder. This world is more like an unfinished suburb than a deserted cemetery.

Chapter 6
The Enemies of Property

ut it is for this especial reason that such an explanation is necessary on the very threshold of the definition of ideals. For owing to that historic fallacy with which I have just dealt, numbers of readers will expect me, when I propound an ideal, to propound a new ideal. Now I have no notion at all of propounding a new ideal. There is no new ideal imaginable by the madness of modern sophists, which will be anything like so startling as fulfilling any one of the old ones. On the day that any copybook maxim is carried out there will be something like an earthquake on the earth. There is only one thing new that can be done under the sun; and that is to look at the sun. If you attempt it on a blue day in June, you will know why men do not look straight at their ideals. There is only one really startling thing to be done with the ideal, and that is to do it. It is to face the flaming logical fact, and its frightful consequences. Christ knew that it would be a more stunning thunderbolt to fulfil the law than to destroy it. It is true of both the cases I have quoted, and of every case. The pagans had always adored purity: Athena, Artemis, Vesta. It was when the virgin martyrs began defiantly to practice purity that they rent them with wild beasts, and rolled them on red-hot coals. The world had always loved the notion of the poor man uppermost; it can be proved by every legend from Cinderella to Whittington, by every poem from the Magnificat to the Marseillaise. The kings went mad against France not because she idealized this ideal, but because she realized it. Joseph of Austria and Catherine of Russia quite agreed that the people should rule; what horrified them was that the people did. The French Revolution, therefore, is the type of all true revolutions, because its ideal is as old as the Old Adam, but its fulfilment almost as fresh, as miraculous, and as new as the New Jerusalem.

But in the modern world we are primarily confronted with the extraordinary spectacle of people turning to new ideals because they have not tried the old. Men have not got tired of Christianity; they have never found enough Christianity to get tired of. Men have never wearied of political justice; they have wearied of waiting for it.

Now, for the purpose of this book, I propose to take only one of these old ideals; but one that is perhaps the oldest. I take the principle of domesticity: the ideal house; the happy family, the holy family of history. For the moment it is only necessary to remark that it is like the church and like the republic, now chiefly assailed by those who have never known it, or by those who have failed to fulfil it. Numberless modern women have rebelled against domesticity in theory because they have never known it in practice. Hosts of the poor are driven to the workhouse without ever having known the house. Generally speaking, the cultured class is shrieking to be let out of the decent home, just as the working class is shouting to be let into it.

Now if we take this house or home as a test, we may very generally lay the simple spiritual foundations of the idea. God is that which can make something out of nothing. Man (it may truly be said) is that which can make something out of anything. In other words, while the joy of God be unlimited creation, the special joy of man is limited creation, the combination of creation with limits. Man's pleasure, therefore, is to possess conditions, but also to be partly possessed by them; to be half-controlled by the flute he plays or by the field he digs. The excitement is to get the utmost out of given conditions; the conditions will stretch, but not indefinitely. A man can write an immortal sonnet on an old envelope, or hack a hero out of a lump of rock. But hacking a sonnet out of a rock would be a laborious business, and making a hero out of an envelope is almost out of the sphere of practical politics. This fruitful strife with limitations, when it concerns some airy entertainment of an educated class, goes by the name of Art. But the mass of men have neither time nor aptitude for the invention of invisible or abstract beauty. For the mass of men the idea of artistic creation can only be expressed by an idea unpopular in present discussions—the idea of property. The average man cannot cut clay into the shape of a man; but he can cut earth into the shape of a garden; and though he arranges it with red geraniums and blue potatoes in alternate straight lines, he is still an artist; because he has chosen. The average man cannot paint the sunset whose colors be admires; but he can paint his own house with what color he chooses, and though he paints it pea green with pink spots, he is still an artist; because that is his choice. Property is merely the art of the democracy. It means that every man should have something that he can shape in his own image, as he is shaped in the image of heaven. But because he is not God, but only a graven image of God, his self-expression must deal with limits; properly with limits that are strict and even small.

I am well aware that the word "property" has been defied in our time by the corruption of the great capitalists. One would think, to hear people talk, that the Rothchilds and the Rockefellers were on the side of property. But obviously they are the enemies of property; because they are enemies of their own limitations. They do not want their own land; but other people's. When they remove their neighbor's landmark, they also remove their own. A man who loves a little triangular field ought to love it because it is triangular; anyone who destroys the shape, by giving him more land, is a thief who has stolen a triangle. A man with the true poetry of possession wishes to see the wall where his garden meets Smith's garden; the hedge where his farm touches Brown's. He cannot see the shape of his own land unless he sees the edges of his neighbor's. It is the negation of property that the Duke of Sutherland should have all the farms in one estate; just as it would be the negation of marriage if he had all our wives in one harem.

Chapter 7
The Free Family

s I have said, I propose to take only one central instance; I will take the institution called the private house or home; the shell and organ of the family. We will consider cosmic and political tendencies simply as they strike that ancient and unique roof. Very few words will suffice for all I have to say about the family itself. I leave alone the speculations about its animal origin and the details of its social reconstruction; I am concerned only with its palpable omnipresence. It is a necessity far mankind; it is (if you like to put it so) a trap for mankind. Only by the hypocritical ignoring of a huge fact can any one contrive to talk of "free love"; as if love were an episode like lighting a cigarette, or whistling a tune. Suppose whenever a man lit a cigarette, a towering genie arose from the rings of smoke and followed him everywhere as a huge slave. Suppose whenever a man whistled a tune he "drew an angel down" and had to walk about forever with a seraph on a string. These catastrophic images are but faint parallels to the earthquake consequences that Nature has attached to sex; and it is perfectly plain at the beginning that a man cannot be a free lover; he is either a traitor or a tied man. The second element that creates the family is that its consequences, though colossal, are gradual; the cigarette produces a baby giant, the song only an infant seraph. Thence arises the necessity for some prolonged system of co-operation; and thence arises the family in its full educational sense.

It may be said that this institution of the home is the one anarchist institution. That is to say, it is older than law, and stands outside the State. By its nature it is refreshed or corrupted by indefinable forces of custom or kinship. This is not to be understood as meaning that the State has no authority over families; that State authority is invoked and ought to be invoked in many abnormal cases. But in most normal cases of family joys and sorrows, the State has no mode of entry. It is not so much that the law should not interfere, as that the law cannot. Just as there are fields too far off for law, so there are fields too near; as a man may see the North Pole before he sees his own backbone. Small and near matters escape control at least as much as vast and remote ones; and the real pains and pleasures of the family form a strong instance of this. If a baby cries for the moon, the policeman cannot procure the moon—but neither can he stop the baby. Creatures so close to each other as husband and wife, or a mother and children, have powers of making each other happy or miserable with which no public coercion can deal. If a marriage could be dissolved every morning it would not give back his night's rest to a man kept awake by a curtain lecture; and what is the good of giving a man a lot of power where he only wants a little peace? The child must depend on the most imperfect mother; the mother may be devoted to the most unworthy children; in such relations legal revenges are vain. Even in the abnormal cases where the law may operate, this difficulty is constantly found; as many a bewildered magistrate knows. He has to save children from starvation by taking away their breadwinner. And he often has to break a wife's heart because her husband has already broken her head. The State has no tool delicate enough to deracinate the rooted habits and tangled affections of the family; the two sexes, whether happy or unhappy, are glued together too tightly for us to get the blade of a legal penknife in between them. The man and the woman are one flesh—yes, even when they are not one spirit. Man is a quadruped. Upon this ancient and anarchic intimacy, types of government have little or no effect; it is happy or unhappy, by its own sexual wholesomeness and genial habit, under the republic of Switzerland or the despotism of Siam. Even a republic in Siam would not have done much towards freeing the Siamese Twins.

The problem is not in marriage, but in sex; and would be felt under the freest concubinage. Nevertheless, the overwhelming mass of mankind has not believed in freedom in this matter, but rather in a more or less lasting tie. Tribes and civilizations differ about the occasions on which we may loosen the bond, but they all agree that there is a bond to be loosened, not a mere universal detachment. For the purposes of this book I am not concerned to discuss that mystical view of marriage in which I myself believe: the great European tradition which has made marriage a sacrament. It is enough to say here that heathen and Christian alike have regarded marriage as a tie; a thing not normally to be sundered. Briefly, this human belief in a sexual bond rests on a principle of which the modern mind has made a very inadequate study. It is, perhaps, most nearly paralleled by the principle of the second wind in walking.

The principle is this: that in everything worth having, even in every pleasure, there is a point of pain or tedium that must be survived, so that the pleasure may revive and endure. The joy of battle comes after the first fear of death; the joy of reading Virgil comes after the bore of learning him; the glow of the sea-bather comes after the icy shock of the sea bath; and the success of the marriage comes after the failure of the honeymoon. All human vows, laws, and contracts are so many ways of surviving with success this breaking point, this instant of potential surrender.

In everything on this earth that is worth doing, there is a stage when no one would do it, except for necessity or honor. It is then that the Institution upholds a man and helps him on to the firmer ground ahead. Whether this solid fact of human nature is sufficient to justify the sublime dedication of Christian marriage is quite an other matter, it is amply sufficient to justify the general human feeling of marriage as a fixed thing, dissolution of which is a fault or, at least, an ignominy. The essential element is not so much duration as security. Two people must be tied together in order to do themselves justice; for twenty minutes at a dance, or for twenty years in a marriage In both cases the point is, that if a man is bored in the first five minutes he must go on and force himself to be happy. Coercion is a kind of encouragement; and anarchy (or what some call liberty) is essentially oppressive, because it is essentially discouraging. If we all floated in the air like bubbles, free to drift anywhere at any instant, the practical result would be that no one would have the courage to begin a conversation. It would be so embarrassing to start a sentence in a friendly whisper, and then have to shout the last half of it because the other party was floating away into the free and formless ether. The two must hold each other to do justice to each other. If Americans can be divorced for "incompatibility of temper" I cannot conceive why they are not all divorced. I have known many happy marriages, but never a compatible one. The whole aim of marriage is to fight through and survive the instant when incompatibility becomes unquestionable. For a man and a woman, as such, are incompatible.

Chapter 8
The Wildness of Domesticity

n the course of this crude study we shall have to touch on what is called the problem of poverty, especially the dehumanized poverty of modern industrialism. But in this primary matter of the ideal the difficulty is not the problem of poverty, but the problem of wealth. It is the special psychology of leisure and luxury that falsifies life. Some experience of modern movements of the sort called "advanced" has led me to the conviction that they generally repose upon some experience peculiar to the rich. It is so with that fallacy of free love of which I have already spoken; the idea of sexuality as a string of episodes. That implies a long holiday in which to get tired of one woman, and a motor car in which to wander looking for others; it also implies money for maintenances. An omnibus conductor has hardly time to love his own wife, let alone other people's. And the success with which nuptial estrangements are depicted in modern "problem plays" is due to the fact that there is only one thing that a drama cannot depict—that is a hard day's work. I could give many other instances of this plutocratic assumption behind progressive fads. For instance, there is a plutocratic assumption behind the phrase "Why should woman be economically dependent upon man?" The answer is that among poor and practical people she isn't; except in the sense in which he is dependent upon her. A hunter has to tear his clothes; there must be somebody to mend them. A fisher has to catch fish; there must be somebody to cook them. It is surely quite clear that this modern notion that woman is a mere "pretty clinging parasite," "a plaything," etc., arose through the somber contemplation of some rich banking family, in which the banker, at least, went to the city and pretended to do something, while the banker's wife went to the Park and did not pretend to do anything at all. A poor man and his wife are a business partnership. If one partner in a firm of publishers interviews the authors while the other interviews the clerks, is one of them economically dependent? Was Hodder a pretty parasite clinging to Stoughton? Was Marshall a mere plaything for Snelgrove?

But of all the modern notions generated by mere wealth the worst is this: the notion that domesticity is dull and tame. Inside the home (they say) is dead decorum and routine; outside is adventure and variety. This is indeed a rich man's opinion. The rich man knows that his own house moves on vast and soundless wheels of wealth, is run by regiments of servants, by a swift and silent ritual. On the other hand, every sort of vagabondage of romance is open to him in the streets outside. He has plenty of money and can afford to be a tramp. His wildest adventure will end in a restaurant, while the yokel's tamest adventure may end in a police-court. If he smashes a window he can pay for it; if he smashes a man he can pension him. He can (like the millionaire in the story) buy an hotel to get a glass of gin. And because he, the luxurious man, dictates the tone of nearly all "advanced" and "progressive" thought, we have almost forgotten what a home really means to the overwhelming millions of mankind.

For the truth is, that to the moderately poor the home is the only place of liberty. Nay, it is the only place of anarchy. It is the only spot on the earth where a man can alter arrangements suddenly, make an experiment or indulge in a whim. Everywhere else he goes he must accept the strict rules of the shop, inn, club, or museum that he happens to enter. He can eat his meals on the floor in his own house if he likes. I often do it myself; it gives a curious, childish, poetic, picnic feeling. There would be considerable trouble if I tried to do it in an A.B.C. tea-shop. A man can wear a dressing gown and slippers in his house; while I am sure that this would not be permitted at the Savoy, though I never actually tested the point. If you go to a restaurant you must drink some of the wines on the wine list, all of them if you insist, but certainly some of them. But if you have a house and garden you can try to make hollyhock tea or convolvulus wine if you like. For a plain, hard-working man the home is not the one tame place in the world of adventure. It is the one wild place in the world of rules and set tasks. The home is the one place where he can put the carpet on the ceiling or the slates on the floor if he wants to. When a man spends every night staggering from bar to bar or from music-hall to music-hall, we say that he is living an irregular life. But he is not; he is living a highly regular life, under the dull, and often oppressive, laws of such places. Some times he is not allowed even to sit down in the bars; and frequently he is not allowed to sing in the music-halls. Hotels may be defined as places where you are forced to dress; and theaters may be defined as places where you are forbidden to smoke. A man can only picnic at home.

Now I take, as I have said, this small human omnipotence, this possession of a definite cell or chamber of liberty, as the working model for the present inquiry. Whether we can give every English man a free home of his own or not, at least we should desire it; and he desires it. For the moment we speak of what he wants, not of what he expects to get. He wants, for instance, a separate house; he does not want a semi-detached house. He may be forced in the commercial race to share one wall with another man. Similarly he might be forced in a three-legged race to share one leg with another man; but it is not so that he pictures himself in his dreams of elegance and liberty. Again, he does not desire a flat. He can eat and sleep and praise God in a flat; he can eat and sleep and praise God in a railway train. But a railway train is not a house, because it is a house on wheels. And a flat is not a house, because it is a house on stilts. An idea of earthy contact and foundation, as well as an idea of separation and independence, is a part of this instructive human picture.

I take, then, this one institution as a test. As every normal man desires a woman, and children born of a woman, every normal man desires a house of his own to put them into. He does not merely want a roof above him and a chair below him; he wants an objective and visible kingdom; a fire at which he can cook what food he likes, a door he can open to what friends he chooses. This is the normal appetite of men; I do not say there are not exceptions. There may be saints above the need and philanthropists below it. Opalstein, now he is a duke, may have got used to more than this; and when he was a convict may have got used to less. But the normality of the thing is enormous. To give nearly everybody ordinary houses would please nearly everybody; that is what I assert without apology. Now in modern England (as you eagerly point out) it is very difficult to give nearly everybody houses. Quite so; I merely set up the desideratum; and ask the reader to leave it standing there while he turns with me to a consideration of what really happens in the social wars of our time.

Chapter 9
History of Hudge and Gudge

here is, let us say, a certain filthy rookery in Hoxton, dripping with disease and honeycombed with crime and promiscuity. There are, let us say, two noble and courageous young men, of pure intentions and (if you prefer it) noble birth; let us call them Hudge and Gudge. Hudge, let us say, is of a bustling sort; he points out that the people must at all costs be got out of this den; he subscribes and collects money, but he finds (despite the large financial interests of the Hudges) that the thing will have to be done on the cheap if it is to be done on the spot. He therefore, runs up a row of tall bare tenements like beehives; and soon has all the poor people bundled into their little brick cells, which are certainly better than their old quarters, in so far as they are weather proof, well ventilated and supplied with clean water. But Gudge has a more delicate nature. He feels a nameless something lacking in the little brick boxes; he raises numberless objections; he even assails the celebrated Hudge Report, with the Gudge Minority Report; and by the end of a year or so has come to telling Hudge heatedly that the people were much happier where they were before. As the people preserve in both places precisely the same air of dazed amiability, it is very difficult to find out which is right. But at least one might safely say that no people ever liked stench or starvation as such, but only some peculiar pleasures en tangled with them. Not so feels the sensitive Gudge. Long before the final quarrel (Hudge v. Gudge and Another), Gudge has succeeded in persuading himself that slums and stinks are really very nice things; that the habit of sleeping fourteen in a room is what has made our England great; and that the smell of open drains is absolutely essential to the rearing of a viking breed.

But, meanwhile, has there been no degeneration in Hudge? Alas, I fear there has. Those maniacally ugly buildings which he originally put up as unpretentious sheds barely to shelter human life, grow every day more and more lovely to his deluded eye. Things he would never have dreamed of defending, except as crude necessities, things like common kitchens or infamous asbestos stoves, begin to shine quite sacredly before him, merely because they reflect the wrath of Gudge. He maintains, with the aid of eager little books by Socialists, that man is really happier in a hive than in a house. The practical difficulty of keeping total strangers out of your bedroom he describes as Brotherhood; and the necessity for climbing twenty-three flights of cold stone stairs, I dare say he calls Effort. The net result of their philanthropic adventure is this: that one has come to defending indefensible slums and still more indefensible slum-landlords, while the other has come to treating as divine the sheds and pipes which he only meant as desperate. Gudge is now a corrupt and apoplectic old Tory in the Carlton Club; if you mention poverty to him he roars at you in a thick, hoarse voice something that is conjectured to be "Do 'em good!" Nor is Hudge more happy; for he is a lean vegetarian with a gray, pointed beard and an unnaturally easy smile, who goes about telling everybody that at last we shall all sleep in one universal bedroom; and he lives in a Garden City, like one forgotten of God.

Such is the lamentable history of Hudge and Gudge; which I merely introduce as a type of an endless and exasperating misunderstanding which is always occurring in modern England. To get men out of a rookery men are put into a tenement; and at the beginning the healthy human soul loathes them both. A man's first desire is to get away as far as possible from the rookery, even should his mad course lead him to a model dwelling. The second desire is, naturally, to get away from the model dwelling, even if it should lead a man back to the rookery. But I am neither a Hudgian nor a Gudgian; and I think the mistakes of these two famous and fascinating persons arose from one simple fact. They arose from the fact that neither Hudge nor Gudge had ever thought for an instant what sort of house a man might probably like for himself. In short, they did not begin with the ideal; and, therefore, were not practical politicians.

We may now return to the purpose of our awkward parenthesis about the praise of the future and the failures of the past. A house of his own being the obvious ideal for every man, we may now ask (taking this need as typical of all such needs) why he hasn't got it; and whether it is in any philosophical sense his own fault. Now, I think that in some philosophical sense it is his own fault, I think in a yet more philosophical sense it is the fault of his philosophy. And this is what I have now to attempt to explain.

Burke, a fine rhetorician, who rarely faced realities, said, I think, that an Englishman's house is his castle. This is honestly entertaining; for as it happens the Englishman is almost the only man in Europe whose house is not his castle. Nearly everywhere else exists the assumption of peasant proprietorship; that a poor man may be a landlord, though he is only lord of his own land. Making the landlord and the tenant the same person has certain trivial advantages, as that the tenant pays no rent, while the landlord does a little work. But I am not concerned with the defense of small proprietorship, but merely with the fact that it exists almost everywhere except in England. It is also true, however, that this estate of small possession is attacked everywhere today; it has never existed among ourselves, and it may be destroyed among our neighbors. We have, therefore, to ask ourselves what it is in human affairs generally, and in this domestic ideal in particular, that has really ruined the natural human creation, especially in this country.

Man has always lost his way. He has been a tramp ever since Eden; but he always knew, or thought he knew, what he was looking for. Every man has a house somewhere in the elaborate cosmos; his house waits for him waist deep in slow Norfolk rivers or sunning itself upon Sussex downs. Man has always been looking for that home which is the subject matter of this book. But in the bleak and blinding hail of skepticism to which he has been now so long subjected, he has begun for the first time to be chilled, not merely in his hopes, but in his desires. For the first time in history he begins really to doubt the object of his wanderings on the earth. He has always lost his way; but now he has lost his address.

Under the pressure of certain upper-class philosophies (or in other words, under the pressure of Hudge and Gudge) the average man has really become bewildered about the goal of his efforts; and his efforts, therefore, grow feebler and feebler. His simple notion of having a home of his own is derided as bourgeois, as sentimental, or as despicably Christian. Under various verbal forms he is recommended to go on to the streets—which is called Individualism; or to the work-house—which is called Collectivism. We shall consider this process somewhat more carefully in a moment. But it may be said here that Hudge and Gudge, or the governing class generally, will never fail for lack of some modern phrase to cover their ancient predominance. The great lords will refuse the English peasant his three acres and a cow on advanced grounds, if they cannot refuse it longer on reactionary grounds. They will deny him the three acres on grounds of State Ownership. They will forbid him the cow on grounds of humanitarianism.

And this brings us to the ultimate analysis of this singular influence that has prevented doctrinal demands by the English people. There are, I believe, some who still deny that England is governed by an oligarchy. It is quite enough for me to know that a man might have gone to sleep some thirty years ago over the day's newspaper and woke up last week over the later newspaper, and fancied he was reading about the same people. In one paper he would have found a Lord Robert Cecil, a Mr. Gladstone, a Mr. Lyttleton, a Churchill, a Chamberlain, a Trevelyan, an Acland. In the other paper he would find a Lord Robert Cecil, a Mr. Gladstone, a Mr. Lyttleton, a Churchill, a Chamberlain, a Trevelyan, an Acland. If this is not being governed by families I cannot imagine what it is. I suppose it is being governed by extraordinary democratic coincidences.

Chapter 10
Oppression by Optimism

ut we are not here concerned with the nature and existence of the aristocracy, but with the origin of its peculiar power, why is it the last of the true oligarchies of Europe; and why does there seem no very immediate prospect of our seeing the end of it? The explanation is simple though it remains strangely unnoticed. The friends of aristocracy often praise it for preserving ancient and gracious traditions. The enemies of aristocracy often blame it for clinging to cruel or antiquated customs. Both its enemies and its friends are wrong. Generally speaking the aristocracy does not preserve either good or bad traditions; it does not preserve anything except game. Who would dream of looking among aristocrats anywhere for an old custom? One might as well look for an old costume! The god of the aristocrats is not tradition, but fashion, which is the opposite of tradition. If you wanted to find an old-world Norwegian head-dress, would you look for it in the Scandinavian Smart Set? No; the aristocrats never have customs; at the best they have habits, like the animals. Only the mob has customs.

The real power of the English aristocrats has lain in exactly the opposite of tradition. The simple key to the power of our upper classes is this: that they have always kept carefully on the side of what is called Progress. They have always been up to date, and this comes quite easy to an aristocracy. For the aristocracy are the supreme instances of that frame of mind of which we spoke just now. Novelty is to them a luxury verging on a necessity. They, above all, are so bored with the past and with the present, that they gape, with a horrible hunger, for the future.

But whatever else the great lords forgot they never forgot that it was their business to stand for the new things, for whatever was being most talked about among university dons or fussy financiers. Thus they were on the side of the Reformation against the Church, of the Whigs against the Stuarts, of the Baconian science against the old philosophy, of the manufacturing system against the operatives, and (to-day) of the increased power of the State against the old-fashioned individualists. In short, the rich are always modern; it is their business. But the immediate effect of this fact upon the question we are studying is somewhat singular.

In each of the separate holes or quandaries in which the ordinary Englishman has been placed, he has been told that his situation is, for some particular reason, all for the best. He woke up one fine morning and discovered that the public things, which for eight hundred years he had used at once as inns and sanctuaries, had all been suddenly and savagely abolished, to increase the private wealth of about six or seven men. One would think he might have been annoyed at that; in many places he was, and was put down by the soldiery. But it was not merely the army that kept him quiet. He was kept quiet by the sages as well as the soldiers;

the six or seven men who took away the inns of the poor told him that they were not doing it for themselves, but for the religion of the future, the great dawn of Protestantism and truth. So whenever a seventeenth century noble was caught pulling down a peasant's fence and stealing his field, the noble pointed excitedly at the face of Charles I or James II (which at that moment, perhaps, wore a cross expression) and thus diverted the simple peasant's attention. The great Puritan lords created the Commonwealth, and destroyed the common land. They saved their poorer countrymen from the disgrace of paying Ship Money, by taking from them the plow money and spade money which they were doubtless too weak to guard. A fine old English rhyme has immortalized this easy aristocratic habit—

You prosecute the man or woman Who steals the goose from off the common, But leave the larger felon loose Who steals the common from the goose.

But here, as in the case of the monasteries, we confront the strange problem of submission. If they stole the common from the goose, one can only say that he was a great goose to stand it. The truth is that they reasoned with the goose; they explained to him that all this was needed to get the Stuart fox over seas. So in the nineteenth century the great nobles who became mine-owners and railway directors earnestly assured everybody that they did not do this from preference, but owing to a newly discovered Economic Law. So the prosperous politicians of our own generation introduce bills to prevent poor mothers from going about with their own babies; or they calmly forbid their tenants to drink beer in public inns. But this insolence is not (as you would suppose) howled at by everybody as outrageous feudalism. It is gently rebuked as Socialism. For an aristocracy is always progressive; it is a form of going the pace. Their parties grow later and later at night; for they are trying to live to-morrow.

Chapter 11
The Homelessness of Jones

hus the Future of which we spoke at the beginning has (in England at least) always been the ally of tyranny. The ordinary Englishman has been duped out of his old possessions, such as they were, and always in the name of progress. The destroyers of the abbeys took away his bread and gave him a stone, assuring him that it was a precious stone, the white pebble of the Lord's elect. They took away his maypole and his original rural life and promised him instead the Golden Age of Peace and Commerce inaugurated at the Crystal Palace. And now they are taking away the little that remains of his dignity as a householder and the head of a family, promising him instead Utopias which are called (appropriately enough) "Anticipations" or "News from Nowhere." We come back, in fact, to the main feature which has already been mentioned. The past is communal: the future must be individualist. In the past are all the evils of democracy, variety and violence and doubt, but the future is pure despotism, for the future is pure caprice. Yesterday, I know I was a human fool, but to-morrow I can easily be the Superman.

The modern Englishman, however, is like a man who should be perpetually kept out, for one reason after another, from the house in which he had meant his married life to begin. This man (Jones let us call him) has always desired the divinely ordinary things; he has married for love, he has chosen or built a small house that fits like a coat; he is ready to be a great grandfather and a local god. And just as he is moving in, something goes wrong. Some tyranny, personal or political, suddenly debars him from the home; and he has to take his meals in the front garden. A passing philosopher (who is also, by a mere coincidence, the man who turned him out) pauses, and leaning elegantly on the railings, explains to him that he is now living that bold life upon the bounty of nature which will be the life of the sublime future. He finds life in the front garden more bold than bountiful, and has to move into mean lodgings in the next spring. The philosopher (who turned him out), happening to call at these lodgings, with the probable intention of raising the rent, stops to explain to him that he is now in the real life of mercantile endeavor; the economic struggle between him and the landlady is the only thing out of which, in the sublime future, the wealth of nations can come. He is defeated in the economic struggle, and goes to the workhouse. The philosopher who turned him out (happening at that very moment to be inspecting the workhouse) assures him that he is now at last in that golden republic which is the goal of mankind; he is in an equal, scientific, Socialistic commonwealth, owned by the State and ruled by public officers; in fact, the commonwealth of the sublime future.

Nevertheless, there are signs that the irrational Jones still dreams at night of this old idea of having an ordinary home. He asked for so little, and he has been offered so much. He has been offered bribes of worlds and systems; he has been offered Eden and Utopia and the New Jerusalem, and he only wanted a house; and that has been refused him.

Such an apologue is literally no exaggeration of the facts of English history. The rich did literally turn the poor out of the old guest house on to the road, briefly telling them that it was the road of progress. They did literally force them into factories and the modern wage-slavery, assuring them all the time that this was the only way to wealth and civilization. Just as they had dragged the rustic from the convent food and ale by saying that the streets of heaven were paved with gold, so now they dragged him from the village food and ale by telling him that the streets of London were paved with gold. As he entered the gloomy porch of Puritanism, so he entered the gloomy porch of Industrialism, being told that each of them was the gate of the future. Hitherto he has only gone from prison to prison, nay, into darkening prisons, for Calvinism opened one small window upon heaven. And now he is asked, in the same educated and authoritative tones, to enter another dark porch, at which he has to surrender, into unseen hands, his children, his small possessions and all the habits of his fathers.

Whether this last opening be in truth any more inviting than the old openings of Puritanism and Industrialism can be discussed later. But there can be little doubt, I think, that if some form of Collectivism is imposed upon England it will be imposed, as everything else has been, by an instructed political class upon a people partly apathetic and partly hypnotized. The aristocracy will be as ready to "administer" Collectivism as they were to administer Puritanism or Manchesterism; in some ways such a centralized political power is necessarily attractive to them. It will not be so hard as some innocent Socialists seem to suppose to induce the Honorable Tomnoddy to take over the milk supply as well as the stamp supply—at an increased salary. Mr. Bernard Shaw has remarked that rich men are better than poor men on parish councils because they are free from "financial timidity." Now, the English ruling class is quite free from financial timidity. The Duke of Sussex will be quite ready to be Administrator of Sussex at the same screw. Sir William Harcourt, that typical aristocrat, put it quite correctly. "We" (that is, the aristocracy) "are all Socialists now."

But this is not the essential note on which I desire to end. My main contention is that, whether necessary or not, both Industrialism and Collectivism have been accepted as necessities—not as naked ideals or desires. Nobody liked the Manchester School; it was endured as the only way of producing wealth. Nobody likes the Marxian school; it is endured as the only way of preventing poverty. Nobody's real heart is in the idea of preventing a free man from owning his own farm, or an old woman from cultivating her own garden, any more than anybody's real heart was in the heartless battle of the machines. The purpose of this chapter is sufficiently served in indicating that this proposal also is a pis aller, a desperate second best—like teetotalism. I do not propose to prove here that Socialism is a poison; it is enough if I maintain that it is a medicine and not a wine.

The idea of private property universal but private, the idea of families free but still families, of domesticity democratic but still domestic, of one man one house—this remains the real vision and magnet of mankind. The world may accept something more official and general, less human and intimate. But the world will be like a broken-hearted woman who makes a humdrum marriage because she may not make a happy one; Socialism may be the world's deliverance, but it is not the world's desire.

Part II: Imperialism, or the Mistake About Man

Chapter 1
The Charm of Jingoism

have cast about widely to find a title for this section; and I confess that the word "Imperialism" is a clumsy version of my meaning. But no other word came nearer; "Militarism" would have been even more misleading, and "The Superman" makes nonsense of any discussion that he enters. Perhaps, upon the whole, the word "Caesarism" would have been better; but I desire a popular word; and Imperialism (as the reader will perceive) does cover for the most part the men and theories that I mean to discuss.

This small confusion is increased, however, by the fact that I do also disbelieve in Imperialism in its popular sense, as a mode or theory of the patriotic sentiment of this country. But popular Imperialism in England has very little to do with the sort of Caesarean Imperialism I wish to sketch. I differ from the Colonial idealism of Rhodes' and Kipling; but I do not think, as some of its opponents do, that it is an insolent creation of English harshness and rapacity. Imperialism, I think, is a fiction created, not by English hardness, but by English softness; nay, in a sense, even by English kindness.

The reasons for believing in Australia are mostly as sentimental as the most sentimental reasons for believing in heaven. New South Wales is quite literally regarded as a place where the wicked cease from troubling and the weary are at rest; that is, a paradise for uncles who have turned dishonest and for nephews who are born tired. British Columbia is in strict sense a fairyland, it is a world where a magic and irrational luck is supposed to attend the youngest sons. This strange optimism about the ends of the earth is an English weakness; but to show that it is not a coldness or a harshness it is quite sufficient to say that no one shared it more than that gigantic English sentimentalist—the great Charles Dickens. The end of "David Copperfield" is unreal not merely because it is an optimistic ending, but because it is an Imperialistic ending. The decorous British happiness planned out for David Copperfield and Agnes would be embarrassed by the perpetual presence of the hopeless tragedy of Emily, or the more hopeless farce of Micawber. Therefore, both Emily and Micawber are shipped off to a vague colony where changes come over them with no conceivable cause, except the climate. The tragic woman becomes contented and the comic man becomes responsible, solely as the result of a sea voyage and the first sight of a kangaroo.

To Imperialism in the light political sense, therefore, my only objection is that it is an illusion of comfort; that an Empire whose heart is failing should be specially proud of the extremities, is to me no more sublime a fact than that an old dandy whose brain is gone should still be proud of his legs. It consoles men for the evident ugliness and apathy of England with legends of fair youth and heroic strenuousness in distant continents and islands. A man can sit amid the squalor of Seven Dials and feel that life is innocent and godlike in the bush or on the veldt. Just so a man might sit in the squalor of Seven Dials and feel that life was innocent and godlike in Brixton and Surbiton. Brixton and Surbiton are "new"; they are expanding; they are "nearer to nature," in the sense that they have eaten up nature mile by mile. The only objection is the objection of fact. The young men of Brixton are not young giants. The lovers of Surbiton are not all pagan poets, singing with the sweet energy of the spring. Nor are the people of the Colonies when you meet them young giants or pagan poets. They are mostly Cockneys who have lost their last music of real things by getting out of the sound of Bow Bells. Mr. Rudyard Kipling, a man of real though decadent genius, threw a theoretic glamour over them which is already fading. Mr. Kipling is, in a precise and rather startling sense, the exception that proves the rule. For he has imagination, of an oriental and cruel kind, but he has it, not because he grew up in a new country, but precisely because he grew up in the oldest country upon earth. He is rooted in a past—an Asiatic past. He might never have written "Kabul River" if he had been born in Melbourne.

I say frankly, therefore (lest there should be any air of evasion), that Imperialism in its common patriotic pretensions appears to me both weak and perilous. It is the attempt of a European country to create a kind of sham Europe which it can dominate, instead of the real Europe, which it can only share. It is a love of living with one's inferiors. The notion of restoring the Roman Empire by oneself and for oneself is a dream that has haunted every Christian nation in a different shape and in almost every shape as a snare. The Spanish are a consistent and conservative people; therefore they embodied that attempt at Empire in long and lingering dynasties. The French are a violent people, and therefore they twice conquered that Empire by violence of arms. The English are above all a poetical and optimistic people; and therefore their Empire is something vague and yet sympathetic, something distant and yet dear. But this dream of theirs of being powerful in the uttermost places, though a native weakness, is still a weakness in them; much more of a weakness than gold was to Spain or glory to Napoleon. If ever we were in collision with our real brothers and rivals we should leave all this fancy out of account. We should no more dream of pitting Australian armies against German than of pitting Tasmanian sculpture against French. I have thus explained, lest anyone should accuse me of concealing an unpopular attitude, why I do not believe in Imperialism as commonly understood. I think it not merely an occasional wrong to other peoples, but a continuous feebleness, a running sore, in my own. But it is also true that I have dwelt on this Imperialism that is an amiable delusion partly in order to show how different it is from the deeper, more sinister and yet more persuasive thing that I have been forced to call Imperialism for the convenience of this chapter. In order to get to the root of this evil and quite un-English Imperialism we must cast back and begin anew with a more general discussion of the first needs of human intercourse.

Chapter 2
Wisdom and the Weather

t is admitted, one may hope, that common things are never commonplace. Birth is covered with curtains precisely because it is a staggering and monstrous prodigy. Death and first love, though they happen to everybody, can stop one's heart with the very thought of them. But while this is granted, something further may be claimed. It is not merely true that these universal things are strange; it is moreover true that they are subtle. In the last analysis most common things will be found to be highly complicated. Some men of science do indeed get over the difficulty by dealing only with the easy part of it: thus, they will call first love the instinct of sex, and the awe of death the instinct of self-preservation. But this is only getting over the difficulty of describing peacock green by calling it blue. There is blue in it. That there is a strong physical element in both romance and the Memento Mori makes them if possible more baffling than if they had been wholly intellectual. No man could say exactly how much his sexuality was colored by a clean love of beauty, or by the mere boyish itch for irrevocable adventures, like running away to sea. No man could say how far his animal dread of the end was mixed up with mystical traditions touching morals and religion. It is exactly because these things are animal, but not quite animal, that the dance of all the difficulties begins. The materialists analyze the easy part, deny the hard part and go home to their tea.

It is complete error to suppose that because a thing is vulgar therefore it is not refined; that is, subtle and hard to define. A drawing-room song of my youth which began "In the gloaming, O, my darling," was vulgar enough as a song; but the connection between human passion and the twilight is none the less an exquisite and even inscrutable thing. Or to take another obvious instance: the jokes about a mother-in-law are scarcely delicate, but the problem of a mother-in-law is extremely delicate. A mother-in-law is subtle because she is a thing like the twilight. She is a mystical blend of two inconsistent things—law and a mother. The caricatures misrepresent her; but they arise out of a real human enigma. "Comic Cuts" deals with the difficulty wrongly, but it would need George Meredith at his best to deal with the difficulty rightly. The nearest statement of the problem perhaps is this: it is not that a mother-in-law must be nasty, but that she must be very nice.

But it is best perhaps to take in illustration some daily custom we have all heard despised as vulgar or trite. Take, for the sake of argument, the custom of talking about the weather. Stevenson calls it "the very nadir and scoff of good conversationalists." Now there are very deep reasons for talking about the weather, reasons that are delicate as well as deep; they lie in layer upon layer of stratified sagacity. First of all it is a gesture of primeval worship. The sky must be invoked; and to begin everything with the weather is a sort of pagan way of beginning everything with prayer. Jones and Brown talk about the weather: but so do Milton and Shelley. Then it is an expression of that elementary idea in politeness—equality. For the very word politeness is only the Greek for citizenship. The word politeness is akin to the word policeman: a charming thought. Properly understood, the citizen should be more polite than the gentleman; perhaps the policeman should be the most courtly and elegant of the three. But all good manners must obviously begin with the sharing of something in a simple style. Two men should share an umbrella; if they have not got an umbrella, they should at least share the rain, with all its rich potentialities of wit and philosophy. "For He maketh His sun to shine ... " This is the second element in the weather; its recognition of human equality in that we all have our hats under the dark blue spangled umbrella of the universe. Arising out of this is the third wholesome strain in the custom; I mean that it begins with the body and with our inevitable bodily brotherhood. All true friendliness begins with fire and food and drink and the recognition of rain or frost. Those who will not begin at the bodily end of things are already prigs and may soon be Christian Scientists. Each human soul has in a sense to enact for itself the gigantic humility of the Incarnation. Every man must descend into the flesh to meet mankind.

Briefly, in the mere observation "a fine day" there is the whole great human idea of comradeship. Now, pure comradeship is another of those broad and yet bewildering things. We all enjoy it; yet when we come to talk about it we almost always talk nonsense, chiefly because we suppose it to be a simpler affair than it is. It is simple to conduct; but it is by no means simple to analyze. Comradeship is at the most only one half of human life; the other half is Love, a thing so different that one might fancy it had been made for another universe. And I do not mean mere sex love; any kind of concentrated passion, maternal love, or even the fiercer kinds of friendship are in their nature alien to pure comradeship. Both sides are essential to life; and both are known in differing degrees to everybody of every age or sex. But very broadly speaking it may still be said that women stand for the dignity of love and men for the dignity of comradeship. I mean that the institution would hardly be expected if the males of the tribe did not mount guard over it. The affections in which women excel have so much more authority and intensity that pure comradeship would be washed away if it were not rallied and guarded in clubs, corps, colleges, banquets and regiments. Most of us have heard the voice in which the hostess tells her husband not to sit too long over the cigars. It is the dreadful voice of Love, seeking to destroy Comradeship.

All true comradeship has in it those three elements which I have remarked in the ordinary exclamation about the weather. First, it has a sort of broad philosophy like the common sky, emphasizing that we are all under the same cosmic conditions. We are all in the same boat, the "winged rock" of Mr. Herbert Trench. Secondly, it recognizes this bond as the essential one; for comradeship is simply humanity seen in that one aspect in which men are really equal. The old writers were entirely wise when they talked of the equality of men; but they were also very wise in not mentioning women. Women are always authoritarian; they are always above or below; that is why marriage is a sort of poetical see-saw. There are only three things in the world that women do not understand; and they are Liberty, Equality, and Fraternity. But men (a class little understood in the modern world) find these things the breath of their nostrils; and our most learned ladies will not even begin to understand them until they make allowance for this kind of cool camaraderie. Lastly, it contains the third quality of the weather, the insistence upon the body and its indispensable satisfaction. No one has even begun to understand comradeship who does not accept with it a certain hearty eagerness in eating, drinking, or smoking, an uproarious materialism which to many women appears only hoggish. You may call the thing an orgy or a sacrament; it is certainly an essential. It is at root a resistance to the superciliousness of the individual. Nay, its very swaggering and howling are humble. In the heart of its rowdiness there is a sort of mad modesty; a desire to melt the separate soul into the mass of unpretentious masculinity. It is a clamorous confession of the weakness of all flesh. No man must be superior to the things that are common to men. This sort of equality must be bodily and gross and comic. Not only are we all in the same boat, but we are all seasick.

The word comradeship just now promises to become as fatuous as the word "affinity." There are clubs of a Socialist sort where all the members, men and women, call each other "Comrade." I have no serious emotions, hostile or other-wise, about this particular habit: at the worst it is conventionality, and at the best flirtation. I am convinced here only to point out a rational principle. If you choose to lump all flowers together, lilies and dahlias and tulips and chrysanthemums and call them all daisies, you will find that you have spoiled the very fine word daisy. If you choose to call every human attachment comradeship, if you include under that name the respect of a youth for a venerable prophetess, the interest of a man in a beautiful woman who baffles him, the pleasure of a philosophical old fogy in a girl who is impudent and innocent, the end of the meanest quarrel or the beginning of the most mountainous love; if you are going to call all these comradeship, you will gain nothing, you will only lose a word. Daisies are obvious and universal and open; but they are only one kind of flower. Comradeship is obvious and universal and open; but it is only one kind of affection; it has characteristics that would destroy any other kind. Anyone who has known true comradeship in a club or in a regiment, knows that it is impersonal. There is a pedantic phrase used in debating clubs which is strictly true to the masculine emotion; they call it "speaking to the question." Women speak to each other; men speak to the subject they are speaking about. Many an honest man has sat in a ring of his five best friends under heaven and forgotten who was in the room while he explained some system.

This is not peculiar to intellectual men; men are all theoretical, whether they are talking about God or about golf. Men are all impersonal; that is to say, republican. No one remembers after a really good talk who has said the good things. Every man speaks to a visionary multitude; a mystical cloud, that is called the club.

It is obvious that this cool and careless quality which is essential to the collective affection of males involves disadvantages and dangers. It leads to spitting; it leads to coarse speech; it must lead to these things so long as it is honorable; comradeship must be in some degree ugly. The moment beauty is mentioned in male friendship, the nostrils are stopped with the smell of abominable things. Friendship must be physically dirty if it is to be morally clean. It must be in its shirt sleeves. The chaos of habits that always goes with males when left entirely to themselves has only one honorable cure; and that is the strict discipline of a monastery. Anyone who has seen our unhappy young idealists in East End Settlements losing their collars in the wash and living on tinned salmon will fully understand why it was decided by the wisdom of St. Bernard or St. Benedict, that if men were to live without women, they must not live without rules. Something of the same sort of artificial exactitude, of course, is obtained in an army; and an army also has to be in many ways monastic; only that it has celibacy without chastity. But these things do not apply to normal married men. These have a quite sufficient restraint on their instinctive anarchy in the savage common-sense of the other sex. There is only one very timid sort of man that is not afraid of women.

Chapter 3
The Common Vision

ow this masculine love of an open and level camaraderie is the life within all democracies and attempts to govern by debate; without it the republic would be a dead formula. Even as it is, of course, the spirit of democracy frequently differs widely from the letter, and a pothouse is often a better test than a Parliament. Democracy in its human sense is not arbitrament by the majority; it is not even arbitrament by everybody. It can be more nearly defined as arbitrament by anybody. I mean that it rests on that club habit of taking a total stranger for granted, of assuming certain things to be inevitably common to yourself and him. Only the things that anybody may be presumed to hold have the full authority of democracy. Look out of the window and notice the first man who walks by. The Liberals may have swept England with an over-whelming majority; but you would not stake a button that the man is a Liberal. The Bible may be read in all schools and respected in all law courts; but you would not bet a straw that he believes in the Bible. But you would bet your week's wages, let us say, that he believes in wearing clothes. You would bet that he believes that physical courage is a fine thing, or that parents have authority over children. Of course, he might be the millionth man who does not believe these things; if it comes to that, he might be the Bearded Lady dressed up as a man. But these prodigies are quite a different thing from any mere calculation of numbers. People who hold these views are not a minority, but a monstrosity. But of these universal dogmas that have full democratic authority the only test is this test of anybody. What you would observe before any newcomer in a tavern—that is the real English law. The first man you see from the window, he is the King of England.

The decay of taverns, which is but a part of the general decay of democracy, has undoubtedly weakened this masculine spirit of equality. I remember that a roomful of Socialists literally laughed when I told them that there were no two nobler words in all poetry than Public House. They thought it was a joke. Why they should think it a joke, since they want to make all houses public houses, I cannot imagine. But if anyone wishes to see the real rowdy egalitarianism which is necessary (to males, at least) he can find it as well as anywhere in the great old tavern disputes which come down to us in such books as Boswell's Johnson. It is worth while to mention that one name especially because the modern world in its morbidity has done it a strange injustice. The demeanor of Johnson, it is said, was "harsh and despotic." It was occasionally harsh, but it was never despotic. Johnson was not in the least a despot; Johnson was a demagogue, he shouted against a shouting crowd. The very fact that he wrangled with other people is proof that other people were allowed to wrangle with him. His very brutality was based on the idea of an equal scrimmage, like that of football. It is strictly true that he bawled and banged the table because he was a modest man. He was honestly afraid of being overwhelmed or even overlooked. Addison had exquisite manners and was the king of his company; he was polite to everybody; but superior to everybody; therefore he has been handed down forever in the immortal insult of Pope—

"Like Cato, give his little Senate laws And sit attentive to his own applause."

Johnson, so far from being king of his company, was a sort of Irish Member in his own Parliament. Addison was a courteous superior and was hated. Johnson was an insolent equal and therefore was loved by all who knew him, and handed down in a marvellous book, which is one of the mere miracles of love.

This doctrine of equality is essential to conversation; so much may be admitted by anyone who knows what conversation is. Once arguing at a table in a tavern the most famous man on earth would wish to be obscure, so that his brilliant remarks might blaze like the stars on the background of his obscurity. To anything worth calling a man nothing can be conceived more cold or cheerless than to be king of your company. But it may be said that in masculine sports and games, other than the great game of debate, there is definite emulation and eclipse. There is indeed emulation, but this is only an ardent sort of equality. Games are competitive, because that is the only way of making them exciting. But if anyone doubts that men must forever return to the ideal of equality, it is only necessary to answer that there is such a thing as a handicap. If men exulted in mere superiority, they would seek to see how far such superiority could go; they would be glad when one strong runner came in miles ahead of all the rest. But what men like is not the triumph of superiors, but the struggle of equals; and, therefore, they introduce even into their competitive sports an artificial equality. It is sad to think how few of those who arrange our sporting handicaps can be supposed with any probability to realize that they are abstract and even severe republicans.

No; the real objection to equality and self-rule has nothing to do with any of these free and festive aspects of mankind; all men are democrats when they are happy. The philosophic opponent of democracy would substantially sum up his position by saying that it "will not work." Before going further, I will register in passing a protest against the assumption that working is the one test of humanity. Heaven does not work; it plays. Men are most themselves when they are free; and if I find that men are snobs in their work but democrats on their holidays, I shall take the liberty to believe their holidays. But it is this question of work which really perplexes the question of equality; and it is with that that we must now deal. Perhaps the truth can be put most pointedly thus: that democracy has one real enemy, and that is civilization. Those utilitarian miracles which science has made are anti-democratic, not so much in their perversion, or even in their practical result, as in their primary shape and purpose. The Frame-Breaking Rioters were right; not perhaps in thinking that machines would make fewer men workmen; but certainly in thinking that machines would make fewer men masters. More wheels do mean fewer handles; fewer handles do mean fewer hands. The machinery of science must be individualistic and isolated. A mob can shout round a palace; but a mob cannot shout down a telephone. The specialist appears and democracy is half spoiled at a stroke.

Chapter 4
The Insane Necessity

he common conception among the dregs of Darwinian culture is that men have slowly worked their way out of inequality into a state of comparative equality. The truth is, I fancy, almost exactly the opposite. All men have normally and naturally begun with the idea of equality; they have only abandoned it late and reluctantly, and always for some material reason of detail. They have never naturally felt that one class of men was superior to another; they have always been driven to assume it through certain practical limitations of space and time.

For example, there is one element which must always tend to oligarchy—or rather to despotism; I mean the element of hurry. If the house has caught fire a man must ring up the fire engines; a committee cannot ring them up. If a camp is surprised by night somebody must give the order to fire; there is no time to vote it. It is solely a question of the physical limitations of time and space; not at all of any mental limitations in the mass of men commanded. If all the people in the house were men of destiny it would still be better that they should not all talk into the telephone at once; nay, it would be better that the silliest man of all should speak uninterrupted. If an army actually consisted of nothing but Hanibals and Napoleons, it would still be better in the case of a surprise that they should not all give orders together. Nay, it would be better if the stupidest of them all gave the orders. Thus, we see that merely military subordination, so far from resting on the inequality of men, actually rests on the equality of men. Discipline does not involve the Carlylean notion that somebody is always right when everybody is wrong, and that we must discover and crown that somebody. On the contrary, discipline means that in certain frightfully rapid circumstances, one can trust anybody so long as he is not everybody. The military spirit does not mean (as Carlyle fancied) obeying the strongest and wisest man. On the contrary, the military spirit means, if anything, obeying the weakest and stupidest man, obeying him merely because he is a man, and not a thousand men. Submission to a weak man is discipline. Submission to a strong man is only servility.

Now it can be easily shown that the thing we call aristocracy in Europe is not in its origin and spirit an aristocracy at all. It is not a system of spiritual degrees and distinctions like, for example, the caste system of India, or even like the old Greek distinction between free men and slaves. It is simply the remains of a military organization, framed partly to sustain the sinking Roman Empire, partly to break and avenge the awful onslaught of Islam. The word Duke simply means Colonel, just as the word Emperor simply means Commander-in-Chief. The whole story is told in the single title of Counts of the Holy Roman Empire, which merely means officers in the European army against the contemporary Yellow Peril. Now in an army nobody ever dreams of supposing that difference of rank represents a difference of moral reality. Nobody ever says about a regiment, "Your Major is very humorous and energetic; your Colonel, of course, must be even more humorous and yet more energetic." No one ever says, in reporting a mess-room conversation, "Lieutenant Jones was very witty, but was naturally inferior to Captain Smith." The essence of an army is the idea of official inequality, founded on unofficial equality. The Colonel is not obeyed because he is the best man, but because he is the Colonel. Such was probably the spirit of the system of dukes and counts when it first arose out of the military spirit and military necessities of Rome. With the decline of those necessities it has gradually ceased to have meaning as a military organization, and become honeycombed with unclean plutocracy. Even now it is not a spiritual aristocracy—it is not so bad as all that. It is simply an army without an enemy—billeted upon the people.

Man, therefore, has a specialist as well as comrade-like aspect; and the case of militarism is not the only case of such specialist submission. The tinker and tailor, as well as the soldier and sailor, require a certain rigidity of rapidity of action: at least, if the tinker is not organized that is largely why he does not tink on any large scale. The tinker and tailor often represent the two nomadic races in Europe: the Gipsy and the Jew; but the Jew alone has influence because he alone accepts some sort of discipline. Man, we say, has two sides, the specialist side where he must have subordination, and the social side where he must have equality. There is a truth in the saying that ten tailors go to make a man; but we must remember also that ten Poets Laureate or ten Astronomers Royal go to make a man, too. Ten million tradesmen go to make Man himself; but humanity consists of tradesmen when they are not talking shop. Now the peculiar peril of our time, which I call for argument's sake Imperialism or Caesarism, is the complete eclipse of comradeship and equality by specialism and domination.

There are only two kinds of social structure conceivable—personal government and impersonal government. If my anarchic friends will not have rules—they will have rulers. Preferring personal government, with its tact and flexibility, is called Royalism. Preferring impersonal government, with its dogmas and definitions, is called Republicanism. Objecting broadmindedly both to kings and creeds is called Bosh; at least, I know no more philosophic word for it. You can be guided by the shrewdness or presence of mind of one ruler, or by the equality and ascertained justice of one rule; but you must have one or the other, or you are not a nation, but a nasty mess. Now men in their aspect of equality and debate adore the idea of rules; they develop and complicate them greatly to excess. A man finds far more regulations and definitions in his club, where there are rules, than in his home, where there is a ruler. A deliberate assembly, the House of Commons, for instance, carries this mummery to the point of a methodical madness. The whole system is stiff with rigid unreason; like the Royal Court in Lewis Carroll. You would think the Speaker would speak; therefore he is mostly silent. You would think a man would take off his hat to stop and put it on to go away; therefore he takes off his hat to walk out and puts it on to stop in. Names are forbidden, and a man must call his own father "my right honorable friend the member for West Birmingham." These are, perhaps, fantasies of decay: but fundamentally they answer a masculine appetite. Men feel that rules, even if irrational, are universal; men feel that law is equal, even when it is not equitable. There is a wild fairness in the thing—as there is in tossing up.

Again, it is gravely unfortunate that when critics do attack such cases as the Commons it is always on the points (perhaps the few points) where the Commons are right. They denounce the House as the Talking-Shop, and complain that it wastes time in wordy mazes. Now this is just one respect in which the Commons are actually like the Common People. If they love leisure and long debate, it is because all men love it; that they really represent England. There the Parliament does approach to the virile virtues of the pothouse.

The real truth is that adumbrated in the introductory section when we spoke of the sense of home and property, as now we speak of the sense of counsel and community. All men do naturally love the idea of leisure, laughter, loud and equal argument; but there stands a specter in our hall. We are conscious of the towering modern challenge that is called specialism or cut-throat competition— Business. Business will have nothing to do with leisure; business will have no truck with comradeship; business will pretend to no patience with all the legal fictions and fantastic handicaps by which comradeship protects its egalitarian ideal. The modern millionaire, when engaged in the agreeable and typical task of sacking his own father, will certainly not refer to him as the right honorable clerk from the Laburnum Road, Brixton. Therefore there has arisen in modern life a literary fashion devoting itself to the romance of business, to great demigods of greed and to fairyland of finance. This popular philosophy is utterly despotic and anti-democratic; this fashion is the flower of that Caesarism against which I am concerned to protest. The ideal millionaire is strong in the possession of a brain of steel. The fact that the real millionaire is rather more often strong in the possession of a head of wood, does not alter the spirit and trend of the idolatry. The essential argument is "Specialists must be despots; men must be specialists. You cannot have equality in a soap factory; so you cannot have it anywhere. You cannot have comradeship in a wheat corner; so you cannot have it at all. We must have commercial civilization; therefore we must destroy democracy." I know that plutocrats have seldom sufficient fancy to soar to such examples as soap or wheat. They generally confine themselves, with fine freshness of mind, to a comparison between the state and a ship. One anti-democratic writer remarked that he would not like to sail in a vessel in which the cabin-boy had an equal vote with the captain. It might easily be urged in answer that many a ship (the Victoria, for instance) was sunk because an admiral gave an order which a cabin-boy could see was wrong. But this is a debating reply; the essential fallacy is both deeper and simpler. The elementary fact is that we were all born in a state; we were not all born on a ship; like some of our great British bankers. A ship still remains a specialist experiment, like a diving-bell or a flying ship: in such peculiar perils the need for promptitude constitutes the need for autocracy. But we live and die in the vessel of the state; and if we cannot find freedom camaraderie and the popular element in the state, we cannot find it at all. And the modern doctrine of commercial despotism means that we shall not find it at all. Our specialist trades in their highly civilized state cannot (it says) be run without the whole brutal business of bossing and sacking, "too old at forty" and all the rest of the filth. And they must be run, and therefore we call on Caesar. Nobody but the Superman could descend to do such dirty work.

Now (to reiterate my title) this is what is wrong. This is the huge modern heresy of altering the human soul to fit its conditions, instead of altering human conditions to fit the human soul. If soap boiling is really inconsistent with brotherhood, so much the worst for soap-boiling, not for brotherhood. If civilization really cannot get on with democracy, so much the worse for civilization, not for democracy. Certainly, it would be far better to go back to village communes, if they really are communes. Certainly, it would be better to do without soap rather than to do without society. Certainly, we would sacrifice all our wires, wheels, systems, specialties, physical science and frenzied finance for one half-hour of happiness such as has often come to us with comrades in a common tavern. I do not say the sacrifice will be necessary; I only say it will be easy.

Part III: Feminism, or the Mistake About Woman

Chapter 1
The Unmilitary Suffragette

t will be better to adopt in this chapter the same process that appeared a piece of mental justice in the last. My general opinions on the feminine question are such as many suffragists would warmly approve; and it would be easy to state them without any open reference to the current controversy. But just as it seemed more decent to say first that I was not in favor of Imperialism even in its practical and popular sense, so it seems more decent to say the same of Female Suffrage, in its practical and popular sense. In other words, it is only fair to state, however hurriedly, the superficial objection to the Suffragettes before we go on to the really subtle questions behind the Suffrage.

Well, to get this honest but unpleasant business over, the objection to the Suffragettes is not that they are Militant Suffragettes. On the contrary, it is that they are not militant enough. A revolution is a military thing; it has all the military virtues; one of which is that it comes to an end. Two parties fight with deadly weapons, but under certain rules of arbitrary honor; the party that wins becomes the government and proceeds to govern. The aim of civil war, like the aim of all war, is peace. Now the Suffragettes cannot raise civil war in this soldierly and decisive sense; first, because they are women; and, secondly, because they are very few women. But they can raise something else; which is altogether another pair of shoes. They do not create revolution; what they do create is anarchy; and the difference between these is not a question of violence, but a question of fruitfulness and finality. Revolution of its nature produces government; anarchy only produces more anarchy. Men may have what opinions they please about the beheading of King Charles or King Louis, but they cannot deny that Bradshaw and Cromwell ruled, that Carnot and Napoleon governed. Someone conquered;

something occurred. You can only knock off the King's head once. But you can knock off the King's hat any number of times. Destruction is finite, obstruction is infinite: so long as rebellion takes the form of mere disorder (instead of an attempt to enforce a new order) there is no logical end to it; it can feed on itself and renew itself forever. If Napoleon had not wanted to be a Consul, but only wanted to be a nuisance, he could, possibly, have prevented any government arising successfully out of the Revolution. But such a proceeding would not have deserved the dignified name of rebellion.

It is exactly this unmilitant quality in the Suffragettes that makes their superficial problem. The problem is that their action has none of the advantages of ultimate violence; it does not afford a test. War is a dreadful thing; but it does prove two points sharply and unanswerably—numbers, and an unnatural valor. One does discover the two urgent matters; how many rebels there are alive, and how many are ready to be dead. But a tiny minority, even an interested minority, may maintain mere disorder forever. There is also, of course, in the case of these women, the further falsity that is introduced by their sex. It is false to state the matter as a mere brutal question of strength. If his muscles give a man a vote, then his horse ought to have two votes and his elephant five votes. The truth is more subtle than that; it is that bodily outbreak is a man's instinctive weapon, like the hoofs to the horse or the tusks to the elephant. All riot is a threat of war; but the woman is brandishing a weapon she can never use. There are many weapons that she could and does use. If (for example) all the women nagged for a vote they would get it in a month. But there again, one must remember, it would be necessary to get all the women to nag. And that brings us to the end of the political surface of the matter. The working objection to the Suffragette philosophy is simply that overmastering millions of women do not agree with it. I am aware that some maintain that women ought to have votes whether the majority wants them or not; but this is surely a strange and childish case of setting up formal democracy to the destruction of actual democracy. What should the mass of women decide if they do not decide their general place in the State? These people practically say that females may vote about everything except about Female Suffrage.

But having again cleared my conscience of my merely political and possibly unpopular opinion, I will again cast back and try to treat the matter in a slower and more sympathetic style; attempt to trace the real roots of woman's position in the western state, and the causes of our existing traditions or perhaps prejudices upon the point. And for this purpose it is again necessary to travel far from the modern topic, the mere Suffragette of today, and to go back to subjects which, though much more old, are, I think, considerably more fresh.

Chapter 2
The Universal Stick

ast your eye round the room in which you sit, and select some three or four things that have been with man almost since his beginning; which at least we hear of early in the centuries and often among the tribes. Let me suppose that you see a knife on the table, a stick in the corner, or a fire on the hearth. About each of these you will notice one speciality; that not one of them is special. Each of these ancestral things is a universal thing; made to supply many different needs; and while tottering pedants nose about to find the cause and origin of some old custom, the truth is that it had fifty causes or a hundred origins. The knife is meant to cut wood, to cut cheese, to cut pencils, to cut throats; for a myriad ingenious or innocent human objects. The stick is meant partly to hold a man up, partly to knock a man down; partly to point with like a finger-post, partly to balance with like a balancing pole, partly to trifle with like a cigarette, partly to kill with like a club of a giant; it is a crutch and a cudgel; an elongated finger and an extra leg. The case is the same, of course, with the fire; about which the strangest modern views have arisen. A queer fancy seems to be current that a fire exists to warm people. It exists to warm people, to light their darkness, to raise their spirits, to toast their muffins, to air their rooms, to cook their chestnuts, to tell stories to their children, to make checkered shadows on their walls, to boil their hurried kettles, and to be the red heart of a man's house and that hearth for which, as the great heathens said, a man should die.

Now it is the great mark of our modernity that people are always proposing substitutes for these old things; and these substitutes always answer one purpose where the old thing answered ten. The modern man will wave a cigarette instead of a stick; he will cut his pencil with a little screwing pencil-sharpener instead of a knife; and he will even boldly offer to be warmed by hot water pipes instead of a fire. I have my doubts about pencil-sharpeners even for sharpening pencils; and about hot water pipes even for heat. But when we think of all those other requirements that these institutions answered, there opens before us the whole horrible harlequinade of our civilization. We see as in a vision a world where a man tries to cut his throat with a pencil-sharpener; where a man must learn single-stick with a cigarette; where a man must try to toast muffins at electric lamps, and see red and golden castles in the surface of hot water pipes.

The principle of which I speak can be seen everywhere in a comparison between the ancient and universal things and the modern and specialist things. The object of a theodolite is to lie level; the object of a stick is to swing loose at any angle; to whirl like the very wheel of liberty. The object of a lancet is to lance; when used for slashing, gashing, ripping, lopping off heads and limbs, it is a disappointing instrument. The object of an electric light is merely to light (a despicable modesty); and the object of an asbestos stove ... I wonder what is the object of an asbestos stove? If a man found a coil of rope in a desert he could at least think of all the things that can be done with a coil of rope; and some of them might even be practical. He could tow a boat or lasso a horse. He could play cat's-cradle, or pick oakum. He could construct a rope-ladder for an eloping heiress, or cord her boxes for a travelling maiden aunt. He could learn to tie a bow, or he could hang himself. Far otherwise with the unfortunate traveller who should find a telephone in the desert. You can telephone with a telephone; you cannot do anything else with it. And though this is one of the wildest joys of life, it falls by one degree from its full delirium when there is nobody to answer you. The contention is, in brief, that you must pull up a hundred roots, and not one, before you uproot any of these hoary and simple expedients. It is only with great difficulty that a modern scientific sociologist can be got to see that any old method has a leg to stand on. But almost every old method has four or five legs to stand on. Almost all the old institutions are quadrupeds; and some of them are centipedes.

Consider these cases, old and new, and you will observe the operation of a general tendency. Everywhere there was one big thing that served six purposes; everywhere now there are six small things; or, rather (and there is the trouble), there are just five and a half. Nevertheless, we will not say that this separation and specialism is entirely useless or inexcusable. I have often thanked God for the telephone; I may any day thank God for the lancet; and there is none of these brilliant and narrow inventions (except, of course, the asbestos stove) which might not be at some moment necessary and lovely. But I do not think the most austere upholder of specialism will deny that there is in these old, many-sided institutions an element of unity and universality which may well be preserved in its due proportion and place. Spiritually, at least, it will be admitted that some all-round balance is needed to equalize the extravagance of experts. It would not be difficult to carry the parable of the knife and stick into higher regions. Religion, the immortal maiden, has been a maid-of-all-work as well as a servant of mankind. She provided men at once with the theoretic laws of an unalterable cosmos and also with the practical rules of the rapid and thrilling game of morality. She taught logic to the student and told fairy tales to the children; it was her business to confront the nameless gods whose fears are on all flesh, and also to see the streets were spotted with silver and scarlet, that there was a day for wearing ribbons or an hour for ringing bells. The large uses of religion have been broken up into lesser specialities, just as the uses of the hearth have been broken up into hot water pipes and electric bulbs. The romance of ritual and colored emblem has been taken over by that narrowest of all trades, modern art (the sort called art for art's sake), and men are in modern practice informed that they may use all symbols so long as they mean nothing by them. The romance of conscience has been dried up into the science of ethics; which may well be called decency for decency's sake, decency unborn of cosmic energies and barren of artistic flower. The cry to the dim gods, cut off from ethics and cosmology, has become mere Psychical Research. Everything has been sundered from everything else, and everything has grown cold. Soon we shall hear of specialists dividing the tune from the words of a song, on the ground that they spoil each other; and I did once meet a man who openly advocated the separation of almonds and raisins. This world is all one wild divorce court; nevertheless, there are many who still hear in their souls the thunder of authority of human habit; those whom Man hath joined let no man sunder.

This book must avoid religion, but there must (I say) be many, religious and irreligious, who will concede that this power of answering many purposes was a sort of strength which should not wholly die out of our lives. As a part of personal character, even the moderns will agree that many-sidedness is a merit and a merit that may easily be overlooked. This balance and universality has been the vision of many groups of men in many ages. It was the Liberal Education of Aristotle; the jack-of-all-trades artistry of Leonardo da Vinci and his friends; the august amateurishness of the Cavalier Person of Quality like Sir William Temple or the great Earl of Dorset. It has appeared in literature in our time in the most erratic and opposite shapes, set to almost inaudible music by Walter Pater and enunciated through a foghorn by Walt Whitman. But the great mass of men have always been unable to achieve this literal universality, because of the nature of their work in the world. Not, let it be noted, because of the existence of their work. Leonardo da Vinci must have worked pretty hard; on the other hand, many a government office clerk, village constable or elusive plumber may do (to all human appearance) no work at all, and yet show no signs of the Aristotelian universalism. What makes it difficult for the average man to be a universalist is that the average man has to be a specialist; he has not only to learn one trade, but to learn it so well as to uphold him in a more or less ruthless society. This is generally true of males from the first hunter to the last electrical engineer; each has not merely to act, but to excel. Nimrod has not only to be a mighty hunter before the Lord, but also a mighty hunter before the other hunters. The electrical engineer has to be a very electrical engineer, or he is outstripped by engineers yet more electrical. Those very miracles of the human mind on which the modern world prides itself, and rightly in the main, would be impossible without a certain concentration which disturbs the pure balance of reason more than does religious bigotry. No creed can be so limiting as that awful adjuration that the cobbler must not go beyond his last. So the largest and wildest shots of our world are but in one direction and with a defined trajectory: the gunner cannot go beyond his shot, and his shot so often falls short; the astronomer cannot go beyond his telescope and his telescope goes such a little way. All these are like men who have stood on the high peak of a mountain and seen the horizon like a single ring and who then descend down different paths towards different towns, traveling slow or fast. It is right; there must be people traveling to different towns; there must be specialists; but shall no one behold the horizon? Shall all mankind be specialist surgeons or peculiar plumbers; shall all humanity be monomaniac? Tradition has decided that only half of humanity shall be monomaniac. It has decided that in every home there shall be a tradesman and a Jack-of-all-trades. But it has also decided, among other things, that the Jack-of-all-trades shall be a Jill-of-all-trades. It has decided, rightly or wrongly, that this specialism and this universalism shall be divided between the sexes. Cleverness shall be left for men and wisdom for women. For cleverness kills wisdom; that is one of the few sad and certain things.

But for women this ideal of comprehensive capacity (or common-sense) must long ago have been washed away. It must have melted in the frightful furnaces of ambition and eager technicality. A man must be partly a one-idead man, because he is a one-weaponed man—and he is flung naked into the fight. The world's demand comes to him direct; to his wife indirectly. In short, he must (as the books on Success say) give "his best"; and what a small part of a man "his best" is! His second and third best are often much better. If he is the first violin he must fiddle for life; he must not remember that he is a fine fourth bagpipe, a fair fifteenth billiard-cue, a foil, a fountain pen, a hand at whist, a gun, and an image of God.

Chapter 3
The Emancipation of Domesticity

nd it should be remarked in passing that this force upon a man to develop one feature has nothing to do with what is commonly called our competitive system, but would equally exist under any rationally conceivable kind of Collectivism. Unless the Socialists are frankly ready for a fall in the standard of violins, telescopes and electric lights, they must somehow create a moral demand on the individual that he shall keep up his present concentration on these things. It was only by men being in some degree specialist that there ever were any telescopes; they must certainly be in some degree specialist in order to keep them going. It is not by making a man a State wage-earner that you can prevent him thinking principally about the very difficult way he earns his wages. There is only one way to preserve in the world that high levity and that more leisurely outlook which fulfils the old vision of universalism. That is, to permit the existence of a partly protected half of humanity; a half which the harassing industrial demand troubles indeed, but only troubles indirectly. In other words, there must be in every center of humanity one human being upon a larger plan; one who does not "give her best," but gives her all.

Our old analogy of the fire remains the most workable one. The fire need not blaze like electricity nor boil like boiling water; its point is that it blazes more than water and warms more than light. The wife is like the fire, or to put things in their proper proportion, the fire is like the wife. Like the fire, the woman is expected to cook: not to excel in cooking, but to cook; to cook better than her husband who is earning the coke by lecturing on botany or breaking stones. Like the fire, the woman is expected to tell tales to the children, not original and artistic tales, but tales—better tales than would probably be told by a first-class cook. Like the fire, the woman is expected to illuminate and ventilate, not by the most startling revelations or the wildest winds of thought, but better than a man can do it after breaking stones or lecturing. But she cannot be expected to endure anything like this universal duty if she is also to endure the direct cruelty of competitive or bureaucratic toil. Woman must be a cook, but not a competitive cook; a school mistress, but not a competitive schoolmistress; a house-decorator but not a competitive house-decorator; a dressmaker, but not a competitive dressmaker. She should have not one trade but twenty hobbies; she, unlike the man, may develop all her second bests. This is what has been really aimed at from the first in what is called the seclusion, or even the oppression, of women. Women were not kept at home in order to keep them narrow; on the contrary, they were kept at home in order to keep them broad. The world outside the home was one mass of narrowness, a maze of cramped paths, a madhouse of monomaniacs. It was only by partly limiting and protecting the woman that she was enabled to play at five or six professions and so come almost as near to God as the child when he plays at a hundred trades. But the woman's professions, unlike the child's, were all truly and almost terribly fruitful; so tragically real that nothing but her universality and balance prevented them being merely morbid. This is the substance of the contention I offer about the historic female position. I do not deny that women have been wronged and even tortured; but I doubt if they were ever tortured so much as they are tortured now by the absurd modern attempt to make them domestic empresses and competitive clerks at the same time. I do not deny that even under the old tradition women had a harder time than men; that is why we take off our hats. I do not deny that all these various female functions were exasperating; but I say that there was some aim and meaning in keeping them various. I do not pause even to deny that woman was a servant; but at least she was a general servant.

The shortest way of summarizing the position is to say that woman stands for the idea of Sanity; that intellectual home to which the mind must return after every excursion on extravagance. The mind that finds its way to wild places is the poet's; but the mind that never finds its way back is the lunatic's. There must in every machine be a part that moves and a part that stands still; there must be in everything that changes a part that is unchangeable. And many of the phenomena which moderns hastily condemn are really parts of this position of the woman as the center and pillar of health. Much of what is called her subservience, and even her pliability, is merely the subservience and pliability of a universal remedy; she varies as medicines vary, with the disease. She has to be an optimist to the morbid husband, a salutary pessimist to the happy-go-lucky husband. She has to prevent the Quixote from being put upon, and the bully from putting upon others. The French King wrote—

"Toujours femme varie Bien fol qui s'y fie,"

but the truth is that woman always varies, and that is exactly why we always trust her. To correct every adventure and extravagance with its antidote in common-sense is not (as the moderns seem to think) to be in the position of a spy or a slave. It is to be in the position of Aristotle or (at the lowest) Herbert Spencer, to be a universal morality, a complete system of thought. The slave flatters; the complete moralist rebukes. It is, in short, to be a Trimmer in the true sense of that honorable term; which for some reason or other is always used in a sense exactly opposite to its own. It seems really to be supposed that a Trimmer means a cowardly person who always goes over to the stronger side. It really means a highly chivalrous person who always goes over to the weaker side; like one who trims a boat by sitting where there are few people seated. Woman is a trimmer; and it is a generous, dangerous and romantic trade.

The final fact which fixes this is a sufficiently plain one. Supposing it to be conceded that humanity has acted at least not unnaturally in dividing itself into two halves, respectively typifying the ideals of special talent and of general sanity (since they are genuinely difficult to combine completely in one mind), it is not difficult to see why the line of cleavage has followed the line of sex, or why the female became the emblem of the universal and the male of the special and superior. Two gigantic facts of nature fixed it thus: first, that the woman who frequently fulfilled her functions literally could not be specially prominent in experiment and adventure; and second, that the same natural operation surrounded her with very young children, who require to be taught not so much anything as everything. Babies need not to be taught a trade, but to be introduced to a world. To put the matter shortly, woman is generally shut up in a house with a human being at the time when he asks all the questions that there are, and some that there aren't. It would be odd if she retained any of the narrowness of a specialist. Now if anyone says that this duty of general enlightenment (even when freed from modern rules and hours, and exercised more spontaneously by a more protected person) is in itself too exacting and oppressive, I can understand the view. I can only answer that our race has thought it worth while to cast this burden on women in order to keep common-sense in the world. But when people begin to talk about this domestic duty as not merely difficult but trivial and dreary, I simply give up the question. For I cannot with the utmost energy of imagination conceive what they mean. When domesticity, for instance, is called drudgery, all the difficulty arises from a double meaning in the word. If drudgery only means dreadfully hard work, I admit the woman drudges in the home, as a man might drudge at the Cathedral of Amiens or drudge behind a gun at Trafalgar. But if it means that the hard work is more heavy because it is trifling, colorless and of small import to the soul, then as I say, I give it up; I do not know what the words mean. To be Queen Elizabeth within a definite area, deciding sales, banquets, labors and holidays; to be Whiteley within a certain area, providing toys, boots, sheets, cakes and books, to be Aristotle within a certain area, teaching morals, manners, theology, and hygiene; I can understand how this might exhaust the mind, but I cannot imagine how it could narrow it. How can it be a large career to tell other people's children about the Rule of Three, and a small career to tell one's own children about the universe? How can it be broad to be the same thing to everyone, and narrow to be everything to someone? No; a woman's function is laborious, but because it is gigantic, not because it is minute. I will pity Mrs. Jones for the hugeness of her task; I will never pity her for its smallness.

But though the essential of the woman's task is universality, this does not, of course, prevent her from having one or two severe though largely wholesome prejudices. She has, on the whole, been more conscious than man that she is only one half of humanity; but she has expressed it (if one may say so of a lady) by getting her teeth into the two or three things which she thinks she stands for. I would observe here in parenthesis that much of the recent official trouble about women has arisen from the fact that they transfer to things of doubt and reason that sacred stubbornness only proper to the primary things which a woman was set to guard. One's own children, one's own altar, ought to be a matter of principle—or if you like, a matter of prejudice. On the other hand, who wrote Junius's Letters ought not to be a principle or a prejudice, it ought to be a matter of free and almost indifferent inquiry. But take an energetic modern girl secretary to a league to show that George III wrote Junius, and in three months she will believe it, too, out of mere loyalty to her employers. Modern women defend their office with all the fierceness of domesticity. They fight for desk and typewriter as for hearth and home, and develop a sort of wolfish wifehood on behalf of the invisible head of the firm. That is why they do office work so well; and that is why they ought not to do it.

Chapter 4
The Romance of Thrift

he larger part of womankind, however, have had to fight for things slightly more intoxicating to the eye than the desk or the typewriter; and it cannot be denied that in defending these, women have developed the quality called prejudice to a powerful and even menacing degree. But these prejudices will always be found to fortify the main position of the woman, that she is to remain a general overseer, an autocrat within small compass but on all sides. On the one or two points on which she really misunderstands the man's position, it is almost entirely in order to preserve her own. The two points on which woman, actually and of herself, is most tenacious may be roughly summarized as the ideal of thrift and the ideal of dignity.

Unfortunately for this book it is written by a male, and these two qualities, if not hateful to a man, are at least hateful in a man. But if we are to settle the sex question at all fairly, all males must make an imaginative attempt to enter into the attitude of all good women toward these two things. The difficulty exists especially, perhaps, in the thing called thrift; we men have so much encouraged each other in throwing money right and left, that there has come at last to be a sort of chivalrous and poetical air about losing sixpence. But on a broader and more candid consideration the case scarcely stands so.

Thrift is the really romantic thing; economy is more romantic than extravagance. Heaven knows I for one speak disinterestedly in the matter; for I cannot clearly remember saving a half-penny ever since I was born. But the thing is true; economy, properly understood, is the more poetic. Thrift is poetic because it is creative; waste is unpoetic because it is waste. It is prosaic to throw money away, because it is prosaic to throw anything away; it is negative; it is a confession of indifference, that is, it is a confession of failure. The most prosaic thing about the house is the dustbin, and the one great objection to the new fastidious and aesthetic homestead is simply that in such a moral menage the dustbin must be bigger than the house. If a man could undertake to make use of all things in his dustbin he would be a broader genius than Shakespeare. When science began to use by-products; when science found that colors could be made out of coaltar, she made her greatest and perhaps her only claim on the real respect of the human soul. Now the aim of the good woman is to use the by-products, or, in other words, to rummage in the dustbin.

A man can only fully comprehend it if he thinks of some sudden joke or expedient got up with such materials as may be found in a private house on a rainy day. A man's definite daily work is generally run with such rigid convenience of modern science that thrift, the picking up of potential helps here and there, has almost become unmeaning to him. He comes across it most (as I say) when he is playing some game within four walls; when in charades, a hearthrug will just do for a fur coat, or a tea-cozy just do for a cocked hat; when a toy theater needs timber and cardboard, and the house has just enough firewood and just enough bandboxes. This is the man's occasional glimpse and pleasing parody of thrift. But many a good housekeeper plays the same game every day with ends of cheese and scraps of silk, not because she is mean, but on the contrary, because she is magnanimous; because she wishes her creative mercy to be over all her works, that not one sardine should be destroyed, or cast as rubbish to the void, when she has made the pile complete.

The modern world must somehow be made to understand (in theology and other things) that a view may be vast, broad, universal, liberal and yet come into conflict with another view that is vast, broad, universal and liberal also. There is never a war between two sects, but only between two universal Catholic Churches. The only possible collision is the collision of one cosmos with another. So in a smaller way it must be first made clear that this female economic ideal is a part of that female variety of outlook and all-round art of life which we have already attributed to the sex: thrift is not a small or timid or provincial thing; it is part of that great idea of the woman watching on all sides out of all the windows of the soul and being answerable for everything. For in the average human house there is one hole by which money comes in and a hundred by which it goes out; man has to do with the one hole, woman with the hundred. But though the very stinginess of a woman is a part of her spiritual breadth, it is none the less true that it brings her into conflict with the special kind of spiritual breadth that belongs to the males of the tribe. It brings her into conflict with that shapeless cataract of Comradeship, of chaotic feasting and deafening debate, which we noted in the last section. The very touch of the eternal in the two sexual tastes brings them the more into antagonism; for one stands for a universal vigilance and the other for an almost infinite output. Partly through the nature of his moral weakness, and partly through the nature of his physical strength, the male is normally prone to expand things into a sort of eternity; he always thinks of a dinner party as lasting all night; and he always thinks of a night as lasting forever. When the working women in the poor districts come to the doors of the public houses and try to get their husbands home, simple minded "social workers" always imagine that every husband is a tragic drunkard and every wife a broken-hearted saint. It never occurs to them that the poor woman is only doing under coarser conventions exactly what every fashionable hostess does when she tries to get the men from arguing over the cigars to come and gossip over the teacups. These women are not exasperated merely at the amount of money that is wasted in beer; they are exasperated also at the amount of time that is wasted in talk. It is not merely what goeth into the mouth but what cometh out the mouth that, in their opinion, defileth a man. They will raise against an argument (like their sisters of all ranks) the ridiculous objection that nobody is convinced by it; as if a man wanted to make a body-slave of anybody with whom he had played single-stick. But the real female prejudice on this point is not without a basis; the real feeling is this, that the most masculine pleasures have a quality of the ephemeral. A duchess may ruin a duke for a diamond necklace; but there is the necklace. A coster may ruin his wife for a pot of beer; and where is the beer? The duchess quarrels with another duchess in order to crush her, to produce a result; the coster does not argue with another coster in order to convince him, but in order to enjoy at once the sound of his own voice, the clearness of his own opinions and the sense of masculine society. There is this element of a fine fruitlessness about the male enjoyments; wine is poured into a bottomless bucket; thought plunges into a bottomless abyss. All this has set woman against the Public House—that is, against the Parliament House. She is there to prevent waste; and the "pub" and the parliament are the very palaces of waste. In the upper classes the "pub" is called the club, but that makes no more difference to the reason than it does to the rhyme. High and low, the woman's objection to the Public House is perfectly definite and rational, it is that the Public House wastes the energies that could be used on the private house.

As it is about feminine thrift against masculine waste, so it is about feminine dignity against masculine rowdiness. The woman has a fixed and very well-founded idea that if she does not insist on good manners nobody else will. Babies are not always strong on the point of dignity, and grown-up men are quite unpresentable. It is true that there are many very polite men, but none that I ever heard of who were not either fascinating women or obeying them. But indeed the female ideal of dignity, like the female ideal of thrift, lies deeper and may easily be misunderstood. It rests ultimately on a strong idea of spiritual isolation; the same that makes women religious. They do not like being melted down; they dislike and avoid the mob. That anonymous quality we have remarked in the club conversation would be common impertinence in a case of ladies. I remember an artistic and eager lady asking me in her grand green drawing-room whether I believed in comradeship between the sexes, and why not. I was driven back on offering the obvious and sincere answer "Because if I were to treat you for two minutes like a comrade you would turn me out of the house." The only certain rule on this subject is always to deal with woman and never with women. "Women" is a profligate word; I have used it repeatedly in this chapter; but it always has a blackguard sound. It smells of oriental cynicism and hedonism. Every woman is a captive queen. But every crowd of women is only a harem broken loose.

I am not expressing my own views here, but those of nearly all the women I have known. It is quite unfair to say that a woman hates other women individually; but I think it would be quite true to say that she detests them in a confused heap. And this is not because she despises her own sex, but because she respects it; and respects especially that sanctity and separation of each item which is represented in manners by the idea of dignity and in morals by the idea of chastity.

Chapter 5
The Coldness of Chloe

e hear much of the human error which accepts what is sham and what is real. But it is worth while to remember that with unfamiliar things we often mistake what is real for what is sham. It is true that a very young man may think the wig of an actress is her hair. But it is equally true that a child yet younger may call the hair of a negro his wig. Just because the woolly savage is remote and barbaric he seems to be unnaturally neat and tidy. Everyone must have noticed the same thing in the fixed and almost offensive color of all unfamiliar things, tropic birds and tropic blossoms. Tropic birds look like staring toys out of a toy-shop. Tropic flowers simply look like artificial flowers, like things cut out of wax. This is a deep matter, and, I think, not unconnected with divinity; but anyhow it is the truth that when we see things for the first time we feel instantly that they are fictive creations; we feel the finger of God. It is only when we are thoroughly used to them and our five wits are wearied, that we see them as wild and objectless; like the shapeless tree-tops or the shifting cloud. It is the design in Nature that strikes us first; the sense of the crosses and confusions in that design only comes afterwards through experience and an almost eerie monotony. If a man saw the stars abruptly by accident he would think them as festive and as artificial as a firework. We talk of the folly of painting the lily; but if we saw the lily without warning we should think that it was painted. We talk of the devil not being so black as he is painted; but that very phrase is a testimony to the kinship between what is called vivid and what is called artificial. If the modern sage had only one glimpse of grass and sky, he would say that grass was not as green as it was painted; that sky was not as blue as it was painted. If one could see the whole universe suddenly, it would look like a bright-colored toy, just as the South American hornbill looks like a bright-colored toy. And so they are—both of them, I mean.

But it was not with this aspect of the startling air of artifice about all strange objects that I meant to deal. I mean merely, as a guide to history, that we should not be surprised if things wrought in fashions remote from ours seem artificial; we should convince ourselves that nine times out of ten these things are nakedly and almost indecently honest. You will hear men talk of the frosted classicism of Corneille or of the powdered pomposities of the eighteenth century, but all these phrases are very superficial. There never was an artificial epoch. There never was an age of reason. Men were always men and women women: and their two generous appetites always were the expression of passion and the telling of truth. We can see something stiff and quaint in their mode of expression, just as our descendants will see something stiff and quaint in our coarsest slum sketch or our most naked pathological play. But men have never talked about anything but important things; and the next force in femininity which we have to consider can be considered best perhaps in some dusty old volume of verses by a person of quality.

The eighteenth century is spoken of as the period of artificiality, in externals at least; but, indeed, there may be two words about that. In modern speech one uses artificiality as meaning indefinitely a sort of deceit; and the eighteenth century was far too artificial to deceive. It cultivated that completest art that does not conceal the art. Its fashions and costumes positively revealed nature by allowing artifice; as in that obvious instance of a barbering that frosted every head with the same silver. It would be fantastic to call this a quaint humility that concealed youth; but, at least, it was not one with the evil pride that conceals old age. Under the eighteenth century fashion people did not so much all pretend to be young, as all agree to be old. The same applies to the most odd and unnatural of their fashions; they were freakish, but they were not false. A lady may or may not be as red as she is painted, but plainly she was not so black as she was patched.

But I only introduce the reader into this atmosphere of the older and franker fictions that he may be induced to have patience for a moment with a certain element which is very common in the decoration and literature of that age and of the two centuries preceding it. It is necessary to mention it in such a connection because it is exactly one of those things that look as superficial as powder, and are really as rooted as hair.

In all the old flowery and pastoral love-songs, those of the seventeenth and eighteenth centuries especially, you will find a perpetual reproach against woman in the matter of her coldness; ceaseless and stale similes that compare her eyes to northern stars, her heart to ice, or her bosom to snow. Now most of us have always supposed these old and iterant phrases to be a mere pattern of dead words, a thing like a cold wall-paper. Yet I think those old cavalier poets who wrote about the coldness of Chloe had hold of a psychological truth missed in nearly all the realistic novels of today. Our psychological romancers perpetually represent wives as striking terror into their husbands by rolling on the floor, gnashing their teeth, throwing about the furniture or poisoning the coffee; all this upon some strange fixed theory that women are what they call emotional. But in truth the old and frigid form is much nearer to the vital fact. Most men if they spoke with any sincerity would agree that the most terrible quality in women, whether in friendship, courtship or marriage, was not so much being emotional as being unemotional.

There is an awful armor of ice which may be the legitimate protection of a more delicate organism; but whatever be the psychological explanation there can surely be no question of the fact. The instinctive cry of the female in anger is *noli me tangere*. I take this as the most obvious and at the same time the least hackneyed instance of a fundamental quality in the female tradition, which has tended in our time to be almost immeasurably misunderstood, both by the cant of moralists and the cant of immoralists. The proper name for the thing is modesty; but as we live in an age of prejudice and must not call things by their right names, we will yield to a more modern nomenclature and call it dignity. Whatever else it is, it is the thing which a thousand poets and a million lovers have called the coldness of Chloe. It is akin to the classical, and is at least the opposite of the grotesque. And since we are talking here chiefly in types and symbols, perhaps as good an embodiment as any of the idea may be found in the mere fact of a woman wearing a skirt. It is highly typical of the rabid plagiarism which now passes everywhere for emancipation, that a little while ago it was common for an "advanced" woman to claim the right to wear trousers; a right about as grotesque as the right to wear a false nose. Whether female liberty is much advanced by the act of wearing a skirt on each leg I do not know; perhaps Turkish women might offer some information on the point. But if the western woman walks about (as it were) trailing the curtains of the harem with her, it is quite certain that the woven mansion is meant for a perambulating palace, not for a perambulating prison. It is quite certain that the skirt means female dignity, not female submission; it can be proved by the simplest of all tests. No ruler would deliberately dress up in the recognized fetters of a slave; no judge would appear covered with broad arrows. But when men wish to be safely impressive, as judges, priests or kings, they do wear skirts, the long, trailing robes of female dignity The whole world is under petticoat government; for even men wear petticoats when they wish to govern.

Chapter 6
The Pedant and the Savage

e say then that the female holds up with two strong arms these two pillars of civilization; we say also that she could do neither, but for her position; her curious position of private omnipotence, universality on a small scale. The first element is thrift; not the destructive thrift of the miser, but the creative thrift of the peasant; the second element is dignity, which is but the expression of sacred personality and privacy. Now I know the question that will be abruptly and automatically asked by all that know the dull tricks and turns of the modern sexual quarrel. The advanced person will at once begin to argue about whether these instincts are inherent and inevitable in woman or whether they are merely prejudices produced by her history and education. Now I do not propose to discuss whether woman could now be educated out of her habits touching thrift and dignity; and that for two excellent reasons. First it is a question which cannot conceivably ever find any answer: that is why modern people are so fond of it. From the nature of the case it is obviously impossible to decide whether any of the peculiarities of civilized man have been strictly necessary to his civilization. It is not self-evident (for instance), that even the habit of standing upright was the only path of human progress. There might have been a quadrupedal civilization, in which a city gentleman put on four boots to go to the city every morning. Or there might have been a reptilian civilization, in which he rolled up to the office on his stomach; it is impossible to say that intelligence might not have developed in such creatures. All we can say is that man as he is walks upright; and that woman is something almost more upright than uprightness.

And the second point is this: that upon the whole we rather prefer women (nay, even men) to walk upright; so we do not waste much of our noble lives in inventing any other way for them to walk. In short, my second reason for not speculating upon whether woman might get rid of these peculiarities, is that I do not want her to get rid of them; nor does she. I will not exhaust my intelligence by inventing ways in which mankind might unlearn the violin or forget how to ride horses; and the art of domesticity seems to me as special and as valuable as all the ancient arts of our race. Nor do I propose to enter at all into those formless and floundering speculations about how woman was or is regarded in the primitive times that we cannot remember, or in the savage countries which we cannot understand. Even if these people segregated their women for low or barbaric reasons it would not make our reasons barbaric; and I am haunted with a tenacious suspicion that these people's feelings were really, under other forms, very much the same as ours. Some impatient trader, some superficial missionary, walks across an island and sees the squaw digging in the fields while the man is playing a flute; and immediately says that the man is a mere lord of creation and the woman a mere serf. He does not remember that he might see the same thing in half the back gardens in Brixton, merely because women are at once more conscientious and more impatient, while men are at once more quiescent and more greedy for pleasure. It may often be in Hawaii simply as it is in Hoxton. That is, the woman does not work because the man tells her to work and she obeys. On the contrary, the woman works because she has told the man to work and he hasn't obeyed. I do not affirm that this is the whole truth, but I do affirm that we have too little comprehension of the souls of savages to know how far it is untrue. It is the same with the relations of our hasty and surface science, with the problem of sexual dignity and modesty. Professors find all over the world fragmentary ceremonies in which the bride affects some sort of reluctance, hides from her husband, or runs away from him. The professor then pompously proclaims that this is a survival of Marriage by Capture. I wonder he never says that the veil thrown over the bride is really a net. I gravely doubt whether women ever were married by capture I think they pretended to be; as they do still.

It is equally obvious that these two necessary sanctities of thrift and dignity are bound to come into collision with the wordiness, the wastefulness, and the perpetual pleasure-seeking of masculine companionship. Wise women allow for the thing; foolish women try to crush it; but all women try to counteract it, and they do well. In many a home all round us at this moment, we know that the nursery rhyme is reversed. The queen is in the counting-house, counting out the money. The king is in the parlor, eating bread and honey. But it must be strictly understood that the king has captured the honey in some heroic wars. The quarrel can be found in moldering Gothic carvings and in crabbed Greek manuscripts. In every age, in every land, in every tribe and village, has been waged the great sexual war between the Private House and the Public House. I have seen a collection of mediaeval English poems, divided into sections such as "Religious Carols," "Drinking Songs," and so on; and the section headed, "Poems of Domestic Life" consisted entirely (literally, entirely) of the complaints of husbands who were bullied by their wives. Though the English was archaic, the words were in many cases precisely the same as those which I have heard in the streets and public houses of Battersea, protests on behalf of an extension of time and talk, protests against the nervous impatience and the devouring utilitarianism of the female. Such, I say, is the quarrel; it can never be anything but a quarrel; but the aim of all morals and all society is to keep it a lovers' quarrel.

Chapter 7
The Modern Surrender of Woman

ut in this corner called England, at this end of the century, there has happened a strange and startling thing. Openly and to all appearance, this ancestral conflict has silently and abruptly ended; one of the two sexes has suddenly surrendered to the other. By the beginning of the twentieth century, within the last few years, the woman has in public surrendered to the man. She has seriously and officially owned that the man has been right all along; that the public house (or Parliament) is really more important than the private house; that politics are not (as woman had always maintained) an excuse for pots of beer, but are a sacred solemnity to which new female worshipers may kneel; that the talkative patriots in the tavern are not only admirable but enviable; that talk is not a waste of time, and therefore (as a consequence, surely) that taverns are not a waste of money. All we men had grown used to our wives and mothers, and grandmothers, and great aunts all pouring a chorus of contempt upon our hobbies of sport, drink and party politics. And now comes Miss Pankhurst with tears in her eyes, owning that all the women were wrong and all the men were right; humbly imploring to be admitted into so much as an outer court, from which she may catch a glimpse of those masculine merits which her erring sisters had so thoughtlessly scorned.

Now this development naturally perturbs and even paralyzes us. Males, like females, in the course of that old fight between the public and private house, had indulged in overstatement and extravagance, feeling that they must keep up their end of the see-saw. We told our wives that Parliament had sat late on most essential business; but it never crossed our minds that our wives would believe it. We said that everyone must have a vote in the country; similarly our wives said that no one must have a pipe in the drawing room. In both cases the idea was the same. "It does not matter much, but if you let those things slide there is chaos." We said that Lord Huggins or Mr. Buggins was absolutely necessary to the country. We knew quite well that nothing is necessary to the country except that the men should be men and the women women. We knew this; we thought the women knew it even more clearly; and we thought the women would say it. Suddenly, without warning, the women have begun to say all the nonsense that we ourselves hardly believed when we said it. The solemnity of politics; the necessity of votes; the necessity of Huggins; the necessity of Buggins; all these flow in a pellucid stream from the lips of all the suffragette speakers. I suppose in every fight, however old, one has a vague aspiration to conquer; but we never wanted to conquer women so completely as this. We only expected that they might leave us a little more margin for our nonsense; we never expected that they would accept it seriously as sense. Therefore I am all at sea about the existing situation; I scarcely know whether to be relieved or enraged by this substitution of the feeble platform lecture for the forcible curtain-lecture. I am lost without the trenchant and candid Mrs. Caudle. I really do not know what to do with the prostrate and penitent Miss Pankhurst. This surrender of the modern woman has taken us all so much by surprise that it is desirable to pause a moment, and collect our wits about what she is really saying.

As I have already remarked, there is one very simple answer to all this; these are not the modern women, but about one in two thousand of the modern women. This fact is important to a democrat; but it is of very little importance to the typically modern mind. Both the characteristic modern parties believed in a government by the few; the only difference is whether it is the Conservative few or Progressive few. It might be put, somewhat coarsely perhaps, by saying that one believes in any minority that is rich and the other in any minority that is mad. But in this state of things the democratic argument obviously falls out for the moment; and we are bound to take the prominent minority, merely because it is prominent. Let us eliminate altogether from our minds the thousands of women who detest this cause, and the millions of women who have hardly heard of it. Let us concede that the English people itself is not and will not be for a very long time within the sphere of practical politics. Let us confine ourselves to saying that these particular women want a vote and to asking themselves what a vote is. If we ask these ladies ourselves what a vote is, we shall get a very vague reply. It is the only question, as a rule, for which they are not prepared. For the truth is that they go mainly by precedent; by the mere fact that men have votes already. So far from being a mutinous movement, it is really a very Conservative one; it is in the narrowest rut of the British Constitution. Let us take a little wider and freer sweep of thought and ask ourselves what is the ultimate point and meaning of this odd business called voting.

Chapter 8
The Brand of the Fleur-de-lis

eemingly from the dawn of man all nations have had governments; and all nations have been ashamed of them. Nothing is more openly fallacious than to fancy that in ruder or simpler ages ruling, judging and punishing appeared perfectly innocent and dignified. These things were always regarded as the penalties of the Fall; as part of the humiliation of mankind, as bad in themselves. That the king can do no wrong was never anything but a legal fiction; and it is a legal fiction still. The doctrine of Divine Right was not a piece of idealism, but rather a piece of realism, a practical way of ruling amid the ruin of humanity; a very pragmatist piece of faith. The religious basis of government was not so much that people put their trust in princes, as that they did not put their trust in any child of man. It was so with all the ugly institutions which disfigure human history. Torture and slavery were never talked of as good things; they were always talked of as necessary evils. A pagan spoke of one man owning ten slaves just as a modern business man speaks of one merchant sacking ten clerks: "It's very horrible; but how else can society be conducted?" A mediaeval scholastic regarded the possibility of a man being burned to death just as a modern business man regards the possibility of a man being starved to death: "It is a shocking torture; but can you organize a painless world?" It is possible that a future society may find a way of doing without the question by hunger as we have done without the question by fire. It is equally possible, for the matter of that, that a future society may reestablish legal torture with the whole apparatus of rack and fagot. The most modern of countries, America, has introduced with a vague savor of science, a method which it calls "the third degree." This is simply the extortion of secrets by nervous fatigue; which is surely uncommonly close to their extortion by bodily pain. And this is legal and scientific in America. Amateur ordinary America, of course, simply burns people alive in broad daylight, as they did in the Reformation Wars. But though some punishments are more inhuman than others there is no such thing as humane punishment. As long as nineteen men claim the right in any sense or shape to take hold of the twentieth man and make him even mildly uncomfortable, so long the whole proceeding must be a humiliating one for all concerned. And the proof of how poignantly men have always felt this lies in the fact that the headsman and the hangman, the jailors and the torturers, were always regarded not merely with fear but with contempt; while all kinds of careless smiters, bankrupt knights and swashbucklers and outlaws, were regarded with indulgence or even admiration. To kill a man lawlessly was pardoned. To kill a man lawfully was unpardonable. The most bare-faced duelist might almost brandish his weapon. But the executioner was always masked.

This is the first essential element in government, coercion; a necessary but not a noble element. I may remark in passing that when people say that government rests on force they give an admirable instance of the foggy and muddled cynicism of modernity. Government does not rest on force. Government is force; it rests on consent or a conception of justice. A king or a community holding a certain thing to be abnormal, evil, uses the general strength to crush it out; the strength is his tool, but the belief is his only sanction. You might as well say that glass is the real reason for telescopes. But arising from whatever reason the act of government is coercive and is burdened with all the coarse and painful qualities of coercion. And if anyone asks what is the use of insisting on the ugliness of this task of state violence since all mankind is condemned to employ it, I have a simple answer to that. It would be useless to insist on it if all humanity were condemned to it. But it is not irrelevant to insist on its ugliness so long as half of humanity is kept out of it.

All government then is coercive; we happen to have created a government which is not only coercive; but collective. There are only two kinds of government, as I have already said, the despotic and the democratic. Aristocracy is not a government, it is a riot; that most effective kind of riot, a riot of the rich. The most intelligent apologists of aristocracy, sophists like Burke and Nietzsche, have never claimed for aristocracy any virtues but the virtues of a riot, the accidental virtues, courage, variety and adventure. There is no case anywhere of aristocracy having established a universal and applicable order, as despots and democracies have often done; as the last Caesars created the Roman law, as the last Jacobins created the Code Napoleon. With the first of these elementary forms of government, that of the king or chieftain, we are not in this matter of the sexes immediately concerned. We shall return to it later when we remark how differently mankind has dealt with female claims in the despotic as against the democratic field. But for the moment the essential point is that in self-governing countries this coercion of criminals is a collective coercion. The abnormal person is theoretically thumped by a million fists and kicked by a million feet. If a man is flogged we all flogged him; if a man is hanged, we all hanged him. That is the only possible meaning of democracy, which can give any meaning to the first two syllables and also to the last two. In this sense each citizen has the high responsibility of a rioter. Every statute is a declaration of war, to be backed by arms. Every tribunal is a revolutionary tribunal. In a republic all punishment is as sacred and solemn as lynching.

Chapter 9
Sincerity and the Gallows

hen, therefore, it is said that the tradition against Female Suffrage keeps women out of activity, social influence and citizenship, let us a little more soberly and strictly ask ourselves what it actually does keep her out of. It does definitely keep her out of the collective act of coercion; the act of punishment by a mob. The human tradition does say that, if twenty men hang a man from a tree or lamp-post, they shall be twenty men and not women. Now I do not think any reasonable Suffragist will deny that exclusion from this function, to say the least of it, might be maintained to be a protection as well as a veto. No candid person will wholly dismiss the proposition that the idea of having a Lord Chancellor but not a Lady Chancellor may at least be connected with the idea of having a headsman but not a headswoman, a hangman but not a hangwoman. Nor will it be adequate to answer (as is so often answered to this contention) that in modern civilization women would not really be required to capture, to sentence, or to slay; that all this is done indirectly, that specialists kill our criminals as they kill our cattle. To urge this is not to urge the reality of the vote, but to urge its unreality. Democracy was meant to be a more direct way of ruling, not a more indirect way; and if we do not feel that we are all jailers, so much the worse for us, and for the prisoners. If it is really an unwomanly thing to lock up a robber or a tyrant, it ought to be no softening of the situation that the woman does not feel as if she were doing the thing that she certainly is doing. It is bad enough that men can only associate on paper who could once associate in the street; it is bad enough that men have made a vote very much of a fiction. It is much worse that a great class should claim the vote be cause it is a fiction, who would be sickened by it if it were a fact. If votes for women do not mean mobs for women they do not mean what they were meant to mean. A woman can make a cross on a paper as well as a man; a child could do it as well as a woman; and a chimpanzee after a few lessons could do it as well as a child. But nobody ought to regard it merely as making a cross on paper; everyone ought to regard it as what it ultimately is, branding the fleur-de-lis, marking the broad arrow, signing the death warrant. Both men and women ought to face more fully the things they do or cause to be done; face them or leave off doing them.

On that disastrous day when public executions were abolished, private executions were renewed and ratified, perhaps forever. Things grossly unsuited to the moral sentiment of a society cannot be safely done in broad daylight; but I see no reason why we should not still be roasting heretics alive, in a private room. It is very likely (to speak in the manner foolishly called Irish) that if there were public executions there would be no executions. The old open-air punishments, the pillory and the gibbet, at least fixed responsibility upon the law; and in actual practice they gave the mob an opportunity of throwing roses as well as rotten eggs; of crying "Hosannah" as well as "Crucify." But I do not like the public executioner being turned into the private executioner. I think it is a crooked oriental, sinister sort of business, and smells of the harem and the divan rather than of the forum and the market place. In modern times the official has lost all the social honor and dignity of the common hangman. He is only the bearer of the bowstring.

Here, however, I suggest a plea for a brutal publicity only in order to emphasize the fact that it is this brutal publicity and nothing else from which women have been excluded. I also say it to emphasize the fact that the mere modern veiling of the brutality does not make the situation different, unless we openly say that we are giving the suffrage, not only because it is power but because it is not, or in other words, that women are not so much to vote as to play voting. No suffragist, I suppose, will take up that position; and a few suffragists will wholly deny that this human necessity of pains and penalties is an ugly, humiliating business, and that good motives as well as bad may have helped to keep women out of it. More than once I have remarked in these pages that female limitations may be the limits of a temple as well as of a prison, the disabilities of a priest and not of a pariah. I noted it, I think, in the case of the pontifical feminine dress. In the same way it is not evidently irrational, if men decided that a woman, like a priest, must not be a shedder of blood.

Chapter 10
The Higher Anarchy

ut there is a further fact; forgotten also because we moderns forget that there is a female point of view. The woman's wisdom stands partly, not only for a wholesome hesitation about punishment, but even for a wholesome hesitation about absolute rules. There was something feminine and perversely true in that phrase of Wilde's, that people should not be treated as the rule, but all of them as exceptions. Made by a man the remark was a little effeminate; for Wilde did lack the masculine power of dogma and of democratic cooperation. But if a woman had said it it would have been simply true; a woman does treat each person as a peculiar person. In other words, she stands for Anarchy; a very ancient and arguable philosophy; not anarchy in the sense of having no customs in one's life (which is inconceivable), but anarchy in the sense of having no rules for one's mind. To her, almost certainly, are due all those working traditions that cannot be found in books, especially those of education; it was she who first gave a child a stuffed stocking for being good or stood him in the corner for being naughty. This unclassified knowledge is sometimes called rule of thumb and sometimes motherwit. The last phrase suggests the whole truth, for none ever called it fatherwit.

Now anarchy is only tact when it works badly. Tact is only anarchy when it works well. And we ought to realize that in one half of the world—the private house—it does work well. We modern men are perpetually forgetting that the case for clear rules and crude penalties is not self-evident, that there is a great deal to be said for the benevolent lawlessness of the autocrat, especially on a small scale; in short, that government is only one side of life. The other half is called Society, in which women are admittedly dominant. And they have always been ready to maintain that their kingdom is better governed than ours, because (in the logical and legal sense) it is not governed at all. "Whenever you have a real difficulty," they say, "when a boy is bumptious or an aunt is stingy, when a silly girl will marry somebody, or a wicked man won't marry somebody, all your lumbering Roman Law and British Constitution come to a standstill. A snub from a duchess or a slanging from a fish-wife are much more likely to put things straight." So, at least, rang the ancient female challenge down the ages until the recent female capitulation. So streamed the red standard of the higher anarchy until Miss Pankhurst hoisted the white flag.

It must be remembered that the modern world has done deep treason to the eternal intellect by believing in the swing of the pendulum. A man must be dead before he swings. It has substituted an idea of fatalistic alternation for the mediaeval freedom of the soul seeking truth. All modern thinkers are reactionaries; for their thought is always a reaction from what went before. When you meet a modern man he is always coming from a place, not going to it. Thus, mankind has in nearly all places and periods seen that there is a soul and a body as plainly as that there is a sun and moon. But because a narrow Protestant sect called Materialists declared for a short time that there was no soul, another narrow Protestant sect called Christian Science is now maintaining that there is no body. Now just in the same way the unreasonable neglect of government by the Manchester School has produced, not a reasonable regard for government, but an unreasonable neglect of everything else. So that to hear people talk to-day one would fancy that every important human function must be organized and avenged by law; that all education must be state education, and all employment state employment; that everybody and everything must be brought to the foot of the august and prehistoric gibbet. But a somewhat more liberal and sympathetic examination of mankind will convince us that the cross is even older than the gibbet, that voluntary suffering was before and independent of compulsory; and in short that in most important matters a man has always been free to ruin himself if he chose. The huge fundamental function upon which all anthropology turns, that of sex and childbirth, has never been inside the political state, but always outside of it. The state concerned itself with the trivial question of killing people, but wisely left alone the whole business of getting them born. A Eugenist might indeed plausibly say that the government is an absent-minded and inconsistent person who occupies himself with providing for the old age of people who have never been infants. I will not deal here in any detail with the fact that some Eugenists have in our time made the maniacal answer that the police ought to control marriage and birth as they control labor and death. Except for this inhuman handful (with whom I regret to say I shall have to deal with later) all the Eugenists I know divide themselves into two sections: ingenious people who once meant this, and rather bewildered people who swear they never meant it—nor anything else. But if it be conceded (by a breezier estimate of men) that they do mostly desire marriage to remain free from government, it does not follow that they desire it to remain free from everything. If man does not control the marriage market by law, is it controlled at all? Surely the answer is broadly that man does not control the marriage market by law, but the woman does control it by sympathy and prejudice. There was until lately a law forbidding a man to marry his deceased wife's sister; yet the thing happened constantly. There was no law forbidding a man to marry his deceased wife's scullery-maid; yet it did not happen nearly so often. It did not happen because the marriage market is managed in the spirit and by the authority of women; and women are generally conservative where classes are concerned. It is the same with that system of exclusiveness by which ladies have so often contrived (as by a process of elimination) to prevent marriages that they did not want and even sometimes procure those they did. There is no need of the broad arrow and the fleur-de lis, the turnkey's chains or the hangman's halter. You need not strangle a man if you can silence him. The branded shoulder is less effective and final than the cold shoulder; and you need not trouble to lock a man in when you can lock him out.

The same, of course, is true of the colossal architecture which we call infant education: an architecture reared wholly by women. Nothing can ever overcome that one enormous sex superiority, that even the male child is born closer to his mother than to his father. No one, staring at that frightful female privilege, can quite believe in the equality of the sexes. Here and there we read of a girl brought up like a tom-boy; but every boy is brought up like a tame girl. The flesh and spirit of femininity surround him from the first like the four walls of a house; and even the vaguest or most brutal man has been womanized by being born. Man that is born of a woman has short days and full of misery; but nobody can picture the obscenity and bestial tragedy that would belong to such a monster as man that was born of a man.

Chapter 11
The Queen and the Suffragettes

ut, indeed, with this educational matter I must of necessity embroil myself later. The fourth section of discussion is supposed to be about the child, but I think it will be mostly about the mother. In this place I have systematically insisted on the large part of life that is governed, not by man with his vote, but by woman with her voice, or more often, with her horrible silence. Only one thing remains to be added. In a sprawling and explanatory style has been traced out the idea that government is ultimately coercion, that coercion must mean cold definitions as well as cruel consequences, and that therefore there is something to be said for the old human habit of keeping one-half of humanity out of so harsh and dirty a business. But the case is stronger still.

Voting is not only coercion, but collective coercion. I think Queen Victoria would have been yet more popular and satisfying if she had never signed a death warrant. I think Queen Elizabeth would have stood out as more solid and splendid in history if she had not earned (among those who happen to know her history) the nickname of Bloody Bess. I think, in short, that the great historic woman is more herself when she is persuasive rather than coercive. But I feel all mankind behind me when I say that if a woman has this power it should be despotic power—not democratic power. There is a much stronger historic argument for giving Miss Pankhurst a throne than for giving her a vote. She might have a crown, or at least a coronet, like so many of her supporters; for these old powers are purely personal and therefore female. Miss Pankhurst as a despot might be as virtuous as Queen Victoria, and she certainly would find it difficult to be as wicked as Queen Bess, but the point is that, good or bad, she would be irresponsible—she would not be governed by a rule and by a ruler. There are only two ways of governing: by a rule and by a ruler. And it is seriously true to say of a woman, in education and domesticity, that the freedom of the autocrat appears to be necessary to her. She is never responsible until she is irresponsible. In case this sounds like an idle contradiction, I confidently appeal to the cold facts of history. Almost every despotic or oligarchic state has admitted women to its privileges. Scarcely one democratic state has ever admitted them to its rights The reason is very simple: that something female is endangered much more by the violence of the crowd. In short, one Pankhurst is an exception, but a thousand Pankhursts are a nightmare, a Bacchic orgie, a Witches Sabbath. For in all legends men have thought of women as sublime separately but horrible in a herd.

Chapter 12
The Modern Slave

ow I have only taken the test case of Female Suffrage because it is topical and concrete; it is not of great moment for me as a political proposal. I can quite imagine anyone substantially agreeing with my view of woman as universalist and autocrat in a limited area; and still thinking that she would be none the worse for a ballot paper. The real question is whether this old ideal of woman as the great amateur is admitted or not. There are many modern things which threaten it much more than suffragism; notably the increase of self-supporting women, even in the most severe or the most squalid employments. If there be something against nature in the idea of a horde of wild women governing, there is something truly intolerable in the idea of a herd of tame women being governed. And there are elements in human psychology that make this situation particularly poignant or ignominious. The ugly exactitudes of business, the bells and clocks the fixed hours and rigid departments, were all meant for the male: who, as a rule, can only do one thing and can only with the greatest difficulty be induced to do that. If clerks do not try to shirk their work, our whole great commercial system breaks down. It is breaking down, under the inroad of women who are adopting the unprecedented and impossible course of taking the system seriously and doing it well. Their very efficiency is the definition of their slavery. It is generally a very bad sign when one is trusted very much by one's employers. And if the evasive clerks have a look of being blackguards, the earnest ladies are often something very like blacklegs. But the more immediate point is that the modern working woman bears a double burden, for she endures both the grinding officialism of the new office and the distracting scrupulosity of the old home. Few men understand what conscientiousness is. They understand duty, which generally means one duty; but conscientiousness is the duty of the universalist. It is limited by no work days or holidays; it is a lawless, limitless, devouring decorum. If women are to be subjected to the dull rule of commerce, we must find some way of emancipating them from the wild rule of conscience. But I rather fancy you will find it easier to leave the conscience and knock off the commerce. As it is, the modern clerk or secretary exhausts herself to put one thing straight in the ledger and then goes home to put everything straight in the house.

This condition (described by some as emancipated) is at least the reverse of my ideal. I would give woman, not more rights, but more privileges. Instead of sending her to seek such freedom as notoriously prevails in banks and factories, I would design specially a house in which she can be free. And with that we come to the last point of all; the point at which we can perceive the needs of women, like the rights of men, stopped and falsified by something which it is the object of this book to expose.

The Feminist (which means, I think, one who dislikes the chief feminine characteristics) has heard my loose monologue, bursting all the time with one pent-up protest. At this point he will break out and say, "But what are we to do? There is modern commerce and its clerks; there is the modern family with its unmarried daughters; specialism is expected everywhere; female thrift and conscientiousness are demanded and supplied. What does it matter whether we should in the abstract prefer the old human and housekeeping woman; we might prefer the Garden of Eden. But since women have trades they ought to have trades unions. Since women work in factories, they ought to vote on factory-acts. If they are unmarried they must be commercial; if they are commercial they must be political. We must have new rules for a new world—even if it be not a better one." I said to a Feminist once: "The question is not whether women are good enough for votes: it is whether votes are good enough for women." He only answered: "Ah, you go and say that to the women chain-makers on Cradley Heath."

Now this is the attitude which I attack. It is the huge heresy of Precedent. It is the view that because we have got into a mess we must grow messier to suit it; that because we have taken a wrong turn some time ago we must go forward and not backwards; that because we have lost our way we must lose our map also; and because we have missed our ideal, we must forget it. "There are numbers of excellent people who do not think votes unfeminine; and there may be enthusiasts for our beautiful modern industry who do not think factories unfeminine." But if these things are unfeminine it is no answer to say that they fit into each other. I am not satisfied with the statement that my daughter must have unwomanly powers because she has unwomanly wrongs. Industrial soot and political printer's ink are two blacks which do not make a white. Most of the Feminists would probably agree with me that womanhood is under shameful tyranny in the shops and mills. But I want to destroy the tyranny. They want to destroy womanhood. That is the only difference.

Whether we can recover the clear vision of woman as a tower with many windows, the fixed eternal feminine from which her sons, the specialists, go forth; whether we can preserve the tradition of a central thing which is even more human than democracy and even more practical than politics; whether, in word, it is possible to re-establish the family, freed from the filthy cynicism and cruelty of the commercial epoch, I shall discuss in the last section of this book. But meanwhile do not talk to me about the poor chain-makers on Cradley Heath. I know all about them and what they are doing. They are engaged in a very wide-spread and flourishing industry of the present age. They are making chains.

Part IV: Education: or the Mistake About the Child

Chapter 1
The Calvinism of To-day

hen I wrote a little volume on my friend Mr. Bernard Shaw, it is needless to say that he reviewed it. I naturally felt tempted to answer and to criticise the book from the same disinterested and impartial standpoint from which Mr. Shaw had criticised the subject of it. I was not withheld by any feeling that the joke was getting a little obvious; for an obvious joke is only a successful joke; it is only the unsuccessful clowns who comfort themselves with being subtle. The real reason why I did not answer Mr. Shaw's amusing attack was this: that one simple phrase in it surrendered to me all that I have ever wanted, or could want from him to all eternity. I told Mr. Shaw (in substance) that he was a charming and clever fellow, but a common Calvinist. He admitted that this was true, and there (so far as I am concerned) is an end of the matter. He said that, of course, Calvin was quite right in holding that "if once a man is born it is too late to damn or save him." That is the fundamental and subterranean secret; that is the last lie in hell.

The difference between Puritanism and Catholicism is not about whether some priestly word or gesture is significant and sacred. It is about whether any word or gesture is significant and sacred. To the Catholic every other daily act is dramatic dedication to the service of good or of evil. To the Calvinist no act can have that sort of solemnity, because the person doing it has been dedicated from eternity, and is merely filling up his time until the crack of doom. The difference is something subtler than plum-puddings or private theatricals; the difference is that to a Christian of my kind this short earthly life is intensely thrilling and precious; to a Calvinist like Mr. Shaw it is confessedly automatic and uninteresting. To me these threescore years and ten are the battle. To the Fabian Calvinist (by his own confession) they are only a long procession of the victors in laurels and the vanquished in chains. To me earthly life is the drama; to him it is the epilogue. Shavians think about the embryo; Spiritualists about the ghost; Christians about the man. It is as well to have these things clear.

Now all our sociology and eugenics and the rest of it are not so much material-ist as confusedly Calvinist, they are chiefly occupied in educating the child before he exists. The whole movement is full of a singular depression about what one can do with the populace, combined with a strange disembodied gayety about what may be done with posterity. These essential Calvinists have, indeed, abolished some of the more liberal and universal parts of Calvinism, such as the belief in an intellectual design or an everlasting happiness. But though Mr. Shaw and his friends admit it is a superstition that a man is judged after death, they stick to their central doctrine, that he is judged before he is born.

In consequence of this atmosphere of Calvinism in the cultured world of to-day, it is apparently necessary to begin all arguments on education with some mention of obstetrics and the unknown world of the prenatal. All I shall have to say, however, on heredity will be very brief, because I shall confine myself to what is known about it, and that is very nearly nothing. It is by no means self-evident, but it is a current modern dogma, that nothing actually enters the body at birth except a life derived and compounded from the parents. There is at least quite as much to be said for the Christian theory that an element comes from God, or the Buddhist theory that such an element comes from previous existences. But this is not a religious work, and I must submit to those very narrow intellectual limits which the absence of theology always imposes. Leaving the soul on one side, let us suppose for the sake of argument that the human character in the first case comes wholly from parents; and then let us curtly state our knowledge rather than our ignorance.

Chapter 2
The Tribal Terror

opular science, like that of Mr. Blatchford, is in this matter as mild as old wives' tales. Mr. Blatchford, with colossal simplicity, explained to millions of clerks and workingmen that the mother is like a bottle of blue beads and the father is like a bottle of yellow beads; and so the child is like a bottle of mixed blue beads and yellow. He might just as well have said that if the father has two legs and the mother has two legs, the child will have four legs. Obviously it is not a question of simple addition or simple division of a number of hard detached "qualities," like beads. It is an organic crisis and transformation of the most mysterious sort; so that even if the result is unavoidable, it will still be unexpected. It is not like blue beads mixed with yellow beads; it is like blue mixed with yellow; the result of which is green, a totally novel and unique experience, a new emotion. A man might live in a complete cosmos of blue and yellow, like the "Edinburgh Review"; a man might never have seen anything but a golden cornfield and a sapphire sky; and still he might never have had so wild a fancy as green. If you paid a sovereign for a bluebell; if you spilled the mustard on the blue-books; if you married a canary to a blue baboon; there is nothing in any of these wild weddings that contains even a hint of green. Green is not a mental combination, like addition; it is a physical result like birth. So, apart from the fact that nobody ever really understands parents or children either, yet even if we could understand the parents, we could not make any conjecture about the children. Each time the force works in a different way; each time the constituent colors combine into a different spectacle. A girl may actually inherit her ugliness from her mother's good looks. A boy may actually get his weakness from his father's strength. Even if we admit it is really a fate, for us it must remain a fairy tale. Considered in regard to its causes, the Calvinists and materialists may be right or wrong; we leave them their dreary debate. But considered in regard to its results there is no doubt about it. The thing is always a new color; a strange star. Every birth is as lonely as a miracle. Every child is as uninvited as a monstrosity.

On all such subjects there is no science, but only a sort of ardent ignorance; and nobody has ever been able to offer any theories of moral heredity which justified themselves in the only scientific sense; that is that one could calculate on them beforehand. There are six cases, say, of a grandson having the same twitch of mouth or vice of character as his grandfather; or perhaps there are sixteen cases, or perhaps sixty. But there are not two cases, there is not one case, there are no cases at all, of anybody betting half a crown that the grandfather will have a grandson with the twitch or the vice. In short, we deal with heredity as we deal with omens, affinities and the fulfillment of dreams. The things do happen, and when they happen we record them; but not even a lunatic ever reckons on them. Indeed, heredity, like dreams and omens, is a barbaric notion; that is, not necessarily an untrue, but a dim, groping and unsystematized notion. A civilized man feels himself a little more free from his family. Before Christianity these tales of tribal doom occupied the savage north; and since the Reformation and the revolt against Christianity (which is the religion of a civilized freedom) savagery is slowly creeping back in the form of realistic novels and problem plays. The curse of Rougon-Macquart is as heathen and superstitious as the curse of Ravenswood; only not so well written. But in this twilight barbaric sense the feeling of a racial fate is not irrational, and may be allowed like a hundred other half emotions that make life whole. The only essential of tragedy is that one should take it lightly. But even when the barbarian deluge rose to its highest in the madder novels of Zola (such as that called "The Human Beast", a gross libel on beasts as well as humanity), even then the application of the hereditary idea to practice is avowedly timid and fumbling. The students of heredity are savages in this vital sense; that they stare back at marvels, but they dare not stare forward to schemes. In practice no one is mad enough to legislate or educate upon dogmas of physical inheritance; and even the language of the thing is rarely used except for special modern purposes, such as the endowment of research or the oppression of the poor.

Chapter 3
The Tricks of Environment

fter all the modern clatter of Calvinism, therefore, it is only with the born child that anybody dares to deal; and the question is not eugenics but education. Or again, to adopt that rather tiresome terminology of popular science, it is not a question of heredity but of environment. I will not needlessly complicate this question by urging at length that environment also is open to some of the objections and hesitations which paralyze the employment of heredity. I will merely suggest in passing that even about the effect of environment modern people talk much too cheerfully and cheaply. The idea that surroundings will mold a man is always mixed up with the totally different idea that they will mold him in one particular way. To take the broadest case, landscape no doubt affects the soul; but how it affects it is quite another matter. To be born among pine-trees might mean loving pine-trees. It might mean loathing pine-trees. It might quite seriously mean never having seen a pine-tree. Or it might mean any mixture of these or any degree of any of them. So that the scientific method here lacks a little in precision. I am not speaking without the book; on the contrary, I am speaking with the blue book, with the guide-book and the atlas. It may be that the Highlanders are poetical because they inhabit mountains; but are the Swiss prosaic because they inhabit mountains? It may be the Swiss have fought for freedom because they had hills; did the Dutch fight for freedom because they hadn't? Personally I should think it quite likely. Environment might work negatively as well as positively. The Swiss may be sensible, not in spite of their wild skyline, but be cause of their wild skyline. The Flemings may be fantastic artists, not in spite of their dull skyline, but because of it.

I only pause on this parenthesis to show that, even in matters admittedly within its range, popular science goes a great deal too fast, and drops enormous links of logic. Nevertheless, it remains the working reality that what we have to deal with in the case of children is, for all practical purposes, environment; or, to use the older word, education. When all such deductions are made, education is at least a form of will-worship; not of cowardly fact-worship; it deals with a department that we can control; it does not merely darken us with the barbarian pessimism of Zola and the heredity-hunt. We shall certainly make fools of ourselves; that is what is meant by philosophy. But we shall not merely make beasts of ourselves; which is the nearest popular definition for merely following the laws of Nature and cowering under the vengeance of the flesh. Education contains much moonshine; but not of the sort that makes mere mooncalves and idiots the slaves of a silver magnet, the one eye of the world. In this decent arena there are fads, but not frenzies. Doubtless we shall often find a mare's nest; but it will not always be the nightmare's.

Chapter 4
The Truth About Education

hen a man is asked to write down what he really thinks on education, a certain gravity grips and stiffens his soul, which might be mistaken by the superficial for disgust. If it be really true that men sickened of sacred words and wearied of theology, if this largely unreasoning irritation against "dogma" did arise out of some ridiculous excess of such things among priests in the past, then I fancy we must be laying up a fine crop of cant for our descendants to grow tired of. Probably the word "education" will some day seem honestly as old and objectless as the word "justification" now seems in a Puritan folio. Gibbon thought it frightfully funny that people should have fought about the difference between the "Homoousion" and the "Homoiousion." The time will come when somebody will laugh louder to think that men thundered against Sectarian Education and also against Secular Education; that men of prominence and position actually denounced the schools for teaching a creed and also for not teaching a faith. The two Greek words in Gibbon look rather alike; but they really mean quite different things. Faith and creed do not look alike, but they mean exactly the same thing. Creed happens to be the Latin for faith.

Now having read numberless newspaper articles on education, and even written a good many of them, and having heard deafening and indeterminate discussion going on all around me almost ever since I was born, about whether religion was part of education, about whether hygiene was an essential of education, about whether militarism was inconsistent with true education, I naturally pondered much on this recurring substantive, and I am ashamed to say that it was comparatively late in life that I saw the main fact about it.

Of course, the main fact about education is that there is no such thing. It does not exist, as theology or soldiering exist. Theology is a word like geology, soldiering is a word like soldering; these sciences may be healthy or no as hobbies; but they deal with stone and kettles, with definite things. But education is not a word like geology or kettles. Education is a word like "transmission" or "inheritance"; it is not an object, but a method. It must mean the conveying of certain facts, views or qualities, to the last baby born. They might be the most trivial facts or the most preposterous views or the most offensive qualities; but if they are handed on from one generation to another they are education. Education is not a thing like theology, it is not an inferior or superior thing; it is not a thing in the same category of terms. Theology and education are to each other like a love-letter to the General Post Office. Mr. Fagin was quite as educational as Dr. Strong; in practice probably more educational. It is giving something—perhaps poison. Education is tradition, and tradition (as its name implies) can be treason.

This first truth is frankly banal; but it is so perpetually ignored in our political prosing that it must be made plain. A little boy in a little house, son of a little tradesman, is taught to eat his breakfast, to take his medicine, to love his country, to say his prayers, and to wear his Sunday clothes. Obviously Fagin, if he found such a boy, would teach him to drink gin, to lie, to betray his country, to blaspheme and to wear false whiskers. But so also Mr. Salt the vegetarian would abolish the boy's breakfast; Mrs. Eddy would throw away his medicine; Count Tolstoi would rebuke him for loving his country; Mr. Blatchford would stop his prayers, and Mr. Edward Carpenter would theoretically denounce Sunday clothes, and perhaps all clothes. I do not defend any of these advanced views, not even Fagin's. But I do ask what, between the lot of them, has become of the abstract entity called education. It is not (as commonly supposed) that the tradesman teaches education plus Christianity; Mr. Salt, education plus vegetarianism; Fagin, education plus crime. The truth is, that there is nothing in common at all between these teachers, except that they teach. In short, the only thing they share is the one thing they profess to dislike: the general idea of authority. It is quaint that people talk of separating dogma from education. Dogma is actually the only thing that cannot be separated from education. It is education. A teacher who is not dogmatic is simply a teacher who is not teaching.

Chapter 5
An Evil Cry

he fashionable fallacy is that by education we can give people something that we have not got. To hear people talk one would think it was some sort of magic chemistry, by which, out of a laborious hotchpotch of hygienic meals, baths, breathing exercises, fresh air and freehand drawing, we can produce something splendid by accident; we can create what we cannot conceive. These pages have, of course, no other general purpose than to point out that we cannot create anything good until we have conceived it. It is odd that these people, who in the matter of heredity are so sullenly attached to law, in the matter of environment seem almost to believe in miracle. They insist that nothing but what was in the bodies of the parents can go to make the bodies of the children. But they seem somehow to think that things can get into the heads of the children which were not in the heads of the parents, or, indeed, anywhere else.

There has arisen in this connection a foolish and wicked cry typical of the confusion. I mean the cry, "Save the children." It is, of course, part of that modern morbidity that insists on treating the State (which is the home of man) as a sort of desperate expedient in time of panic. This terrified opportunism is also the origin of the Socialist and other schemes. Just as they would collect and share all the food as men do in a famine, so they would divide the children from their fathers, as men do in a shipwreck. That a human community might conceivably not be in a condition of famine or shipwreck never seems to cross their minds. This cry of "Save the children" has in it the hateful implication that it is impossible to save the fathers; in other words, that many millions of grown-up, sane, responsible and self-supporting Europeans are to be treated as dirt or debris and swept away out of the discussion; called dipsomaniacs because they drink in public houses instead of private houses; called unemployables because nobody knows how to get them work; called dullards if they still adhere to conventions, and called loafers if they still love liberty. Now I am concerned, first and last, to maintain that unless you can save the fathers, you cannot save the children; that at present we cannot save others, for we cannot save ourselves. We cannot teach citizenship if we are not citizens; we cannot free others if we have forgotten the appetite of freedom. Education is only truth in a state of transmission; and how can we pass on truth if it has never come into our hand? Thus we find that education is of all the cases the clearest for our general purpose. It is vain to save children; for they cannot remain children. By hypothesis we are teaching them to be men; and how can it be so simple to teach an ideal manhood to others if it is so vain and hopeless to find one for ourselves?

I know that certain crazy pedants have attempted to counter this difficulty by maintaining that education is not instruction at all, does not teach by authority at all. They present the process as coming, not from the outside, from the teacher, but entirely from inside the boy. Education, they say, is the Latin for leading out or drawing out the dormant faculties of each person. Somewhere far down in the dim boyish soul is a primordial yearning to learn Greek accents or to wear clean collars; and the schoolmaster only gently and tenderly liberates this imprisoned purpose. Sealed up in the newborn babe are the intrinsic secrets of how to eat asparagus and what was the date of Bannockburn. The educator only draws out the child's own unapparent love of long division; only leads out the child's slightly veiled preference for milk pudding to tarts. I am not sure that I believe in the derivation; I have heard the disgraceful suggestion that "educator," if applied to a Roman schoolmaster, did not mean leading our young functions into freedom; but only meant taking out little boys for a walk. But I am much more certain that I do not agree with the doctrine; I think it would be about as sane to say that the baby's milk comes from the baby as to say that the baby's educational merits do. There is, indeed, in each living creature a collection of forces and functions; but education means producing these in particular shapes and training them to particular purposes, or it means nothing at all. Speaking is the most practical instance of the whole situation. You may indeed "draw out" squeals and grunts from the child by simply poking him and pulling him about, a pleasant but cruel pastime to which many psychologists are addicted. But you will wait and watch very patiently indeed before you draw the English language out of him. That you have got to put into him; and there is an end of the matter.

Chapter 6
Authority The Unavoidable

ut the important point here is only that you cannot anyhow get rid of authority in education; it is not so much (as poor Conservatives say) that parental authority ought to be preserved, as that it cannot be destroyed. Mr. Bernard Shaw once said that he hated the idea of forming a child's mind. In that case Mr. Bernard Shaw had better hang himself; for he hates something inseparable from human life. I only mentioned educere and the drawing out of the faculties in order to point out that even this mental trick does not avoid the inevitable idea of parental or scholastic authority. The educator drawing out is just as arbitrary and coercive as the instructor pouring in; for he draws out what he chooses. He decides what in the child shall be developed and what shall not be developed. He does not (I suppose) draw out the neglected faculty of forgery. He does not (so far at least) lead out, with timid steps, a shy talent for torture. The only result of all this pompous and precise distinction between the educator and the instructor is that the instructor pokes where he likes and the educator pulls where he likes. Exactly the same intellectual violence is done to the creature who is poked and pulled. Now we must all accept the responsibility of this intellectual violence. Education is violent; because it is creative. It is creative because it is human. It is as reckless as playing on the fiddle; as dogmatic as drawing a picture; as brutal as building a house. In short, it is what all human action is; it is an interference with life and growth. After that it is a trifling and even a jocular question whether we say of this tremendous tormentor, the artist Man, that he puts things into us like an apothecary, or draws things out of us, like a dentist.

The point is that Man does what he likes. He claims the right to take his mother Nature under his control; he claims the right to make his child the Superman, in his image. Once flinch from this creative authority of man, and the whole courageous raid which we call civilization wavers and falls to pieces. Now most modern freedom is at root fear. It is not so much that we are too bold to endure rules; it is rather that we are too timid to endure responsibilities. And Mr. Shaw and such people are especially shrinking from that awful and ancestral responsibility to which our fathers committed us when they took the wild step of becoming men. I mean the responsibility of affirming the truth of our human tradition and handing it on with a voice of authority, an unshaken voice. That is the one eternal education; to be sure enough that something is true that you dare to tell it to a child. From this high audacious duty the moderns are fleeing on every side; and the only excuse for them is, (of course,) that their modern philosophies are so half-baked and hypothetical that they cannot convince themselves enough to convince even a newborn babe. This, of course, is connected with the decay of democracy; and is somewhat of a separate subject. Suffice it to say here that when I say that we should instruct our children, I mean that we should do it, not that Mr. Sully or Professor Earl Barnes should do it. The trouble in too many of our modern schools is that the State, being controlled so specially by the few, allows cranks and experiments to go straight to the schoolroom when they have never passed through the Parliament, the public house, the private house, the church, or the marketplace. Obviously, it ought to be the oldest things that are taught to the youngest people; the assured and experienced truths that are put first to the baby. But in a school to-day the baby has to submit to a system that is younger than himself. The flopping infant of four actually has more experience, and has weathered the world longer, than the dogma to which he is made to submit. Many a school boasts of having the last ideas in education, when it has not even the first idea; for the first idea is that even innocence, divine as it is, may learn something from experience. But this, as I say, is all due to the mere fact that we are managed by a little oligarchy; my system presupposes that men who govern themselves will govern their children. To-day we all use Popular Education as meaning education of the people. I wish I could use it as meaning education by the people.

The urgent point at present is that these expansive educators do not avoid the violence of authority an inch more than the old school masters. Nay, it might be maintained that they avoid it less. The old village schoolmaster beat a boy for not learning grammar and sent him out into the playground to play anything he liked; or at nothing, if he liked that better. The modern scientific schoolmaster pursues him into the playground and makes him play at cricket, because exercise is so good for the health. The modern Dr. Busby is a doctor of medicine as well as a doctor of divinity. He may say that the good of exercise is self-evident; but he must say it, and say it with authority. It cannot really be self-evident or it never could have been compulsory. But this is in modern practice a very mild case. In modern practice the free educationists forbid far more things than the old-fashioned educationists. A person with a taste for paradox (if any such shameless creature could exist) might with some plausibility maintain concerning all our expansion since the failure of Luther's frank paganism and its replacement by Calvin's Puritanism, that all this expansion has not been an expansion, but the closing in of a prison, so that less and less beautiful and humane things have been permitted. The Puritans destroyed images; the Rationalists forbade fairy tales. Count Tostoi practically issued one of his papal encyclicals against music; and I have heard of modern educationists who forbid children to play with tin soldiers. I remember a meek little madman who came up to me at some Socialist soiree or other, and asked me to use my influence (have I any influence?) against adventure stories for boys. It seems they breed an appetite for blood. But never mind that; one must keep one's temper in this madhouse. I need only insist here that these things, even if a just deprivation, are a deprivation. I do not deny that the old vetoes and punishments were often idiotic and cruel; though they are much more so in a country like England (where in practice only a rich man decrees the punishment and only a poor man receives it) than in countries with a clearer popular tradition—such as Russia. In Russia flogging is often inflicted by peasants on a peasant. In modern England flogging can only in practice be inflicted by a gentleman on a very poor man. Thus only a few days ago as I write a small boy (a son of the poor, of course) was sentenced to flogging and imprisonment for five years for having picked up a small piece of coal which the experts value at 5d. I am entirely on the side of such liberals and humanitarians as have protested against this almost bestial ignorance about boys. But I do think it a little unfair that these humanitarians, who excuse boys for being robbers, should denounce them for playing at robbers. I do think that those who understand a guttersnipe playing with a piece of coal might, by a sudden spurt of imagination, understand him playing with a tin soldier. To sum it up in one sentence: I think my meek little madman might have understood that there is many a boy who would rather be flogged, and unjustly flogged, than have his adventure story taken away.

Chapter 7
The Humility of Mrs. Grundy

n short, the new education is as harsh as the old, whether or no it is as high. The freest fad, as much as the strictest formula, is stiff with authority. It is because the humane father thinks soldiers wrong that they are forbidden; there is no pretense, there can be no pretense, that the boy would think so. The average boy's impression certainly would be simply this: "If your father is a Methodist you must not play with soldiers on Sunday. If your father is a Socialist you must not play with them even on week days." All educationists are utterly dogmatic and authoritarian. You cannot have free education; for if you left a child free you would not educate him at all. Is there, then, no distinction or difference between the most hidebound conventionalists and the most brilliant and bizarre innovators? Is there no difference between the heaviest heavy father and the most reckless and speculative maiden aunt? Yes; there is. The difference is that the heavy father, in his heavy way, is a democrat. He does not urge a thing merely because to his fancy it should be done; but, because (in his own admirable republican formula) "Everybody does it." The conventional authority does claim some popular mandate; the unconventional authority does not. The Puritan who forbids soldiers on Sunday is at least expressing Puritan opinion; not merely his own opinion. He is not a despot; he is a democracy, a tyrannical democracy, a dingy and local democracy perhaps; but one that could do and has done the two ultimate virile things—fight and appeal to God. But the veto of the new educationist is like the veto of the House of Lords; it does not pretend to be representative. These innovators are always talking about the blushing modesty of Mrs. Grundy. I do not know whether Mrs. Grundy is more modest than they are; but I am sure she is more humble.

But there is a further complication. The more anarchic modern may again attempt to escape the dilemma by saying that education should only be an enlargement of the mind, an opening of all the organs of receptivity. Light (he says) should be brought into darkness; blinded and thwarted existences in all our ugly corners should merely be permitted to perceive and expand; in short, enlightenment should be shed over darkest London. Now here is just the trouble; that, in so far as this is involved, there is no darkest London. London is not dark at all; not even at night. We have said that if education is a solid substance, then there is none of it. We may now say that if education is an abstract expansion there is no lack of it. There is far too much of it. In fact, there is nothing else.

There are no uneducated people. Everybody in England is educated; only most people are educated wrong. The state schools were not the first schools, but among the last schools to be established; and London had been educating

Londoners long before the London School Board. The error is a highly practical one. It is persistently assumed that unless a child is civilized by the established schools, he must remain a barbarian. I wish he did. Every child in London becomes a highly civilized person. But here are so many different civilizations, most of them born tired. Anyone will tell you that the trouble with the poor is not so much that the old are still foolish, but rather that the young are already wise. Without going to school at all, the gutter-boy would be educated. Without going to school at all, he would be over-educated. The real object of our schools should be not so much to suggest complexity as solely to restore simplicity. You will hear venerable idealists declare we must make war on the ignorance of the poor; but, indeed, we have rather to make war on their knowledge. Real educationists have to resist a kind of roaring cataract of culture. The truant is being taught all day. If the children do not look at the large letters in the spelling-book, they need only walk outside and look at the large letters on the poster. If they do not care for the colored maps provided by the school, they can gape at the colored maps provided by the Daily Mail. If they tire of electricity, they can take to electric trams. If they are unmoved by music, they can take to drink. If they will not work so as to get a prize from their school, they may work to get a prize from Prizy Bits. If they cannot learn enough about law and citizenship to please the teacher, they learn enough about them to avoid the policeman. If they will not learn history forwards from the right end in the history books, they will learn it backwards from the wrong end in the party newspapers. And this is the tragedy of the whole affair: that the London poor, a particularly quick-witted and civilized class, learn everything tail foremost, learn even what is right in the way of what is wrong. They do not see the first principles of law in a law book; they only see its last results in the police news. They do not see the truths of politics in a general survey. They only see the lies of politics, at a General Election.

But whatever be the pathos of the London poor, it has nothing to do with being uneducated. So far from being without guidance, they are guided constantly, earnestly, excitedly; only guided wrong. The poor are not at all neglected, they are merely oppressed; nay, rather they are persecuted. There are no people in London who are not appealed to by the rich; the appeals of the rich shriek from every hoarding and shout from every hustings. For it should always be remembered that the queer, abrupt ugliness of our streets and costumes are not the creation of democracy, but of aristocracy. The House of Lords objected to the Embankment being disfigured by trams. But most of the rich men who disfigure the street-walls with their wares are actually in the House of Lords. The peers make the country seats beautiful by making the town streets hideous. This, however, is parenthetical. The point is, that the poor in London are not left alone, but rather deafened and bewildered with raucous and despotic advice. They are not like sheep without a shepherd. They are more like one sheep whom twenty-seven shepherds are shouting at. All the newspapers, all the new advertisements, all the new medicines and new theologies, all the glare and blare of the gas and brass of modern times—it is against these that the national school must bear up if it can. I will not question that our elementary education is better than barbaric ignorance. But there is no barbaric ignorance. I do not doubt that our schools would be good for uninstructed boys. But there are no uninstructed boys. A modern London school ought not merely to be clearer, kindlier, more clever and more rapid than ignorance and darkness. It must also be clearer than a picture postcard, cleverer than a Limerick competition, quicker than the tram, and kindlier than the tavern. The school, in fact, has the responsibility of universal rivalry. We need not deny that everywhere there is a light that must conquer darkness. But here we demand a light that can conquer light.

Chapter 8
The Broken Rainbow

will take one case that will serve both as symbol and example: the case of color. We hear the realists (those sentimental fellows) talking about the gray streets and the gray lives of the poor. But whatever the poor streets are they are not gray; but motley, striped, spotted, piebald and patched like a quilt. Hoxton is not aesthetic enough to be monochrome; and there is nothing of the Celtic twilight about it. As a matter of fact, a London gutter-boy walks unscathed among furnaces of color. Watch him walk along a line of hoardings, and you will see him now against glowing green, like a traveler in a tropic forest; now black like a bird against the burning blue of the Midi; now passant across a field gules, like the golden leopards of England. He ought to understand the irrational rapture of that cry of Mr. Stephen Phillips about "that bluer blue, that greener green." There is no blue much bluer than Reckitt's Blue and no blacking blacker than Day and Martin's; no more emphatic yellow than that of Colman's Mustard. If, despite this chaos of color, like a shattered rainbow, the spirit of the small boy is not exactly intoxicated with art and culture, the cause certainly does not lie in universal grayness or the mere starving of his senses. It lies in the fact that the colors are presented in the wrong connection, on the wrong scale, and, above all, from the wrong motive. It is not colors he lacks, but a philosophy of colors. In short, there is nothing wrong with Reckitt's Blue except that it is not Reckitt's. Blue does not belong to Reckitt, but to the sky; black does not belong to Day and Martin, but to the abyss. Even the finest posters are only very little things on a very large scale. There is something specially irritant in this way about the iteration of advertisements of mustard: a condiment, a small luxury; a thing in its nature not to be taken in quantity. There is a special irony in these starving streets to see such a great deal of mustard to such very little meat. Yellow is a bright pigment; mustard is a pungent pleasure. But to look at these seas of yellow is to be like a man who should swallow gallons of mustard. He would either die, or lose the taste of mustard altogether.

Now suppose we compare these gigantic trivialities on the hoardings with those tiny and tremendous pictures in which the mediaevals recorded their dreams; little pictures where the blue sky is hardly longer than a single sapphire, and the fires of judgment only a pigmy patch of gold. The difference here is not merely that poster art is in its nature more hasty than illumination art; it is not even merely that the ancient artist was serving the Lord while the modern artist is serving the lords. It is that the old artist contrived to convey an impression that colors really were significant and precious things, like jewels and talismanic stones. The color was often arbitrary; but it was always authoritative. If a bird was blue, if a tree was golden, if a fish was silver, if a cloud was scarlet, the artist managed to convey that these colors were important and almost painfully intense; all the red red-hot and all the gold tried in the fire. Now that is the spirit touching color which the schools must recover and protect if they are really to give the children any imaginative appetite or pleasure in the thing. It is not so much an indulgence in color; it is rather, if anything, a sort of fiery thrift. It fenced in a green field in heraldry as straitly as a green field in peasant proprietorship. It would not fling away gold leaf any more than gold coin; it would not heedlessly pour out purple or crimson, any more than it would spill good wine or shed blameless blood. That is the hard task before educationists in this special matter; they have to teach people to relish colors like liquors. They have the heavy business of turning drunkards into wine tasters. If even the twentieth century succeeds in doing these things, it will almost catch up with the twelfth.

The principle covers, however, the whole of modern life. Morris and the merely aesthetic mediaevalists always indicated that a crowd in the time of Chaucer would have been brightly clad and glittering, compared with a crowd in the time of Queen Victoria. I am not so sure that the real distinction is here. There would be brown frocks of friars in the first scene as well as brown bowlers of clerks in the second. There would be purple plumes of factory girls in the second scene as well as purple lenten vestments in the first. There would be white waistcoats against white ermine; gold watch chains against gold lions. The real difference is this: that the brown earth-color of the monk's coat was instinctively chosen to express labor and humility, whereas the brown color of the clerk's hat was not chosen to express anything. The monk did mean to say that he robed himself in dust. I am sure the clerk does not mean to say that he crowns himself with clay. He is not putting dust on his head, as the only diadem of man. Purple, at once rich and somber, does suggest a triumph temporarily eclipsed by a tragedy. But the factory girl does not intend her hat to express a triumph temporarily eclipsed by a tragedy; far from it. White ermine was meant to express moral purity; white waistcoats were not. Gold lions do suggest a flaming magnanimity; gold watch chains do not. The point is not that we have lost the material hues, but that we have lost the trick of turning them to the best advantage. We are not like children who have lost their paint box and are left alone with a gray lead-pencil. We are like children who have mixed all the colors in the paint-box together and lost the paper of instructions. Even then (I do not deny) one has some fun.

Now this abundance of colors and loss of a color scheme is a pretty perfect parable of all that is wrong with our modern ideals and especially with our modern education. It is the same with ethical education, economic education, every sort of education. The growing London child will find no lack of highly controversial teachers who will teach him that geography means painting the map red; that economics means taxing the foreigner, that patriotism means the peculiarly un-English habit of flying a flag on Empire Day. In mentioning these examples specially I do not mean to imply that there are no similar crudities and popular fallacies upon the other political side. I mention them because they constitute a very special and arresting feature of the situation. I mean this, that there were always Radical revolutionists; but now there are Tory revolutionists also. The modern Conservative no longer conserves. He is avowedly an innovator. Thus all the current defenses of the House of Lords which describe it as a bulwark against the mob, are intellectually done for; the bottom has fallen out of them; because on five or six of the most turbulent topics of the day, the House of Lords is a mob itself; and exceedingly likely to behave like one.

Chapter 9
The Need for Narrowness

hrough all this chaos, then we come back once more to our main conclusion. The true task of culture to-day is not a task of expansion, but very decidedly of selection—and rejection. The educationist must find a creed and teach it. Even if it be not a theological creed, it must still be as fastidious and as firm as theology. In short, it must be orthodox. The teacher may think it antiquated to have to decide precisely between the faith of Calvin and of Laud, the faith of Aquinas and of Swedenborg; but he still has to choose between the faith of Kipling and of Shaw, between the world of Blatchford and of General Booth. Call it, if you will, a narrow question whether your child shall be brought up by the vicar or the minister or the popish priest. You have still to face that larger, more liberal, more highly civilized question, of whether he shall be brought up by Harmsworth or by Pearson, by Mr. Eustace Miles with his Simple Life or Mr. Peter Keary with his Strenuous Life; whether he shall most eagerly read Miss Annie S. Swan or Mr. Bart Kennedy; in short, whether he shall end up in the mere violence of the S. D. F., or in the mere vulgarity of the Primrose League. They say that nowadays the creeds are crumbling; I doubt it, but at least the sects are increasing; and education must now be sectarian education, merely for practical purposes. Out of all this throng of theories it must somehow select a theory; out of all these thundering voices it must manage to hear a voice; out of all this awful and aching battle of blinding lights, without one shadow to give shape to them, it must manage somehow to trace and to track a star.

I have spoken so far of popular education, which began too vague and vast and which therefore has accomplished little. But as it happens there is in England something to compare it with. There is an institution, or class of institutions, which began with the same popular object, which has since followed a much narrower object, but which had the great advantage that it did follow some object, unlike our modern elementary schools.

In all these problems I should urge the solution which is positive, or, as silly people say, "optimistic." I should set my face, that is, against most of the solutions that are solely negative and abolitionist. Most educators of the poor seem to think that they have to teach the poor man not to drink. I should be quite content if they teach him to drink; for it is mere ignorance about how to drink and when to drink that is accountable for most of his tragedies. I do not propose (like some of my revolutionary friends) that we should abolish the public schools. I propose the much more lurid and desperate experiment that we should make them public. I do not wish to make Parliament stop working, but rather to make it work; not to shut up churches, but rather to open them; not to put out the lamp of learning or destroy the hedge of property, but only to make some rude effort to make universities fairly universal and property decently proper.

In many cases, let it be remembered, such action is not merely going back to the old ideal, but is even going back to the old reality. It would be a great step forward for the gin shop to go back to the inn. It is incontrovertibly true that to mediaevalize the public schools would be to democratize the public schools. Parliament did once really mean (as its name seems to imply) a place where people were allowed to talk. It is only lately that the general increase of efficiency, that is, of the Speaker, has made it mostly a place where people are prevented from talking. The poor do not go to the modern church, but they went to the ancient church all right; and if the common man in the past had a grave respect for property, it may conceivably have been because he sometimes had some of his own. I therefore can claim that I have no vulgar itch of innovation in anything I say about any of these institutions. Certainly I have none in that particular one which I am now obliged to pick out of the list; a type of institution to which I have genuine and personal reasons for being friendly and grateful: I mean the great Tudor foundations, the public schools of England. They have been praised for a great many things, mostly, I am sorry to say, praised by themselves and their children. And yet for some reason no one has ever praised them the one really convincing reason.

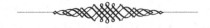

Chapter 10
The Case for the Public Schools

he word success can of course be used in two senses. It may be used with reference to a thing serving its immediate and peculiar purpose, as of a wheel going around; or it can be used with reference to a thing adding to the general welfare, as of a wheel being a useful discovery. It is one thing to say that Smith's flying machine is a failure, and quite another to say that Smith has failed to make a flying machine. Now this is very broadly the difference between the old English public schools and the new democratic schools. Perhaps the old public schools are (as I personally think they are) ultimately weakening the country rather than strengthening it, and are therefore, in that ultimate sense, inefficient. But there is such a thing as being efficiently inefficient. You can make your flying ship so that it flies, even if you also make it so that it kills you. Now the public school system may not work satisfactorily, but it works; the public schools may not achieve what we want, but they achieve what they want. The popular elementary schools do not in that sense achieve anything at all. It is very difficult to point to any guttersnipe in the street and say that he embodies the ideal for which popular education has been working, in the sense that the fresh-faced, foolish boy in "Etons" does embody the ideal for which the headmasters of Harrow and Winchester have been working. The aristocratic educationists have the positive purpose of turning out gentlemen, and they do turn out gentlemen, even when they expel them. The popular educationists would say that they had the far nobler idea of turning out citizens. I concede that it is a much nobler idea, but where are the citizens? I know that the boy in "Etons" is stiff with a rather silly and sentimental stoicism, called being a man of the world. I do not fancy that the errand-boy is rigid with that republican stoicism that is called being a citizen. The schoolboy will really say with fresh and innocent hauteur, "I am an English gentleman." I cannot so easily picture the errand-boy drawing up his head to the stars and answering, "Romanus civis sum." Let it be granted that our elementary teachers are teaching the very broadest code of morals, while our great headmasters are teaching only the narrowest code of manners. Let it be granted that both these things are being taught. But only one of them is being learned.

It is always said that great reformers or masters of events can manage to bring about some specific and practical reforms, but that they never fulfill their visions or satisfy their souls. I believe there is a real sense in which this apparent platitude is quite untrue. By a strange inversion the political idealist often does not get what he asks for, but does get what he wants. The silent pressure of his ideal lasts much longer and reshapes the world much more than the actualities by which he attempted to suggest it. What perishes is the letter, which he thought so practical.

What endures is the spirit, which he felt to be unattainable and even unutterable. It is exactly his schemes that are not fulfilled; it is exactly his vision that is fulfilled. Thus the ten or twelve paper constitutions of the French Revolution, which seemed so business-like to the framers of them, seem to us to have flown away on the wind as the wildest fancies. What has not flown away, what is a fixed fact in Europe, is the ideal and vision. The Republic, the idea of a land full of mere citizens all with some minimum of manners and minimum of wealth, the vision of the eighteenth century, the reality of the twentieth. So I think it will generally be with the creator of social things, desirable or undesirable. All his schemes will fail, all his tools break in his hands. His compromises will collapse, his concessions will be useless. He must brace himself to bear his fate; he shall have nothing but his heart's desire.

Now if one may compare very small things with very great, one may say that the English aristocratic schools can claim something of the same sort of success and solid splendor as the French democratic politics. At least they can claim the same sort of superiority over the distracted and fumbling attempts of modern England to establish democratic education. Such success as has attended the public schoolboy throughout the Empire, a success exaggerated indeed by himself, but still positive and a fact of a certain indisputable shape and size, has been due to the central and supreme circumstance that the managers of our public schools did know what sort of boy they liked. They wanted something and they got something; instead of going to work in the broad-minded manner and wanting everything and getting nothing.

The only thing in question is the quality of the thing they got. There is something highly maddening in the circumstance that when modern people attack an institution that really does demand reform, they always attack it for the wrong reasons. Thus many opponents of our public schools, imagining themselves to be very democratic, have exhausted themselves in an unmeaning attack upon the study of Greek. I can understand how Greek may be regarded as useless, especially by those thirsting to throw themselves into the cut throat commerce which is the negation of citizenship; but I do not understand how it can be considered undemocratic. I quite understand why Mr. Carnegie has a hatred of Greek. It is obscurely founded on the firm and sound impression that in any self-governing Greek city he would have been killed. But I cannot comprehend why any chance democrat, say Mr. Quelch, or Mr. Will Crooks, I or Mr. John M. Robertson, should be opposed to people learning the Greek alphabet, which was the alphabet of liberty. Why should Radicals dislike Greek? In that language is written all the earliest and, Heaven knows, the most heroic history of the Radical party. Why should Greek disgust a democrat, when the very word democrat is Greek?

A similar mistake, though a less serious one, is merely attacking the athletics of public schools as something promoting animalism and brutality. Now brutality, in the only immoral sense, is not a vice of the English public schools. There is much moral bullying, owing to the general lack of moral courage in the public-school atmosphere. These schools do, upon the whole, encourage physical courage; but they do not merely discourage moral courage, they forbid it. The ultimate result of the thing is seen in the egregious English officer who cannot even endure to wear a bright uniform except when it is blurred and hidden in the smoke of battle. This, like all the affectations of our present plutocracy, is an entirely modern thing. It was unknown to the old aristocrats. The Black Prince would certainly have asked that any knight who had the courage to lift his crest among his enemies, should also have the courage to lift it among his friends. As regards moral courage, then it is not so much that the public schools support it feebly, as that they suppress it firmly. But physical courage they do, on the whole, support; and physical courage is a magnificent fundamental. The one great, wise Englishman of the eighteenth century said truly that if a man lost that virtue he could never be sure of keeping any other. Now it is one of the mean and morbid modern lies that physical courage is connected with cruelty. The Tolstoian and Kiplingite are nowhere more at one than in maintaining this. They have, I believe, some small sectarian quarrel with each other, the one saying that courage must be abandoned because it is connected with cruelty, and the other maintaining that cruelty is charming because it is a part of courage. But it is all, thank God, a lie. An energy and boldness of body may make a man stupid or reckless or dull or drunk or hungry, but it does not make him spiteful. And we may admit heartily (without joining in that perpetual praise which public-school men are always pouring upon themselves) that this does operate to the removal of mere evil cruelty in the public schools. English public school life is extremely like English public life, for which it is the preparatory school. It is like it specially in this, that things are either very open, common and conventional, or else are very secret indeed. Now there is cruelty in public schools, just as there is kleptomania and secret drinking and vices without a name. But these things do not flourish in the full daylight and common consciousness of the school, and no more does cruelty. A tiny trio of sullen-looking boys gather in corners and seem to have some ugly business always; it may be indecent literature, it may be the beginning of drink, it may occasionally be cruelty to little boys. But on this stage the bully is not a braggart. The proverb says that bullies are always cowardly, but these bullies are more than cowardly; they are shy.

As a third instance of the wrong form of revolt against the public schools, I may mention the habit of using the word aristocracy with a double implication. To put the plain truth as briefly as possible, if aristocracy means rule by a rich ring, England has aristocracy and the English public schools support it. If it means rule by ancient families or flawless blood, England has not got aristocracy, and the public schools systematically destroy it. In these circles real aristocracy, like real democracy, has become bad form. A modern fashionable host dare not praise his ancestry; it would so often be an insult to half the other oligarchs at table, who have no ancestry. We have said he has not the moral courage to wear his uniform; still less has he the moral courage to wear his coat-of-arms. The whole thing now is only a vague hotch-potch of nice and nasty gentlemen. The nice gentleman never refers to anyone else's father, the nasty gentleman never refers to his own. That is the only difference, the rest is the public-school manner. But Eton and Harrow have to be aristocratic because they consist so largely of parvenues. The public school is not a sort of refuge for aristocrats, like an asylum, a place where they go in and never come out. It is a factory for aristocrats; they come out without ever having perceptibly gone in. The poor little private schools, in their old-world, sentimental, feudal style, used to stick up a notice, "For the Sons of Gentlemen only." If the public schools stuck up a notice it ought to be inscribed, "For the Fathers of Gentlemen only." In two generations they can do the trick.

Chapter 11
The School for Hypocrites

hese are the false accusations; the accusation of classicism, the accusation of cruelty, and the accusation of an exclusiveness based on perfection of pedigree. English public-school boys are not pedants, they are not torturers; and they are not, in the vast majority of cases, people fiercely proud of their ancestry, or even people with any ancestry to be proud of. They are taught to be courteous, to be good tempered, to be brave in a bodily sense, to be clean in a bodily sense; they are generally kind to animals, generally civil to servants, and to anyone in any sense their equal, the jolliest companions on earth. Is there then anything wrong in the public-school ideal? I think we all feel there is something very wrong in it, but a blinding network of newspaper phraseology obscures and entangles us; so that it is hard to trace to its beginning, beyond all words and phrases, the faults in this great English achievement.

Surely, when all is said, the ultimate objection to the English public school is its utterly blatant and indecent disregard of the duty of telling the truth. I know there does still linger among maiden ladies in remote country houses a notion that English schoolboys are taught to tell the truth, but it cannot be maintained seriously for a moment. Very occasionally, very vaguely, English schoolboys are told not to tell lies, which is a totally different thing. I may silently support all the obscene fictions and forgeries in the universe, without once telling a lie. I may wear another man's coat, steal another man's wit, apostatize to another man's creed, or poison another man's coffee, all without ever telling a lie. But no English school-boy is ever taught to tell the truth, for the very simple reason that he is never taught to desire the truth. From the very first he is taught to be totally careless about whether a fact is a fact; he is taught to care only whether the fact can be used on his "side" when he is engaged in "playing the game." He takes sides in his Union debating society to settle whether Charles I ought to have been killed, with the same solemn and pompous frivolity with which he takes sides in the cricket field to decide whether Rugby or Westminster shall win. He is never allowed to admit the abstract notion of the truth, that the match is a matter of what may happen, but that Charles I is a matter of what did happen—or did not. He is Liberal or Tory at the general election exactly as he is Oxford or Cambridge at the boat race. He knows that sport deals with the unknown; he has not even a notion that politics should deal with the known. If anyone really doubts this self-evident proposition, that the public schools definitely discourage the love of truth, there is one fact which I should think would settle him. England is the country of the Party System, and it has always been chiefly run by public-school men. Is there anyone out of Hanwell who will maintain that the Party System, whatever its conveniences or inconveniences, could have been created by people particularly fond of truth?

The very English happiness on this point is itself a hypocrisy. When a man really tells the truth, the first truth he tells is that he himself is a liar. David said in his haste, that is, in his honesty, that all men are liars. It was afterwards, in some leisurely official explanation, that he said the Kings of Israel at least told the truth. When Lord Curzon was Viceroy he delivered a moral lecture to the Indians on their reputed indifference to veracity, to actuality and intellectual honor. A great many people indignantly discussed whether orientals deserved to receive this rebuke; whether Indians were indeed in a position to receive such severe admonition. No one seemed to ask, as I should venture to ask, whether Lord Curzon was in a position to give it. He is an ordinary party politician; a party politician means a politician who might have belonged to either party. Being such a person, he must again and again, at every twist and turn of party strategy, either have deceived others or grossly deceived himself. I do not know the East; nor do I like what I know. I am quite ready to believe that when Lord Curzon went out he found a very false atmosphere. I only say it must have been something startlingly and chokingly false if it was falser than that English atmosphere from which he came. The English Parliament actually cares for everything except veracity. The public-school man is kind, courageous, polite, clean, companionable; but, in the most awful sense of the words, the truth is not in him.

This weakness of untruthfulness in the English public schools, in the English political system, and to some extent in the English character, is a weakness which necessarily produces a curious crop of superstitions, of lying legends, of evident delusions clung to through low spiritual self-indulgence. There are so many of these public-school superstitions that I have here only space for one of them, which may be called the superstition of soap. It appears to have been shared by the ablutionary Pharisees, who resembled the English public-school aristocrats in so many respects: in their care about club rules and traditions, in their offensive optimism at the expense of other people, and above all in their unimaginative plodding patriotism in the worst interests of their country. Now the old human common sense about washing is that it is a great pleasure. Water (applied externally) is a splendid thing, like wine. Sybarites bathe in wine, and Nonconformists drink water; but we are not concerned with these frantic exceptions. Washing being a pleasure, it stands to reason that rich people can afford it more than poor people, and as long as this was recognized all was well; and it was very right that rich people should offer baths to poor people, as they might offer any other agreeable thing—a drink or a donkey ride. But one dreadful day, somewhere about the middle of the nineteenth century, somebody discovered (somebody pretty well off) the two great modern truths, that washing is a virtue in the rich and therefore a duty in the poor. For a duty is a virtue that one can't do. And a virtue is generally a duty that one can do quite easily; like the bodily cleanliness of the upper classes. But in the public-school tradition of public life, soap has become creditable simply because it is pleasant. Baths are represented as a part of the decay of the Roman Empire; but the same baths are represented as part of the energy and rejuvenation of the British Empire. There are distinguished public school men, bishops, dons, headmasters, and high politicians, who, in the course of the eulogies which from time to time they pass upon themselves, have actually identified physical cleanliness with moral purity. They say (if I remember rightly) that a public-school man is clean inside and out. As if everyone did not know that while saints can afford to be dirty, seducers have to be clean. As if everyone did not know that the harlot must be clean, because it is her business to captivate, while the good wife may be dirty, because it is her business to clean. As if we did not all know that whenever God's thunder cracks above us, it is very likely indeed to find the simplest man in a muck cart and the most complex blackguard in a bath.

There are other instances, of course, of this oily trick of turning the pleasures of a gentleman into the virtues of an Anglo-Saxon. Sport, like soap, is an admirable thing, but, like soap, it is an agreeable thing. And it does not sum up all mortal merits to be a sportsman playing the game in a world where it is so often necessary to be a workman doing the work. By all means let a gentleman congratulate himself that he has not lost his natural love of pleasure, as against the blase, and unchildlike. But when one has the childlike joy it is best to have also the childlike unconsciousness; and I do not think we should have special affection for the little boy who ever lastingly explained that it was his duty to play Hide and Seek and one of his family virtues to be prominent in Puss in the Corner.

Another such irritating hypocrisy is the oligarchic attitude towards mendicity as against organized charity. Here again, as in the case of cleanliness and of athletics, the attitude would be perfectly human and intelligible if it were not maintained as a merit. Just as the obvious thing about soap is that it is a convenience, so the obvious thing about beggars is that they are an inconvenience. The rich would deserve very little blame if they simply said that they never dealt directly with beggars, because in modern urban civilization it is impossible to deal directly with beggars; or if not impossible, at least very difficult. But these people do not refuse money to beggars on the ground that such charity is difficult. They refuse it on the grossly hypocritical ground that such charity is easy. They say, with the most grotesque gravity, "Anyone can put his hand in his pocket and give a poor man a penny; but we, philanthropists, go home and brood and travail over the poor man's troubles until we have discovered exactly what jail, reformatory, workhouse, or lunatic asylum it will really be best for him to go to." This is all sheer lying. They do not brood about the man when they get home, and if they did it would not alter the original fact that their motive for discouraging beggars is the perfectly rational one that beggars are a bother. A man may easily be forgiven for not doing this or that incidental act of charity, especially when the question is as genuinely difficult as is the case of mendicity. But there is something quite pestilently Pecksniffian about shrinking from a hard task on the plea that it is not hard enough. If any man will really try talking to the ten beggars who come to his door he will soon find out whether it is really so much easier than the labor of writing a check for a hospital.

Chapter 12
The Staleness of the New Schools

or this deep and disabling reason therefore, its cynical and abandoned indifference to the truth, the English public school does not provide us with the ideal that we require. We can only ask its modern critics to remember that right or wrong the thing can be done; the factory is working, the wheels are going around, the gentlemen are being produced, with their soap, cricket and organized charity all complete. And in this, as we have said before, the public school really has an advantage over all the other educational schemes of our time. You can pick out a public-school man in any of the many companies into which they stray, from a Chinese opium den to a German Jewish dinner-party. But I doubt if you could tell which little match girl had been brought up by undenominational religion and which by secular education. The great English aristocracy which has ruled us since the Reformation is really, in this sense, a model to the moderns. It did have an ideal, and therefore it has produced a reality.

We may repeat here that these pages propose mainly to show one thing: that progress ought to be based on principle, while our modern progress is mostly based on precedent. We go, not by what may be affirmed in theory, but by what has been already admitted in practice. That is why the Jacobites are the last Tories in history with whom a high-spirited person can have much sympathy. They wanted a specific thing; they were ready to go forward for it, and so they were also ready to go back for it. But modern Tories have only the dullness of defending situations that they had not the excitement of creating. Revolutionists make a reform, Conservatives only conserve the reform. They never reform the reform, which is often very much wanted. Just as the rivalry of armaments is only a sort of sulky plagiarism, so the rivalry of parties is only a sort of sulky inheritance. Men have votes, so women must soon have votes; poor children are taught by force, so they must soon be fed by force; the police shut public houses by twelve o'clock, so soon they must shut them by eleven o'clock; children stop at school till they are fourteen, so soon they will stop till they are forty. No gleam of reason, no momentary return to first principles, no abstract asking of any obvious question, can interrupt this mad and monotonous gallop of mere progress by precedent. It is a good way to prevent real revolution. By this logic of events, the Radical gets as much into a rut as the Conservative. We meet one hoary old lunatic who says his grandfather told him to stand by one stile. We meet another hoary old lunatic who says his grandfather told him only to walk along one lane.

I say we may repeat here this primary part of the argument, because we have just now come to the place where it is most startlingly and strongly shown. The final proof that our elementary schools have no definite ideal of their own is the fact that they so openly imitate the ideals of the public schools. In the elementary schools we have all the ethical prejudices and exaggerations of Eton and Harrow carefully copied for people to whom they do not even roughly apply. We have the same wildly disproportionate doctrine of the effect of physical cleanliness on moral character. Educators and educational politicians declare, amid warm cheers, that cleanliness is far more important than all the squabbles about moral and religious training. It would really seem that so long as a little boy washes his hands it does not matter whether he is washing off his mother's jam or his brother's gore. We have the same grossly insincere pretense that sport always encourages a sense of honor, when we know that it often ruins it. Above all, we have the same great upperclass assumption that things are done best by large institutions handling large sums of money and ordering everybody about; and that trivial and impulsive charity is in some way contemptible. As Mr. Blatchford says, "The world does not want piety, but soap—and Socialism." Piety is one of the popular virtues, whereas soap and Socialism are two hobbies of the upper middle class.

These "healthy" ideals, as they are called, which our politicians and schoolmasters have borrowed from the aristocratic schools and applied to the democratic, are by no means particularly appropriate to an impoverished democracy. A vague admiration for organized government and a vague distrust of individual aid cannot be made to fit in at all into the lives of people among whom kindness means lending a saucepan and honor means keeping out of the workhouse. It resolves itself either into discouraging that system of prompt and patchwork generosity which is a daily glory of the poor, or else into hazy advice to people who have no money not to give it recklessly away. Nor is the exaggerated glory of athletics, defensible enough in dealing with the rich who, if they did not romp and race, would eat and drink unwholesomely, by any means so much to the point when applied to people, most of whom will take a great deal of exercise anyhow, with spade or hammer, pickax or saw. And for the third case, of washing, it is obvious that the same sort of rhetoric about corporeal daintiness which is proper to an ornamental class cannot, merely as it stands, be applicable to a dustman. A gentleman is expected to be substantially spotless all the time. But it is no more discreditable for a scavenger to be dirty than for a deep-sea diver to be wet. A sweep is no more disgraced when he is covered with soot than Michael Angelo when he is covered with clay, or Bayard when he is covered with blood. Nor have these extenders of the public-school tradition done or suggested anything by way of a substitute for the present snobbish system which makes cleanliness almost impossible to the poor; I mean the general ritual of linen and the wearing of the cast-off clothes of the rich. One man moves into another man's clothes as he moves into another man's house. No wonder that our educationists are not horrified at a man picking up the aristocrat's second-hand trousers, when they themselves have only taken up the aristocrat's second-hand ideas.

Chapter 13
The Outlawed Parent

here is one thing at least of which there is never so much as a whisper inside the popular schools; and that is the opinion of the people. The only persons who seem to have nothing to do with the education of the children are the parents. Yet the English poor have very definite traditions in many ways. They are hidden under embarrassment and irony; and those psychologists who have disentangled them talk of them as very strange, barbaric and secretive things. But, as a matter of fact, the traditions of the poor are mostly simply the traditions of humanity, a thing which many of us have not seen for some time. For instance, workingmen have a tradition that if one is talking about a vile thing it is better to talk of it in coarse language; one is the less likely to be seduced into excusing it. But mankind had this tradition also, until the Puritans and their children, the Ibsenites, started the opposite idea, that it does not matter what you say so long as you say it with long words and a long face. Or again, the educated classes have tabooed most jesting about personal appearance; but in doing this they taboo not only the humor of the slums, but more than half the healthy literature of the world; they put polite nose-bags on the noses of Punch and Bardolph, Stiggins and Cyrano de Bergerac. Again, the educated classes have adopted a hideous and heathen custom of considering death as too dreadful to talk about, and letting it remain a secret for each person, like some private malformation. The poor, on the contrary, make a great gossip and display about bereavement; and they are right. They have hold of a truth of psychology which is at the back of all the funeral customs of the children of men. The way to lessen sorrow is to make a lot of it. The way to endure a painful crisis is to insist very much that it is a crisis; to permit people who must feel sad at least to feel important. In this the poor are simply the priests of the universal civilization; and in their stuffy feasts and solemn chattering there is the smell of the baked meats of Hamlet and the dust and echo of the funeral games of Patroclus.

The things philanthropists barely excuse (or do not excuse) in the life of the laboring classes are simply the things we have to excuse in all the greatest monuments of man. It may be that the laborer is as gross as Shakespeare or as garrulous as Homer; that if he is religious he talks nearly as much about hell as Dante; that if he is worldly he talks nearly as much about drink as Dickens. Nor is the poor man without historic support if he thinks less of that ceremonial washing which Christ dismissed, and rather more of that ceremonial drinking which Christ specially sanctified. The only difference between the poor man of to-day and the saints and heroes of history is that which in all classes separates the common man who can feel things from the great man who can express them. What he feels is merely the heritage of man. Now nobody expects of course that the cabmen and coal-heavers can be complete instructors of their children any more than the squires and colonels and tea merchants are complete instructors of their children. There must be an educational specialist in loco parentis. But the master at Harrow is in loco parentis; the master in Hoxton is rather contra parentem. The vague politics of the squire, the vaguer virtues of the colonel, the soul and spiritual yearnings of a tea merchant, are, in veritable practice, conveyed to the children of these people at the English public schools. But I wish here to ask a very plain and emphatic question. Can anyone alive even pretend to point out any way in which these special virtues and traditions of the poor are reproduced in the education of the poor? I do not wish the coster's irony to appeal as coarsely in the school as it does in the tap room; but does it appear at all? Is the child taught to sympathize at all with his father's admirable cheerfulness and slang? I do not expect the pathetic, eager pietas of the mother, with her funeral clothes and funeral baked meats, to be exactly imitated in the educational system; but has it any influence at all on the educational system? Does any elementary schoolmaster accord it even an instant's consideration or respect? I do not expect the schoolmaster to hate hospitals and C.O.S. centers so much as the schoolboy's father; but does he hate them at all? Does he sympathize in the least with the poor man's point of honor against official institutions? Is it not quite certain that the ordinary elementary schoolmaster will think it not merely natural but simply conscientious to eradicate all these rugged legends of a laborious people, and on principle to preach soap and Socialism against beer and liberty? In the lower classes the school master does not work for the parent, but against the parent. Modern education means handing down the customs of the minority, and rooting out the customs of the majority. Instead of their Christlike charity, their Shakespearean laughter and their high Homeric reverence for the dead, the poor have imposed on them mere pedantic copies of the prejudices of the remote rich. They must think a bathroom a necessity because to the lucky it is a luxury; they must swing Swedish clubs because their masters are afraid of English cudgels; and they must get over their prejudice against being fed by the parish, because aristocrats feel no shame about being fed by the nation.

Chapter 14
Folly and Female Education

t is the same in the case of girls. I am often solemnly asked what I think of the new ideas about female education. But there are no new ideas about female education. There is not, there never has been, even the vestige of a new idea. All the educational reformers did was to ask what was being done to boys and then go and do it to girls; just as they asked what was being taught to young squires and then taught it to young chimney sweeps. What they call new ideas are very old ideas in the wrong place. Boys play football, why shouldn't girls play football; boys have school colors, why shouldn't girls have school-colors; boys go in hundreds to day-schools, why shouldn't girls go in hundreds to day-schools; boys go to Oxford, why shouldn't girls go to Oxford—in short, boys grow mustaches, why shouldn't girls grow mustaches—that is about their notion of a new idea. There is no brain-work in the thing at all; no root query of what sex is, of whether it alters this or that, and why, anymore than there is any imaginative grip of the humor and heart of the populace in the popular education. There is nothing but plodding, elaborate, elephantine imitation. And just as in the case of elementary teaching, the cases are of a cold and reckless inappropriateness. Even a savage could see that bodily things, at least, which are good for a man are very likely to be bad for a woman. Yet there is no boy's game, however brutal, which these mild lunatics have not promoted among girls. To take a stronger case, they give girls very heavy home-work; never reflecting that all girls have home-work already in their homes. It is all a part of the same silly subjugation; there must be a hard stick-up collar round the neck of a woman, because it is already a nuisance round the neck of a man. Though a Saxon serf, if he wore that collar of cardboard, would ask for his collar of brass.

It will then be answered, not without a sneer, "And what would you prefer? Would you go back to the elegant early Victorian female, with ringlets and smelling-bottle, doing a little in water colors, dabbling a little in Italian, playing a little on the harp, writing in vulgar albums and painting on senseless screens? Do you prefer that?" To which I answer, "Emphatically, yes." I solidly prefer it to the new female education, for this reason, that I can see in it an intellectual design, while there is none in the other. I am by no means sure that even in point of practical fact that elegant female would not have been more than a match for most of the inelegant females. I fancy Jane Austen was stronger, sharper and shrewder than Charlotte Bronte; I am quite certain she was stronger, sharper and shrewder than George Eliot. She could do one thing neither of them could do: she could coolly and sensibly describe a man. I am not sure that the old great lady who could only smatter Italian was not more vigorous than the new great lady who can only stammer American; nor am I certain that the bygone duchesses who were scarcely successful when they painted Melrose Abbey, were so much more weak-minded than the modern duchesses who paint only their own faces, and are bad at that. But that is not the point. What was the theory, what was the idea, in their old, weak water-colors and their shaky Italian? The idea was the same which in a ruder rank expressed itself in home-made wines and hereditary recipes; and which still, in a thousand unexpected ways, can be found clinging to the women of the poor. It was the idea I urged in the second part of this book: that the world must keep one great amateur, lest we all become artists and perish. Somebody must renounce all specialist conquests, that she may conquer all the conquerors. That she may be a queen of life, she must not be a private soldier in it. I do not think the elegant female with her bad Italian was a perfect product, any more than I think the slum woman talking gin and funerals is a perfect product; alas! there are few perfect products. But they come from a comprehensible idea; and the new woman comes from nothing and nowhere. It is right to have an ideal, it is right to have the right ideal, and these two have the right ideal. The slum mother with her funerals is the degenerate daughter of Antigone, the obstinate priestess of the household gods. The lady talking bad Italian was the decayed tenth cousin of Portia, the great and golden Italian lady, the Renascence amateur of life, who could be a barrister because she could be anything. Sunken and neglected in the sea of modern monotony and imitation, the types hold tightly to their original truths. Antigone, ugly, dirty and often drunken, will still bury her father. The elegant female, vapid and fading away to nothing, still feels faintly the fundamental difference between herself and her husband: that he must be Something in the City, that she may be everything in the country.

There was a time when you and I and all of us were all very close to God; so that even now the color of a pebble (or a paint), the smell of a flower (or a firework), comes to our hearts with a kind of authority and certainty; as if they were fragments of a muddled message, or features of a forgotten face. To pour that fiery simplicity upon the whole of life is the only real aim of education; and closest to the child comes the woman—she understands. To say what she understands is beyond me; save only this, that it is not a solemnity. Rather it is a towering levity, an uproarious amateurishness of the universe, such as we felt when we were little, and would as soon sing as garden, as soon paint as run. To smatter the tongues of men and angels, to dabble in the dreadful sciences, to juggle with pillars and pyramids and toss up the planets like balls, this is that inner audacity and indifference which the human soul, like a conjurer catching oranges, must keep up forever. This is that insanely frivolous thing we call sanity. And the elegant female, drooping her ringlets over her water-colors, knew it and acted on it. She was juggling with frantic and flaming suns. She was maintaining the bold equilibrium of inferiorities which is the most mysterious of superiorities and perhaps the most unattainable. She was maintaining the prime truth of woman, the universal mother: that if a thing is worth doing, it is worth doing badly.

Part V: The Home of Man

Chapter 1
The Empire of the Insect

A cultivated Conservative friend of mine once exhibited great distress because in a gay moment I once called Edmund Burke an atheist. I need scarcely say that the remark lacked something of biographical precision; it was meant to. Burke was certainly not an atheist in his conscious cosmic theory, though he had not a special and flaming faith in God, like Robespierre. Nevertheless, the remark had reference to a truth which it is here relevant to repeat. I mean that in the quarrel over the French Revolution, Burke did stand for the atheistic attitude and mode of argument, as Robespierre stood for the theistic. The Revolution appealed to the idea of an abstract and eternal justice, beyond all local custom or convenience. If there are commands of God, then there must be rights of man. Here Burke made his brilliant diversion; he did not attack the Robespierre doctrine with the old mediaeval doctrine of jus divinum (which, like the Robespierre doctrine, was theistic), he attacked it with the modern argument of scientific relativity; in short, the argument of evolution. He suggested that humanity was everywhere molded by or fitted to its environment and institutions; in fact, that each people practically got, not only the tyrant it deserved, but the tyrant it ought to have. "I know nothing of the rights of men," he said, "but I know something of the rights of Englishmen." There you have the essential atheist. His argument is that we have got some protection by natural accident and growth; and why should we profess to think beyond it, for all the world as if we were the images of God! We are born under a House of Lords, as birds under a house of leaves; we live under a monarchy as niggers live under a tropic sun; it is not their fault if they are slaves, and it is not ours if we are snobs. Thus, long before Darwin struck his great blow at democracy, the essential of the Darwinian argument had been already urged against the French Revolution. Man, said Burke in effect, must adapt himself to everything, like an animal; he must not try to alter everything, like an angel.

The last weak cry of the pious, pretty, half-artificial optimism and deism of the eighteenth century came in the voice of Sterne, saying, "God tempers the wind to the shorn lamb." And Burke, the iron evolutionist, essentially answered, "No; God tempers the shorn lamb to the wind." It is the lamb that has to adapt himself. That is, he either dies or becomes a particular kind of lamb who likes standing in a draught.

The subconscious popular instinct against Darwinism was not a mere offense at the grotesque notion of visiting one's grandfather in a cage in the Regent's Park. Men go in for drink, practical jokes and many other grotesque things; they do not much mind making beasts of themselves, and would not much mind having beasts made of their forefathers. The real instinct was much deeper and much more valuable. It was this: that when once one begins to think of man as a shifting and alterable thing, it is always easy for the strong and crafty to twist him into new shapes for all kinds of unnatural purposes. The popular instinct sees in such developments the possibility of backs bowed and hunch-backed for their burden, or limbs twisted for their task. It has a very well-grounded guess that whatever is done swiftly and systematically will mostly be done by a successful class and almost solely in their interests. It has therefore a vision of inhuman hybrids and half-human experiments much in the style of Mr. Wells's "Island of Dr. Moreau." The rich man may come to breeding a tribe of dwarfs to be his jockeys, and a tribe of giants to be his hall-porters. Grooms might be born bow-legged and tailors born cross-legged; perfumers might have long, large noses and a crouching attitude, like hounds of scent; and professional wine-tasters might have the horrible expression of one tasting wine stamped upon their faces as infants. Whatever wild image one employs it cannot keep pace with the panic of the human fancy, when once it supposes that the fixed type called man could be changed. If some millionaire wanted arms, some porter must grow ten arms like an octopus; if he wants legs, some messenger-boy must go with a hundred trotting legs like a centipede. In the distorted mirror of hypothesis, that is, of the unknown, men can dimly see such monstrous and evil shapes; men run all to eye, or all to fingers, with nothing left but one nostril or one ear. That is the nightmare with which the mere notion of adaptation threatens us. That is the nightmare that is not so very far from the reality.

It will be said that not the wildest evolutionist really asks that we should become in any way unhuman or copy any other animal. Pardon me, that is exactly what not merely the wildest evolutionists urge, but some of the tamest evolutionists too. There has risen high in recent history an important cultus which bids fair to be the religion of the future—which means the religion of those few weak-minded people who live in the future. It is typical of our time that it has to look for its god through a microscope; and our time has marked a definite adoration of the insect. Like most things we call new, of course, it is not at all new as an idea; it is only new as an idolatry. Virgil takes bees seriously but I doubt if he would have kept bees as carefully as he wrote about them. The wise king told the sluggard to watch the ant, a charming occupation—for a sluggard. But in our own time has appeared a very different tone, and more than one great man, as well as numberless intelligent men, have in our time seriously suggested that we should study the insect because we are his inferiors. The old moralists merely took the virtues of man and distributed them quite decoratively and arbitrarily among the animals. The ant was an almost heraldic symbol of industry, as the lion was of courage, or, for the matter of that, the pelican of charity. But if the mediaevals had been convinced that a lion was not courageous, they would have dropped the lion and kept the courage; if the pelican is not charitable, they would say, so much the worse for the pelican. The old moralists, I say, permitted the ant to enforce and typify man's morality; they never allowed the ant to upset it. They used the ant for industry as the lark for punctuality; they looked up at the flapping birds and down at the crawling insects for a homely lesson. But we have lived to see a sect that does not look down at the insects, but looks up at the insects, that asks us essentially to bow down and worship beetles, like ancient Egyptians.

Maurice Maeterlinck is a man of unmistakable genius, and genius always carries a magnifying glass. In the terrible crystal of his lens we have seen the bees not as a little yellow swarm, but rather in golden armies and hierarchies of warriors and queens. Imagination perpetually peers and creeps further down the avenues and vistas in the tubes of science, and one fancies every frantic reversal of proportions; the earwig striding across the echoing plain like an elephant, or the grasshopper coming roaring above our roofs like a vast aeroplane, as he leaps from Hertfordshire to Surrey. One seems to enter in a dream a temple of enormous entomology, whose architecture is based on something wilder than arms or backbones; in which the ribbed columns have the half-crawling look of dim and monstrous caterpillars; or the dome is a starry spider hung horribly in the void. There is one of the modern works of engineering that gives one something of this nameless fear of the exaggerations of an underworld; and that is the curious curved architecture of the under ground railway, commonly called the Twopenny Tube. Those squat archways, without any upright line or pillar, look as if they had been tunneled by huge worms who have never learned to lift their heads. It is the very underground palace of the Serpent, the spirit of changing shape and color, that is the enemy of man.

But it is not merely by such strange aesthetic suggestions that writers like Maeterlinck have influenced us in the matter; there is also an ethical side to the business. The upshot of M. Maeterlinck's book on bees is an admiration, one might also say an envy, of their collective spirituality; of the fact that they live only for something which he calls the Soul of the Hive. And this admiration for the communal morality of insects is expressed in many other modern writers in various quarters and shapes; in Mr. Benjamin Kidd's theory of living only for the evolutionary future of our race, and in the great interest of some Socialists in ants, which they generally prefer to bees, I suppose, because they are not so brightly colored. Not least among the hundred evidences of this vague insectolatry are the floods of flattery poured by modern people on that energetic nation of the Far East of which it has been said that "Patriotism is its only religion"; or, in other words, that it lives only for the Soul of the Hive. When at long intervals of the centuries Christendom grows weak, morbid or skeptical, and mysterious Asia begins to move against us her dim populations and to pour them westward like a dark movement of matter, in such cases it has been very common to compare the invasion to a plague of lice or incessant armies of locusts. The Eastern armies were indeed like insects; in their blind, busy destructiveness, in their black nihilism of personal outlook, in their hateful indifference to individual life and love, in their base belief in mere numbers, in their pessimistic courage and their atheistic patriotism, the riders and raiders of the East are indeed like all the creeping things of the earth. But never before, I think, have Christians called a Turk a locust and meant it as a compliment. Now for the first time we worship as well as fear; and trace with adoration that enormous form advancing vast and vague out of Asia, faintly discernible amid the mystic clouds of winged creatures hung over the wasted lands, thronging the skies like thunder and discoloring the skies like rain; Beelzebub, the Lord of Flies.

In resisting this horrible theory of the Soul of the Hive, we of Christendom stand not for ourselves, but for all humanity; for the essential and distinctive human idea that one good and happy man is an end in himself, that a soul is worth saving. Nay, for those who like such biological fancies it might well be said that we stand as chiefs and champions of a whole section of nature, princes of the house whose cognizance is the backbone, standing for the milk of the individual mother and the courage of the wandering cub, representing the pathetic chivalry of the dog, the humor and perversity of cats, the affection of the tranquil horse, the loneliness of the lion. It is more to the point, however, to urge that this mere glorification of society as it is in the social insects is a transformation and a dissolution in one of the outlines which have been specially the symbols of man. In the cloud and confusion of the flies and bees is growing fainter and fainter, as is finally disappearing, the idea of the human family. The hive has become larger than the house, the bees are destroying their captors; what the locust hath left, the caterpillar hath eaten; and the little house and garden of our friend Jones is in a bad way.

Chapter 2
The Fallacy of the Umbrella

hen Lord Morley said that the House of Lords must be either mended or ended, he used a phrase which has caused some confusion; because it might seem to suggest that mending and ending are somewhat similar things. I wish specially to insist on the fact that mending and ending are opposite things. You mend a thing because you like it; you end a thing because you don't. To mend is to strengthen. I, for instance, disbelieve in oligarchy; so I would no more mend the House of Lords than I would mend a thumbscrew. On the other hand, I do believe in the family; therefore I would mend the family as I would mend a chair; and I will never deny for a moment that the modern family is a chair that wants mending. But here comes in the essential point about the mass of modern advanced sociologists. Here are two institutions that have always been fundamental with mankind, the family and the state. Anarchists, I believe, disbelieve in both. It is quite unfair to say that Socialists believe in the state, but do not believe in the family; thousands of Socialists believe more in the family than any Tory. But it is true to say that while anarchists would end both, Socialists are specially engaged in mending (that is, strengthening and renewing) the state; and they are not specially engaged in strengthening and renewing the family. They are not doing anything to define the functions of father, mother, and child, as such; they are not tightening the machine up again; they are not blackening in again the fading lines of the old drawing. With the state they are doing this; they are sharpening its machinery, they are blackening in its black dogmatic lines, they are making mere government in every way stronger and in some ways harsher than before. While they leave the home in ruins, they restore the hive, especially the stings. Indeed, some schemes of labor and Poor Law reform recently advanced by distinguished Socialists, amount to little more than putting the largest number of people in the despotic power of Mr. Bumble. Apparently, progress means being moved on—by the police.

The point it is my purpose to urge might perhaps be suggested thus: that Socialists and most social reformers of their color are vividly conscious of the line between the kind of things that belong to the state and the kind of things that belong to mere chaos or uncoercible nature; they may force children to go to school before the sun rises, but they will not try to force the sun to rise; they will not, like Canute, banish the sea, but only the sea-bathers. But inside the outline of the state their lines are confused, and entities melt into each other. They have no firm instinctive sense of one thing being in its nature private and another public, of one thing being necessarily bond and another free. That is why piece by piece, and quite silently, personal liberty is being stolen from Englishmen, as personal land has been silently stolen ever since the sixteenth century.

I can only put it sufficiently curtly in a careless simile. A Socialist means a man who thinks a walking-stick like an umbrella because they both go into the umbrella-stand. Yet they are as different as a battle-ax and a bootjack. The essential idea of an umbrella is breadth and protection. The essential idea of a stick is slenderness and, partly, attack. The stick is the sword, the umbrella is the shield, but it is a shield against another and more nameless enemy—the hostile but anonymous universe. More properly, therefore, the umbrella is the roof; it is a kind of collapsible house. But the vital difference goes far deeper than this; it branches off into two kingdoms of man's mind, with a chasm between. For the point is this: that the umbrella is a shield against an enemy so actual as to be a mere nuisance; whereas the stick is a sword against enemies so entirely imaginary as to be a pure pleasure. The stick is not merely a sword, but a court sword; it is a thing of purely ceremonial swagger. One cannot express the emotion in any way except by saying that a man feels more like a man with a stick in his hand, just as he feels more like a man with a sword at his side. But nobody ever had any swelling sentiments about an umbrella; it is a convenience, like a door scraper. An umbrella is a necessary evil. A walking-stick is a quite unnecessary good. This, I fancy, is the real explanation of the perpetual losing of umbrellas; one does not hear of people losing walking sticks. For a walking-stick is a pleasure, a piece of real personal property; it is missed even when it is not needed. When my right hand forgets its stick may it forget its cunning. But anybody may forget an umbrella, as anybody might forget a shed that he has stood up in out of the rain. Anybody can forget a necessary thing.

If I might pursue the figure of speech, I might briefly say that the whole Collectivist error consists in saying that because two men can share an umbrella, therefore two men can share a walking-stick. Umbrellas might possibly be replaced by some kind of common awnings covering certain streets from particular showers. But there is nothing but nonsense in the notion of swinging a communal stick; it is as if one spoke of twirling a communal mustache. It will be said that this is a frank fantasia and that no sociologists suggest such follies. Pardon me if they do. I will give a precise parallel to the case of confusion of sticks and umbrellas, a parallel from a perpetually reiterated suggestion of reform. At least sixty Socialists out of a hundred, when they have spoken of common laundries, will go on at once to speak of common kitchens. This is just as mechanical and unintelligent as the fanciful case I have quoted. Sticks and umbrellas are both stiff rods that go into holes in a stand in the hall. Kitchens and washhouses are both large rooms full of heat and damp and steam. But the soul and function of the two things are utterly opposite. There is only one way of washing a shirt; that is, there is only one right way. There is no taste and fancy in tattered shirts. Nobody says, "Tompkins likes five holes in his shirt, but I must say, give me the good old four holes." Nobody says, "This washerwoman rips up the left leg of my pyjamas; now if there is one thing I insist on it is the right leg ripped up." The ideal washing is simply to send a thing back washed. But it is by no means true that the ideal cooking is simply to send a thing back cooked. Cooking is an art; it has in it personality, and even perversity, for the definition of an art is that which must be personal and may be perverse. I know a man, not otherwise dainty, who cannot touch common sausages unless they are almost burned to a coal. He wants his sausages fried to rags, yet he does not insist on his shirts being boiled to rags. I do not say that such points of culinary delicacy are of high importance. I do not say that the communal ideal must give way to them. What I say is that the communal ideal is not conscious of their existence, and therefore goes wrong from the very start, mixing a wholly public thing with a highly individual one. Perhaps we ought to accept communal kitchens in the social crisis, just as we should accept communal cat's-meat in a siege. But the cultured Socialist, quite at his ease, by no means in a siege, talks about communal kitchens as if they were the same kind of thing as communal laundries. This shows at the start that he misunderstands human nature. It is as different as three men singing the same chorus from three men playing three tunes on the same piano.

Chapter 3
The Dreadful Duty of Gudge

n the quarrel earlier alluded to between the energetic Progressive and the obstinate Conservative (or, to talk a tenderer language, between Hudge and Gudge), the state of cross-purposes is at the present moment acute. The Tory says he wants to preserve family life in Cindertown; the Socialist very reasonably points out to him that in Cindertown at present there isn't any family life to preserve. But Hudge, the Socialist, in his turn, is highly vague and mysterious about whether he would preserve the family life if there were any; or whether he will try to restore it where it has disappeared. It is all very confusing. The Tory sometimes talks as if he wanted to tighten the domestic bonds that do not exist; the Socialist as if he wanted to loosen the bonds that do not bind anybody. The question we all want to ask of both of them is the original ideal question, "Do you want to keep the family at all?" If Hudge, the Socialist, does want the family he must be prepared for the natural restraints, distinctions and divisions of labor in the family. He must brace himself up to bear the idea of the woman having a preference for the private house and a man for the public house. He must manage to endure somehow the idea of a woman being womanly, which does not mean soft and yielding, but handy, thrifty, rather hard, and very humorous. He must confront without a quiver the notion of a child who shall be childish, that is, full of energy, but without an idea of independence; fundamentally as eager for authority as for information and butter-scotch. If a man, a woman and a child live together any more in free and sovereign households, these ancient relations will recur; and Hudge must put up with it. He can only avoid it by destroying the family, driving both sexes into sexless hives and hordes, and bringing up all children as the children of the state—like Oliver Twist. But if these stern words must be addressed to Hudge, neither shall Gudge escape a somewhat severe admonition. For the plain truth to be told pretty sharply to the Tory is this, that if he wants the family to remain, if he wants to be strong enough to resist the rending forces of our essentially savage commerce, he must make some very big sacrifices and try to equalize property. The overwhelming mass of the English people at this particular instant are simply too poor to be domestic. They are as domestic as they can manage; they are much more domestic than the governing class; but they cannot get what good there was originally meant to be in this institution, simply because they have not got enough money. The man ought to stand for a certain magnanimity, quite lawfully expressed in throwing money away: but if under given circumstances he can only do it by throwing the week's food away, then he is not magnanimous, but mean. The woman ought to stand for a certain wisdom which is well expressed in valuing things rightly and guarding money sensibly; but how is she to guard money if there is no money to guard? The child ought to look on his mother as a fountain of natural fun and poetry; but how can he unless the fountain, like other fountains, is allowed to play? What chance have any of these ancient arts and functions in a house so hideously topsy-turvy; a house where the woman is out working and the man isn't; and the child is forced by law to think his schoolmaster's requirements more important than his mother's? No, Gudge and his friends in the House of Lords and the Carlton Club must make up their minds on this matter, and that very quickly. If they are content to have England turned into a beehive and an ant-hill, decorated here and there with a few faded butterflies playing at an old game called domesticity in the intervals of the divorce court, then let them have their empire of insects; they will find plenty of Socialists who will give it to them. But if they want a domestic England, they must "shell out," as the phrase goes, to a vastly greater extent than any Radical politician has yet dared to suggest; they must endure burdens much heavier than the Budget and strokes much deadlier than the death duties; for the thing to be done is nothing more nor less than the distribution of the great fortunes and the great estates. We can now only avoid Socialism by a change as vast as Socialism. If we are to save property, we must distribute property, almost as sternly and sweepingly as did the French Revolution. If we are to preserve the family we must revolutionize the nation.

Chapter 4
A Last Instance

nd now, as this book is drawing to a close, I will whisper in the reader's ear a horrible suspicion that has sometimes haunted me: the suspicion that Hudge and Gudge are secretly in partnership. That the quarrel they keep up in public is very much of a put-up job, and that the way in which they perpetually play into each other's hands is not an everlasting coincidence. Gudge, the plutocrat, wants an anarchic industrialism; Hudge, the idealist, provides him with lyric praises of anarchy. Gudge wants women-workers because they are cheaper; Hudge calls the woman's work "freedom to live her own life." Gudge wants steady and obedient workmen, Hudge preaches teetotalism–to workmen, not to Gudge–Gudge wants a tame and timid population who will never take arms against tyranny; Hudge proves from Tolstoi that nobody must take arms against anything. Gudge is naturally a healthy and well-washed gentleman; Hudge earnestly preaches the perfection of Gudge's washing to people who can't practice it. Above all, Gudge rules by a coarse and cruel system of sacking and sweating and bi-sexual toil which is totally inconsistent with the free family and which is bound to destroy it; therefore Hudge, stretching out his arms to the universe with a prophetic smile, tells us that the family is something that we shall soon gloriously outgrow.

I do not know whether the partnership of Hudge and Gudge is conscious or unconscious. I only know that between them they still keep the common man homeless. I only know I still meet Jones walking the streets in the gray twilight, looking sadly at the poles and barriers and low red goblin lanterns which still guard the house which is none the less his because he has never been in it.

Chapter 5
Conclusion

ere, it may be said, my book ends just where it ought to begin. I have said that the strong centers of modern English property must swiftly or slowly be broken up, if even the idea of property is to remain among Englishmen. There are two ways in which it could be done, a cold administration by quite detached officials, which is called Collectivism, or a personal distribution, so as to produce what is called Peasant Proprietorship. I think the latter solution the finer and more fully human, because it makes each man as somebody blamed somebody for saying of the Pope, a sort of small god. A man on his own turf tastes eternity or, in other words, will give ten minutes more work than is required. But I believe I am justified in shutting the door on this vista of argument, instead of opening it. For this book is not designed to prove the case for Peasant Proprietorship, but to prove the case against modern sages who turn reform to a routine. The whole of this book has been a rambling and elaborate urging of one purely ethical fact. And if by any chance it should happen that there are still some who do not quite see what that point is, I will end with one plain parable, which is none the worse for being also a fact.

A little while ago certain doctors and other persons permitted by modern law to dictate to their shabbier fellow-citizens, sent out an order that all little girls should have their hair cut short. I mean, of course, all little girls whose parents were poor. Many very unhealthy habits are common among rich little girls, but it will be long before any doctors interfere forcibly with them. Now, the case for this particular interference was this, that the poor are pressed down from above into such stinking and suffocating underworlds of squalor, that poor people must not be allowed to have hair, because in their case it must mean lice in the hair. Therefore, the doctors propose to abolish the hair. It never seems to have occurred to them to abolish the lice. Yet it could be done. As is common in most modern discussions the unmentionable thing is the pivot of the whole discussion. It is obvious to any Christian man (that is, to any man with a free soul) that any coercion applied to a cabman's daughter ought, if possible, to be applied to a Cabinet Minister's daughter. I will not ask why the doctors do not, as a matter of fact apply their rule to a Cabinet Minister's daughter. I will not ask, because I know. They do not because they dare not. But what is the excuse they would urge, what is the plausible argument they would use, for thus cutting and clipping poor children and not rich? Their argument would be that the disease is more likely to be in the hair of poor people than of rich. And why? Because the poor children are forced (against all the instincts of the highly domestic working classes) to crowd together in close rooms under a wildly inefficient system of public instruction;

and because in one out of the forty children there may be offense. And why? Because the poor man is so ground down by the great rents of the great ground landlords that his wife often has to work as well as he. Therefore she has no time to look after the children, therefore one in forty of them is dirty. Because the workingman has these two persons on top of him, the landlord sitting (literally) on his stomach, and the schoolmaster sitting (literally) on his head, the workingman must allow his little girl's hair, first to be neglected from poverty, next to be poisoned by promiscuity, and, lastly, to be abolished by hygiene. He, perhaps, was proud of his little girl's hair. But he does not count.

Upon this simple principle (or rather precedent) the sociological doctor drives gayly ahead. When a crapulous tyranny crushes men down into the dirt, so that their very hair is dirty, the scientific course is clear. It would be long and laborious to cut off the heads of the tyrants; it is easier to cut off the hair of the slaves. In the same way, if it should ever happen that poor children, screaming with toothache, disturbed any schoolmaster or artistic gentleman, it would be easy to pull out all the teeth of the poor; if their nails were disgustingly dirty, their nails could be plucked out; if their noses were indecently blown, their noses could be cut off. The appearance of our humbler fellow-citizen could be quite strikingly simplified before we had done with him. But all this is not a bit wilder than the brute fact that a doctor can walk into the house of a free man, whose daughter's hair may be as clean as spring flowers, and order him to cut it off. It never seems to strike these people that the lesson of lice in the slums is the wrongness of slums, not the wrongness of hair. Hair is, to say the least of it, a rooted thing. Its enemy (like the other insects and oriental armies of whom we have spoken) sweep upon us but seldom. In truth, it is only by eternal institutions like hair that we can test passing institutions like empires. If a house is so built as to knock a man's head off when he enters it, it is built wrong.

The mob can never rebel unless it is conservative, at least enough to have conserved some reasons for rebelling. It is the most awful thought in all our anarchy, that most of the ancient blows struck for freedom would not be struck at all to-day, because of the obscuration of the clean, popular customs from which they came. The insult that brought down the hammer of Wat Tyler might now be called a medical examination. That which Virginius loathed and avenged as foul slavery might now be praised as free love. The cruel taunt of Foulon, "Let them eat grass," might now be represented as the dying cry of an idealistic vegetarian. Those great scissors of science that would snip off the curls of the poor little school children are ceaselessly snapping closer and closer to cut off all the corners and fringes of the arts and honors of the poor. Soon they will be twisting necks to suit clean collars, and hacking feet to fit new boots. It never seems to strike them that the body is more than raiment; that the Sabbath was made for man; that all institutions shall be judged and damned by whether they have fitted the normal flesh and spirit. It is the test of political sanity to keep your head. It is the test of artistic sanity to keep your hair on.

Now the whole parable and purpose of these last pages, and indeed of all these pages, is this: to assert that we must instantly begin all over again, and begin at the other end. I begin with a little girl's hair. That I know is a good thing at any rate. Whatever else is evil, the pride of a good mother in the beauty of her daughter is good. It is one of those adamantine tendernesses which are the touchstones of every age and race. If other things are against it, other things must go down. If landlords and laws and sciences are against it, landlords and laws and sciences must go down. With the red hair of one she-urchin in the gutter I will set fire to all modern civilization. Because a girl should have long hair, she should have clean hair; because she should have clean hair, she should not have an unclean home: because she should not have an unclean home, she should have a free and leisured mother; because she should have a free mother, she should not have an usurious landlord; because there should not be an usurious landlord, there should be a redistribution of property; because there should be a redistribution of property, there shall be a revolution. That little urchin with the gold-red hair, whom I have just watched toddling past my house, she shall not be lopped and lamed and altered; her hair shall not be cut short like a convict's; no, all the kingdoms of the earth shall be hacked about and mutilated to suit her. She is the human and sacred image; all around her the social fabric shall sway and split and fall; the pillars of society shall be shaken, and the roofs of ages come rushing down, and not one hair of her head shall be harmed.

Three Notes

Chapter 1
On Female Suffrage

Not wishing to overload this long essay with too many parentheses, apart from its thesis of progress and precedent, I append here three notes on points of detail that may possibly be misunderstood.

The first refers to the female controversy. It may seem to many that I dismiss too curtly the contention that all women should have votes, even if most women do not desire them. It is constantly said in this connection that males have received the vote (the agricultural laborers for instance) when only a minority of them were in favor of it. Mr. Galsworthy, one of the few fine fighting intellects of our time, has talked this language in the "Nation." Now, broadly, I have only to answer here, as everywhere in this book, that history is not a toboggan slide, but a road to be reconsidered and even retraced. If we really forced General Elections upon free laborers who definitely disliked General Elections, then it was a thoroughly undemocratic thing to do; if we are democrats we ought to undo it. We want the will of the people, not the votes of the people; and to give a man a vote against his will is to make voting more valuable than the democracy it declares.

But this analogy is false, for a plain and particular reason. Many voteless women regard a vote as unwomanly. Nobody says that most voteless men regarded a vote as unmanly. Nobody says that any voteless men regarded it as unmanly. Not in the stillest hamlet or the most stagnant fen could you find a yokel or a tramp who thought he lost his sexual dignity by being part of a political mob. If he did not care about a vote it was solely because he did not know about a vote; he did not understand the word any better than Bimetallism. His opposition, if it existed, was merely negative. His indifference to a vote was really indifference.

But the female sentiment against the franchise, whatever its size, is positive. It is not negative; it is by no means indifferent. Such women as are opposed to the change regard it (rightly or wrongly) as unfeminine. That is, as insulting certain affirmative traditions to which they are attached. You may think such a view prejudiced; but I violently deny that any democrat has a right to override such prejudices, if they are popular and positive. Thus he would not have a right to make millions of Moslems vote with a cross if they had a prejudice in favor of voting with a crescent. Unless this is admitted, democracy is a farce we need scarcely keep up. If it is admitted, the Suffragists have not merely to awaken an indifferent, but to convert a hostile majority.

Chapter 2
On Cleanliness in Education

n re-reading my protest, which I honestly think much needed, against our heathen idolatry of mere ablution, I see that it may possibly be misread. I hasten to say that I think washing a most important thing to be taught both to rich and poor. I do not attack the positive but the relative position of soap. Let it be insisted on even as much as now; but let other things be insisted on much more. I am even ready to admit that cleanliness is next to godliness; but the moderns will not even admit godliness to be next to cleanliness. In their talk about Thomas Becket and such saints and heroes they make soap more important than soul; they reject godliness whenever it is not cleanliness. If we resent this about remote saints and heroes, we should resent it more about the many saints and heroes of the slums, whose unclean hands cleanse the world. Dirt is evil chiefly as evidence of sloth; but the fact remains that the classes that wash most are those that work least. Concerning these, the practical course is simple; soap should be urged on them and advertised as what it is—a luxury. With regard to the poor also the practical course is not hard to harmonize with our thesis. If we want to give poor people soap we must set out deliberately to give them luxuries. If we will not make them rich enough to be clean, then emphatically we must do what we did with the saints. We must reverence them for being dirty.

Chapter 3
On Peasant Proprietorship

have not dealt with any details touching distributed ownership, or its possibility in England, for the reason stated in the text. This book deals with what is wrong, wrong in our root of argument and effort. This wrong is, I say, that we will go forward because we dare not go back. Thus the Socialist says that property is already concentrated into Trusts and Stores: the only hope is to concentrate it further in the State. I say the only hope is to unconcentrate it; that is, to repent and return; the only step forward is the step backward.

But in connection with this distribution I have laid myself open to another potential mistake. In speaking of a sweeping redistribution, I speak of decision in the aim, not necessarily of abruptness in the means. It is not at all too late to restore an approximately rational state of English possessions without any mere confiscation. A policy of buying out landlordism, steadily adopted in England as it has already been adopted in Ireland (notably in Mr. Wyndham's wise and fruitful Act), would in a very short time release the lower end of the see-saw and make the whole plank swing more level. The objection to this course is not at all that it would not do, only that it will not be done. If we leave things as they are, there will almost certainly be a crash of confiscation. If we hesitate, we shall soon have to hurry. But if we start doing it quickly we have still time to do it slowly.

This point, however, is not essential to my book. All I have to urge between these two boards is that I dislike the big Whiteley shop, and that I dislike Socialism because it will (according to Socialists) be so like that shop. It is its fulfilment, not its reversal. I do not object to Socialism because it will revolutionize our commerce, but because it will leave it so horribly the same.

Book Catalog

Works by Our Authors

- *The Opium of Happiness* by Jeremy Hausotter. This book examines the Church's teachings on drugs and marijuana. It also contains about 70 pages of appendices of hard to find Church documents discussing drugs. ISBN: 978-1-964170-54-1
- *How to Win Tic Tac Toe Like a Champion* by Jeremy Hausotter. ISBN: 978-1-964170-58-9

Theology & Philosophy

- *Select Works* by St. Ambrose. ISBN: 978-1-964170-44-2
- St. Thomas Aquinas

    - *The Summa Theologiae: Prima Pars*, Q. 1-119. ISBN: 978-1-964170-23-7
    - *The Summa Theologiae: Prima Secundae*, Q. 1-114. ISBN: 978-1-964170-24-4
    - *The Summa Theologiae: Secunda Secundae*, Q. 1-189. ISBN: 978-1-964170-25-1
    - *The Summa Theologiae: Tertia Pars*, Q. 1-90. ISBN: 978-1-964170-27-5
    - *The Summa Theologiae: Supplementum*, Q. 1-99. ISBN: 978-1-964170-28-2

- *The Life of St. Anthony* by St. Athanasius. ISBN: 978-1-964170-20-6
- *Select Works and Letters* by St. Athanasius. ISBN: 978-1-964170-67-1
- St. Augustine

    - *On Christian Doctrine*. ISBN: 978-1-964170-74-9
    - *Select Doctrinal and Moral Treatises*. ISBN: 978-1-964170-63-3
    - *The Anti-Donatist Works*. ISBN: 978-1-964170-40-4
    - *The Anti-Manichean Works*. ISBN: 978-1-964170-67-1
    - *The Anti-Pelagian Works*. ISBN: 978-1-964170-65-7

- *The Art of Dying Well* by St. Robert Bellarmine. ISBN: 978-1-964170-62-6
- *Select Letters and Orations* by St. Gregory Nazianzen. ISBN: 978-1-964170-56-5
- St. John Henry Newman

    - *An Essay in Aid of a Grammar of Assent*. ISBN: 978-1-964170-52-7
    - *The Complete Parochial and Plain Sermons*, volumes 1-4. ISBN: 978-1-964170-22-0
    - *The Complete Parochial and Plain Sermons*, volumes 5-8. ISBN: 978-1-964170-66-4
    - *The Complete Historical Sketches*, volumes 1-3. ISBN: 978-1-964170-71-8
    - *On the Development of Christian Doctrine*. ISBN: 978-1-964170-48-0
    - *Sermons Preached on Various Occasions*. ISBN: 978-1-964170-50-3

- *The Problem of Form in Painting and Sculpture* by Adolf von Hildebrand. ISBN: 978-1-964170-60-2

Papal Documents

- The Papal Writings of John Paul II

    - Vol. 1, *The Complete Encyclicals*. ISBN: 978-1-964170-21-3
    - Vol. 2, *Redemptor Hominis*. ISBN: 978-1-964170-00-8
    - Vol. 3, *Dives in Misericordia*. ISBN: 978-1-964170-01-5

- Vol. 4, *Laborem Exercens*. ISBN: 978-1-964170-02-2
- Vol. 11, *Veritatis Splendor*. ISBN: 978-1-964170-09-1
- Vol. 12, *Evangelium Vitae*. ISBN: 978-1-964170-10-7
- Vol. 14, *Fides et Ratio*. ISBN: 978-1-964170-12-1
- The Papal Writings of Benedict XVI
  - Vol. 1, *Select Papal Writings: The Encyclicals, Apostolic Exhortations, and Select Other Writings.* ISBN: 978-1-964170-14-5

Classics

- The G.K. Chesterton Collection
  - Nonfiction
    * *The Defendant, Varied Types, Heretics, All Things Considered.* ISBN: 978-1-964170-79-4
    * *Tremendous Trifles, Orthodoxy, What's Wrong with the World.* ISBN: 978-1-964170-81-7
- The Complete Works of Fyodor Dostoevsky
  - Vol. 8, *The Minor Novels and Novellas: The Insulted and the Injured, The House of the Dead.* ISBN: 978-1-964170-17-6
  - Vol. 9, *The Complete Short Stories*. ISBN: 978-1-964170-18-3
- *The Wind in the Willows* by Kenneth Grahame. ISBN: 978-1-964170-46-6
- Greek and Roman Classics
  - Vol. 1, *Homer's The Iliad and the Odyssey*, translated by Alexander Pope. ISBN: 978-1-964170-15-2
  - Vol. 4, *Commentaries* by Julius Caesar. ISBN: 978-1-964170-72-5
- Norse Classics
  - Vol. 1, *The Poetic and Prose Eddas*. ISBN: 978-1-964170-37-4
  - Vol. 2, *The Heimskringla*. ISBN: 978-1-964170-39-8
  - Vol. 3, *The Nibelungenlied* (prose translation). ISBN: 978-1-964170-33-6
  - Vol. 4, *The Norse Sagas, Part 1*. ISBN: 978-1-964170-35-0
  - Vol. 5, *The Norse Sagas, Part 2*. ISBN: 978-1-964170-29-9
  - Vol. 6, *The Norse Sagas, Part 3*. ISBN: 978-1-964170-31-2
- 20,000 *Leagues Under the Sea* by Jules Verne. ISBN: 978-1-964170-42-8

Forthcoming Titles

- A volume on the dogma *no salvation outside of the Church* by Jeremy Hausotter.
- A volume on the hermeneutics of Vatican II by Jeremy Hausotter.
- The *Summa Contra Gentiles* by St. Thomas Aquinas.

Made in the USA
Las Vegas, NV
26 December 2024

15432544R00213